Crime and Corruption in Organizations

Psychological and Behavioral Aspects of Risk Series

Series Editors: Professor Cary L. Cooper and Professor Ronald J. Burke

Risk management is an ongoing concern for modern organizations in terms of their finance, their people, their assets, their projects and their reputation. The majority of the processes and systems adopted are very financially oriented or fundamentally mechanistic; often better suited to codifying and recording risk, rather than understanding and working with it. Risk is fundamentally a human construct; how we perceive and manage it is dictated by our attitude, behavior and the environment or culture within which we work. Organizations that seek to mitigate, manage, transfer or exploit risk need to understand the psychological factors that dictate the response and behaviors of their employees, their high-flyers, their customers and their stakeholders.

This series, edited by two of the most influential writers and researchers on organizational behavior and human psychology explores the psychological and behavioral aspects of risk; the factors that:

- define our attitudes and response to risk,
- are important in understanding and managing 'risk managers', and
- dictate risky behavior in individuals at all levels.

Titles Currently in the Series Include:

New Directions in Organisational Psychology and Behavioural Medicine
Edited by Alexander-Stamatios Antoniou and Cary Cooper

Risky Business
Psychological, Physical and Financial Costs of High Risk Behavior in Organizations
Edited by Ronald J. Burke and Cary L. Cooper

Safety Culture
Assessing and Changing the Behaviour of Organizations
John Bernard Taylor

Crime and Corruption in Organizations

Why It Occurs and What To Do About It

RONALD J. BURKE,
EDWARD C. TOMLINSON
and
CARY L. COOPER

GOWER

© Ronald J. Burke, Edward C. Tomlinson and Cary L. Cooper 2011

All rights reserved. No part of this publication may be reproduced, stored in a retrieval system or transmitted in any form or by any means, electronic, mechanical, photocopying, recording or otherwise without the prior permission of the publisher.

Ronald J. Burke, Edward C. Tomlinson and Cary L. Cooper have asserted their moral right under the Copyright, Designs and Patents Act, 1988, to be identified as the editors of this work.

Gower Applied Business Research
Our programme provides leaders, practitioners, scholars and researchers with thought provoking, cutting edge books that combine conceptual insights, interdisciplinary rigour and practical relevance in key areas of business and management.

Published by
Gower Publishing Limited
Wey Court East
Union Road
Farnham
Surrey, GU9 7PT
England

Ashgate Publishing Company
Suite 420
101 Cherry Street
Burlington,
VT 05401-4405
USA

www.gowerpublishing.com

British Library Cataloguing in Publication Data
Crime and corruption in organizations : why it occurs and what to do about it.
-- (Psychological and behavioural aspects of risk)
1. Employee crimes. 2. Employee crimes--Prevention.
3. White collar crimes. 4. White collar crimes--
Prevention. 5. Corporations--Corrupt practices.
6. Corporations--Corrupt practices--Prevention.
7. Organizational behavior. 8. Professional ethics.
I. Series II. Burke, Ronald J. III. Tomlinson, Edward C. IV. Cooper, Cary L.
364.1'68-dc22

ISBN: 978-0-566-08981-7 (hbk)
       978-1-4094-1260-1 (ebk)

Library of Congress Cataloging-in-Publication Data
Crime and corruption in organizations : why it occurs and what to do about it / [edited] by Ronald J. Burke, Edward C. Tomlinson and Cary L. Cooper.
    p. cm. -- (Psychological and behavioural aspects of risk)
  Includes index.
  ISBN 978-0-566-08981-7 (hbk.) 1. Corporations--Corrupt practices. 2. Business ethics.
  3. Commercial crimes. I. Burke, Ronald J. II. Tomlinson, Edward C. III. Cooper, Cary L.
  HV6768.C72 2010
  658.4'73--dc22

2010015717

Printed and bound in Great Britain by
MPG Books Group, UK

Contents

List of Figures	vii
List of Tables	ix
List of Contributors	xi
Acknowledgements	xix

PART I	INTRODUCTION	
1	Crime and Corruption in Organizations Ronald J. Burke	3

PART II	CAUSES OF CRIME AND CORRUPTION IN ORGANIZATIONS	
2	Show Me the Money Ronald J. Burke	69
3	Predicting Workplace Misconduct Using Personality and Academic Behaviors Thomas H. Stone, I. M. Jawahar, and Jennifer L. Kisamore	97
4	The Role of Trust in Employee Theft Edward C. Tomlinson	121
5	The Influence of National Culture on the Rationalization of Corruption Amy Guerber, Aparna Rajagoplan, and Vikas Anand	143

PART III	COSTS OF CRIME AND CORRUPTION IN ORGANIZATIONS	
6	The Debilitating Effects of Fraud in Organizations Conan C. Albrecht, Matthew L. Sanders, Daniel V. Holland, and Chad Albrecht	163

7	A Re-examination of the Withdrawal Syndrome vis-à-vis Organizational Ethics in Schools *Zehava Rosenblatt and Orly Shapira-Lishchinsky*	187
PART IV	**CORRUPTION IN THE PROFESSIONS**	
8	Making Sense of Academic Misconduct *Alison L. Antes and Michael D. Mumford*	215
9	Medicines and Money: The Corruption of Clinical Information *Joel Lexchin*	249
PART V	**REDUCING CRIME AND CORRUPTION IN ORGANIZATIONS**	
10	How to Minimize Corruption in Business Organizations: Developing and Sustaining an Ethical Corporate Culture *Mark S. Schwartz*	273
11	Confronting Corruption Using Integrity Pacts: The Case of Nigeria *Wesley Cragg, Uwafiokun Idemudia, and Bronwyn Best*	297
12	Easy Prey Canadians *L. S. (Al) Rosen*	323
Index		*345*

List of Figures

Figure 3.1	Results of structural equation model—full mediation model	110
Figure 5.1	Cultural values	152
Figure 6.1	Amount embezzled at odd-year intervals	166
Figure 6.2	The fraud triangle	168
Figure 6.3	The Ethics Development Model	176
Figure 6.4	Fraud detection method breakdown	178
Figure 7.1	The interaction effect of distributive justice and affective commitment on lateness	200
Figure 7.2	Summary of coefficient modeling results of the relationship between teachers' perceptions of formal ethical climate and absence frequency, mediated by affective commitment	200
Figure 7.3	Summary of the results of the relationship of ethical variables with intent to leave, mediated by affective and normative commitment	201
Figure 8.1	Sense-making model of ethical decision-making	224
Figure 10.1	The three elements of an ethical corporate culture	291
Figure 11.1	Constituent states of the Niger Delta, Nigeria	305

List of Tables

Table 3.1	Means, standard deviations, and correlations between study variables	109
Table 5.1	Rationalization techniques: description and summary	146
Table 6.1	Types of fraud	165
Table 6.2	Income statement	167
Table 8.1	Taxonomy of ethical dimensions of academic work	221
Table 8.2	Strategies facilitating sense-making	225
Table 11.1	The IP implementation plan and progress achieved	320

List of Contributors

The Editors

Ronald J. Burke is Professor of Organizational Behavior, Schulich School of Business, York University, Toronto, Canada. He has been the editor or co-editor of 31 books and has published over 500 journal articles. He was the founding editor of the Canadian Journal of Administrative Sciences and has served on the editorial boards of over 20 journals. His current research interests include work and health, crime and corruption in organizations, occupational health and safety, corporate reputation, and women in management. He has participated in numerous management development courses and consulted with both private- and public-sector organizations on human resource management issues.

Cary L. Cooper is Distinguished Professor of Organizational Psychology and Health at Lancaster University Management School. He is the author of over 100 books (on occupational stress, women at work and industrial and organizational psychology), has written over 400 scholarly articles and is a frequent contributor to national newspapers, TV and radio.

Professor Cooper is a Fellow of the British Academy of Management and of the Academy of Management (having also won the 1998 Distinguished Service Award). In 2001 he was awarded a CBE in the Queen's Birthday Honours List for his contribution to organizational health. He was also the lead scientist to the UK Government Office for Science on their Foresight programme on Mental Capital and Well Being (2007–2008) and was appointed a member of the expert group on establishing guidance for the National Institute for Health and Clinical Excellence on "promoting mental wellbeing through productive and healthy working conditions," 2009. Professor Cooper is Chair of the UK's Academy of Social Sciences.

Edward C. Tomlinson is Associate Professor of Management and Mulwick Scholar in the Boler School of Business at John Carroll University. He received his PhD from the Fisher College of Business at Ohio State University. His primary research interests include interpersonal trust, behavioral integrity, and deviant workplace behavior. His research has been published in journals including the *Academy of Management Review*, *International Journal of Conflict*

Management, Journal of Applied Psychology, Journal of Management, and *Journal of Management Education.* He currently serves on the inaugural editorial board of *Journal of Trust Research*

The Contributors

Chad O. Albrecht is an Assistant Professor at Utah State University. Chad's research focuses on organizational fraud and corruption from a managerial perspective. Chad has co-authored four books on fraud and published in multiple outlets including the *Journal of Business Ethics, Internal Auditing, Corporate Finance Review,* and the *International Journal of Human Resource Management.* Chad serves as an associate editor for *Cross Cultural Management: An International Journal.* Chad received his PhD from ESADE Business School in Barcelona, Spain.

Conan C. Albrecht is Professor of Information Systems and eBusiness Fellow at Brigham Young University. He teaches classes in enterprise development, middleware, and network programming. Conan actively researches fraud detection techniques and online group dynamics. He previously held a faculty position as the Director of Programming for the Center for the Management of Information for the University of Arizona. Conan has published articles on fraud detection and information theory in the *Journal of Forensic Accounting, Journal of Accounting, Communications of the ACM, Decision Support Systems, Information and Management,* and many other academic and professional outlets.

Vikas Anand received his PhD from Arizona State University and an MBA in International Business from the Indian Institute of Foreign Trade. He also holds a Bachelor's degree in Engineering and a Master's degree in Physics. His major areas of research include corruption and ethics in organizations, knowledge management in organizations, and trends in the globalization of business practices such as outsourcing. He has published and presented his work on business ethics and knowledge management in several research and practitioner outlets, such as the *Academy of Management Review, Research in Organizational Behavior, Academy of Management Executive,* and so on. Prior to his academic career, he was a manager in two large multinational corporations and worked extensively on marketing and strategic planning positions in various parts of Africa and Asia.

Alison L. Antes, PhD, is Assistant Professor of Organizational Leadership in the Department of Political Science and Criminal Justice, Northern Kentucky University, having gained a PhD in Industrial and Organizational Psychology at the University of Oklahoma. Alison has worked for five years on a grant sponsored by the National Institutes of Health and Office of Research Integrity, examining ethical decision-making and ethics instruction. She also collaborated with the Graduate College at the University of Oklahoma to implement a campus-wide ethics training program for graduate students. In addition to ethics, Alison's research interests include organizational leadership and creative problem-solving.

Bronwyn Best holds an HonsBA and MA from the University of Toronto and an MBA from the Schulich School of Business, York University. She runs her own cross-cultural management and international business ethics consultancy, Heiwa Business International, and has served as the Executive Director of Transparency International Canada, since November 1997. Prior to this, she worked with the Asia Pacific Foundation of Canada, the Canadian Chamber of Commerce, and the Department of Foreign Affairs and International Trade. Ms Best has published on the role of bribery and corruption in global ethical decision-making by business and government.

Wesley Cragg is Professor Emeritus and Senior Scholar in the Department of Philosophy and the Schulich School of Business at York University, Toronto, Canada. He has published widely in Canadian and international journals and has written and edited books on topics in business ethics, corporate citizenship, bribery and corruption, occupational ethics, moral education, applied ethics, moral, political and social philosophy, philosophy of law and philosophy of punishment. Dr Cragg is currently Project Director for the SSHRC-funded Canadian Business Ethics Research Network (CBERN). Funded by the Canadian Social Science and Humanities Research Council and other donors, CBERN's goal is to encourage, support and raise the profile of business ethics research in Canada.

Amy Guerber is a doctoral student in Management at the Sam M. Walton College of Business, University of Arkansas. She is currently engaged in research aimed at understanding distinctions between deliberative and non-deliberative ethical decision-making, as well as predicting which type of ethical decision-making is most likely in a given situation. She is also involved in research designed to understand the factors that shape public perceptions about the ethicality of organizational decisions. Her future research interests include understanding the effects of moral recognition on information-seeking behaviors and other decision-making processes.

Daniel V. Holland is an Assistant Professor of Entrepreneurship at Utah State University. His research centers on entrepreneurial decision-making, ethics, and social responsibility and has been published in outlets such as *Entrepreneurship, Theory, and Practice* and *Frontiers of Entrepreneurship Research*. Dan received his PhD from Indiana University and his MBA and Bachelor of Science from Brigham Young University. Prior to joining academe, Dan worked for several years in a variety of engineering, marketing, and management roles in the high-tech industry.

Uwafiokun Idemudia received his PhD from Lancaster University in the United Kingdom. He is an Assistant Professor of International Development and African Studies and the coordinator of the African Studies Programme at York University, Toronto, Canada. He also teaches in the Business and Society programme at York. His recent publications have appeared in *Journal of Business Ethics, Journal of Corporate Citizenship, Resource Policy, Journal of International Development*, and *Conflict Security and Development*.

I. M. "Jim" Jawahar holds a PhD from Oklahoma State University and is currently Professor of Management and Chairperson of the Department of Management and Quantitative Methods at Illinois State University. His research interests include performance appraisal, fairness, citizenship and counterproductive behaviors, stress and academic integrity. Jim received the Dale Yoder and Herb Heneman Research Award from the Society for Human Resource Management. His research has appeared in the *Academy of Management Review, Journal of Applied Psychology, Personnel Psychology, Journal of Labor Research, Journal of Management, Group and Organization Management*, and *Human Relations*. Jim serves on the editorial boards of *Group and Organization Management* and *Journal of Managerial Psychology*. He is a co-editor of *Career Development International*.

Jennifer L. Kisamore holds a PhD from the University of South Florida and is currently an Associate Professor of Psychology at the University of Oklahoma in Tulsa, teaching human resource management courses in the department's Organizational Dynamics program. Her research interests include citizenship and counterproductive work behaviors, methodological issues in measurement, and academic integrity. Jennifer's research has appeared in journals including *Organizational Research Methods, Journal of Business Ethics*, and the *International*

Journal of Selection and Assessment. She currently serves on the editorial board of *Career Development International*.

Joel Lexchin received his MD from the University of Toronto in 1977 and for the past 22 years has been an emergency physician at the University Health Network. He is currently a Professor in the School of Health Policy and Management at York University and an Associate Professor in the Department of Family and Community Medicine at the University of Toronto. He has been a consultant for the province of Ontario, various arms of the Canadian federal government, the World Health Organization, the government of New Zealand and the Australian National Prescribing Service. Joel is the author or co-author of over 90 peer-reviewed articles on topics such as physician prescribing behavior, pharmaceutical patent issues, the drug approval process, and prescription drug promotion.

Michael D. Mumford, PhD, is a George Lynn Cross Distinguished Research Professor at the University of Oklahoma where he directs the Center for Applied Social Research. Dr Mumford is a Fellow of the American Psychological Association (Divisions 3, 5, 14), the Society of Industrial and Organizational Psychology, and the American Psychological Society. He has written more than 200 articles on creativity, innovation, planning, leadership, and ethics and serves as Senior Editor of *The Leadership Quarterly*. Dr Mumford has also worked as principal investigator on grants totaling more than US$25 million from agencies such as the National Science Foundation, the National Institutes of Health, and the Department of Defense.

Aparna Rajagopalan is a doctoral student in the Sam M. Walton School of Business, University of Arkansas. Her educational background includes a Masters degree in Business Administration and an undergraduate degree in commerce. Her research interests include organizational corruption, organizational accounts, and business ethics. She is currently exploring the believability of organizational accounts in response to corruption.

Lawrence S. ("Al") Rosen graduated from the University of British Columbia with an undergraduate degree and later obtained a PhD and MBA from the University of Washington. In 1990 he founded Rosen & Associates Limited, a forensic and investigative accounting and auditing firm. He has given independent opinions on hundreds of litigation-related engagements across Canada, and in the US, including the Courts of British Columbia, Alberta, Quebec, Ontario and New York, and has provided an affidavit for the Supreme

Court of Canada. Dr Rosen is a member of several accounting associations in the US, China and Canada, as well as the author or co-author of several books and hundreds of articles in various publications. He is a frequent writer for *Canadian Business* magazine. He has previously held the positions of instructor or Professor of Accounting at the University of British Columbia, the University of Washington, the University of Alberta, and York University. In addition, he served as a technical advisor to three Auditors' General of Canada for 15 years.

Zehava Rosenblatt is a member of the Faculty of Education, University of Haifa, Israel, where she heads the Center for School Evaluation and Administration. She taught in John M. Olin School of Business in Washington University, and in the School of Education in the University of Illinois at Chicago. Zehava specializes in human resource management and organizational behavior and has published extensively on topics such as job design, job insecurity, and withdrawal behaviors. She is a member of the editorial board of the *Journal of Educational Administration*. Zehava is currently involved in a large-scale intervention project in Israeli public schools.

Matthew L. Sanders holds a PhD from the University of Colorado at Boulder and is currently an Assistant Professor of Speech Communication at Utah State University. His areas of specialization include organizations and social change, social entrepreneurship, and leadership communication. His current research focuses on how values such as integrity and kindness underlie effective leadership as well as the ways in which non-profit organizations and social entrepreneurs evoke and resist business discourses in the pursuit of social goals.

Mark Schwartz is Assistant Professor of Corporate Governance, Law and Ethics at Atkinson's School of Administrative Studies, York University, Toronto. Dr Schwartz received his PhD from the Schulich School of Business, York University, in 1999, specializing in the field of business ethics. His research interests include corporate ethics programs, corporate social responsibility, Jewish business ethics, corporate governance and ethics, and ethical investment. Dr Schwartz is also a Research Fellow for the Center for Business Ethics (Bentley College) and the Jerusalem Center for Business Ethics (Jerusalem College of Technology). He has consulted for a number of companies on business ethics-related matters.

Orly Shapira-Lishchinsky, PhD, is a faculty member in the Department of Educational Administration, in Bar-Ilan University, Israel. Her research areas include organizational ethics, teachers' withdrawal behaviors (lateness, absenteeism, intent to leave), and simulation-based workshops for educational leaders.

Her recent publications include articles in *Educational Administration Quarterly*, *Qualitative Health Research*, *Journal of Business Ethics*, and *Sex Roles*. She is a member of the editorial board of *Creative Education Journal*. Orly won the 2009 Emerald/EFMD Outstanding Doctoral Research Award in the Education and Leadership Strategy category for her research on organizational ethics and teachers' work withdrawal behaviors.

Thomas H. Stone holds a PhD from the University of Minnesota and is currently Professor of Management at Oklahoma State University. Tom has served on the faculties of the University of Iowa, University of Minnesota, York University, and McMaster University. His research interests include performance appraisal, leadership, decision-making, citizenship and counterproductive behaviors, stress, and academic integrity. Tom's research has appeared in *Journal of Applied Psychology*, *The Leadership Quarterly*, *Academy of Management Review*, *Journal of Business Ethics*, and *Canadian Journal of Administrative Studies* amongst others. He is also Associate Editor of *Career Development International*.

Acknowledgements

I became interested in crime and corruption in organizations in a somewhat serious way about 2 years ago. I started clipping stories from local newspapers until I became overwhelmed by the quantity of this material. Crime and corruption are major worldwide organizational and societal problems that have huge individual, organizational and societal costs. And though increasing attention has been paid to them, there are no signs that crime and corruption is decreasing. I hope this volume continues to keep crime and corruption on the front burner.

I thank my two colleagues. Cary Cooper and I have worked together for some time. We joke about continuing our collaboration until we are in our 90s. This is my first venture with Ed Tomlinson, a valued colleague, who has made significant contributions to our understanding of crime and corruption and what to do about it. His input shaped the direction of this collection.

I thank our international authors for contributing their current thinking on this important topic.

York University provided partial support for the preparation of this volume.

My family continues to be a source of support and joy for me. Thanks guys.

Finally, I acknowledge the continuing interest and support for our work provided by Jonathan Norman and the staff at Gower Publishing. Jonathan realized the importance of better understanding of the psychological and social determinants and costs of risky behavior in organizations and continues to champion these efforts.

Ronald J. Burke
Toronto, Canada

PART I
Introduction

Crime and Corruption in Organizations[1]

Ronald J. Burke

This chapter serves as an introduction to understanding the causes and consequences of crime and corruption in organizations, and suggests what individuals, organizations, and societies can do to reduce corruption. It identifies central concepts and themes in this area and ends with a summary of the chapters that follow.

Ashforth et al. (2007, p. 671) define corruption as "the illicit use of one's position or power for perceived personal or collective gain." Corruption includes terms such as corporate wrongdoing, management fraud, and illegal corporate behavior (Zahra, Priem, and Rasheed, 2005). Examples include embezzlement, insider trading, the padding of one's expenses, paying a bribe to get a contract, altering a financial document, and individuals receiving money or being promoted for altering a financial document. Consider the following. Intel Corp., the giant manufacturer of computer chips, is now facing new anti-trust charges alleging that it threatened other computer manufacturers and paid billions of dollars in kickbacks to stop them from using a competitor's chips (Diaz, 2009). Intel has already paid a US$1.45 billion fine to settle anti-trust charges in Europe. The company controls 80 percent of the market, and its practices were stated as harming consumers, other companies and levels of government (Associated Press, 2009a).

In another example, JP Morgan Chase & Co. agreed to pay more than US$700 million to settle charges that it made unlawful payments to friends of public officials to win municipal bond business. As is often the case, the company neither admitted nor denied any wrongdoing (Gordon, 2009).

In December 2009 the US Securities and Exchange Commission (SEC) charged three former executives of now-bankrupt lender New Century

---

1 Preparation of this chapter was supported in part by York University.

Financial Corp. with fraud for misleading investors by misrepresenting their financial circumstances (US Securities and Exchange Commission, 2009).

Finally, the top pasta-makers in Italy were charged with price-fixing. Twenty-six Italian pasta-makers, working as a cartel, were convicted in February 2009 of raising prices to consumers by as much as 36 percent and were fined €12.5 million for restricting competition (BBC News, 2009a).

How Common is Crime and Corruption?

The 2009 PricewaterhouseCoopers *Global Economic Crime Survey* found that 83 percent of economic crime in 2008 stemmed from "asset misappropriation" or, in plain language, stealing from work—a crime admitted to by 56 percent of men and 76 percent of women responding to the survey. The most common items stolen were office supplies and electronics.

The Association of Certified Fraud Examiners (2009) noted that 55.4 percent of certified fraud examiners believed that corporate fraud had risen during 2008-2009 due to the financial meltdown; 49.1 percent blamed financial pressures for the increase, and 88 percent believed that fraud would continue to increase during 2010. Embezzlement—fraud perpetrated by company employees—increased most strongly during the economic downturn. Ryan (2009), in an interview with Martin Kenney, quoted Kenney as saying that, in his estimate, white-collar theft had grown to US$1 billion per month between 2006 and 2009.

A survey by *Sales and Marketing Management Magazine* found that 49 percent of sales managers admitted that their sales representatives lied on sales calls, 34 percent admitted to having heard sales reps make unrealistic promises to customers, and 30 percent admitted that they had customers who demanded kickbacks for buying products or services (Bucaro, 2006).

One can also make a distinction between illegal and unethical behaviors. Illegal behaviors would include stealing, and unethical behaviors would include giving clients small gifts at Christmas. Some behaviors, such as bribery, are both illegal and unethical. Turning to employee theft, defined as the "unauthorized appropriation of company property by employees either for one's own use or for sale to another" (Greenberg, 1995, p. 154), there is evidence that this type of crime has increased during the current economic downturn. In February 2010 Sergey Aleynikov, a former computer programmer with Goldman Sachs, was indicted on charges of stealing computer codes for high-frequency trading software worth millions of dollars to the bank (Bray and Bunge, 2010). He faces the prospect of a possible 25-year prison term. Intellectual property, as well as more tangible things such as merchandise, can be stolen.

The US National Retail Foundation (2009) reported that shoplifting, termed retail shrinkage, rose only 0.08 percent in 2008, but this amounted to US$1.7 billion more in losses year-over-year. Total shrinkage in 2008 was US$36.5 billion, with three-quarters of retailers saying that the problem is getting worse. Employees account for more theft and fraud than do customers or clients: 43 percent versus 36 percent of unexplained losses. Employees fail to ring up sales to friends, or falsely ring up sales returns and put this money on to gift cards. In a strange twist, a British priest, Father Tim Jones of St Lawrence and St Hilda parishes in York, told his congregation that shoplifting was acceptable behavior by those in need when they were desperate, but only from large organizations which would pass this loss on to other consumers in the form of higher prices (Aitchison, 2009). Recent estimates place the annual cost to US organizations from fraud and theft at US$994 billion (ACFE, 2008). Crime and corruption are major problems in organizations.

People sometimes lie on their income tax forms, not declaring all of their income if there is no chance of being caught. Thus, waiters and waitresses at restaurants sometimes do not declare all their tips. Another poll of Canadians, conducted in April 2009, reported that 19 percent of females and 29 percent of males said they would lie in response to the question "Would you lie (leave information off your tax return or make write-offs you couldn't back up) if you knew you wouldn't get caught?" As an example, Bernard Kerik, former New York City Police Commissioner, admitted that he lied to the White House while being considered for the position of Homeland Security Chief in 2004. Kerik, a hero following 9/11, admitted eight crimes in all, including lying on tax returns and accepting US$250,000 worth of home renovations as a payback from a company to which he had awarded a public contract. He was eventually sentenced to four years' imprisonment (Bone, 2010).

- This fact is reflected in *The Insider*, a paper run by undergraduate business students at my university. Several issues in 2009–2010 each carried a story under the heading "Criminal of the month." The criminal profiled in October 2009 was John Rigas, currently in prison and formerly CEO of Adelphia. The Rigas family (two sons also worked in the company) was charged with personally misusing US$100 million of corporate funds and hiding US$2.3 billion of debt from investors. John Rigas spent US$12 million on building a personal golf course and US$26 million on buying the timberland around his house to preserve the view. Other expenditures included US$6,000 on shipping Christmas trees to his daughter's house in New York and buying 17 company cars. The November "criminal of the month" was Sir Allen Stanford who was charged with, and later imprisoned for, a US$7 billion swindle, money-laundering, and a total of 21 criminal charges. The December "criminal of the month" was Richard Scrushy, former CEO of HealthSouth Corporation, who is currently in prison for accounting fraud.

Almost 10 million Americans were victims of identity theft in 2008 according to Miller-McCune.com (Beale, 2009). The methods used ranged from high-tech hacking to stealing wallets and documents.

The Spread of Corruption Within an Organization

Although corruption generally begins with one individual, it typically spreads to other participants (Zyglidopoulos and Fleming, 2008, 2009). Anand, Ashforth, and Joshi (2005) identified six rationalizations individuals used to justify their corrupt actions to themselves, while also reducing regrets and guilt feelings arising from their corrupt behavior. These were: denial of responsibility, denial of injury, denial of victim, social weighting, appeal to higher loyalties, and balancing the ledger. They also proposed three socialization processes that lead people into participating in corrupt acts: cooptation, incrementalism, and compromise. Finally, they identified some external facilitating factors supporting an individual's participation in corrupt acts: group attractiveness and a social cocoon, the mutual support of rationalization and socialization, and the use of euphemistic language.

In a series of experiments, Gino, Ayal, and Ariely (2009) show that unethical behavior by individuals depends less on their simple calculation of cost-benefit analyses than on the social norms reflected in the dishonesty of others and on the visibility of that dishonesty.

Bernard Madoff did not act alone. His key lieutenant, Frank DiPascali, was found guilty of participating in the fraud and sentenced. Two of his computer specialists have also recently been charged with knowingly producing false financial statements. And another half-dozen employees and family members are also being investigated. Madoff's two sons, his brother, and a niece were also sued in September 2009 to recover US$198 million for defrauded investors (Clark, 2009).

Sir Allen Stanford also did not act alone. James Davis, CFO of Stanford Financial Group Co. pleaded guilty to helping Stanford in his US$7 billion Ponzi scheme[2] (Daker, 2009). Three other executives at his companies were also

---

2 A Ponzi scheme involves using money from new investors to pay older investors, with the Ponzi scheme originator using incoming money to meet his or her own needs. Little or no

charged, and the CEO of Antigua's Financial Services Regulatory Commission was indicted for taking bribes from Stanford to stop investigations.

Edward Okun, convicted of a massive fraud and sentenced to jail for 100 years, was also joined in his schemes by his lawyer, members of his former law firm, and Wachovia Corp. in their work for Okun's firm, 1031 Tax Group LLC (Larson, 2009).

Corruption is likely to spread or exist if managers and co-workers observe unethical behavior but ignore it. Managers and colleagues are more likely to ignore unethical behavior when they perceive that it might cause them harm (Gino, Moore, and Bazerman 2008a, 2008b).

Gino and Bazerman (2009) found, in a series of laboratory experiments, that individuals were more likely to accept another's unethical behavior when this unethical behavior increased only gradually rather than dramatically—a "slippery slope effect."

Financial Fraud

Obviously most fraud involves money.

In October 2009 US investigators charged six securities professionals with insider trading involving hedge funds. One of those charged, Raj Rajaratnam, the founder of the Galleon Group and manager of its hedge funds, is one of America's richest men. The investigation was triggered by increases in stock purchase just before an announcement of a company takeover. Investigators said that these individuals gained about US$25 million by investing on the basis of tips from a hedge fund credit rating firm and staff at other companies (Associated Press, 2009b). A few weeks later, the number of individuals charged had risen to 20, including lawyers and Wall Street professionals (Reuters, 2009a). Anil Kumar, a former McKinsey director, pleaded guilty to providing inside information to the Galleon Group. Others have pleaded guilty as well, and have agreed to testify against Rajaratnam (Glovin, 2010).

After a long battle against extradition from Canada, Rakesh Saxena, former treasury advisor to the Bangkok Bank of Commerce, whose failure contributed to the Asian financial crisis in 1997, was charged with embezzling Bt140 million. In addition, he has been charged with approving fraudulent loans worth Bt1.65 million from the bank to a company which he owned (*Bangkok Post*, 2010).

Optionable, Inc., a New York brokerage firm at the center of a US$853 million commodities trading scandal in September 2009, was alleged to have given two former Bank of Montreal (BMO) employees lavish gifts, including

---

money is actually invested.

gambling trips, meals, tickets, and expensive car and limousine services. BMO was also duped into paying the two men US$23 million in compensation and bonuses, and Optionable millions of dollars in fees and commissions (Trichur, 2009).

BAE Systems Plc, Europe's largest defense contractor, agreed to pay US$450 million to the UK and the US after pleading guilty to making false statements about deals with other countries (Reuters, 2010a).

In February 2010 Bank of America reached a US$150 million settlement with the US SEC, averting a lawsuit alleging that the bank concealed its knowledge of losses at Merrill Lynch before Bank of America obtained funds from the US government (Reuters, 2010b). Ken Lewis, then CEO of Bank of America, was twice named Banker of the Year by *American Banker* before his current fall from grace.

The reputations of executives in the financial services sector have taken a huge blow. Yet, apparently some bankers have "thin skins." In December 2009 Hugh McGee, a Wall Street banker earning an eight-figure salary, wrote a letter to the board of trustees of his son's private school asking that a teacher and two other staff members be fired. Why? The teacher apparently referred to bankers as "sleazeballs" (Quinn, 2009).

Thousands of individuals hide money in offshore accounts so they can avoid paying income taxes to their home countries. The US government estimates that it loses about US$100 billion per year in tax revenue because of money being hidden in offshore banks and other tax evasion schemes. Pressure on Switzerland, among other countries, has resulted in these countries providing information to the US on such individuals, who have been offered one year—ending in 2010—to make full disclosure of these assets or risk criminal charges.

In 2009 almost 7,000 Canadian tax cheats, holding Can$1.66 billion in hidden assets, voluntarily came forward to disclose these assets and offshore accounts to the Canada Revenue Agency after Canadian tax officials met with the Swiss USB bank to find out about Canadian assets hidden in offshore accounts. These individuals will only have to pay taxes and accrued interest on these monies and no other financial penalty. Canada does not have as strong laws against tax evasion as do other countries (Wednesday-Night.com, 2009). It is also alleged that the staff of Canada's largest brokerage firm, RBC Dominion, helped clients hide wealth in Liechtenstein (McArthur, 2009).

IF IT'S TOO GOOD TO BE TRUE, IT ISN'T

In November 2009 the SEC charged four people and two companies with organizing a US$30 million Ponzi scheme targeting elderly investors and those approaching retirement. Individuals were encouraged to liquidate the equity on their homes and their retirement funds with the promise of 17 percent to "hundreds of percent" annual return on their investment (Stempel, 2009). In June 2009 Weizhen Tang, a Toronto resident who proclaimed himself as the "Chinese Warren Buffet," was charged by the US SEC with running a multimillion-dollar Ponzi scheme. According to the Ontario Securities Commission, which is also investigating the case, his scheme offered investors weekly profits of 1 percent funded not by bona fide investments on the stock market, but by money deposited in the scheme by fresh investors (Schecter, 2009). Having reached a settlement with the SEC without admitting liability, Tang returned to Canada, was arrested and briefly jailed before being granted bail. The OSC case is still ongoing (Pazzano, 2010).

AND IT MIGHT BE GIBBERISH

Geraint Anderson, formerly a stock analyst at Dresdner Kleinwort, a London-based stock brokerage, in his 2008 book, *Cityboy: Beer and Loathing in the Square Mile*, wrote that much of what he and his colleagues told their clients was "utter gibberish." Anderson was earning a salary of several hundreds of thousands of pounds at the time.

INNOCENT VICTIMS

There have been tens of thousands of innocent victims of fraud, who have lost their money when the fraud has been found out or the Ponzi scheme has failed. There are also tens of thousands of innocent victims who worked for organizations involved in fraud that collapsed, though they had no part in the fraudulent activity. These individuals are likely to have been associated with their failed organization for some time and have greater difficulty gaining new employment. Employees of smaller firms that collapsed because of fraud will face greater difficulties than those of large firms (e.g., Enron, Arthur Andersen) as they will be seen as having been closer to the corruption. Individuals looking for new jobs need to be careful what they say about their former failed (corrupt) employer in their job applications as badmouthing their former employer is likely to be viewed negatively. However, they do need to stress their lack of culpability. Bernard Madoff's two sons have been unemployed since the scandal broke. Madoff's assistant, Eleanor Squillari, indicated that she could never get a job in finance and was contemplating a career in cosmetology. Elaine Solomon, assistant to Bernard Madoff's brother, Peter, indicated difficulties in finding another job, and Peter Madoff stated that he was "forcibly retired" (Lucchetti, 2009).

Job counselors suggest the following advice:

- Learn to overcome your anger.
- Quit your fraudulent firm before being laid off.
- Provide a reference who can attest to your honesty.
- Be ready to provide ethical work examples.
- Be prepared to take a job with lower pay.
- Consider consulting or part-time work to get started.
- Start your own business with the help of former clients and co-workers.
- Switch professions or industries.

HOW TO AVOID BEING "MADOFFED"

Although crooks form only a minority of those providing financial advice, recent high-profile scandals (Madoff, Earl Jones, the Norbourg Group), have led some writers to offer firms advice on how to avoid being "Madoffed." Here are some examples of their guidance.

- Don't focus on the advisor's claimed track record; instead, check out his or her auditor.
- Ask how the advisor gets his or her ideas and recommendations.
- Find out which associations the advisor belongs to.
- Ask direct questions about what the advisor will add to the company.
- Ask how the advisor is paid. Who holds the money? If it is the advisor, is there a trustee?
- Investigate the advisor's lifestyle (lavish?).
- Ask securities regulators if your advisor is in good standing.

Fraud by Misrepresentation

PUTTING SCIENCE ON THE PAYROLL

Merck, the makers of Vioxx, an arthritis drug, is just one of several pharmaceutical companies that have come under scrutiny on account of their research and marketing activities. It was estimated that between 1999 and 2004 more than 27 million patients suffered fatal and non-fatal heart attacks that might have been avoided if those patients had taken a competitor's drug instead (MSNBC, 2004). During that period, however, Merck allegedly played down or misrepresented the risks of dying for patients taking its Vioxx medication. In 2007 Merck, without admitting liability, agreed to pay US$4.85 billion into a trust fund to settle claims against it.

Since then, it has emerged that Merck employees "ghostwrote" academic papers reporting trial results and review papers promoting the drug, according to studies published in April, 2008 in the *Journal of the American Medical Association* (Goldstein, 2008). Apparently, Merck paid academics and physicians to put their names on manuscripts before they were submitted to journals for publication.

Staying with healthcare, in September 2009 pharmaceutical giant Pfizer agreed to plead guilty to US criminal charges involving the promotion and sale of Bextra, a pain medication, and will pay US$2.3 billion to settle charges that it improperly marketed 13 medications. Pfizer claimed that these drugs helped conditions for which they were not approved (Thomaselli, 2009). Some critics maintained that this fine was relatively small, given the profits that Pfizer made from the sale of these medications (Angell, 2004). Pfizer also received negative publicity for testing drugs on children in Africa yet not selling the drugs in Africa because of their high prices (Goos, 2007).

Four pharmaceutical firms (Bayer AG, Eli Lilly & Co., Cephalon, and Amylin Pharmaceuticals Inc.) were asked by the US Food and Drug Administration to stop using misleading promotions for some of their products in which they exaggerated the benefits and downplayed the risks (Reuters, 2010c).

It has been noted that the Vioxx heart risk could have been found several years earlier if Pfizer data had been available to outside researchers (Steenhuysen, 2009). This is not to attack Pfizer, but to suggest that making such data publicly available would help the pharmaceutical industry as a whole.

Spielmans, Biehn, and Sawrey (2010) reported that pharmaceutical companies sometimes report findings from parts of the same study several times, each publication showing the benefits of the drug. Thus one study reports data collected after 12 weeks while a second study reports data collected after 16 weeks.

In summary, the pharmaceutical industry has been found to create fake academic journals, submit falsified manuscripts to real academic journals, and submit falsified manuscripts to leading academic publications. Merck allegedly paid publishing company Elsevier to print nine fake academic journals without acknowledging their links to Merck, with 13 more journals being discussed. Merck suppressed data indicating that two of its drugs were no better than cheaper generic alternatives. Eli Lilly & Co. allegedly has employees who act as ghostwriters for academic journal articles that put the company's products in a favorable light. Merck and Pfizer, it has been claimed, also follow this practice (Laidlow, 2009). All of this is in the name of marketing their products.

Researchers have found copies of internal documents destroyed by Imperial Tobacco Canada, indicating not only that cigarettes were addictive and caused cancer, but that filter-tip cigarettes conferred little, if any, protection. The company studies were carried out in the late 1960s through the early 1980s, and the evidence was destroyed in the early 1990s, probably to avoid damaging tobacco sales (Brunner, 2009). In 1998, the tobacco industry in the US agreed to pay US$246 billion to state governments over 25 years to cover the costs of healthcare to people with smoking-related illnesses. The reality inherent in all these examples is that science is always politicized; you cannot separate science from politics.

Another type of fraud, more common among academics, involves fabricating the results of one's studies. In October 2009 a South Korean court handed down a suspended two-year prison sentence to Hwang Woo-suk for falsifying the results of some of his stem-cell experiments (BBC News, 2009b). In 2004 Hwang achieved some fame for a paper published in *Science*, claiming that he had created the world's first stem-cell line from a cloned human embryo – the journal subsequently withdrew the paper when the fraud allegations surfaced. Academics also sometimes engage in plagiarism—the use of writing by another academic without attribution.

There have also been concerns raised about universities, and their professors, becoming too closely tied with business organizations in their quest for financial support (Woodhouse, 2009) and the effects this has sometimes had on academic freedom.

DOING GOOD BUT BEHAVING BADLY

Lying, cheating, and stealing are complex behaviors. Mazar and Zhong (2009) found, in a series of experiments, that university students who bought products deemed to be morally good (green products) later behaved badly (lying, cheating, and stealing). It seemed that doing good gave them permission to behave badly.

LITTLE WHITE LIES?

Rutherford, Buller, and Stebbins (2009) note that entrepreneurs lack legitimacy in the start-up phases of their enterprises. They have no history, capital, employees, suppliers, or customers. To counteract this, they engage in "legitimacy lies"—the intentional misrepresentation of facts. This lying involves information on organizational size, length of operations, amount of expertise possessed, number of employees, number of previous clients, and making promises that they cannot deliver on.

Even established firms tell "little white lies." Rogers Communications Inc., a Canadian provider of cable and telephone services, was ordered by the British Columbia courts to drop its claim that it has "Canada's most reliable" wireless network. Rogers had previously claimed that it was also Canada's fastest network, but has since discontinued this advertising (Sturgeon, 2009).

NOT SO "LITTLE WHITE LIES"

Apparently there is a market for "fake" university degrees. Several institutions now sell university degrees of various types (business, liberal arts) and at various levels (BA, MA, PhD). An enterprising graduate of my university, Peng Sun, sold degrees from my university for Can$3,000 and an MBA degree for Can$4,000. Sun claimed to have sold hundreds of York University and University of Toronto degrees. Interestingly, Sun was never charged with a crime. Some of the purchasers were from China and preferred to buy the degrees rather than spend three to five years acquiring them legitimately (Brazao, 2008a). A woman from Grenade now living in Canada, Quami Frederick, bought an undergraduate degree from a diploma mill on the Internet and was admitted to a prestigious law school in Canada. The law school found out about this when she was in her final year and removed her from the program; she also lost a summer articling job with a law firm as a result (Brazao, 2008b). My university and others now use an online service to almost instantly verify degrees.

People who lie on their resumés pay a price. Anyone caught lying about their degrees or reasons for their current unemployment, for example, can be fired.

The late Ali Kordan, an ally of the Iranian President, was fired from his job as interior minister in 2008 when he was found to have lied about having received an honorary doctorate from Oxford University (Theodoulou, 2008). His claims to having a master's and bachelor's degree from Iranian universities were also found to be lies.

Employee Theft and Fraud as Job Enrichment

Almost 40 years ago *Psychology Today* published an article titled "A little larceny can do a lot for employee morale." According to Zeitlin (1971), employee theft allows employees to release their frustration, gives employees opportunities for job enrichment, and reduces the need for management to provide salary increases. Allowing workers to steal, Zeitlin contends, will make them happier and more productive. There must be a lot of happy employees out there. However, it is unlikely that this message would have much traction today.

JOB ENRICHMENT AS AN ANTIDOTE TO EMPLOYEE THEFT AND FRAUD

There is evidence that employees who experience job satisfaction or whose current jobs match their long-term career goals are less likely to engage in workplace misconduct, including theft (Harris and Benson, 1998; Huiras, Uggen, and McMorris, 2000).

Government Fraud and Corruption

> **"Karzai vows to crack down on self"***
>
> Hamid Karzai, the President of Afghanistan, has been told that he and his country must reduce rampant corruption. At the opening of a three-day anti-corruption conference, Karzai defended the Mayor of Kabul, a friend and ally, as a good man even though he had just been sentenced to four years in prison for corruption.
>
> **The Onion*, December 2, 2009.

The current president of Pakistan, Asif Ali Zardari, widower of the slain Pakistani politician, Benazir Bhutto, is a billionaire. He accumulated much of his fortune during his wife's two terms in government, when he was known as "Mr Ten Percent." In 1990 and 1991 he was charged with fraud and corruption and imprisoned, but the charges were dropped (GlobalSecurity.org, n.d.). And, as the current president, he has immunity from prosecution.

On 28 September 2009 former Peruvian President Alberto Fujimori pleaded guilty to wiretapping opponents and paying bribes to politicians and journalists to support his 2000 re-election campaign. He received an eight-year sentence to be served concurrently with his 25-year sentence for human rights abuses (Boucaud, 2009).

One day after Mahmoud Abbas's former anti-corruption czar, Fahmi Shabaneh, threatened to expose unsavory practices at the highest levels of Fatah, the Palestinian Authority issued a warrant for his arrest on charges of "collaboration with Israel." The former corruption czar had issued an ultimatum to Abbas to remove all corrupt officials or he would start naming names. Shabaneh indicated that many senior officials of the Palestinian Authority were allegedly involved in the theft of public funds and in sex scandals (Toameh, 2010).

The Chernobyl nuclear reactor exploded on April 26, 1986. In 1997 the Canadian government, along with other G-7 governments, sent money (in this case, Can$71 million) to enclose the remaining reactor buildings in an effort to seal off leaking radiation. As of February 2010 no work has begun on this project. Instead, it is thought that Ukrainian officials have fraudulently taken the money for their own enrichment (*Globe and Mail*, 2010a).

Former Costa Rican president, Rafael Calderón, was found guilty of embezzlement and sentenced to five years' imprisonment in October 2009. Calderón was accused of receiving over US$500,000 in 2004 from a Finnish government loan to Costa Rica's social security system (Associated Press, 2009c).

Also in October 2009 Jacques Chirac, former president of France, was ordered to stand trial for embezzlement and breach of trust during his time as mayor of Paris. He is accused of using City Hall funds to pay dozens of people in fictitious jobs (Associated Press, 2009d).

In December 2009 Jesse Chacon, a government minister and close friend of Venezuelan President Hugo Chavez, resigned as part of a growing banking scandal that has implicated businessmen with ties to his government. Several bankers are in custody and some banks have been closed (Reuters, 2009b).

As this chapter was being written (February 2010) a presidential election was being held in the Ukraine. Both the challenger (Yanukovych), who had a small lead, and the incumbent (Tymoshenko) accused each other of fraud, vote-rigging and vote-buying.

The World Bank Institute has estimated that the total amount of bribes paid by companies per year may be US$1 trillion (Rose-Ackerman, 2007) and that this corruption costs US$80 billion per year. The National Audit Office estimated that Chinese officials misused or embezzled about US$35 billion in the first 11 months of 2009. This included money-laundering, issuing fraudulent loans, and cheating the government through the purchase or sale of state land or mining rights. More than 1,000 state officials face prosecution (Barboza, 2009).

According to Ernst & Young's *10th Global Fraud Survey*, conducted in 2007 and 2008, 24 percent of executive respondents had experienced an incident of bribery or corruption, 23 percent indicated that they had been asked to pay a bribe to win or retain business, and 18 percent believed that they had lost business because of bribes paid by a competitor. In addition, over a third of respondents felt that corruption was increasing (Ernst & Young, 2008, pp. 5–6).

The costs of corruption are huge and include less organizational and country growth, lower levels of public spending on education and healthcare, less revenue from taxes, greater political instability, and lower levels of direct foreign investment (Fisman and Svensson, 2007; Rodriguez, Uhlenbruck, and Eden, 2005).

In June 2009 Ikea announced that it was suspending investment in Russia because of widespread corruption and demands for bribes. The company claimed that it was overcharged millions of dollars for electricity and had to pay bribes before a completed store could be opened. Ikea's action could encourage other foreign countries and businesses to make the same decision, which will damage Russia's reputation as a place to do business. It also hurts the Russian economy since Ikea creates jobs and provides relatively low-cost products to consumers. Russian President Dimitri Medvedev has acknowledged that corruption is a significant problem in Russia and has made curbing it a priority (Kramer, 2009).

Israel was granted membership in the OECD beginning in 2010 but, before joining, had to renounce bribery in arms sales. As the OECD was prepared to award Israel membership, four Israelis were arrested for bribing an African defense minister to purchase Israeli-made weapons (*Globe and Mail*, 2010b).

Although Gabon is a relatively poor country, when Gabon's President Omar Bongo died in June 2009 at the age of 73, he was one of the world's richest men — his family owned more property in Paris than that of any other country leader. Bongo had 66 bank accounts, 183 cars, 39 luxury properties in France, and huge government constructions in Libreville, the capital of Gabon, which were basically monuments to himself. Visitors to a government minister's house spoke of the latest flat-screen televisions, expensive electronic gadgets, and a garage full of expensive cars. In the "Bongo system," fueled by oil monies, it was said that you had to bring a suitcase to Bongo's palace to take home money, as the president only dealt in cash. Most people in Gabon live on US$2 a day (Nossiter, 2009).

Corrupt money continues to flow into the US even though tighter legislation on money-laundering passed after 9/11 was supposed to make this more difficult. Jennifer Douglas, a US citizen and fourth wife of a former vice-president of Nigeria, allegedly helped her husband bring US$40 million into the US. The son of the president of Equatorial Guinea used US lawyers, bankers, real estate agents, and escrow agents to move US$110 million into the US. He bought a US$30 million home in Malibu, California, and a US$38.5 million Gulfstream jet. The daughter of Omar Bongo, president of Gabon, had

US$1 million in her safe deposit box and stated that her father brought it into the US using his diplomatic status (Abrams, 2010).

Cross-cultural Views on Ethics, Fraud and Corruption

Albrecht and Albrecht (2009a) note that crime and corruption in organizations exist in all countries. In addition, fraud and corruption in one part of the world has effects on businesses and governments in other parts of the world. The authors organized a special issue of the *International Journal of Cross Cultural Management* (Albrecht and Albrecht, 2009b) showing how different cultures develop norms about fraud and corruption based on different conceptions of human nature, how cultural characteristics impact on corruption, differences in manager and employee attitudes toward corruption, and the likelihood of bribery and financial statement manipulations in various countries.

Every country in the world views bribery as a criminal act, yet bribery, though varying across countries, is commonplace (Eicher, 2009; Hopton, 2009)). Bribery has both a supply and a demand side. Individuals demand bribes, and firms provide bribes. Some firms are more likely to offer or pay bribes than are others. Some firms seek a competitive advantage and are more willing to offer passive or active bribes. Passive bribes are used to avoid sanctions or punishments; active bribes are used to obtain influence (win contracts, get favorable decisions on regulations, get favorable government policies). The degree of bribery is influenced by the context of the firm's home country and the pressures faced by the firm. Martin et al. (2007) investigated the effects of cultural values and firm characteristics on bribery activities. They considered data from 376 firms from 38 countries in examining the role of cultural factors, social institutions, and a firm's local financial constraints as predictors of a firm's propensity to offer bribes and found that higher levels of bribery were associated with more individualistic countries, social welfare-oriented countries displayed less bribery, and countries with stronger political constraints showed even lower levels of bribery.

A report by the UN Office on Drugs and Crime (UNODC) states that half the Afghans surveyed indicated they had been forced to pay a bribe to a public official during 2009, and that the average bribe amounted to US$160—from an average annual per capita income of only US$425. From these statistics, the total paid in bribes across the whole the country was estimated to be U$2.5 billion per year—equal to 23 percent of Afghanistan's GDP. Moreover, 38 percent of Afghans considered paying a kickback to speed up administrative procedures to be the norm (UNODC, 2010, p. 4).

The Canadian government has proposed changes that will make it more difficult for white-collar criminals to get early parole. Currently, white-collar criminals can request parole after serving only one-sixth of their sentence and receive full parole after serving just one-third of their sentence.

COUNTRIES HAVING THE MOST AND LEAST FRAUD

In its survey of 3,000 companies in 54 countries, PricewaterhouseCoopers (PwC) found that the four countries having the highest levels of fraud (in descending order) were Russia, South Africa, Kenya, and Canada. Other high-fraud countries, after Canada, were Mexico, Ukraine, the UK, New Zealand, and Australia. Low levels of fraud were found in Japan, Hong Kong, Turkey, Netherlands, Romania, Finland, and Switzerland (PricewaterhouseCoopers, 2009, p. 10). In their annual report Transparency International (TI) ranked Russia at 146, a ranking similar to Kenya and Ecuador (TI, 2009). Fifty-six percent of Canadian companies reported economic crimes in 2008. Twenty-seven percent of all the companies surveyed worldwide estimated their fraud-related losses at more than US$500,000 (TI, 2009, p. 13), with 67 percent of companies reporting asset misappropriation as the most common type of fraud, followed by accounting fraud and bribery (TI, 2009, p. 6). The economic meltdown also contributed to both motivation and opportunity to engage in fraud. However, the level of actual fraud is likely to be higher worldwide as it often goes undetected. Bribery and intellectual property infringements were relatively low in Canada compared to the other countries in the survey. The high levels of overall fraud in Canada are the result of more reported instances due to better detection, as well as the relatively light penalties for the offense.

According to TI (2009), the least corrupt governments were New Zealand, Denmark, Singapore, Sweden, Switzerland, Finland, Netherlands, Australia, Canada, and Iceland. The most corrupt governments in the same survey were Somalia, Afghanistan, Burma (Myanmar), Sudan, Iraq, Chad, Uzbekistan, Turkmenistan, Iran, and Haiti. China and Russia were the most improved countries.

Conflicts of Interest

Conflicts of interest abound. Consider the following:

- Nearly one-third of published cancer studies reported a conflict of interest. Research funded by the pharmaceutical industry

was more likely to focus on treatment than on prevention, risk factors, screening or diagnostic methods, and more likely to use study designs that yielded results favorable to the drug company concerned (UMHS News, 2009).
- Stock market analysts making a buy recommendation of risky stock known to be "junk" to other clients to keep current clients happy. But this is tricky. Joseph Hirko, former chairman and CEO of Enron Broadband Section (EBS), the Internet Division of Enron, was sentenced to 16 months' imprisonment and required to pay US$7 million for falsely promoting EBS to analysts to increase the company's stock price. Hirko admitted that Enron's broadband operating system could not do what it had been promoted to do (Fowler, 2009). But Hertz Global Holdings, Inc. has, ironically, sued an analyst, as well as Jack Zwingli, CEO of Integrity Inc., for including Hertz among 20 large companies that might go bankrupt in 2010 (Reuters, 2009c).
- Brian Kennedy, stock analyst at Jefferies & Co. was forced to quit his job after making a "sell" recommendation on shares of CardioNet Inc. He was the target of a complaint filed by CardioNet with the SEC and by some executives at his own firm (Armstrong, 2009).
- Steve Frustaglio's two companies received Can$1 million in untendered jobs for the region of Vaughn, just north of Toronto, while his mother, Joyce Frustaglio was a councilor for the region. The son submitted bids of under Can$3,000 which did not require competitive tendering, and the Vaughn administration was unaware of all the work that his companies were doing in various departments (Gombu, 2009). Another example of transactions that do not pass the "bad smell test."
- Hazel McCallion, Mayor of Mississauga, a small city on the outskirts of Toronto, is currently (July 2010) on trial for allegedly violating the Municipal Conflict of Interest Act. She stands accused of being heavily involved with negotiations to push forward a bid by World Class Developments to build several condominiums and a hotel in the city centre and claims to have been unaware that her son was a principal of that company. Her son would have gained Can$10 million if the deal had gone through. Without coming to a firm conclusion on the outcome of this case, it does not "look good" (O'Toole, 2010).

Moore et al. (2006) write about what they term the "moral seduction" of auditors who, they believe, face widespread conflicts of interest. They identify three threats to the independence of auditors: executives of organizations hire and fire auditors; auditors often take positions with client organizations; and auditors today provide more than just auditing services to clients. Organizations are more likely to hire and retain auditors who support their actions. Auditors taking jobs with their employing organizations forge a common identity. And, as auditors provide a wider array of services to their client organizations, they are more likely to rate their own initiatives as satisfactory. These factors subtly color the judgment of the supposedly objective outsiders.

Moore et al. (2006) and Bazerman et al. (2006) offer some suggestions for reducing conflicts of interest common to auditors. These include: more penalties for organizational corruption; more severe punishment for corrupt individuals; tighter regulation of auditors; limiting auditors to providing only auditing services; requiring organizations to change their auditing firm every five years; prohibiting auditors from taking jobs with their clients; requiring auditors to make independent assessments of a company's financial statements rather than ratifying the client organization's assessments; and requiring that auditing firms be chosen by the boards of directors rather than by senior organizational executives.

A World of Cheats?

There is evidence that corruption is widespread and worldwide. Corruption has been with us for centuries, despite efforts to limit or stop it. In fact, it may be on the increase. Corruption is also much more common in some countries than in others. Are we becoming nations (or a world) of cheats?

Consider the world of athletics. This is timely since the Winter Olympics were held in Vancouver in early 2010 and the World Cup was held in South Africa in mid-2010.

- In 1976 at the Montreal Olympic Games, East Germany won 40 gold medals in total, second only to the Soviet Union. It was later disclosed that hundreds of East German athletes had been using banned steroids for years. Newly uncovered documents indicate that East German officials dumped leftover serum and syringes in the St Lawrence River (Canadian Press, 2009a)
- Six athletes failed a retroactive drugs test 15 months after participating in the Beijing Olympics after several professional cyclists, including an Olympic medalist, tested positive for the performance-enhancing drug CERA in another competition

in 2008. Five athletes were subsequently disqualified, and two were stripped of their Olympic medals (Roadcycling.com, 2010; Wikipedia, 2010).
- Thirty athletes hoping to participate in the 2010 Winter Olympic Games held in Vancouver (February 12-28) were banned from competing after testing positive in drugs tests.
- Mark McGwire, a baseball player who set the record for home runs in a single season in 1998, confirmed on January 11, 2010 what lots of people already knew—he was taking steroids. This was five years after testifying before the US Congress and refusing to answer a direct question on drug use (Heakes, 2010).
- South African runner Caster Semenya won a women's race, but it is not yet clear whether she is a woman or a man. However, although no evidence was provided, Semenya was given permission to run as a woman in July 2010.
- A scandal has hit lawn bowling. Four members of a New Zealand team were found guilty of match-fixing in the Asia-Pacific Championship tournament, deliberately losing a match to Thailand, so that the team would then be drawn against a weaker opponent (Associated Press, 2010).
- In November 2009 Tim Donaghy, a referee in the National Basketball Association, was released from prison after serving 13 months for wire fraud[3] and gambling felonies. Donaghy bet on over 100 games, using the money to refurbish his home, and eventually provided information to organized crime (Donaghy, 2009).
- Canadian Richard Pound, International Olympic Committee member, stated in January 2010 that he believed that corruption is still a problem with the judging of figure skating. In the 2002 Winter Olympics, a scandal blew up when a French judge awarded higher marks to the Russian figure skating pair than to the Canadian pair who had skated flawlessly, thereby denying the Canadians the gold medal. The French judge allegedly admitted that she had been pressured by the Russians, although she subsequently retracted this. However, subsequent investigations concluded that the judge had indeed been pressured, and a second gold medal was awarded to the Canadians (Associated Press, 2002).

---

3   Wire fraud, in the US Code, is any criminally fraudulent activity that has involved any kind of electronic communication at any point in the fraud. Using electronic communications in the perpetration of any part of a fraud incurs a more severe penalty than for fraud conducted without the use of electronic communications.

- The Renault Formula One team was sanctioned in September 2009 for ordering Nelson Piquet Jr to deliberately crash his car into a concrete wall, a life-threatening move, so that his teammate Fernando Alonso would win the 2008 Singapore Grand Prix (Formula 1, 2009). Piquet has since left the Renault racing team.
- Unseen by any of the referees, French soccer player Thierry Henry touched the ball with his hand, resulting in the winning goal in the World Cup qualifying match in which France beat Ireland to advance to the 2010 World Cup in Johannesburg, South Africa. Once the handball was caught on videotape and replayed countless times, Henry admitted the foul, but he did not acknowledge it during the game. Apparently athletes in all sports are loath to admit infractions that the referees miss. What message is this sending to youngsters starting out in their own sports activities? If you cheat you can win?
- In November 2009 about 200 European soccer matches came under investigation in Switzerland and eight other countries. Players, referees, coaches, and officials were believed to have been bribed by a criminal gang who made money from betting on the matches' outcomes. Fifteen people in Germany and two in Switzerland were arrested (BBC News, 2009c).

Now consider the world of politics. There is increasing evidence that Hamid Karzai, sworn in as president in November 2009 for another five-year term, "stole" the election by engaging in fraud (ballot-stuffing, intimidation, bribery). However, he refused to replace the man (his loyal friend) who headed up the fraudulent election because a run-off election was to be held. Various countries providing troops in Afghanistan have been putting Karzai under intense pressure to reduce corruption. He has now bowed to these demands and, in November 2009, began an investigation of 15 of his close supporters and colleagues (Farmer, 2009). Time will tell if he acts on instances of corruption in a country noted for high levels of corruption.

Why are people dishonest? Mazar, Amir, and Ariely (2008) argue that although individuals like to think of themselves as honest, being dishonest has benefits. Their research indicates that people resolve this discrepancy by behaving dishonestly enough to gain but honestly enough to convince themselves of their honesty. They do this by ignoring moral standards and by rationalizing their conduct.

Cheating in high school and university is common. Interestingly, business students were found to cheat more in university than did students in other majors or disciplines (McCabe, Trevino, and Butterfield, 2001). And although most students believe that cheating is unethical, many still cheat. The best predictor of student cheating was student perceptions that their peers cheat (McCabe, Trevino, and Butterfield, 2002). Cheating behavior is trivialized as a result. Unfortunately, cheating in schools is likely to develop into cheating at work (Nonis and Swift, 2001). High ideals of honesty and character seem to have fallen short as more and more individuals and their families use any unethical or illegal advantage at their disposal in their pursuit of advantage, success, fame, and money.

Early in 2010, 19 professors, students and mediators from Zagreb University Faculty of Economics were convicted of corruption in the form of a bribery scheme which guaranteed that the students would pass their exams in exchange for money. Individual students were found to have paid professors up to €2,000 for their pass grades (SETimes.com, 2010).

Causes of Crime and Corruption

Before moving to a consideration of specific aspects of crime and corruption, their consequences and how we fight or control them, let us consider why crime and corruption occur.

Kish-Gephart, Harrison, and Trevino (2010) undertook a meta-analysis on research findings examining bad apples (individuals), bad cases (moral issues), and bad barrels (work environments). They considered the following antecedents of unethical intention or behavioral choices.

Individual characteristics (bad apples)

1. Psychological:
   - cognitive moral development
   - idealism
   - relativism
   - Machiavellianism
   - locus of control
   - job satisfaction.

2. Demographics:
   - gender
   - age
   - education level.

Moral issue characteristics (bad cases)

- Concentration of affect
- Magnitude of consequences
- Probability of effect
- Proximity
- Social consensus
- Temporal immediacy
- General moral intensity.

Organizational environment characteristics (bad barrels)

- Egoism, ethical climate
- Benevolent ethical climate
- Principled ethical climate
- Ethical culture
- Code of conduct
- Code enforcement.

The authors found support for the relationship between many of these antecedents and ethical intentions and ethical behaviors. In addition, they found that there were multiple sources on unethical choice (all three groups of antecedents) and that these often work in impulsive and automatic, rather than more thoughtful and deliberative, ways. Broader conceptions of work environment had weaker relationships with ethical intention than did more focused assessments of ethical climate. Surprisingly, the presence of a code of conduct was unrelated to ethical intentions, but the enforcement of codes of conduct was related to ethical intentions. Let us now consider some of these antecedents in more detail.

MORAL DEVELOPMENT AND MORAL DISENGAGEMENT

Some individuals are more likely to behave in ethical and moral ways than are others. What characteristics do moral and ethical individuals possess? Two stable individual difference factors have been found to be associated with ethical decision-making: levels of moral development and moral disengagement.

Kohlberg (1984) proposed and validated a six-stage theory of increasingly complex moral development.

- *Stage 1: obedience and punishment orientation*. Individuals believe that they must act according to set rules or laws.

- *Stage 2: individualism and exchange*. Individuals can hold different views based on their own interests.
- *Stage 3: good interpersonal relationships*. Individuals act on the basis of good motives and supportive feelings.
- *Stage 4: maintaining the social order*. Individuals act in accordance with laws and authorities to maintain the social order.
- *Stage 5: social contract and individual rights*. Individuals believe that everyone wants certain basic rights and some democratic procedures for changing laws and bettering society.
- *Stage 6: universal principles*. Individuals hold universal principles (e.g., justice for all).

The fifth and sixth stages are typically grouped together. Individuals capable of reasoning at the fifth and sixth stages are less likely to engage in unethical behaviors.

Individuals are also more likely to make unethical decisions when they become morally disengaged (Bandura, 1986). Moral disengagement frees individuals from self-sanctions and the guilt that accompanies engaging in behavior that violates their internal ethical standards. Bandura identified eight interrelated moral disengagement mechanisms, including empathy, moral identity, trait cynicism, and chance locus of control—the belief that individuals have little control over events in their lives.

FOLLOW THE MONEY!

Consider the following.

- The highest paid US CEO, Stephen Schwarzman, who set his own salary, received US$702 million in 2008; the second highest salary, received by Larry Ellison, was US$556.9 million (Reuters, 2009d). Although Schwarzman and Ellison have never been charged with any crime, they do illustrate the huge sums of money paid to corporate executives. Ellison also co-owns one of the world's largest yachts, reflecting the lifestyles of "the rich and famous."
- Bernard Madoff, convicted of running a Ponzi scheme that lost billions and sentenced to 150 years in prison, owned three luxury homes, a boat, expensive jewelry, and art. Not every Madoff client was ripped off, however. Some, such as Jeffry Picower, who made over US$7 billion and owned luxury homes in Manhattan, Palm Beach and Greenwich, Connecticut, made huge gains in the early

years of Madoff's scheme. Picower, who had been informed that the government was going to charge him and come after this money, died of a heart attack while swimming in his pool at his Florida home on Sunday October 25, 2009. He had been in poor health and had heart disease, and his death was ruled as accidental (Efrati, 2009). One can only speculate on the role played by the upcoming fraud charges and trial.

- A Canadian financial adviser, Earl Jones, was convicted in January 2010 for operating a Ponzi scheme that cost his clients about Can$50 million. Jones took almost Can$3 million in payments from his company, as well as Can $593,000 for his children's schooling and other expenses, Can$169,000 for car purchases, and transferred Can$497,000 to Bermuda (Canadian Press, 2009b). Jones and his wife reportedly spent Can$70,000 a month on jet-setting and dining. Maxine Jones, who is in the process of divorcing her husband, had hundreds of thousands of dollars placed in her bank account each year, but apparently never asked her soon to be ex-husband where it came from (CBC News, 2009b). The money was used to pay for the couple's daughters' weddings, the purchase of three condos, household furnishings and landscaping, three cars, and memberships at the Royal Montreal Golf club and the Boca Raton Resort Club.
- When Scott Rothstein, a Florida-based US lawyer, was indicted for running a Ponzi scheme in November, 2009 federal agents seized his assets. These included 20 luxury cars (including three Ferraris, two Rolls-Royces, and a 2009 Bugatti Veyron valued at over US$1 million), 15 properties (including a South Beach mansion formerly owned by Gianni Versace), three boats (a 26-meter Warren yacht, a 10-meter Aquariva and a 17-meter Sea Ray), and money deposited in Moroccan bank accounts (Zand, 2010). These assets were put up for sale.
- There is recent evidence that people who participate in Ponzi schemes do so at the suggestion and invitation of their friends (LeBor, 2009). Affinity fraud, fraud among friends, starts with a few people making money and then inviting friends to take part.
- The mayors of three New Jersey cities, two state legislators, along with five rabbis and dozens of other public officials, were arrested on July 23, 2009 in 54 locations in New York and New Jersey on charges of corruption and money-laundering. Public officials allegedly took bribes from developers in exchange for their help in

getting projects and permits prioritized and steering work to them. The money-laundering scheme stretched as far afield as Israel (Temple-Raston, 2009).

A common theme runs through these examples of individual and organizational corruption—greed. That is, in the vast majority of cases, money was involved, and individuals and/or organizations engaged in corruption for financial benefits, either directly or indirectly.

The recent failures of Wall Street financial institutions were attributed, in part, to compensation systems that rewarded executives for taking excessive risk (Cohan, 2009; Tett, 2009). Jeffrey Immelt, current CEO of GE, in a speech to military students at West Point on December 9, 2009, stated that "rewards became perverted" and "tough-mindedness was replaced by meanness and greed" (Immelt, 2009, p. 6). A Statistics Canada survey indicated that wages rose a paltry 1.6 percent in 2009 while earnings of business managers increased by 17 percent, more than ten times as much. It seems that those who caused the economic crisis were not affected by it (Statistics Canada, 2010).

Leaders of some developed countries (e.g., France, the UK, the US) have discussed the possibility of regulating "excessive" executive compensation, but these efforts are not widely supported by the business community. Some financial institutions have indicated that they will alter their pay practices, but it is too soon to see what this entails and what effect it will have. US President Barack Obama has moved to regulate (i.e., reduce) the salaries of a small number of executives of companies that received financial bail-outs from the US government (i.e., the taxpayers). The banking and financial sectors have been "warned to change their ways" in many industrialized countries (e.g., Canada, France, the UK, the US) and the G20 as a whole, but it is too soon to tell whether they understand the message. Bonuses, if they are to be paid, should be tied to long-term performance. Banks need to build up larger capital reserves in case of emergencies. Risky financial practices need to be curtailed. The banking and financial services sectors need to be more tightly controlled. Capital should be available for loans instead of bonuses. Unfortunately, it looks as if the banking and financial sectors are tone-deaf. They continue to argue that paying out huge bonuses is necessary and that the inequality between Wall Street and Main Street will lead to future prosperity for all. They continue to lobby against global and national legislative changes. John Thain, who lost his job as CEO of Merrill Lynch after its sale to Bank of America, was vilified in the press for spending huge sums of money redecorating his office. He has made speeches indicating what might be done to prevent the financial crisis from happening again and has also said that it is "very unfortunate" that the

American Dream "has been kind of demonized now." Was he referring to the US$1.2 million office refurbishment (Huffington Post, 2009)? In addition to greed, it is likely that managerial incompetence also played a role in the 2008 financial meltdown.

A recent International Monetary Fund (IMF) working paper titled *A Fistful of Dollars: Lobbying and the Financial Crisis* (Igan, Mishra, and Tressel, 2009) reported a direct link between the amount of money spent by mortgage lending organizations on lobbying efforts aimed at politicians and engaging in high-risk lending. This money was spent in an attempt to limit legislation that would curtail their efforts to lend to high-risk borrowers.

But it does appear that the Obama administration may be serious about reform. It plans to cut the salaries of the top 25 earners of seven firms that received financial bail-outs by 90 percent. In addition, any of these 125 individuals wanting extra perks (e.g., private planes, limos, company cars, country-club memberships) have to receive government permission first. The US government also passed a financial-sector reform package in 2010.

Several financial institutions in various countries (e.g., Canada, the UK, France, the US) have indicated that they will be changing their pay practices so that performance-based pay is tied to longer-term growth, and some have indicated the possibility of clawing back some of the bonus money already paid.

Unfortunately, at the end of 2009 banking executives saw fit to award themselves record bonuses on the basis of recent improvements in the sector's financial health. In the UK, the chancellor, Alastair Darling, responded by imposing a one-off 50 percent tax on all banking bonuses exceeding £25,000. This raised a massive £2 billion for the UK Treasury (GAAPweb.com, 2010). Obviously the banking industry was not amused.

HUBRIS AND ARROGANCE

Many individuals implicated in major fraud cases (e.g., Allen Stanford, Dennis Kozlowski, Garth Drabinsky) have huge egos and seem almost larger than life. Drabinsky wrote a book earlier in his career titled *Closer to the Sun* (1995), equating himself with Icarus, the legendary figure in Greek mythology, who fell to earth after getting too close to the sun and having his wings burned. These individuals have high levels of pride and self-confidence, giving them the sense that they can accomplish anything (see Nocera, 2008, for examples of how pride, ego, and revenge come together to make some "bad guys"). Engaging in fraud may become necessary to fulfill their dreams.

MAKING THE NUMBERS

Executives of public companies in particular face pressures from various stakeholders to achieve financial goals (Lanchester, 2010). CEOs then place pressure on their managers to deliver short-term results (Schweitzer, Ordonez, and Douma, 2004). When these financial goals prove difficult to achieve, managers may resort to aggressive or illegal accounting practices (Swartz and Watkins, 2003). Harris and Bromiley (2007) found that both top management compensation and poor organizational performance in relation to aspirations increased the likelihood of financial misrepresentation.

Thus, "failing to make the numbers" has great consequences for senior managers, increasing the pressure to "cook the books." As a result there has also been a corresponding increase in the number of organizations worldwide that have had to restate their earnings when "errors" have been discovered.

In order to make the numbers, and to keep alive the prospect of receiving a large bonus, executives downsize to reduce head-count, switch to less expensive part-time staff instead of full-time staff, reduce staff benefits and perks, and delay necessary investments in infrastructure and repairs. However, while all this may make them look good in the short run, it creates problems in the longer term. A recent example of this is famed former GE executive Robert Nardelli who became CEO at Home Depot. He instituted many of these changes, but found that he had to undo them because company performance suffered.

Ethical Work Climates

Victor and Cullen (1988) found that employees who rated their work climates higher on ethics also reported observing fewer ethical lapses. But what is an ethical work climate? An ethical work climate is based on employee perceptions of the organization's practices and procedures relating to ethical issues. It spells out the correct response for an individual to make in a situation that has ethical dimensions. Aspects of a work climate that spell out ethical behaviors at work, procedures that one should employ in these situations, and one's professional and occupational ethics obtained from training and education all come together in creating an ethical work climate (Stevens, 2009), highlighting the appropriate course of action. However, an ethical code by itself is not enough to ensure ethical behaviors. Germany's Siemens AG had to pay around €1.5 billion in penalties in 2008 after pleading guilty to corruption charges, even though the company had a strong code prohibiting bribery. Enron had a lengthy code of ethics as well. So you need more than words on paper.

Costs of Corruption

A new arcade game has been raking in the money in a UK seaside town. The game, "Whack a banker" is based on the older "Whack a mole" game, with the bankers here being bald and looking the same since most people see bankers as faceless. Players try to hit as many bankers as they can in 30 seconds. If the player manages to hit enough bankers in a set time, a voice says: "You win. We retire. Thank you very much to the taxpayer for paying our pensions." Replacing worn-out mallets has become a real challenge (BBC News, 2009d).

Corruption inflicts a cost on individuals, organizations, society, and whole countries (Nofsinger and Kim, 2003). Individuals who are convicted of taking part in corruption may experience pangs of guilt and shame and face penalties of varying degrees of harshness, including making financial restitution, serving prison sentences, loss of reputation, loss of their means of earning a living, and, in some cases, loss of family through divorce. Organizations lose reputation, money, and chances of long-term survival (Clarke, Dean, and Oliver, 2003). Firms guilty of corruption also face greater scrutiny and diminished future performance, including a decline in the quality of their network partners and their cohesion (Sullivan, Haunschild and Page, 2007) and bankruptcy in some cases (e.g., Arthur Andersen). Societies lose trust in their institutions (Wall Street executives, lawyers) and in their elected officials, and fewer young women and men pursue their careers in these occupations. Cynicism is heightened (Pirson, 2009). Finally, countries lose opportunities for investment and growth, respect in the broader international community, and their influence in making the world a better place—the moral high ground. All of these factors contribute to what many see as a crisis of confidence in corporations (Child, 2002; Child and Rodrigues, 2003; Kochan, 2002; Gioia, 2002)

Nortel Networks, once a highly successful Canadian high-tech company, is now working its way through bankruptcy. One factor leading to this situation was the major accounting scandal the company experienced in 2004, which resulted in multiple financial restatements, the departure of company leaders, a damaged reputation, depleted management resources, and huge expenses. In addition to the financial costs associated with the accounting scandal, skeptical investors, and a weakening market, the company subsequently found it difficult to attract outstanding board members, all of which exacerbated its spiral of decline.

FAILED INVESTMENT IN TRUST

Historically, people have willingly put their faith and trust in members of particular professions or occupations, including the clergy, auditors, politicians, lawyers, doctors, corporate executives, and police officers. Unfortunately, too many people have experienced a betrayal of this trust.

Although the pharmaceutical industry has developed a number of life-saving and health-enhancing drugs, it has come under increasing scrutiny and encountered growing cynicism (Santoro and Gorrie, 2005) on account of unethical practices; the "grand bargain" between the pharmaceutical industry and society is becoming frayed. Huge industry profits, along with unethical practices, no longer balance the benefits received by members of society.

Lawyers and police officers who should know better, given their roles and status, are sometimes guilty of betraying our trust. Slayton (2007) described the criminal behavior of a small number of Canadian lawyers who engaged in theft and fraud, abused financial relationships, helped clients steal money, and engaged in drug use and sexual relations with their clients. In December 2009, US border agents and customs inspectors were found to have accepted money and sex to help Mexican drug smugglers get around heightened border security measures. One inspector, Luis Alarid, accepted US$200,000 which he used to buy a motorcycle, flat-screen TVs, and a laptop computer among other things. Customs officers earn an average of US$70,000 a year, so a bribe can be attractive to some (Archibold, 2009).

The Royal Canadian Mounted Police (RCMP) has come under some scrutiny and attracted negative publicity for their use of tasers to disarm individuals, occasionally causing death. Like many Canadian police forces, the RCMP investigates itself, and it is typical for these investigative bodies to find no violations. In August 2009 the RCMP rejected a report recommending that it should stop investigating itself in serious incidents involving a killing.

According to Human Rights Watch (2009), police in Rio de Janeiro and São Paulo Brazil killed more than 11,000 people in six years. Rio police killed one of every 23 people arrested, São Paulo police killed one of every 348 people arrested, while US police killed one of every 37,000 people arrested. Brazilian police in these cities attribute the deaths to resisting arrest. Human Rights Watch labels many of these deaths as execution-style slayings.

There are also more dramatic costs of fraud and corruption. A Kuwaiti businessman linked to Citigroup and charged in the US with corruption, Hazem al-Braikan, committed suicide in July 2009. A Toronto lawyer, Gil Cornblum, accused of insider trading resulting in a multi-million-dollar fraud, committed suicide just one day before the Ontario Securities and Exchange Commission was to announce a settlement agreement with the now deceased and his co-conspirator (Wallace, 2009).

Bankers have now replaced lawyers at the bottom of the trust totem pole. Leaders of various countries have described their banking executives as arrogant, greedy, lacking humility, and disgraceful. There has been a huge erosion of trust in the financial services sector. Banker jokes have replaced lawyer jokes. The Second City Comedy troupe in Toronto titled one of their shows "0 down, 100% screwed" to reflect this.

In an extreme case, a group of wealthy German pensioners kidnapped and tortured a financial advisor who lost €2.5 million of their savings which he had invested in the Florida property market (Pidd, 2010). Although this case did not involve fraud, and likely did not involve incompetence given the sudden economic meltdown, it illustrates the anger felt by large numbers of ordinary people against the financial system and its executives..

The Pew Research Center in the US surveyed Americans on their perceptions of which professions contribute "a lot" to society's well-being. The top three contributors were the military (84 percent), teachers (77 percent) and scientists (70 percent); the bottom four were journalists (38 percent), artists (31 percent), lawyers (23 percent) and business executives (21 percent) (Pew Research Center, 2009).

RECOVERING FROM PUBLICLY KNOWN ACTS OF CORRUPTION

Many countries believe in second chances. Thus, individuals convicted of engaging in criminal, fraudulent or corrupt behavior have opportunities for redemption. In the US and UK, recent examples of individuals who have rebuilt their careers, lives and reputations include Michael Milliken, Martha Stewart, and Sir Jeffrey Archer. Other individuals are in the process of recovery, including Michael Vick, the US professional football player sent to prison for bankrolling a dog-fighting ring, and Michael McCain, CEO of McCain Foods, whose firm had to deal with a listeria crisis resulting from tainted meat, which killed some consumers and resulted in a US$28 million class-action settlement.

Lloyd Blankfein, CEO of Goldman Sachs, apologized on November 17, 2009 for the firm's role in the global financial crisis, particularly the sub-prime mortgage fiasco. Goldman Sachs had come under intense criticism over the previous year, likely contributing to this apology. Blankfein admitted that Goldman, the largest and most powerful investment bank in the world, participated in "things that were clearly wrong" (Harper and Townsend, 2009).

While having some common elements, individual and organizational recoveries from acts of corruption and bad behavior also have some differences. Both involve marketing (oneself and the company) and both need to acknowledge the damage done and offer to fix it. Both individuals and companies have to be contrite. And both individuals and companies have to earn back trust. Personal reputation is affected to a large degree by individual charisma and likeability (e.g., Bill Clinton). Individuals can give back to their communities (e.g., Eliot Spitzer, former governor of New York, involved in a call-girl scandal and now teaching an undergraduate course on Law and Public Policy for little money at City College of New York). But unlike companies, individuals have no one to blame but themselves; companies can fire people, blame individuals, and change personnel. However, for both individuals and companies, recovery will take a long time.

Indeed, can organizations recover when their corrupt or unethical behavior becomes public knowledge? Some organizations have been unable to survive this situation (e.g., Enron, Arthur Andersen). But organizational death is not inevitable. Pfarrer et al. (2008) have developed a four-stage model for increasing the speed with which, and likelihood that, an organization will recover following a publicly-known corrupt or unethical act that places stakeholders at risk. Their model has the following stages:

1. discovering the facts of the corruption (conducting an internal investigation, undertaking due diligence, offering voluntary disclosure, engaging in public cooperation);
2. providing an appropriate explanation for the corruption (acknowledging the wrongdoing, expressing regret, accepting responsibility, offering amends, making an apology);
3. doing penance and accepting and serving a fair punishment (accepting the verdict, serving time, acknowledging the equitable punishment);
4. making internal and external rehabilitative changes (changing people and reward structures, portraying a new image externally, developing a new mission statement).

Individuals and organizations can rebound from widely known acts of corruption if they deal with the transgression openly and honestly and then act responsibly. The old public relations strategies and spin no longer work.

Reducing Corruption

On the other side of the coin, ethical organizations may reap dividends (Simons, 2009), making it important to increase ethical behavior of both individuals and organizations (Schwartz, 2009; Torres, 2009).

INDIVIDUALS' CHOICES AND ACTIONS

Individuals can choose to act in ways that reduce corruption in their workplaces (Beenen and Pinto, 2009; Watkins, 2003). They could share their concerns with a trusted co-worker about anything that they think might be inappropriate. They could discuss their concerns with their supervisors. They could then choose to become whistleblowers, using the company's hotline to report their concerns. And, as a last resort, they might get legal or other advice from outside if there is no internal reporting system in their organization. Using their interview with Sherron Watkins, formerly with Enron, Beenen and Pinto (2003) label individual actions using the terms "perceive," "probe," "protest," and "persist." It is clear that as one moves along this continuum of individual action, the associated costs become greater to all concerned.

MBA EDUCATION

Business schools may have an important role to play in raising ethical concerns and impacting on future levels of corruption (Adler, 2002; Gioia, 2003). All business schools nowadays are likely to offer either a course or a module with a course on business ethics.

McCabe and his colleagues (McCabe, Trevino, and Butterfield, 1999; McCabe and Trevino, 1993) found that having students sign an honor code prohibiting cheating resulted in a dramatic drop in cheating incidents in school. An increasing number of business schools around the globe are having their graduates sign an oath that they will behave in an ethical way when they graduate: "I solemnly swear never to become Bernie Madoff," as one writer put it. It is not clear, however, whether signing such oaths will make any difference when graduates enter the world of work, although it is clear that MBA graduates who have taken ethics courses and signed the oath will know the correct verbal responses to give. But making MBA students ethical is something else. MBA graduates who behave unethically after taking the ethics courses will at least be unable to claim ignorance of their behavior. But, more basically, can ethical behavior be taught? A student's ethical character is likely set years before he or she enters an MBA program. As a result, I have become increasingly skeptical about the value of ethics education for MBA students.

Nevertheless there are concerns that the teaching of business ethics in business schools is still a marginal part of most MBA programs. Most business schools emphasize content from economists, termed agency theory, which suggests that people are selfish, and want, and try to get, as much as they can for themselves in a dog-eat-dog world (Sutton, Ferraro, and Pfeffer, 2005). In addition, concerns have been raised about the effectiveness of teaching business ethics to adults; some critics maintain that the best time to address ethics is when boys and girls are very young.

It has been observed that graduating MBA students are arrogant, have inflated egos, unrealistic expectations of their worth, and a sense of entitlement. When I left my office recently, on the day that our incoming MBA students were arriving for their first day on campus, I noticed some large posters on which the top line—in bold print—said "Ruling the world starts here." This highlights the challenge facing the teaching of management in business schools—if, indeed, it can even be learned here (Mintzberg, 2004).

A recent study by Dincer, Gregory-Allen, and Shawky (2010) looked at whether money managers who have achieved the prestigious Chartered Financial Analyst (CFA) designation did better than those with an MBA as against those without those credentials. The authors found that neither designation had a meaningful effect on performance, but managers with a CFA build significantly less risky portfolios than managers with MBAs. This might add another factor in explaining the difficulties on Wall Street in recent years. Interestingly, fewer MBAs are now seeking work there, reflecting not only the decline in hiring, but also the negative attitudes being directed there.

The recent economic downturn that occurred on the watch of business-school-trained executives has caused many to criticize business school education. About 40 percent of the graduates of the world's best business schools worked on Wall Street where they presumably applied what they had learned. Many academics have accepted at least part of the blame for the meltdown and have attempted to reform MBA programs. Some schools have added a few new courses in business ethics, ethical marketing, and ethical finance, and some schools have added a voluntary pledge to behave honorably. But these changes have been small. Business schools need to take a more critical look at what they teach and be more critical of their concepts, theories and those who practice them.

Controlling Corruption

Jérôme Kerviel, a trader employed by French bank Société Générale, lost almost €5 billion through rogue betting in 2007, leaving the bank close to collapse in January 2008. He was charged with forgery, breach of trust, and unauthorized computer use in September 2009 and faces up to five years in prison and a fine of €375,000 if convicted. Kerviel claims that he acted with the tacit knowledge and agreement of his superiors; the bank is claiming that he acted alone. The trial will begin in June 2010. Regardless of whether he acted alone or with the knowledge of his superiors, there is clearly something wrong with the bank's control systems for this to have occurred at all. The French Banking Commission fined Société Générale €4 million for serious shortcomings in its internal controls, leading to the trading losses, and the bank has admitted not only management failures and weaknesses, but also a failure to follow up at least 74 trading alerts since 2006 (*New York Times*, 2010).

An approach commonly advocated for controlling corruption is the imposition of organizational controls. Almost all large organizations have an ethics office and officer(s). However, there have to be doubts about the adequacy of internal controls in many organizations if Jérôme Kerviel could run up such huge losses through unauthorized trading.

Lange (2007) provides a multidimensional conception of organizational corruption control. He identifies four types of corruption controls based on (1) a focus on targets, either process or outcomes, and (2) an emphasis on transmission channels, either administrative or social/cultural. Process targets emphasize individual behaviors; outcome targets focus on rewards or punishments based on behaviors. Administrative transmission channels emphasize formal rules, routines, and structures which are again coercive (using rewards and punishments); and social/cultural transmission channels focus on beliefs and norms.

Albrecht and his colleagues (Albrecht, Albrecht, and Albrecht, 2004; Albrecht, Albrecht, and Dolan, 2007) propose three broad strategies for reducing corruption following from their "corruption triangle" approach: reducing the opportunities for corruption through better oversight, monitoring, and controls; reducing the pressures that individuals feel they are under to make the numbers at all costs; and hiring ethical staff.

Anand, Ashforth, and Joshi (2005) describe ways of preventing corruption-related rationalization and socialization, and reducing these if they already exist. For prevention, they advocate fostering awareness of these processes through discussion, through training sessions, and through encouraging introspection into how employees do their jobs on a daily basis and identifying any ethical implications that emerge from this analysis. They also propose that performance evaluations go beyond just "the numbers," and suggest that organizations would benefit if they created an ethical organizational environment. Finally, they argue that top management should serve as ethical role models. In terms of reducing existing forces of rationalization and socialization, Anand et al. suggest first uncovering these forces, making their reversal a critical need, and moving quickly to address these, sometimes using external change agents who can bring in an external perspective and represent a new way of operating.

The Association of Certified Fraud Examiners indicated that expense account abuse accounted for 13 percent of all fraud in the US in 2008, and an increasing number of employers are carefully monitoring their employees' expense claims. Employees at all organizational levels have been found to be using their employers as their own piggy banks, charging them for gym memberships, nannies, cleaning, gardening, expensive lunches, dry-cleaning, golf lessons, escorts, and expenses incurred by other family members. There are plenty of outrageous examples of such behavior. Conrad Black, currently serving time in a Florida prison after being convicted of fraud at Hollinger, ran what has been called a "corporate kleptocracy." Black charged Hollinger US$24,950 for "summer drinks," US$90,000 to spruce up his Rolls Royce, and thousands of dollars for exercise equipment, silverware for his corporate jet, and clothing (Kirby, 2009). Dennis Kozlowski, former CEO of Tyco, charged his firm US$11 million for antiques and furnishings for his multimillion-dollar homes in Florida and New York and US$1 million for a fortieth birthday party for his then wife, as well as US$6,000 for the infamous floral patterned shower curtain (Maremont and Cohen, 2002).

Employees are increasingly being terminated for expense account abuse. But organizations must first indicate to all employees that this is a fireable offense and have convincing evidence that such an offense has been committed. Forensic accounting has become a growth industry. There are software programs now available for tracking employees' expenses, and an ever increasing number of firms are making use of these services. However, organizations need to find ways of monitoring employees' activities without making them feel like criminals or children.

Several instances of real or potential conflicts of interest have been raised involving individuals serving on city and municipal governing bodies in Canada (and the House of Commons in the UK, among other places). The Catholic School Board in Toronto has had issues with elected board members' conflicts of interest, unauthorized benefits, and lavish expenditures (lingerie, mini-bar alcohol, Caribbean vacations).The board held a one-day crash course on November 21, 2009 for anyone interested in running for trusteeship in their next election. The session covered topics such as campaign tricks, conflict of interest laws, and the job of a trustee (Yang, 2009).

REDUCING FINANCIAL FRAUD

Individuals such as Bernie Madoff, Marc Drier, Allen Stanford and Earl Jones, among countless others, have given financial investing a bad name. The investment industry clearly has to rebuild investor trust. Financial professionals could undertake the following actions.

- Obtain the necessary education and credentials to become accredited and professional.
- Explain their credentials to clients.
- Speak out against others who are offering financial advisory services but seem to lack professional credentials.

Investors also need to act in ways that prevent them from falling victim to fraud. The following actions might help.

- Work with a well-established and reputable firm.
- Find out more about the financial advisor's credentials, experience and services.
- Ask the advisor for references.
- Spread investments over more than one advisor.

REDUCING EMPLOYEE THEFT

Rosenbaum (1976) has shown that using weighted application blank scores in the employee selection process and scheduling differential surveillance for potential high-risk employees can reduce employee theft.

WHISTLEBLOWING

"In a time of universal deceit telling the truth is a revolutionary act."
George Orwell

Time magazine chose three female whistleblowers—Cynthia Cooper of Worldcom, Coleen Rowley of the FBI, and Sherron Watkins of Enron—as their Persons of the Year in 2002. Miceli, Near, and Dworkin (2009, p. 379) define whistleblowing as follows: "Whistle-blowing—when current or former employees disclose illegal, immoral, or illegitimate organizational activity to parties they believe may be able to stop it." The authors indicate how whistleblowing can help organizations by saving money and reputation, improving employee satisfaction and preventing reactions that would encourage government regulation. Whistleblowing can provide an organization with critical information and is vital to organizational learning, self-correction, and improvement (Armenakis, 2004; Martin, 2009). But most organizations do not do a good job of organizational learning: they have difficulty learning in "normal" times and even more difficulty in "trying times," which is what whistleblowing creates. So it is no surprise that few managers encourage their staff to become whistleblowers. Miceli, Near, and Dworkin (2009, 2008) offer organizations some suggestions to ensure that whistleblowing occurs when necessary. These include: banning retaliation, hiring employees likely to blow the whistle when they see something wrong, communicating codes of ethics and anti-retaliation policies throughout the organization, training managers how to handle concerns without retaliation, indicating to employees what the organization considers wrong, creating channels for reporting wrongdoing, providing incentives to report concerns, and investigating all complaints thoroughly.

In November 2009 a Canadian diplomat, Richard Colvin, gave testimony before a Canadian House of Commons committee on memos he sent in 2007 to numerous Canadian government and military leaders about the abuse of Afghans arrested by Canadian forces and then turned over to Afghan soldiers, many of whom were later tortured. Many of the Afghans picked up were civilians—taxi-drivers and farmers—not Taliban insurgents. Colvin's testimony was perceived as putting the Canadian government in a bad light and as giving ammunition to opposition parties to attack the government. As a response to Colvin, the government—his employer—came down on him like a ton of bricks, attacking his credibility by saying that his testimony was full of holes (Brennan and Woods, 2009). On December 8, 2009 almost 50 former Canadian ambassadors signed a letter protesting against the Canadian government's treatment of Colvin, suggesting that his treatment would send a chill over the foreign service, silencing dissent. And on December 9, 2009 the commander of the Canadian Forces, Walter Natynczyk, made statements supporting Colvin's claims. As of April 2010 this affair is still playing itself out in the form of hearings conducted by the Canadian Military Police Complaints Commission, despite efforts by the government to prevent them, and Colvin has held to his story (Voltairenet.org, 2010). Colvin is a whistleblower. I have discussed the Colvin case with a small group of young employed professionals, and the majority indicated that they would never do what Colvin is doing. Most whistleblowers face difficult choices, the majority being "punished" in some way (Martin, 2003). This is a sad commentary on truth in organizations!

What is interesting and perhaps not surprising is the response of Colvin's colleagues who are failing to stand up to defend or support him. Some are afraid to speak out since they have spent a lifetime in the government bureaucracy and fear for their jobs and pensions, or they fear being transferred to lower-paid, less interesting jobs, and are intimidated by the attacks on Colvin or their lack of rights under Canadian law. The Canadian laws on whistleblowing do not offer as much protection as laws elsewhere (e.g., the US, Israel).

But some whistleblowers achieve a happy ending. John Kopchinski, a former salesman for Pfizer, was awarded US$51.5 million as a result of his whistleblower lawsuit against his former employer. Kopchinski was upset at the way in which Pfizer marketed Bextra, feeling that Pfizer put profits before the health of customers, and filed a lawsuit against the company. He was immediately fired by Pfizer, and he and his family were forced to live on about one-third of his former salary over the six years it took to conclude the court case. Kopchinski and five other Pfizer salesmen filed their charges under the US False Claims Act under which individuals might get rewarded by exposing corporate wrongdoings (Reuters, 2009e).

CORPORATE CODES OF ETHICS

A code of ethics has been defined as "a written, distinct, and formal document which consists of moral standards used to guide employee and/or corporate behavior" (Schwartz, 2004, p. 324). Codes of ethics detail the values of an organization: what is acceptable and what is not, the standards and values that should guide all employees' behavior. As a consequence of the increasing emphasis on ethical behavior in organizations, at least 58 percent of the world's largest 100 firms have now written ethical codes (Kapstein, 2004).

Codes of ethics can serve a number of critical functions. They provide firms with a legal self-defense by making it clear to employees what behaviors are unacceptable (Stevens, 2009). They indicate ethical and moral values that should govern individual actions within a firm. Written codes of ethics can have value in reducing corruption. Important sources of support include: ethical leadership; an awareness of the code of ethics through constant communication; articulating clear standards; firm consequences for violating ethical guidelines; holding open discussions of the code in both formal and informal settings; fostering an understanding of the code of ethics; and embedding the code in the living system of the firm (Mays, 2009; Weaver, Trevino, and Agle, 2005).

PROVIDING BUSINESS ETHICS INFORMATION TO EMPLOYEES

A global organization with headquarters in the US distributes "Business Ethics Bulletins" to all employees on a semi-regular basis as issues, both positive and negative, occur. One such bulletin indicated three "incidents"—a vendor slipping gift cards into the purse of a company buyer who returned the gift cards and reminded the vendor of the organization's policies regarding gifts, a potential customer who indicated that he would consider purchasing organization products for a kickback which was refused by the salesperson, an organization buyer who solicited kickbacks and was terminated for this behavior—and key lessons that should be learnt (e.g., what is appropriate or, conversely, unacceptable employee behavior, where to get organizational ethics training if required, a brief summary of the organization's standing on gifts, and how employees can report concerns about illegal activity). These bulletins serve to keep the organization's position on unethical behavior visible and central.

ETHICAL LEADERSHIP

Cultural values emanate from the top levels of organizations, so it is not surprising that the role of CEOs and board members has received attention in this context. Schwartz, Dunfee, and Kline (2005) suggest six universal core ethical values for CEOs and corporate board members: honesty, integrity, loyalty, responsibility, fairness and citizenship. Freeman, Moriarty, and Stewart (2009) identify ten facets of ethical leaders from the perspective of the leaders themselves. Becoming an ethical leader is relatively simple, beginning with an examination of one's own behavior and values and taking responsibility for the effects of one's actions on various stakeholders. The authors indicate the kinds of questions that leaders need to ask themselves and suggest that employees need to challenge whether or not their organization is living up to its values, a view seconded by Kochan (2003). Trevino, Hartman, and Brown (2000) provide some indicators of how managers develop reputations for ethical leadership as well.

Others (e.g., Grojean et al., 2004; Gowri, 2007; Mendonca, 2001; Moore, 2005; Wright and Goodstein, 2007) have suggested a rationale as to why ethical leadership has a significant role in creating an ethical culture. But little research has yet examined this proposition.

Neubert et al. (2009) present empirical evidence supporting links between ethical leadership, perceptions of ethical climate, and staff job satisfaction and affective organizational commitment. They collected data from 250 full-time employees from various companies and found that ethical leadership had both direct and indirect effects on staff outcomes—an indirect effect of ethical leadership on staff outcomes through perceptions of ethical climate and a direct effect of ethical leadership on the two staff outcomes—job satisfaction and organizational commitment.

GOVERNMENT REGULATIONS

The Chinese government executed two people, a dairy farmer and a milk salesman, on November 24, 2009 for their roles in selling contaminated baby formula. The men added melamine to milk powder, raising its protein content to boost profits, killing at least six babies and making 300,000 others sick, many with kidney stones or kidney failure. Nineteen other people were convicted and received lesser sentences. One was sentenced to life in prison and others received 5–15 years in prison (BBC News, 2009e). These would not be considered light sentences in Canada. Citizens affected by these products were offered money by both the firms in question and the government to not pursue lawsuits. In a different incident, the former chairman of a large state-owned holding company, Li Peiying, was also executed after being found guilty of accepting about US$3.7 million in bribes and embezzling U$11.2 million (*Guardian*, 2009).

Several of Canada's largest financial institutions have been fined Can$138.8 million to settle allegations of wrongdoing for their contribution to the asset-backed commercial paper debacle in 2007 (Yew, 2009). Britain's banking regulator fined the Toronto Dominion Bank's London unit £7 million for repeated failings in the systems and controls it uses to price sophisticated financial products (FSA, 2009). The latest failing involved the discovery that a trader had lied about the value of the securities he traded.

If one is going to become a criminal, it is better to do so in Canada than in the US as Canadian prison sentences are significantly shorter. Consider the following: David Radler, sentenced to 29 months for one count of fraud and awarded full parole after ten months; Julius Melnetizer, sentenced to nine years for 43 charges of fraud totaling over Can$67 million and received full parole after two and a half years; Alan Eagleson, sentenced to 18 months and a Can$1 million fine for six counts of fraud and received a full parole after 6 months; Harold Ballard sentenced to three years for 49 counts of theft and fraud and served one year; and Garth Drabinsky, sentenced to seven years for two counts of fraud but currently out on appeal. If sentenced to seven years, Drabinsky could be out of prison within one year. Drabinsky has appealed his sentence and is currently out on bail (as of June 2010), so he might not begin his prison sentence anytime soon. By contrast, one day before Drabinsky was sentenced in Canada, a Canadian now living and working in the US, Edward Okun, was found guilty of 23 counts of conspiracy, wire fraud, money-laundering, smuggling and perjury and sentenced to 100 years in prison for stealing US$126 million. In October 2009, however, the Canadian government indicated that it will be introducing legislation to increase penalties for white-collar criminals.

The US Securities and Exchange Commission (SEC) received several warnings about the activities of Bernard Madoff but did not undertake a competent investigation. Inexperience and incompetence helped Madoff's schemes go undetected. As a response to this, the US SEC is considering the creation of a "fraud college" to train staff in spotting fraud, and as of September 2009, 300 SEC employees were being trained. In November 2009 the Obama administration created a task force to address and crack down on financial fraud.

Unfortunately, memories seem to be short. The passage of new legislation is moving very slowly, and it appears that the changes being considered will have effects only at the margin (Rosen, 2009). It seems that Wall Street is moving back to business pretty much as usual.

Monitoring National and International Corruption

Transparency International (TI) publishes an annual survey and ranking of levels of corruption in the public sector in over 150 countries (de Sousa and Larmour, 2009). TI defines corruption as "the abuse of public office for private gain" (e.g., bribery of public officials, kickbacks in public bidding and procurement, embezzlement of public funds) more likely to be associated with weak anti-corruption policies. TI's corruption index is a composite measure that includes multiple expert opinion surveys from at least three sources. These data serve several useful purposes in the reduction of national and international corruption. These purposes include providing a metric of levels of corruption within a given country, serving as a benchmark allowing comparisons across countries, and making it possible to document country improvements or declines over time. In addition, they make countries accountable for their high levels of corruption.

Are We Making Progress?

My review of the newspaper articles and academic journals suggests that we are not making progress. Through a content analysis of 180 articles published in *Business Week*, *Fortune* and *Forbes* magazines, Hannah and Zatzick (2008) found no evidence that the landmark business scandals in the early years of the twenty-first century had any impact on the use, role or relevance of ethics in these magazines' portrayals of organizational leaders five years before and five years after the scandals. Apparently, organizational leaders must still deliver profits above all else.

Delving into the organizational crime and corruption literature (e.g., Nocera, 2008) has been an eye-opening but somewhat depressing experience for me. I have come to realize the magnitude of the corruption challenge, the difficulties in reducing corruption, and why so little headway has been made to date. But there are some small but uneven signs of progress being made. We know more now about the causes of crime and corruption (Lefkowitz, 2009). There is also more media coverage devoted to issues of crime and corruption in organizations and their costs, more ethics education for students and managers, more organizations developing "real" codes of ethical conduct, and more efforts made to help developing countries create the policies and institutional infrastructure likely to reduce bribery and corruption. We also have a greater understanding of how to reduce employee theft (Tomlinson, 2009). But these efforts are only a start. We hope that this collection lays out clearly what needs to be done and why acting now is so critical (Friedland, 2009). Organizations face choices in their responses to crime and corruption, some more desirable than others (Anand et al., 2009).

In recent years capitalism has come under scrutiny and attack just as it did several hundred years ago when people were forced to work in mines and factories rather than continuing to work as farmers and craftsmen in their smaller communities (Allaire and Firsirotu, 2009). As a result, companies came to dominate and destroy some parts of the world (Bown, 2009). In his third encyclical, *Charity in Truth* (July 2009) Pope Benedict denounced profit as the only goal, and condemned corruption and illegality of both politicians and business, arguing that the economy must have moral character. The past few years have shown that unbridled and unregulated capitalism can have a "dark side" (Patel, 2010; Yaziji, 2008). It is too soon to tell whether these critiques will have a lasting effect on the nature of capitalism in the future. Capitalism has made the world a better place for many, but only when it is a servant rather than a master of human needs. Bettering oneself, working hard and obtaining rewards for these efforts are laudatory. Being rewarded for providing a service that others want and will pay for fulfills an important need (Anderson, 2009; Crawford, 2009).

I end up being moderately optimistic that things will improve over the next few years. As it now stands, corporate morality has become an oxymoron. But the ethical shortfalls and greed of the past decade has encouraged discussion of ethical issues, and an increasing number of individuals, organizations and governments have committed to behaving in more ethical, transparent, and accountable ways. And, as always, actions speak louder than words.

About This Book

Here, in Part I of this book, I have set the stage for the chapters that follow by laying out central concepts, theories, causes and consequences of crime and corruption in organizations, illustrated by vignettes from the print media. I began by offering a definition of corruption along with some examples. This was followed by a discussion of various types of corruption undertaken by individuals, groups, organizations, and industries in which factors associated with the spread of corruption in organizations were identified. I then considered financial fraud and how it occurs, profiling examples of corruption in specific sectors (e.g., pharmaceuticals, academia, government). Societies have different views of ethics, fraud and corruption and this was explored next. Common conflicts of interest were identified and causes of crime and corruption, both individual and organizational, were considered. Consequences such as diminished trust, wasted resources, and lower performance were noted. Individuals and organizations that engage in crime and corruption and are caught can recover from damaged reputations, and suggestions for achieving this were offered. The chapter concluded with a review of avenues for reducing crime and corruption. These include individual actions, education, organizational controls, whistleblowing, corporate codes of ethics, government regulations, and monitoring of national and international levels of corruption.

Part II considers some of the causes of crime and corruption in organizations. Several accounts of the causes of the recent worldwide financial crisis have identified the greed of individuals working in banking and financial services as a major factor. In Chapter 2, I suggest that greed underlies almost all acts of crime and corruption in organizations. I provide examples showing that money was at the heart of many recent acts of corruption in organizations. These individuals used their ill-gotten gains to maintain lavish lifestyles. These excesses allowed them to join an elite club and be envied and respected. Individuals working together in organizations engaged in corrupt acts to make their organizations look more profitable than they really were so that they appeared successful in the marketplace, gaining high stock prices as a result. Such cheating appears to be widespread—anything to gain an upper hand. Marketing efforts in a capitalistic society fosters the need for money. Individuals are then driven to becoming wealthy and getting rich quickly. Conspicuous consumption is everywhere. Unfortunately, money does not guarantee happiness. Money can be useful, however, in meeting a variety of needs and values, and, in fact, does increase happiness if spent on others or spent on experiences. However, time affluence is more satisfying than material affluence to many. I conclude the chapter with suggestions on how individuals and organizations can downplay the importance of money. Although difficult, changing capitalism in ways that reduce greed excess and materialism is one avenue for reducing crime and corruption in and outside organizations.

Thomas Stone, Jim Jawahar, and Jennifer Kisamore (Chapter 3) consider the possible beginnings of unethical or illegal behaviors, focusing on schools. Cheating and unethical behavior occur in high schools, colleges, and universities worldwide. Cheating in graduate schools is increasing, and business students are the worst offenders. It has also been reported that cheating in school is associated with committing unethical or illegal behaviors at work. Stone, Jawahar, and Kisamore link unethical and illegal work behaviors to aspects of broader indicators of job performance, particularly organizational citizenship behaviors (OCB) and counterproductive work behaviors (CWB) which have been shown to be negatively related. They then examine personality and integrity (lack of cheating in school) as antecedents of both OCB and CWB in a sample of 227 employed students, considering three Big Five personality factors and two samples of academic integrity. They find that both cheating and reporting of cheating in school predicted CWB. Personality factors had little effect. Finally, the authors advocate the use of well-established objective behavioral indices to avoid the hiring of "bad apples."

Ed Tomlinson (Chapter 4) suggests that employee theft appears to be on the increase. He examines the role of trust in employee theft; if employees do not trust the executives who manage their organizations, they may be more likely to steal. He begins by reviewing a prominent model of organizational trust and then links this model to studies of employee theft. Depending on one's viewpoint, trust can be positively or negatively related to employee theft. In addition, other factors likely moderate the trust and employee theft relationship (e.g., employee need, opportunity). When employees trust their employer, theft is likely to be low. Tomlinson concludes with some managerial implications. Managers should place trust only in those found to be trustworthy. The use of integrity tests for employees has shown value. Managers can create a workplace environment that maintains and strengthens integrity; ethics training is one possibility here. Managers can balance trust and control of employees. Managers can assess the risk involved in a particular situation; hence the use of greater monitoring and control. Finally, employees are more likely to trust a trustworthy employer.

Cultures differ in their views and acceptance of corruption. Yet, in all cultures, corruption eventually becomes routinized and accepted. Which cultural factors or values influence the types of rationalization for corruption that individuals use? In Chapter 5 Amy Guerber, Aparna Rajagopalan, and Vikas Anand consider the influence of national culture on individuals' adoption of different rationalization techniques to account for acts of corruption.

As well as shaping individual values, culture is important in indicating which behaviors and which justifications individuals view as acceptable or unacceptable. The authors use Schwartz's cultural framework (Schwartz, 2006) to describe national culture and consider the rationalizations of justifications and excuses. Justifications involve accepting responsibility for an act but denying its negative effects; excuses involve admitting that the act was negative but denying responsibility for it. They include two justifications (appeal to higher authorities, denial of injury), two social excuses (denial of victim, social weighting), and three contextual excuses (denial of responsibility, denial of illegality, metaphor of the ledger). Schwartz's cultural dimensions include autonomy/embeddedness, egalitarianism/hierarchy, and harmony/mastery. The authors then describe how various cultural dimensions increase the use of particular rationalizations. This chapter opens up several important research avenues toward better understanding cultural differences in ethical behaviors and their interpretation.

Part III examines some of the costs of crime and corruption in organizations. In Chapter 6 Conan Albrecht, Mathew Sanders, David Holland, and Chad Albrecht suggest that modern technology has led to a greater number of potential victims and fraud on a larger scale. They review various types of fraud (e.g., employee embezzlement, vendor fraud, customer fraud, managerial fraud, and consumer fraud). Using two case studies they consider how fraud affects organizations. They then examine known perpetrators of fraud, concluding that it was difficult to know how to identify them in advance since they look pretty much like the rest of us. Fraud occurs when perceived pressures, perceived opportunities and rationalizations come together—the fraud triangle. Pressures include greed and various addictions. Opportunity presents itself when controls are weak. Rationalizations allow the individual to commit fraud without threatening the self-concept. The authors go on to explain why some fraud is committed by groups of individuals using French's and Raven's five bases of power as explanatory concepts. They conclude with suggestions for reducing fraud. These include tone at the top and sound governance, hiring, education and training efforts, integrity risk and control assessments, reporting and monitoring procedures, fraud auditing, and rigorous investigation and follow-up. They identify potential symptoms of fraud (e.g., accounting anomalies, control weaknesses). While tip-offs are the most common fraud detection method, organizations can be more proactive in identifying fraud, and they outline a method of data-driven fraud protection without having evidence that fraud might exist.

Zehava Rosenblatt and Orly Shapira-Lishchinsky (Chapter 7) examine the relationship between organizational ethics and withdrawal behaviors (lateness, absences, intent to leave) among Israeli schoolteachers. These withdrawal behaviors are dysfunctional to their schools. Three ethics concepts are included: ethical climate, organizational justice, and tendency to misbehavior. Ethics are embedded in each of the three withdrawal behaviors: both students and colleagues are short-changed when teachers "withdraw." And organizational ethics reflect values that influence teacher behaviors. Rosenblatt and Shapira-Lishchinsky see organizational commitments as a mediator of the ethics-withdrawal behaviors relationship. Data were collected from over 1,000 teachers in the largest private high-school network in Israel (over 50 schools) over a five-month period. Each of the ethical climate measures (climate, justice, and acceptance of misbehavior) was related to one or more of the withdrawal behaviors. The authors suggest that school leadership should consistently focus on organizational ethics in order to maintain teacher work presence and school loyalty.

Crime and corruption occur in all professions, and Part IV considers two of them. First, Alison Antes and Michael Mumford (Chapter 8) look at academic misconduct, defined as "the violation of standard codes of scholarly conduct and ethical behavior." Ethically questionable behavior among academics is common, with about 30 percent of academics admitting minor forms of misconduct, a figure likely to be an underestimate. The issue has become more important as more academics work with industry. The authors begin by reviewing the nature of academic work which, they find, is complex, ambiguous, competitive and high-pressure, and requires collaboration and peer review. They then give examples of academic misconduct, including fabrication of data, falsification of results, and plagiarism and identify several consequences of such behavior (wasting money, physical harm, public distrust of researchers and research, whistleblowing, damaged careers and reputations). Antes and Mumford go on to offer a model that not only explores the sources of academic misconduct (e.g., field socialization, work environment, experiential learning and personality), but also develops strategies for improving ethical decision-making (e.g., recognizing the circumstances, seeking help, questioning one's own judgment). They conclude with suggestions for overcoming academic misconduct. These include codes of conduct, policies and oversight, ethics instruction, sense-making strategies, changing the demands placed on academics, improving openness and fairness of reward systems, and monitoring work environments.

In Chapter 9 Joel Lexchin reviews the literature on corruption in the pharmaceutical industry, providing concrete and detailed case studies that indicate various ways in which the pharmaceutical industry engages in "questionable" or corrupt practices. These practices are unfortunately industry-wide and include: biasing the conduct of clinical research; questionable communication between drug companies and drug regulators on safety issues; selective and distorted publication of research findings; hiring ghostwriters to endorse company products and communicate what drug companies want; promoting products for unauthorized uses; "seducing" medical students and doctors into using their products; and attacking individuals and groups critical of the industry and its policies. Lexchin provides evidence and discussion in each of these areas, and then asks whether there are any solutions to these concerns. Correctly noting that drug companies do not break any laws and that government fines for misconduct are less than the profits these companies make and so have little deterrent value, or even little or no effect on company reputations, he advocates that society change its views about what should be the legitimate initiatives of drug companies—likely to be a long and slow process.

Part V concludes the collection with an examination of ways of reducing crime and corruption in organizations. Mark Schwartz (Chapter 11) focuses on the development and maintenance of an ethical corporate culture as a way of minimizing corruption in organizations. Ethical cultures by themselves, however, are not enough: there will always be "bad apples." But a majority of employees will be swayed by an ethical organizational culture. Schwartz proposes that three elements are needed as central building blocks of an ethical culture: a set of core ethical values spread throughout the organization; the establishment of a formal ethics program (e.g., ethics code, training, hotline, an ethics officer); and the continuous presence of ethical leadership. He offers a list of core ethical values and suggests how they might be disseminated throughout an organization (e.g., through policies, processes, practices) and goes on to elaborate on elements of an ethics program (e.g., a code of ethics, support from senior management and boards of directors, ethics training, enforcement). Schwartz concludes with a discussion of the important role of ethical leadership, providing examples of senior executives who have demonstrated this behavior and others who have not.

In Chapter 11 Wesley Cragg, Uwafiaokun Idemudia, and Bronwyn Best offer a case study of reducing corruption in the Nigerian oil sector. They begin by reviewing bribery and corruption in an international context and then provide vivid examples of bribery, suggesting a variety of reasons why it occurs; bribery has many uses. After describing various legislative efforts to reduce corruption, they introduce the Integrity Pact (IP), a concept developed by Transparency International (TI) to help governments, business, and civil society work together to combat corruption in public contracting, which is currently being used by TI in several countries and in various sectors. An IP is a process that creates an agreement between a government and all bidders for a public-sector contract, and its implementation is monitored by a third party. The authors describe IPs and when IPs work best, as well as what they have learnt from successful implementations of IPs. Moving on to the case study, they then describe how an IP was developed in Nigeria to address corruption in the Niger Delta in the extraction of oil, laying out the six stages taken to develop this IP—a long and slow process. A key stage was the initial conference that tackled several thorny issues—vital if progress was to be made. The next stages were then identified, and some progress was made. This case study offers a useful model for addressing corruption in government contracting, particularly in developing countries.

In a blistering critique, Al Rosen (Chapter 12) believes that Canada is easy prey for securities frauds. He notes that protection against fraud is weak. Canada has no national regulatory or prosecution system. Investment fund managers do not get reported as their organizations do not want to publicize their weaknesses. Canadian regulatory bodies may not follow up with criminal cases, although the US has successfully prosecuted the perpetrators. Canada has weak financial and auditing rules thereby lowering auditors' obligations. Directors of Canadian companies have few legal obligations. When flaws have been noted in Canada's regulatory practices, few changes have been enacted. Rosen reviews Ponzi schemes in Canada, showing that swindlers receive relatively light sentences, using recent examples (e.g., Nortel Networks) to drive home his points. Rosen then describes commonly used "tricks" (e.g., hiding liabilities and expenses, self-dealing). It is not a comforting picture.

A New "Bottom Line"

It is possible for companies to be effective and embrace strong humane values and follow them, despite pressures from a highly competitive business environment. Kanter (2009) profiles a number of successful companies, which she terms "vanguard companies," which focus on the long term, resisting short-term financial pressures. Vanguard companies engage in more socially responsible activities. De Luque et al. (2008) found that CEOs' emphasis on economic values was associated with followers' perceptions of autocratic leadership, whereas CEOs' emphasis on stakeholder values was associated with followers' perceptions of visionary leadership, which was related to employees' extra effort, which was related in turn to firm performance.

References

Abrams, J. (2010) "US Senate: Atiku Akubar, others brought 'dirty money' to US banks," February 4, at: http://thewillnigeria.com/business/3619-SENATE-Atiku-Abubakar-Others-Brought-Dirty-Money-Banks.html.

ACFE (2008) *Report to the Nation on Occupational Fraud and Abuse*, Austin, TX: Association of Certified Fraud Examiners. Available at: http://www.acfe.com/documents/2008-rttn.pdf.

Adler, P. S. (2002) "Corporate scandals: It's time for reflection in business schools," *Academy of Management Executive*, 16, 148–149.

Aitchison, G. (2009) "'It's okay to shoplift' says Father Tim Jones, parish priest of St Lawrence and St Hilda," December 21, at: http://www.yorkpress.co.uk/news/4813836._It_s_okay_to_shoplift__says_York_priest/.

Albrecht, C. and Albrecht, C. (2009a). "International ethics, fraud, and corruption: A cross-cultural perspective," guest editorial, *International Journal of Cross Cultural Management*, 16, 237–240.

Albrecht, C. and Albrecht, C. (2009b) "International ethics, fraud and corruption: A cross-cultural perspective," *International Journal of Cross Cultural Management*, 16, 237–326.

Albrecht, W. S., Albrecht, C. C., and Albrecht, C. (2004) "Fraud and corporate executives: Agency stewardship and broken trust," *Journal of Forensic Accounting*, 5, 109–130.

Albrecht, C., Albrecht, C. C., and Dolan, S. (2007) "Financial fraud: The how and why," *European Business Forum*, 29, 35–39.

Allaire, Y. and Firsirotu, M. (2009) *Black Markets ... and Business Blues: The Man-made Crisis of 2007–2009 and the Road to a New Capitalism*, Paris: FI Press.

Anand, V., Ashforth, B. E., and Joshi, M. (2005) "Business as usual: The acceptance and perpetuation of corruption in organizations," *Academy of Management Executive*, 19, 9–23.

Anand, V., Ellstrand, A., Rajagopalan, A., and Joshi, M. (2009) "Organizational responses to allegations of corruption," in R. J. Burke and C. L. Cooper (eds) *Research Companion to Corruption in Organizations*, Cheltenham, UK: Edward Elgar, pp. 217–230.

Anderson, G. (2008) *Cityboy: Beer and Loathing in the Square Mile*, London: Headline Book Publishers.

Anderson, R. C. (2009) *Confessions of a Radical Industrialist: Profits, People, Purpose—Doing Business by Respecting the Earth*, New York: St Martin's Press.

Angell, M. (2004) *The Truth About the Drug Companies: How They Deceive Us and What To Do About It*, New York: Random House.

Archibold, R. C. (2009) "Hired by Customs, but working for Mexican cartels," *New York Times*, December 17, at: http://www.nytimes.com/2009/12/18/us/18corrupt.html.

Armenakis, A. (2004) "Making a difference by speaking out: Jeff Wigand says exactly what's on his mind," *Journal of Management Inquiry*, 1, 355–362.

Armstrong, D. (2009) "Analyst's 'sell' call ends up as 'bye' call," *Wall Street Journal*, November 20, at: http://online.wsj.com/article/NA_WSJ_PUB:SB10001424052748704538404574542082056152414.html.

Ashforth, B. E., Gioia, D. A., Robinson, S. L., and Trevino, L. K. (2007) "Reviewing organizational corruption in organizations," *Academy of Management Review*, 33, 670–684.

Associated Press (2002) "French judge, fed chief suspended three years," May 1, at: http://lubbockonline.com/stories/050102/pro_0501020059.shtml.

Associated Press (2009a) "Intel hit with more antitrust charges in FTC suit," December 16, at: http://www.physorg.com/news180181446.html.

Associated Press (2009b) "Six people charged in insider trading case," October 16, at: http://www.msnbc.msn.com/id/33343905/ns/business-us_business/.

Associated Press (2009c) "Costa Rica ex-leader jailed for embezzlement," 6 October, at: http://www.msnbc.msn.com/id/33184912/.

Associated Press (2009d) "Jacques Chirac to stand trial for 'corruption'," October 30, at: http://www.independent.co.uk/news/world/europe/jacques-chirac-to-stand-trial-for-corruption-1811887.html.

Associated Press (2010) "Lawn bowls team guilty of match-fixing," January 12, at: http://news.smh.com.au/breaking-news-sport/lawn-bowls-team-guilty-of-matchfixing-20100112-m3c6.html.

Association of Certified Fraud Examiners (2009) *Occupational Fraud: A Study of the Impact of an Economic Recession*, at: http://www.acfe.com/documents/occupational-fraud.pdf.

Bandura, A. (1986) *Social Foundations of Thought and Actions: A Social Cognition Theory*, Englewood Cliffs, NJ: Prentice-Hall.

Bangkok Post (2010) "Prosecutors charge Saxena," January 28, at: http://www.bangkokpost.com/news/local/166770/prosecutors-charge-saxena.

Barboza, D. (2009) "China finds huge fraud by officials," *New York Times*, December 29, at: http://www.nytimes.com/2009/12/30/world/asia/30fraud.html.

Bazerman, M. H., Moore, D. A., Tetlock, P. E., and Tanlu, L. (2006) "Reports of solving the conflicts of interest in auditing are highly exaggerated," *Academy of Management Review*, 31, 43–49.

BBC News (2009a) "Italy investigates pasta makers over 'price fixing'," December 16, at: http://news.bbc.co.uk/1/hi/world/europe/8415265.stm.

BBC News (2009b) "S Korea clone scientist convicted," October 26, at: http://news.bbc.co.uk/1/hi/world/asia-pacific/8325377.stm.

BBC News (2009c) "Match-fixing inquiry probes 200 European football games," November 20, at: http://news.bbc.co.uk/1/hi/world/europe/8370748.stm.

BBC News (2009d) "Bankers 'whacked' in arcade game," December 13, at: http://news.bbc.co.uk/1/hi/england/suffolk/8410453.stm.

BBC News (2009e) "China executes two over tainted milk powder scandal," November 24, at: http://news.bbc.co.uk/1/hi/world/asia-pacific/8375638.stm.

Beale, L. (2009) "The low-tech reality of identity theft," November 13, at: http://www.miller-mccune.com/legal-affairs/the-low-tech-reality-of-identity-theft-5149/.

Beenen, G. and Pinto, J. (2009) "Resisting organizational-level corruption: An interview with Sherron Watkins," *Academy of Management Learning and Education*, 8, 275–289.

Bone, J. (2010) "Ex-New York police chief Bernard Kerik gets four-year term for tax fraud," *The Times*, February 19, at: http://www.timesonline.co.uk/tol/news/world/us_and_americas/article7032860.ece.

Boucaud, S. (2009) "Peru ex-president Fujimori pleads guilty to illegal wiretapping and bribery," *The Jurist*, September 29, at: http://jurist.law.pitt.edu/paperchase/2009/09/peru-ex-president-pleads-guilty-to.php.

Bown, S. R. (2009) *Merchant Kings: When Companies Ruled the World, 1600–1900*, Toronto: Douglas & McIntyre.

Bray, C. and Bunge, J. (2010) "Goldman programmer indicted for trade secrets theft," *Wall Street Journal*, February 12, at: http://online.wsj.com/article/SB10001424052748703382904575059660427173510.html.

Brazao, D. (2008a) "Phony degree scam exposed," *Toronto Star*, December 7, at: http://www.thestar.com/article/549772.

Brazao, D. (2008b) "Phony degrees catch up to buyers," *Toronto Star*, December 13, at: http://www.thestar.com/news/canada/article/553330.

Brennan, R. J. and Wood, A. (2009) "Canada shamed on Afghan prisoner torture," November 19, at: http://www.thestar.com/news/canada/afghanmission/article/727879--canada-shamed-on-torture.

Brunner, S. (2009) "Imperial Tobacco Canada destroyed documents containing studies on the health effects of smoking," October 15, at: http://www.medicalnewstoday.com/articles/167430.php.

Bucaro, F. (2006) "How do you spell success ... E-T-H-I-C-S," November 1, at: http://www.eyesonsales.com/content/article/how_do_you_spell_success_e_t_h_i_c_s/.

Canadian Press (2009a) "Stasi dumped syringes in St. Lawrence in 1976: Report," November 8, at: http://www.cbc.ca/sports/amateur/story/2009/11/08/sp-syringes-olympics-east-germany.html.

Canadian Press (2009b) "Accused swindler withdrew $12 million," August 19, at: http://www.thestar.com/article/682707.

CBC News (2009a) "Son of mob boss Rizzuto killed in Montreal: Report," December 28, at: http://www.cbc.ca/canada/montreal/story/2009/12/28/montreal-police-investigation.html.

CBC News (2009b) "Jones's wife denies knowledge of fraud," November 26, at: http://www.cbc.ca/canada/montreal/story/2009/11/26/montreal-jones-ponzi-fraud.html.

Child, J. (2002) "The international crisis of confidence in corporations," *The Academy of Management Executive*, 18, 145–147.

Child, J. and Rodrigues, S. (2003) "The international crisis of confidence in corporations," *Journal of Management and Governance*, 7, 233–240.

Clark, A. (2009) "Bernard Madoff's family sued for nearly $200m," at: http://www.guardian.co.uk/business/2009/oct/02/bernard-madoff-family-sued.

Clarke, F., Dean, G., and Oliver, K. (2003) *Corporate Collapse: Accounting, Regulatory and Ethical Failure*, Cambridge, UK: Cambridge University Press.

Cohan, W. D. (2009) *House of Cards: A Tale of Hubris and Wretched Excess on Wall Street*, New York: Doubleday.

Crawford, M. B. (2009) *Shopcraft as Soulcraft: An Inquiry into the Value of Work*, New York: Penguin.

Daker, S. (2009) "Stanford Financial's No. 2 is guilty," *Wall Street Journal*, August 28, at: http://online.wsj.com/article/SB125138421669063741.html.

de Luque, M. S., Washburn, N. T., Waldman, D. A., and House, R. J. (2008) "Unrequited profit: How stakeholder and economic values relate to subordinates' perceptions of leadership and firm performance," *Administrative Science Quarterly*, 53, 626–654.

de Sousa, L. and Larmour, P (2009) "Transparency International: Global franchising and the war of information against corruption," in R. J. Burke and C. L. Cooper (eds) *Research Companion to Corruption in Organizations*, Cheltenham, UK: Edward Elgar, pp. 269–284.

Diaz, S. (2009) "New York AG files antitrust charges against Intel: Alleges bribery, coercion," November 4, at: http://www.zdnet.com/blog/btl/new-york-ag-files-antitrust-charges-against-intel-alleges-bribery-coercion/26903.

Dincer, O. C., Gregory-Allen, R. B., and Shawky, H. A. (2010) "Are you smarter than a CFA'er?" unpublished working paper, Illinois State University, Normal, IL.

Donaghy, T. (2009) *Personal Foul: A First Person Account of the Scandal that Rocked the NBA*, Tampa, FL: VTi Group Inc.

Drabinsky, G. (1995) *Closer to the Sun*, Toronto: McClelland & Stewart.

Efrati, A. (2009) "Lawyer: Heart attack killed Picower," *Wall Street Journal*, October 27, at: http://online.wsj.com/article/SB125657674277308509.html.

Eicher, S (2009) *Corruption in International Business: The Challenge of Cultural and Legal Diversity*, Burlington, VT: Gower.

Ernst & Young (2008) *Corruption or Compliance—Weighing the Costs: 10th Global Fraud Survey*, at: http://www.ey.com/Publication/vwLUAssets/Weighing_the_costs_of_corruption_or_compliance:_10th_Global_Fraud_Survey/$FILE/EY_10th_Global_Fraud_Survey.pdf.

Farmer, B. (2009) "Karzai under pressure after investigators target 15 officials on corruption charges," November 23, at: http://www.telegraph.co.uk/news/worldnews/asia/afghanistan/6636999/Karzai-under-pressure-after-investigations-target-15-officials-on-corruption-charges.html.

Fisman, R. and Svensson, J. (2007) "Are corruption and taxation really harmful to growth? Firm-level evidence," *Journal of Development Economics*, 83, 63–75.

Formula 1 (2009) "Renault handed suspended F1 ban," September 21, at: http://news.bbc.co.uk/sport1/hi/motorsport/formula_one/8266090.stm.

Fowler, T. (2009) "The fall of Enron: Former broadband CEO given 16-month sentence," *Houston Chronicle*, September 28, at: http://www.chron.com/disp/story.mpl/special/enron/6641962.html.

Freeman, R. E., Moriarty, B., and Stewart, L. A. (2009) "What is ethical leadership?" in R. J. Burke and C. L. Cooper (eds) *Research Companion to Corruption in Organizations*, Cheltenham, UK: Edward Elgar, pp. 192–205.

Friedland, J. (2009) *Doing Well and Good: The Human Face of the New Capitalism*, Charlotte, NC: Information Age Publishing.

FSA (2009) "Toronto Dominion fined £7m for repeated failings," FSA/PN/175/2009, December 17, at: http://www.fsa.gov.uk/pages/Library/Communication/PR/2009/175.shtml.

GAAPweb.com (2010) "Darling: Bank bonuses tax raises £2 bn," March 26, at: http://www.gaapweb.com/News/2329-Darling-Bank-bonuses-tax-raises-2bn.html.

Gino, F. and Bazerman, M. H. (2009) "When misconduct goes unnoticed: The acceptability of gradual erosion in others' unethical behavior," *Journal of Experimental Social Psychology*, 45, 208–219.

Gino, F., Ayal, S., and Ariely, D. (2009) "Contagion and differentiation in unethical behavior: The effect of one bad apple on the barrel," *Psychological Science*, 20, 393–398.

Gino, F., Moore, D. A., and Bazerman, M. H. (2008a) *See No Evil: When We Overlook Other People's Unethical Behavior*, Working Paper No. 08-045, Cambridge, MA: Harvard Business School.

Gino, F., Moore, D. A., and Bazerman, M. H. (2008b) *No Harm, No Foul: The Outcome of Bias in Ethical Judgments*, Working Paper No. 08-080, Cambridge, MA: Harvard Business School.

Gioia, D. A. (2002) "Business education's role in the crisis of corporate confidence," *Academy of Management Executive*, 16, 142–144.

Gioia, D. A. (2003) "Teaching teachers to teach corporate governance differently," *Journal of Management and Governance*, 7, 255–262.

GlobalSecurity.org (n.d.) "Asif Zardari," at: http://www.globalsecurity.org/military/world/pakistan/asif-zardari.htm.

Globe and Mail (2010a) "Chernobyl: Leaking radiation and sucking money," February 3, at: http://politifi.com/news/Chernobyl-Leaking-radiation-and-sucking-up-Canadian-money-166451.html.

Globe and Mail (2010b) "Foreign Corrupt Practices Act: Israel's membership in OECD at risk due to bribery allegations," January 29, at: http://obtaining foreignevidence.blogspot.com/2010/01/foreign-corrupt-practices-act-israels.html.

Glovin, D. (2010) "Kumar pleads guilty in Galleon case, admits accepting cash," January 8, at: http://www.bloomberg.com/apps/news?pid=20601087&sid=aD2QccHUAzpk.

Goldstein, J. (2008) "Ghost of Vioxx still haunts Merck," April 15, at: http://blogs.wsj.com/health/2008/04/15/ghost-of-vioxx-still-haunts-merck/.

Gombu, P. (2009) "1M in jobs for politician's son," *Toronto Star*, November 26, at: http://www.thestar.com/news/gta/article/730989---1m-in-jobs-for-politicians-son.

Goos, H. (2007) "Nigeria takes on Pfizer over controversial drug test," November 16, at: http://www.spiegel.de/international/world/0,1518,517805,00.html.

Gordon, M. (2009), "Morgan Chase forfeits $700 million in bribe scandal," November 4, at: http://www.gata.org/node/7978.

Gowri, A. (2007) "On corporate virtue," *Journal of Business Ethics*, 70, 391–400.

Green, P. S. (2009) "Merrill's Thain said to pay $1.2 million to decorator," January 23, at: http://www.bloomberg.com/apps/news?pid=20601087&sid=aFcrG8er4FRw&refer=home.

Greenberg, J. (1995) "Employee theft" in N. Nicholson (ed.) *The Blackwell Encyclopedic Dictionary of Organizational Behavior*, Oxford: Blackwell, pp. 154–155.

Grojean, M. W., Resick, C. J., Dickson, M. W., and Smith, D. B. (2004) "Leaders, values, and organizational climate: Examining leadership strategies for

establishing an organizational climate regarding ethics," *Journal of Business Ethics*, 55, 223–241.
Guardian (2009) "Former Beijing airport chief executed for corruption," August 7, at: http://www.guardian.co.uk/world/2009/aug/07/beijing-airport-chief-executed-corruption/print.
Hannah, D. R. and Zatzick, C. D. (2008) "An examination of leader portrayals in the US business press following the landmark scandals of the early 21st century," *Journal of Business Ethics*, 79, 361–377.
Harper, C. and Townsend, M. (2009) "Blankfein apologizes for Goldman Sachs role in crisis," November 17, at: http://www.bloomberg.com/apps/news?pid =20601103&sid=aeV9jwqKKrEw.
Harris, D. K. and Benson, M. L. (1998) "Nursing home theft: The hidden problem," *Journal of Aging Studies*, 12, 57–67.
Harris, J. and Bromiley, P. (2007) "Incentive to cheat: The influence of executive compensation and firm performance on financial misrepresentation," *Organization Science*, 18, 350–379.
Heakes, G. (2010) "Baseball star McGwire admits steroid use," January 11, at: http://www.google.com/hostednews/afp/article/ALeqM5jjskiQh63ZGfn A5q4bQxbMqLArnQ.
Hopton, D. (2009) *Money Laundering*, Burlington, VT: Gower.
Huffington Post (2009) "John Thain, ex-Merrill chief complains: It's unfortunate the American Dream has been 'demonized'," October 7, at: http://www. huffingtonpost.com/2009/10/07/john-thain-its-unfortunat_n_312524.html.
Huiras, J., Uggen, C., and McMorris, B. (2000) "Career jobs, survival jobs, and employee deviance: A social investment model of workplace misconduct," *Sociological Quarterly*, 41, 245–263.
Human Rights Watch (2009) "Brazil: Curb police violence in Rio, São Paulo," December 8, at: http://www.hrw.org/en/news/2009/12/08/brazil-curb-police-violence-rio-s-o-paolo.
Igan, D., Mishra, I., and Tressel, T. (2009) *A Fistful of Dollars: Lobbying and the Financial Crisis*, IMF Working Paper WP/09/28. Available at: http://www.imf. org/external/pubs/ft/wp/2009/wp09287.pdf.
Immelt, J. (2009) "Renewing American leadership," speech delivered at West Point, December 9. Available at: http://files.gereports.com/wp-content/ uploads/2009/12/90304-2-JRI-Speech-Reprint1-557.qxd_8.5x11.pdf.
Kanter, R. M. (2009) *Supercorp: How Vanguard Companies Create Innovation, Profits, Growth and Social Good*, New York: Crown Publishing.
Kapstein, M. (2004) "Business codes of multinational firms: What do they say?" *Journal of Business Ethics*, 79, 13–31.

Kirby, J. (2009) "Forensic accounting: Expenses," *Canadian Business*, October 12, at: http://www.canadianbusiness.com/managing/strategy/article.jsp?content=20091012_10019_10019&ref=related&page=2.

Kish-Gephart, J. J., Harrison, D. A., and Treviño, L. K. (2010) "Bad apples, bad cases, and bad barrels: Meta-analytic evidence about sources of unethical decisions at work," *Journal of Applied Psychology*, 95, 1–31.

Kochan, T. A. (2002) "Addressing the crisis of confidence in corporations: Root causes, victims, and strategies for reform," *Academy of Management Executive*, 16, 139–141.

Kochan, T. A. (2003) "Restoring trust in American corporations: Addressing the real cause," *Journal of Management and Governance*, 7, 223–231.

Kohlberg, L. (1984) *Essays on Moral Development*. Vol. 2: *The Psychology of Moral Development: The Nature and Validity of Moral Stages*, San Francisco, CA: Harper and Row.

Kramer, A. E. (2009) "Ikea plans to halt investment in Russia," *New York Times*, June 23, at: http://www.nytimes.com/2009/06/24/business/global/24ruble.html.

Laidlow, S. (2009) "Drug 'reports' found to be faked," *Toronto Star*, June 22, at: http://www.thestar.com/living/article/654423.

Lanchester, J. (2010) *I.O.U.: Why Everyone Owes Everyone and No One Can Pay*, New York: Simon & Schuster.

Lange, D. A. (2007) "A multidimensional conceptualization of organizational corruption control," *Academy of Management Review*, 33, 710–729.

Larson, E. (2009) "Wachovia will pay $45 million to end Okun fraud suits," August 18, at: http://www.bloomberg.com/apps/news?pid=newsarchive&sid=ahBqLp5hxPM0.

Lefkowitz, J. (2009) "Individual and organizational antecedents of misconduct in organizations: What do we (believe that we) know, and on what bases do we (believe that we) know it?" in R. J. Burke and C. L. Cooper (eds) *Research Companion to Corruption in Organizations*, Cheltenham, UK: Edward Elgar, pp. 60–91.

Lucchetti, A. (2009) "Not exactly a résumé highlight: Madoff work," *Wall Street Journal*, December 11, at: http://online.wsj.com/article/SB10001424052748704825504574586340365352928.html.

Maremont, M. and Cohen, L. P. (2002) "Tyco spent millions for benefit of Kozlowski, its former CEO: Company secretly forgave loans, financed extravagant lifestyle," *Wall Street Journal*, August 7, at: http://www.mindfully.org/Industry/Tyco-Spent-Millions-Kozlowski7aug02.htm.

Martin, B. (2003) "Illusions of whistle blower protection," *UTS Law Review*, 5, 119–130.

Martin, B. (2009) "Corruption, outrage and whistle-blowing" in R. J. Burke and C. L. Cooper (eds) *Research Companion to Corruption in Organizations*, Cheltenham, UK: Edward Elgar, pp. 206–216.

Martin, K. D., Cullen, J. B., Johnson, J. L., and Parboteeah, K. P. (2007) "Deciding to bribe: A cross-level analysis of firm and home country influences on bribery activity," *Academy of Management Journal*, 50, 1401–1422.

Mays, S. (2009) "Transforming the ethical cultures of organizations" in J. Friedland (ed.) *Doing Well and Good: The Human Face of the New Capitalism*, Charlotte, NC: Information Age Publishing, pp. 87–112.

Mazar, N. and Zhong, B. (2009) "Do green products make us better people?" *Psychological Science*, 21, 494–498.

Mazar, N., Amir, O., and Ariely, D. (2008) "The dishonesty of honest people: A theory of self-concept maintenance," *Journal of Marketing Research*, 45, 633–644.

McArthur, G. (2009) "Canada's largest brokerage scheme linked to alleged tax-haven scheme," *Globe and Mail*, December 14, at: http://www.theglobeandmail.com/news/national/canadas-largest-brokerage-firm-linked-to-alleged-tax-haven-scheme/article1399215/.

McCabe D. L. and Trevino, L. K. (1993) "Academic dishonesty: Honor codes and other contextual influences," *Journal of Higher Education*, 64, 522–538.

McCabe, D. L., Trevino, L. K., and Butterfield, K. D. (1999) "Academic integrity in honor code and non-honor code environments: A qualitative investigation," *Journal of Higher Education*, 70, 211–234.

McCabe, D. L., Treviño, L. K., and Butterfield, K. D. (2001) "Cheating in academic institutions: A decade of research," *Ethics and Behavior*, 11, 219–233.

McCabe, D. L., Treviño, L. K., and Butterfield, K. D. (2002) "Honor codes and other contextual influences on academic integrity: A replication and extension of modified honor code settings," *Research in Higher Education*, 43, 29–45.

Mendonca, M. (2001) "Preparing for ethical leadership in organizations," *Canadian Journal of Administrative Science*, 18, 266–276.

Miceli, M. P., Near, J. P., and Dworkin, T. M. (2008) *Whistle-blowing in Organizations*, New York: Taylor & Francis.

Miceli, M. P., Near, J. P., and Dworkin, T. M. (2009) "A word to the wise: How managers and policy-makers can encourage employees to report wrongdoing," *Journal of Business Ethics*, 86, 379–396.

Mintzberg, H. (2004) *Managers Not MBAs*, San Francisco, CA: Berrett-Koehler.

MNSBC (2010) "Report: Vioxx linked to thousands of deaths," October 6, at: http://www.msnbc.msn.com/id/6192603/.

Moore, D. A., Tetlock, P. E., Tanlu, L., and Bazerman, M. H. (2006) "Conflicts of interest and the case of auditor independence: Moral seduction and strategic issue cycling," *Academy of Management Review*, 31, 10–29.

Moore, G. (2005) "Corporate character: Modern virtue ethics and the virtuous corporation," *Business Ethics Quarterly*, 15, 659–685.

Neubert, M. J., Carlson, D. S., Kacmar, K. M., Roberts, J. A., and Chonko, L. B. (2009) "The virtuous influence of ethical leadership behavior: Evidence from the field," *Journal of Business Ethics*, 90, 157–170.

New York Times (2010) "Jérôme Kerviel," Times Topics, June 11, at: http://topics.nytimes.com/topics/reference/timestopics/people/k/jerome_kerviel/index.html.

Nocera, J. (2008) *Good Guys & Bad Guys*, New York: Portfolio.

Nofsinger, J. and Kim, K. (2003) *Infectious Greed: Restoring Confidence in America's Companies*, Upper Saddle River, NJ: Prentice Hall.

Nonis, S. and Swift, C. O. (2001) "An examination of the relationship between academic dishonesty and workplace dishonesty: A multi-campus investigation," *Journal of Education for Business*, 77, 69–77.

Nossiter, A. (2009) "Underneath palatial skin, corruption rules Gabon," *New York Times International*, September 15, at: http://www.wehaitians.com/underneath%20palatial%20skin%20corruption%20rules%20gabon.html.

NRF Foundation (2009) "Troubled economy increases shoplifting rates according to national retail security survey," at: http://www.nrf.com/modules.php?name=News&op=viewlive&sp_id=746.

O'Connor, J. P., Priem, R. L., Coombs, J. E., and Gilley, K. M. (2006) "Do CEO stock options prevent or promote fraudulent financial reporting?" *Academy of Management Journal*, 49, 483–500.

O'Toole, M. (2010) "Mississauga's invulnerable matriarch Hazel McCallion may finally be wounded," *National Post*, July 31, at: http://news.nationalpost.com/2010/07/31/mississauga%E2%80%99s-invulnerable-matriarch-hazel-mccallion-may-finally-be-wounded/.

Patel, R. (2010) *The Value of Nothing: Why Everything Costs So Much More Than We Think*, New York: HarperCollins.

Pazzano, S. "'Chinese Warren Buffet' gets bail," April 21, at: http://www.torontosun.com/news/torontoandgta/2010/04/20/13658511.html.

Pew Research Center (2009) *Public Praises Science: Scientists Faults Public and Media*, Washington, DC: Pew Research Center.

Pfarrer, M. D., DeCelles, K. A., Smith, K. G., and Taylor, M. S. (2008) "After the fall: Reintegrating the corrupt organization," *Academy of Management Review*, 33, 730–749.

Pidd, H. (2010) "German pensioners found guilty of kidnapping financial adviser," March 23, at: http://www.guardian.co.uk/world/2010/mar/23/german-pensioners-guilty-kidnap-financial-adviser.

Pirson, M. (2009) "Facing the stakeholder trust gap" in J. Friedland (ed.) *Doing Well and Good: The Human Face of the New Capitalism*, Charlotte, NC: Information Age Publishing.

PriceWaterhouseCoopers (2009) *The Global Economic Crime Survey*. Available at: http://www.pwc.com/gx/en/economic-crime-survey/index.jhtml.

Quinn, J. (2009) "Barclays banker Hugh McGee wants son's teacher fired for 'sleazeball' comment," *Daily Telegraph*, December 2, at: http://www.telegraph.co.uk/finance/newsbysector/banksandfinance/6712738/Barclays-banker-Hugh-McGee-wants-sons-teacher-fired-for-sleazeball-comment.html.

Reuters (2009a) "Insider trading probe ensnares 14 more," November 5, at: http://www.reuters.com/article/idUSTRE5A42XF20091105.

Reuters (2009b) "Science & Technology Minister Jesse Chacon resigns in wake of bank purge," December 6, at: http://www.vheadline.com/readnews.asp?id=86738.

Reuters (2009c) "Hertz sues analyst who said it could go bankrupt," September 28, at: http://www.reuters.com/article/idCNN287287720090928?rpc=44.

Reuters (2009d) "Highest paid CEOs in U.S. include Stephen Schwarzman, Larry Ellison, Michael Jeffries," August 14, at: http://www.nydailynews.com/money/2009/08/17/2009-08-17_highest_paid_ceos_in_us_.html.

Reuters (2009e) "Pfizer whistleblower's ordeal reaps big rewards," September 2, at: http://www.reuters.com/article/idUSN021592920090902.

Reuters (2010a) "BAE reaches $450 million settlement with U.S., Britain," February 5, at: http://www.thestar.com/business/article/689640--optionable-plied-former-traders-with-gifts-bmo.

Reuters (2010b) "Judge OKs 'half-baked' SEC-Bank of America accord," February 22, at: http://www.reuters.com/article/idUSTRE61G4AY20100222.

Reuters (2010c) "US FDA warnings target four drug companies," January 12, at: http://www.reuters.com/article/idUSTRE60B5KW20100112.

Roadcycling.com (2010) "Beijing Olympics medalist Rebellin loses medal and doping appeal," July 30, at: http://www.roadcycling.com/articles/Beijing-Olympics-Medalist-Rebellin-Loses-Medal-and-Doping-Appeal_003780.shtml.

Rodriguez, P., Uhlenbruck, K., and Eden, L. (2005) "Government corruption and the entry strategies of multi-nationals," *Academy of Management Review*, 30, 383–396.

Rose-Ackerman, R. (2007) *International Handbook on the Consequences of Corruption*, Cheltenham, UK: Edward Elgar.

Rosen, L. S. (2009) "Canadian corporate corruption" in R. J. Burke and C. L. Cooper (eds) *Research Companion to Corruption in Organizations*, Cheltenham, UK: Edward Elgar, pp. 285–298.

Rosenbaum, R. W. (1976) "Predictability of employee theft using weighted application blanks," *Journal of Applied Psychology*, 61, 94–98.

Rutherford, M. W., Buller, P. F., and Stebbins, J. M. (2009) "Ethical consideration of the legitimacy lie," *Entrepreneurship: Theory and Practice*, 34, 949–964.

Ryan, N. (2009) "Never mind the death threats," *Report on Business*, November, 54–58.

Santoro, M. A. and Gorrie, T. H. (2005) *Ethics and the Pharmaceutical Industry*, Cambridge, UK: Cambridge University Press.

Schecter, B. (2009) "Chinese Warren Buffet faces judgment in U.S.," *Financial Post*, July 27, at: http://www.financialpost.com/story.html?id=1834267.

Schwartz, M. S. (2004) "Effective corporate codes of ethics: Perceptions of code users," *Journal of Business Ethics*, 55, 323–343.

Schwartz, M. S. (2009) "Beyond the bottom line: A shifting paradigm for business?" in J. Friedland (ed.) *Doing Well and Good: The Human Face of the New Capitalism*, Charlotte, NC: Information Age Publishing, pp. 131–149.

Schwartz, M. S., Dunfee, T. W., and Kline, M. J. (2005) "Tone at the top: An ethics code for directors," *Journal of Business Ethics*, 58, 79–100.

Schwartz, S. H. (2006) "A theory of cultural value orientations: Explication and applications," *Comparative Sociology*, 5, 137–182.

Schweitzer, M. E., Ordonez, L., and Douma, B. (2004) "Goal setting as a motivator of unethical behavior," *Academy of Management Journal*, 47, 422–432.

SETimes.com (2010) "Croatian court convicts professors of corruption," February 2, at: http://www.setimes.com/cocoon/setimes/xhtml/en_GB/news briefs/setimes/newsbriefs/2010/02/02/nb-10.

Simons, T. (2009) "The integrity dividend and doing good" in J. Friedland (ed.) *Doing Well and Good: The Human Face of the New Capitalism*, Charlotte, NC: Information Age Publishing, pp. 151–166.

Slayton, P. (2007) *Lawyers Gone Bad: Money, Sex and Madness in the Canadian Legal Profession*, New York: Penguin.

Spielmans, G. I., Biehn, T. L., and Sawrey, D. C. (2010) "A case study of salami slicing: Pooled analyses of Duloxatine for depression," *Psychotherapy and Psychosomatics*, 79, 97–106.

Statistics Canada (2010) *Labor Force Survey*, Ottawa, ON: Statistics Canada.

Steenhuyssen, J. (2009) "Vioxx risks could have been detected earlier: Study," November 23, at: http://www.reuters.com/article/idUSTRE 5AM4MV20091123.

Stempel, J. (2009) "SEC file charges over 'green' scheme," November 16, at: http://www.reuters.com/article/idUSTRE5AF50W20091116.

Stevens, B. (2008) "Corporate ethical codes: Effective instruments for influencing behavior," *Journal of Business Ethics*, 78, 601–609.

Stevens, B. (2009) "Corporate ethical codes as a vehicle of reducing corruption in organizations" in R. J. Burke and C. L. Cooper (eds) *Research Companion to Corruption in Organizations*, Cheltenham, UK: Edward Elgar, pp. 252–268.

Sturgeon, J. (2009) "Court rules Rogers must drop 'most reliable network' claim," November 25, at: http://www2.canada.com/topics/technology/story.html?id=2263461.

Sullivan, B. N, Haunschild, P., and Page, K. (2007) "Organizations non gratae? The impact of unethical corporate acts on inter-organizational networks," *Organization Science*, 18, 55–72.

Sutton, R., Ferraro, F., and Pfeffer, J. (2005) "Economic language and assumptions: How theory can become self-fulfilling," *Academy of Management Review*, 30, 8–24.

Swartz, M. and Watkins, S. (2003) *Power Failure: The Inside Story of the Collapse of Enron*, New York: Currency/Doubleday.

Temple-Raston (2009) "3 N. J. mayors arrested in major corruption probe," July 23, at: http://www.npr.org/templates/story/story.php?storyId=106918289.

Tett, G. (2009) *Fool's Gold: How the Bold Dream of a Small Tribe at J. P. Morgan was Corrupted by Wall Street Greed*, New York: The Free Press.

Theodoulou, M. (2008) "Iranian interior minister sacked over fake Oxford degree," *The Times*, November 5, at: http://www.timesonline.co.uk/tol/news/world/middle_east/article5079422.ece. Thomaselli, R. (2009) "Pfizer to pay $2.3 billion in fraudulent-marketing suit," September 2, at: http://adage.com/article?article_id=138763.

Toameh, K. A. (2010) "PA issues arrest warrant for Shabeneh," *Jerusalem Post*, November 2, at: http://www.jpost.com/MiddleEast/Article.aspx?id=168375.

Tomlinson, E. C. (2009) "Reducing employee theft: Weighing the evidence on intervention effectiveness" in R. J. Burke and C. L. Cooper (eds) *Research Companion to Corruption in Organizations*, Cheltenham, UK: Edward Elgar, pp. 231–251.

Torres, M. B. (2009) "Getting business off steroids" in J. Friedland (ed.) *Doing Well and Good: The Human Face of the New Capitalism*, Charlotte, NC: Information Age Publishing, pp. 3–30.

Transparency International (2009) "Corruption Perceptions Index 2009," at: http://www.transparency.org/policy_research/surveys_indices/cpi/2009/cpi_2009_table.

Treviño, L. K., Hartman, L. P., and Brown, M. (2000) "Moral person and moral manager: How executives develop a reputation for ethical leadership," *California Management Review*, 42, 128–142.

Trichur, R. (2009) "Optionable 'plied' former traders with gifts: BMO," *Toronto Star*, September 2, at: http://www.thestar.com/business/article/689640--optionable-plied-former-traders-with-gifts-bmo.

UMHS News (2009) "29% of cancer studies report conflict of interest," May 11, at: http://www2.med.umich.edu/prmc/media/newsroom/details.cfm?ID=1147.

UNODC (2010) *Corruption in Afghanistan: Bribery as Reported by the Victims*, January, at: http://www.unodc.org/documents/data-and-analysis/Afghanistan/Afghanistan-corruption-survey2010-Eng.pdf.

US Securities and Exchange Commission (SEC) (2009) "SEC charges former officers of subprime lender New Century with fraud," press release 2009-258, at: http://www.sec.gov/news/press/2009/2009-258.htm.

Victor, B. and Cullen, J. B. (1988) "The organizational basis of ethical work climates," *Administrative Science Quarterly*, 33, 101–125.

Voltairenet.org (2010) "Richard Colvin sticks to his testimony on torture in Afghanistan," April 16, at: http://www.voltairenet.org/article164982.html.

Wallace, K. (2009) "Toronto lawyer commits suicide after admitting multi-million-dollar insider trading," October 28, at: http://www.canada.com/news/Toronto+lawyer+commits+suicide+after+admitting+million+dollar+insider+trading/2152225/story.html.

Watkins, S. (2003) "Ethical conflicts at Enron: Moral responsibility in corporate capitalism," *Academy of Management Executive*, 45, 6–19.

Weaver, G. R., Treviño, L. K., and Agle, B. (2005) "'Somebody I look up to': Ethical role models in organizations," *Organizational Dynamics*, 34, 313–330.

Wednesday-Night.com (2009) "Thousands of tax cheats fess up," December 5, at: http://www.wednesday-night.com/newtax.asp.

Westmarland, L. (2005) "Police ethics and integrity: Breaking the blue code of silence," *Policing and Society*, 15, 145–165.

Wikipedia (2010) "Use of performance-enhancing drugs in the Olympic Games," at: http://en.wikipedia.org/wiki/Use_of_performance-enhancing_drugs_in_the_Olympic_Games.

Woodhouse, H. (2009) *Selling Out: Academic Freedom and the Corporate Market*, Montreal and Kingston: McGill-Queen's University Press.

Wright, T. A. and Goodstein, J. (2007) "Character is not 'dead' in management research: A review of individual character and organizational-level virtue," *Journal of Management*, 33, 928–958.

Yang, J. (2009) "Trustee offers basic training for candidates," November 23, at: http://www.parentcentral.ca/parent/education/schoolsandresources/article/729375--trustee-offers-basic-training-for-candidates.

Yaziji, M. (2008) "Time to rethink capitalism?" *Harvard Business Review*, November, 27–28.

Yew, M. A-T. (2009) "ABCP penalties to total $138.8 million," 22 December, at: http://www.thestar.com/business/bank/article/741675--abcp-penalties-to-total-138-8m.

Zahra, S. A., Priem, R. L., and Rasheed, A. A. (2005) "The antecedents and consequences of top management fraud," *Journal of Management*, 31, 803–828.

Zand, J. (2010) "Disbarred Fla. Attorney Scott Rothstein's guilty plea in Ponzi scheme," January 27, at: http://blogs.findlaw.com/courtside/2010/01/disbarred-fla-attorney-scott-rothsteins-guilty-plea-in-ponzi-scheme.html.

Zeitlin, L. R. (1971) "A little larceny can do a lot for employee morale," *Psychology Today*, 5, 22, 24, 25, 64.

Zhang, X., Bartol, K. M. K., Smith, K. G., Pfarrer, M. D., and Khanin, D. M. (2008) "CEOs on the edge: Earnings manipulation and stock-based incentive misalignment," *Academy of Management Journal*, 51, 241–258.

Zyglidopoulos, S. C. and Fleming, P. J. (2008) "Ethical distance in corrupt firms: How do innocent bystanders become guilty perpetrators?" *Journal of Business Ethics*, 78, 265–274.

Zyglidopoulos, S. C. and Fleming, P. J. (2009) "The escalation of corruption" in R. J. Burke and C. L. Cooper (eds) *Research Companion to Corruption in Organizations*, Cheltenham, UK: Edward Elgar, pp. 104–119.

PART II
Causes of Crime and Corruption in Organizations

2

Show Me the Money[1]
Ronald J. Burke

Introduction

> "Greed—noun—avarice, insatiable desire or covetousness."
> *Cassell's Concise Dictionary (1997)*

This chapter is about money and greed. It builds on and updates my earlier chapter in the *Research Companion to Corruption in Organizations* (Burke, 2009). This collection begins with a chapter on greed because I believe that greed underlies almost all acts of crime and corruption in organizations. When Willie Sutton, a famous American bank robber, was arrested yet again following another bank robbery, he was asked why he continued to rob banks and he replied, "That's where the money is." Crime and corruption seem to be flourishing today in organizations because "that's where the money is."

Consider the following examples.

In October 2009 Anthony Marshall, the 85-year-old son of philanthropist Brooke Astor, and his former lawyer were convicted of charges of mishandling the late socialite's US$180 million estate. He was prosecuted after Marshall's son accused his father of mistreating his grandmother who was suffering from Alzheimer's disease. Brooke Astor's nurse stated that Marshall "dragged" Mrs Astor to a meeting in which her will was amended to give him control of most of her estate (Leonard, 2009).

Ao Man-long, Macao's highest-level official ever convicted of corruption, was sentenced to 27 years in prison on January 30, 2008, for taking contract kickbacks in the construction industry. He was found guilty of taking millions of dollars in bribes, laundering money and abusing his power to help developers get construction contracts. His properties and US$31 million of his assets were seized (Macau, 2008).

---

[1] The preparation of this chapter was supported in part by York University.

Ikea decided to end its investment in Russia in 2009 because of pervasive corruption and demands for bribes. Dimitri Medvedev, the Russian president, has admitted that corruption is a national problem and reducing corruption is one of his main goals (Kramer, 2009).

Eight of the 12 baseball players who hit over 40 home runs in the 1998 season have been linked to steroid use (NPR, 2009). There were financial benefits—both short- and long-term—for these achievements, particularly if they were done drug-free. Some of these men may be denied admittance into baseball's Hall of Fame in the future as a consequence.

Michael Misick, the former premier of Turks and Caicos, resigned in March 2009 accused of corruption. He, too, had a lavish lifestyle. His wife claimed she was allocated up to US$200,000 a month for clothes and paid US$300,000 by the Tourism Board to pose in a swimsuit for an ad campaign. The couple also maintained an US$8 million mansion and traveled around the world in a private jet. The islands were also plagued by patronage, kickbacks, low property evaluations to insiders, low-interest loans to insiders, and high limits to credit cards issued to politicians in exchange for favorable votes on development projects (*The Independent*, 2009).

Earl Jones, a Montreal-based financial planner, disappeared in the middle of July 2009 with Can$30-50 million of investor funds unaccounted for—Canada's answer to Bernard Madoff (*National Post*, 2009a). He later returned to Montreal and was convicted of fraud in January 2010.

In February 2008 Merck agreed to pay US$671 million to settle claims that it overcharged Medicaid for three popular drugs and gave doctors discounts and gifts so they would prescribe its products. Merck said, however, that the settlement did not constitute an admission of any liability or wrongdoing (Johnson, 2008).

Reshma Jagri and colleagues (2010) at the University of Michigan reviewed 1,534 cancer studies published in eight top-ranked medical journals. More than a third indicated a conflict of interest (industry funding, industry authors). Studies having a conflict of interest were more likely to report the benefits of particular drugs, thereby providing financial benefits to the drug manufacturers.

A number of institutions selling bogus university degrees have sprung up over the past 20 years. For a fee—typically US$1,000-2,000—these institutions will sell you any number and types of university degree. Bogus degrees have been estimated by the FBI as a billion-dollar-per-year industry. The institutions make money with little investment of resources; individuals who purchase these bogus degrees save both time and money required in actually obtaining a university degree. In addition, individuals with bogus degrees increase their career prospects and incomes—unless they get found out. Ironically, a woman with a bogus degree obtained a job in a college registrar's office where one of her duties was to authenticate applicants' degrees! In addition, individuals with bogus degrees in nursing and medicine, to cite only two professions, have apparently worked successfully in them.

And the frauds just keep on coming and seem to be getting larger.

Bernard Madoff was charged in late 2008 with running a Ponzi scheme that bilked investors of US$50 billion over the past two decades. Madoff should have known better; he had previously been a board member on the NASDAQ. Madoff, at the time of his arrest, had a house in Palm Beach, Florida, a villa in France, a beach house on Long Island, two planes at his disposal around the clock, yachts moored in both Florida and France, and millions of dollars in jewelry. He belonged to an expensive country club in a town (Palm Beach) that epitomizes conspicuous consumption and lavish entertainment. Leamer, in *Madness under the Royal Palms: Love and Death behind the Gates* (2009) noted that Palm Beach was about money and that Madoff was liked because he had money; should your money disappear, you were likely to be dropped. Madoff scammed money from wealthy individuals, charitable organizations, and banks hoping to benefit from the large financial increases that he promised and initially delivered (Arvedlund, 2009; Kirtzman, 2009; Oppenheimer, 2009). When he admitted to the scheme, these investors lost their money. Charitable organizations were no longer able to provide their services, and some individual investors were forced to sell their homes when they realized they had no money. Madoff continued to live in his US$7 million Manhattan apartment, apologizing to his neighbors for the disturbance caused to them by reporters at his apartment door. He was found guilty in early 2009 and sentenced to 150 years in prison.

In late 2009 Salah Ezzedine, a Shiite business man in Lebanon, and his partner Youseff Faour were arrested and charged with cheating investors out of millions of dollars, perhaps up to US$1 billion. Ezzedine's financial company had promised investors as much as 40 percent annual return on their money. Ezzedine owned one of Lebanon's major religious publishing houses, was active in charitable works in Lebanon (building mosques), and had business interests in oil and iron in Eastern Europe. These investments lost money in 2008 as oil prices fell, and Ezzedine may have tried to compensate for these losses by taking money from his investors (Naharnet.com, 2009).

Cricket impresario Sir Allen Stanford was charged in February 2009 with financial fraud of over US$8 billion. He was knighted by Antigua and Barbuda in 2006, and much of his work was carried out and headquartered in the Caribbean. In 2008 he organized a million-dollar-a-man, winner-take-all cricket contest between England and a team of West Indian all-stars. At the time of his being charged with fraud, Stanford owed the US government US$212 million in back taxes for 2007 and 2008 (Huffington Post, 2009).

Stanford had the following assets when charged: US$2 billion in cash, a 120-foot yacht, a fleet of six aircraft worth US$100 million, a restaurant, real estate on various islands in the Caribbean, including houses in St Croix and Antigua, Wackenhut Castle (18,000 square feet, 57 rooms) a 24/7 chauffeur-driven Lincoln Navigator vehicle for use by the children, and two Mercedes. Records show that he also spent US$75,000 on children's Christmas gifts and vacations and US$9,000 on gifts for his children's teachers (*Financial Times*, 2009). Stanford, not Johnny Depp, was the real pirate of the Caribbean.

Edward Okun, sentenced to 100 years in prison for fraud in August 2009, used the money as a "personal piggy bank" to fund his divorce and buy jewelry for his new wife as well as expensive dinners with friends. He also owned a 131-foot yacht, several mansions, a jet and a helicopter (Larson, 2009).

Gary Sorenson, a Canadian accused of running a Ponzi scheme that defrauded investors of Can$100 million was arrested upon his return to Canada on September 29, 2009. He had been living in Honduras in a multimillion-dollar mansion and had access to a private jet. A co-accused, Milowe Brost, was arrested about two weeks earlier (Seskus, Cryderman, and Massinon, 2009).

In June 2010 Hafiz Malik, a store owner, having pleaded guilty to stealing a winning Can$5.4 million lottery ticket from the rightful ticket owners in June 2004, was sentenced to one year in jail. Malik used the money to buy a Can$1 million mansion, a Land Rover and a Mercedes (Torstar Network, 2010).

Melissa King, a union employee, was charged in December 2009 with embezzling US$42 million from the union's employee benefits fund. Ms King spent a lot of the money on her stable of showjumping horses, including more than US$3 million on horse-related expenses, US$7.3 million on her American Express account, more than US$300,000 at Nieman Marcus, US$713,000 at a Californian jewelry store, and thousands of dollars on clothes and presents for friends (Buettner, 2010).

Executives at Lehman Brothers Holdings Inc. and Bear Stearns made US$2.5 billion from 2000 to 2008, indicating that their pay policies likely encouraged the risk-taking that caused these companies to fail according to a discussion paper titled *The Wages of Failure* published by Harvard Law School (Bebchuk, Cohen, and Spamann, 2010). The top five officials at Lehman, which filed for bankruptcy in September 2008, earned US$1.03 billion in cash bonuses and proceeds from equity sales during this period. Top executives at Bear Stearns made US$1.46 billion in the years before JP Morgan Chase & Co. agreed to buy the firm in 2008. Any losses that these executives may have suffered as their firms were failing were more than offset by financial pay-outs during the preceding eight years

After Me, You're Next

Ten US companies (United Airlines, US Airways, among others) paid senior executives US$350 million in the five years before they were forced to drop their underfunded pension plans for employees. One airline company was US$979 million short in required pension contributions while its top three executives earned US$5.5 million in compensation. Another company paid four executives US$120 million during two bankruptcies. Benefits to retirees were cut by as much as two-thirds in some cases while executives were awarded salary increases, stock options, and retention bonuses (Rosenkrantz, 2009).

Nortel Networks was one of Canada's premier high-tech companies a decade ago. It fell on hard times and went bankrupt in 2009. Executives, however, continue to receive bonuses, in part to keep them while winding down the company. Seventy-two Nortel executives will get US$7.5 million in bonuses in addition to their regular salaries, yet retirees, those who lost their jobs, and those unable to work because of disability will likely receive severely reduced or no pension benefits. Former CEO Mike Zafirovski claimed US$12.2 million in back pay and bonuses, and in March 2009 about 1,000 executives of the failed company were awarded US$45 million in retention bonuses (Evans, 2009a, 2009b; Reuters, 2009).

Goldman Sachs received a US$10 billion bail-out from US taxpayers. In return, it proposed to pay its management executives US$17 billion in year-end bonuses, but apparently changed its mind in the face of public outcry and awarded instead US$20 million in stock which has to be retained for five years and is subject to review if employees are later found to be taking unacceptable risks. Top traders not on the management committee, however, are still able to earn large cash bonuses (Johansmeyer, 2009). The irony is that there is little or no evidence that suggests that the awarding of bonuses based on job performance actually increases job performance. Indeed, the prospect of a large bonus may increase performance expectations, resulting in increased levels of stress and *lower* performance. Individuals come to expect bonuses regardless of how they perform. And senior executives themselves believe that bonuses have little or no effect on how their companies or executives perform.

The backlash against excessive executive pay, bonuses not based on performance, denial of retiree benefits while executives still get large bonuses, and cuts in the workforce while executives keep their jobs has resulted in a growth in executive protection services. Executives have had their homes defaced and received death threats. In response to these potential threats, companies have hired security personnel to protect executives, their families, and their workplaces against violence. Companies have always protected their executives from external threats (e.g., by providing protective services while doing business in Mexico City to prevent kidnapping), but many of the threats today are internal.

And although unemployment remains high, the modest recovery in the financial sector suggests that executive bonuses and pay will continue to remain high, increasing the tension between Wall Street and Main Street.

Mintzberg, Simons, and Basu (2002) believe that over the past two decades North America has glorified self-interest; they use the term "selfishness" to capture this. Greed is rampant, and organizations seem to exist only to provide benefits to shareholders.

At the Trough

There has been a seemingly endless list of men and women—elected officials, government bureaucrats and private-sector executives—abusing their office. Consider the following:

- Jean-Louis Roy, president of the federally-funded Canadian Rights and Democracy organization claimed expenses over a three-year period for 46 nights in Paris even though Rights and Democracy has no program there, did not reimburse personal expenses, and dined with employees at taxpayers' expense (*National Post*, 2009b).
- Gordon Brown, the former British prime minister, agreed to repay £12,415 of expenses for cleaning, gardening and decorating (Winnett, 2009) following the publication of MPs' expenses claims by the *Daily Telegraph* in 2009. Following the revelations, about 175 parliamentarians voluntarily repaid almost £300,000 (Stratton, 2009). Among the more interesting claims were those for cleaning a swimming pool, cleaning a moat, a duck house, chauffeur-driven cars to football matches, mortgage interest on a house that didn't exist, and payments to a daughter while claiming she wasn't a daughter by using an assumed name (Telegraph.co.uk, 2009). After an audit of MPs' expenses claims between 2004 and 2008 carried out by Sir Thomas Legg, 373 MPs were asked to repay a total of £1.11 million. The largest individual payback (£42,458) was made by millionaire

Labour MP Barbara Follett for expenses relating to mobile security patrols at her second home, an excessive number of telephone lines, fine art insurance, boiler insurance which was submitted and paid twice, and pest control at an address that was not her second home. The lowest repayment, by the Labour MP for Ilford South, was 40p (BBC News, 2010). Many of the MPs who made the more outrageous claims either stood down or were ousted at the 2010 General Election, and several former MPs now face criminal charges for fraud.

- John O'Donoghue, Speaker of Ireland's parliament, stepped down when details of his lavish spending and foreign travel were made public. Between 2002 and 2008 O'Donoghue spent over €600,000, including more than €900 a night on hotel rooms in Liverpool, Paris and Venice, and €473 to travel by car between two terminals of the same airport (Sharrock, 2009).
- In September 2009 the head of the Ontario Lottery and Gaming Corp was fired and the entire board resigned after questions were raised about spending. These individuals charged the Ontario government for pen refills, the cancelation of a deposit on a Florida condominium, a nanny to facilitate attendance at meetings and a car wash (CBC News, 2009).
- The head of eHealth, a unit charged with computerizing Ontario's health information was fired in June 2009 for awarding Can$5 million of untendered consulting contracts to former associates, who besides being paid a high daily rate, billed the taxpayers for answering e-mails and getting cups of coffee (Dearing, 2009).

Business leaders are now rated lower than politicians and lawyers! A recent poll by the Kennedy School of Government at Harvard University found that only 10 percent of Americans believe that business leaders generally work for the greater good of society; most (52 percent) believe that corporate executives work mainly to benefit themselves, while 31 percent said that they work to benefit just a small segment of society with special interests (Center for Public Leadership, 2009). Business leaders, to some, represent bad apples, in bad barrels, in bad forests (Colvin, 2004).

The Salaries of CEOs

Although the worldwide economic recession has had major effects on employment, job prospects and wages, CEOs still are raking it in. In 2008, salaries paid to the top 100 Canadian CEOs, were 174 times greater than the average Canadian's salary. Between 1998 and 2008, the average Canadian lost 6 percent when inflation was factored in, while CEOs' salaries outpaced inflation by 70 percent (CBC News, 2010).

The Canadian experience is not unique. Stephen Hester, CEO of the Royal Bank of Scotland, admitted that even his parents believe that he is paid too much (Prynn and Duncan, 2010). It is not surprising, then, that governments in several countries (France, the UK, the US) want to either limit CEO pay and pay increases or impose additional taxes on those earning very high salaries.

Interestingly, according to Guner, Malmendier, and Tate (2008), corporate boards of directors which have more highly paid CEOs as members award these individuals higher levels of salary and salary increases. In addition, corporate directors with financial expertise tend to exert considerable influence in board deliberations, but not necessarily in the interest of shareholders.

The Wages of Sin

THE WAGES OF SIN MAY BE MORE WAGES

A small consulting niche has emerged to assist white-collar criminals make the transition from life on the outside to life in prison. Former criminals provide coaching assistance on the dos and don'ts of prison life.

Nick Leeson, released after serving four years in a Singapore prison for his rogue trading of US$1.3 billion that caused the collapse of Barings Bank, is on the lecture circuit telling what he learned from this incident (wished he had someone to talk to when the losses were small) and how it happened (not enough financial controls, overly complex financial instruments that many people did not understand). Leeson charges £6–10,000 per speech.

There has also been an upsurge in individuals and firms providing services in forensic accounting, the detection of fraud, and the undertaking of efforts to recover stolen monies.

Ryan (2009) chronicles the activities of Martin Kenney, a Canadian living in the Caribbean, whose firm pursues fraud artists. Kenney moved to the Caribbean because that is where much of the fraudulently-obtained money ends up.

THE WAGES OF SIN MAY BE A "GET OUT OF JAIL FREE" CARD

In March 2009 Broadway producers Garth Drabinsky and Myron Gottlieb were found guilty in Toronto of perpetuating a multimillion-dollar fraud with Livent.

At their pre-sentencing hearing their lawyers presented letters of support from dozens of directors, writers and performers who had benefited in some way from their association with Drabinsky and Gottleib. They also suggested that Drabrinsky and Gottlieb be given two years' less a day house arrest followed by three years' probation during which time they could present lectures to university students on business ethics (Acharya and Yew, 2009). Would this be similar to having Bernard Madoff lecture on how to start and maintain a Ponzi scheme, bank robbers on how to rob banks, and individuals convicted of fraud indicating how this was undertaken?

THE WAGES OF SIN AND INCOMPETENCE MAY BE MORE WAGES

AIG is a large US company that was on the verge of bankruptcy for encouraging and supporting bad loans and mortgages to individuals who could not afford them and survives today on money provided by American taxpayers. Its new CEO, Robert Benmosche, spent most of his first month with the company working from his US$1 million villa overlooking the Croatian Adriatic coast while simultaneously overseeing the grape harvest at his vineyard north of Dubrovnik. He pointed out that he was able to keep in touch with AIG business through satellite technology, the Internet and conference calls (Clark, 2009). It is a dirty job but somebody has to do it!

THE WAGES OF SIN MAY BE DIFFICULTY IN FINDING ANOTHER JOB

In October 2009, a year after Lehman Brothers filed for bankruptcy, some of the company's former senior executives were still unemployed. It is difficult to find another job when one is a senior executive of a firm that engaged in massive fraud. These individuals earned high salaries before their firm dissolved but will now have to learn to live with much less. Here are their employment statuses as they stood at the end of 2009:

- Richard Fuld, CEO—still unemployed
- Joseph Gregory, President—still unemployed
- Bart McDade, President—unemployed again after a two-month stay at Barclays
- Erin Callan, CFO—possibly employed, but on a leave of absence
- Rich McKinney, Head of American Securitized Products—employed
- Ted Janulis, Head of Mortgage Capital—retired.

The Financial Benefits of Cheating

Individuals cheat because they believe that they can gain an advantage. In the short run these ill-gotten advantages may give the individual a feeling of superiority and, in the long run, they may lead to greater success that will ultimately increase fame and fortune (Callahan, 2004). Students cheat in lower-level schools to raise their marks and get into better universities. Students in universities cheat so that they can get better marks and obtain better jobs, with business school students cheating more than students in other academic programs. People buy fake degrees from bogus universities to obtain higher-paying jobs. Individuals cheat on their expense accounts and on their income taxes. People place their money in offshore accounts so that they won't have to pay income tax on it. People cheat in sports so that they can become celebrities and earn money from product endorsements. An increasing number of organizations have to restate their financial earnings to make them appear more successful in the eyes of investors (Albrecht, Albrecht, and Dolan, 2007). Cheating becomes important for success—particularly in financial terms—in a winner-take-all environment (Frank and Cook, 1995).

Enough is Enough

Citizens in the developed world have decried the salaries paid to executives, particularly those in companies that have failed to perform and, in some cases, have gone bankrupt. Why did the executives of the three failing Detroit automakers fly to Washington in expensive corporate jets? Why would an executive of a Wall Street financial institution that received a government bail-out spend over US$100,000 on office decorations? President Obama's imposition of a salary cap of US$500,000 for executives of firms that have received government bail-outs reflects this anger. But, despite the economic downturn in 2008, at least 5,000 Wall Street bankers earned bonuses of over US$1 million that year (Story and Dash, 2009). The message: if the bank does well, you are paid well; if the bank does poorly, you are still paid well; and if the bank does very poorly and has to be bailed out with taxpayers' money, you are still paid well. In March 2009, 15 AIG employees, perhaps shamed by media attention, decided to give back their bonuses (McCool and Zuill, 2009).

The Billionaire Club—Growing but Falling on Hard Times?

The latest data on billionaires reveals that the economic recession has taken its toll, with the numbers of billionaires down in almost all countries, particularly in Russia where the numbers have fallen from 101 in 2007 to 62 in 2010 (Wikipedia, 2010a, 2010b). China, however, now has 64 US dollar billionaires, ranking second only to the US, up from none in 2003. It has also been suggested that China has some billionaires who have not yet been identified. In addition, India now has 49 billionaires. Interestingly, a higher proportion of billionaires in China and India are self-made as opposed to having inherited their wealth, which is more common in the UK and the US. Deng Xiaoping, a former leader of the Chinese Communist Party, once said that "to get rich is glorious." It seems that the Chinese are getting the message and liking it, judging by the number of BMWs and Mercedes parked by the luxury shops in Shanghai.

But even the rich have to cut back when the economy sours. A story in the *National Post* (March 27, 2008, FP3) noted that wives of two senior investment bankers at Bear Stearns canceled pricey home decorating projects two days after the firm's near-failure. It also became much easier to get a table at top restaurants at the last minute. Tens of thousands of financial service employees lost their jobs in the first three months of 2008. CEOs of the largest US companies had the value of their stock, equity awards, and bonus pay-outs fall 42 percent in 2008 according to Watson Wyatt Worldwide (Towers Watson, 2009), but the recent recovery has turned this around somewhat.

Don't Blame Adam Smith

> *"The point is, ladies and gentlemen, that: Greed, for lack of a better word is good. Greed is right; greed works. Greed clarifies, cuts through, and captures the essence of the evolutionary spirit. Greed, in all of its forms—greed for life, for money, for love, knowledge—has marked the upward surge of mankind and greed—you mark my words—will not only save Teldar Paper but that other malfunctioning corporation called the USA."*
>
> Gordon Gecko (played by Michael Douglas) in the movie *Wall Street (1987)*, written and directed by Oliver Stone

Some people blame Adam Smith for encouraging greed. In *The Wealth of Nations*, Smith proposed that "selfishness" was a driver of progress and growth: the desire for more money benefited everyone because this extra money produced more jobs and sales. Smith believed that, in general, honest people able to freely pursue their own interests would fare better than they would if someone controlled what they did. Individuals' self-interests would reduce inefficiencies and allocate resources where they would most benefit the larger society. Some misinterpreted his work to suggest that greed was good and that unfettered greed was even better. But Smith thought that such "selfishness" was self-regulating or at least had some limits. Smith's first book, *The Theory of Moral Sentiments*, on which *The Wealth of Nations* is built, is less well-known, but in it he stated that individuals would also be interested in the well-being of others. Adam Smith is getting "a bad rap".

Can Money Buy Happiness?

"Too many people spend money they haven't earned on things they don't want to impress people they don't like."

Will Smith

Many developed and developing countries hold the belief that, through hard work, people can better themselves—the Horatio Alger "rags to riches" story. Betterment in this case is always in economic and financial terms. The dream in most countries is to become rich. There have never been more materialistic societies than the ones we live in today.

F. Scott Fitzgerald, author of *The Great Gatsby*, wrote "Let me tell you about the very rich. They are different from you and me." Ernest Hemingway is said to have responded: "Yes. They have more money." Leamer (2009) provides a vivid and disquieting portrait of how the super-rich who live in Palm Beach, Florida (at least some of the year) spend their lives. People here form their social groups according to how much money they have. He observed tension between those with "old money" and those with "new money," and between Gentiles and Jews. Residents of Palm Beach belong to very expensive country clubs, eat at high-priced restaurants, and attend dozens of social events each year. Yet few seem to have found joy. Unfortunately, for many of them there is always someone richer and/or better socially connected than they are.

Here are some signs that materialism and conspicuous consumption are pervasive (see Burke, 2009 for a more complete discussion of these).

THE BRITNEY SPEARS EFFECT—GREED AMONG CHILDREN

Children today want to live "celebrity lifestyles" epitomized by the latest mobile phone applications and designer clothes. Chaplin and John (2007) studied materialism and self-esteem among children and teenagers aged between 8 and 18, and found that children with low self-esteem valued cars, money, and jewelry whereas children with high self-esteem valued family, friends, hobbies, and sporting activities. The link between materialism and low self-esteem was strongest among 12–14-year-olds. Schor (2004) observed that children believed that their clothes and brands described who they were and defined their social status.

PRETENDING THAT YOU ARE RICH

Nowadays, more people who are not rich can appear to be rich. There is a huge black market for counterfeit goods carrying famous brand names such as Louis Vuitton, Nike, Chanel, Gucci, Versace, Armani, Rolex, and Prada (Phillips, 2005). Most fake goods sold in Canada are manufactured in China. The production and sale of these fake brands is a crime that harms legitimate business (Nunes and Mulani, 2008). Yet many people believe that it is acceptable to buy fake items bearing an expensive logo in order to pretend that they have money.

KEEPING UP WITH THE JONESES

George (1997) observed that employees too often choose income over family and leisure, and then work longer hours. This gives them additional income with which they can acquire products and services that are being marketed in a wide variety of ways and media. Managers and employing organizations sometimes use working longer hours and "face time" as indicators of commitment to the workplace; this leads to higher evaluations of employees who work long hours and greater rewards, which in turn leads to a "rat race" atmosphere (Landers, Rebitzer, and Taylor, 1996).

THE WORK AND SPEND TREADMILL

The work and spend treadmill results from "keeping up with the Joneses." Schor (1991) noted that employees become trapped in a work and spend cycle; employees work more hours to earn more income to acquire more possessions in order to feel successful.

The Downside of Materialism

"Self worth and net worth are not the same."

Rick Warren

Materialism has been defined as:

> ... a value that guides people's choices and conduct in a variety of situations including, but not limited to, consumption arenas. With respect to consumption, materialism will influence the type and quantity of goods purchased. Beyond consumption, materialism will influence the allocation of a variety of resources, including time. A materialist, for instance, might choose to work longer hours and earn more money instead of using that time for leisure activities. (Richins and Dawson, 1992, p. 307)

Richins and Dawson (1992) developed a measure of materialism with three components: acquisition centrality, acquisition as the pursuit of happiness, and possessions-defined success. High scorers desired a higher level of income, placed greater emphasis on financial security and less on interpersonal relationships, preferred to spend more on themselves and less on others, engaged in fewer voluntary simplicity behaviors (trying to leave a smaller footprint on the planet), and were less satisfied with their lives. There is also evidence that materialism has increased over the past 80 years (Belk and Pollay, 1985).

Whybrow (2005) notes that the compulsive quest for more has negative effects on both health and happiness. He cites growing evidence that increases in material wealth have not enhanced individual well-being (see also Csikszentmihalyi, 1999; Diener and Seligman, 2004). Sirgy (1998) theorized that materialists in fact experience greater dissatisfaction with their standard of living than do non-materialists. Kasser (2002), after reviewing the scientific evidence relating materialism to happiness, concluded that pursuing wealth not only fails to lead to happiness, but also makes many people less happy, even when they become wealthy (Easterbrook, 2004; Frank, 1999).

Materialism does, however, have some good aspects. Some employees will work harder to increase their material possessions. High levels of materialism can therefore increase the profitability of organizations, allowing them to prosper, invest more heavily in innovation and the creation of new products, and achieve greater productivity, ultimately raising the living standards of countless others.

What Do We Know About Money?

The US actress and singer Sophie Tucker once said: "I've been rich and I've been poor. Believe me, honey, rich is better." Yet, although rich people tend to be happier than poor people, the effects are small.

The psychology of money has been a neglected topic. Money is a taboo subject (Furnham and Argyle, 1998). Here are some things we know about money (Diener et al., 1999):

- People in wealthier nations are happier than people in poorer nations.
- Increases in national wealth within developed countries have not, over recent decades, been associated with increases in happiness.
- Within-nation differences in wealth show only small positive correlations with happiness.
- Increases in personal wealth do not typically result in increased happiness.
- People who strongly desire wealth and money are less happy than those who do not. Thus, avoiding poverty, living in a rich country, and emphasizing goals other than wealth are associated with higher levels of happiness.

There is only a very small correlation—generally around 0.15 to 0.20—between income and satisfaction. Several hypotheses have been offered to explain this low relationship. These include the following:

- Adaptation—we get used to the income very quickly.
- Comparison—there is always someone richer than you are.
- Alternatives—as we get more money, other things (leisure, family) seem more valuable. There are other important sources of happiness than money—family, friends, leisure, health.
- Worry—once we have money we are free to worry about things other than money. There is, however, a strong relationship between income and happiness among those with lower incomes. For this group, money buys the things they need or want.

The gist of this evidence is that higher levels of income do not buy people happiness. Instead, people get satisfaction from relationships with family and friends, the love they give and receive, and the meaning they get from work, service, hobbies, and religion. Happiness depends heavily on individual character—some people will always smile while others will always complain—and national culture: Swedes and Danes are happier than Americans who, in turn, are happier than the French, Germans, and Italians.

Izzo (2005) interviewed 235 people 60 years of age and older, identified as "wise elders" by thousands of people on his e-mail list, about things they would like to do before they died. He found a few common themes: make love a priority, live in the moment, and understand that happiness comes from inside. Almost none of the "wise elders" mentioned reading a book to find out about places you must see or the things you must do before you die. Instead, most of the secrets to happiness in old age involved "What can I give?" not "What can I take?"

Kasser and Sheldon (2009) believed that having more time, termed "time affluence," would be a more important contributor to happiness or well-being than would money, termed "material affluence." Both time and money are finite resources; they can be saved, spent or wasted. Their thinking went as follows. It takes time to participate in satisfying activities and events (Lyubomirsky, Sheldon, and Schkade, 2005). Time is also needed for personal growth, relationships, and civic contribution (Kasser, 2002). And time constraints can limit the experience of flow (Csikszcentmihalyi, 1999) and mindfulness (Brown and Ryan, 2003), important factors that contribute to happiness.

Kasser and Sheldon (2009) considered the relationship between time and material affluence and measures of job and family satisfaction in three studies. In the first study they found that time affluence predicted both job and family satisfaction, controlling for material affluence measured by income. In the second study, they found that short-term changes in outcomes were related to changes in time affluence (about a month lag), controlling for changes in material affluence. And in another study they discovered that both mindfulness and need satisfaction partially mediated the relationship between time affluence and well-being. Thus, having more time contributed more strongly to happiness than did having more money. But here are some encouraging conclusions.

THE GOOD LIFE MAY BE LESS COSTLY THAN ONE THINKS

Most individuals think that an increase in their income will make them happier and a decrease in income will make them less happy. Aknin, Norton, and Dunn (2009) asked 429 people earning a wide range of incomes (US$5,000 to over US$200,000) to rate their own happiness and then predict how happy they and others would be at different lower and higher income levels. The authors found that people overestimated the connection between money and happiness. Respondents underestimated the happiness of those earning less.

They correctly predicted that people earning high incomes would be happier than those on moderate incomes. People at all income levels have financial expenditures (car payments, mortgages etc.) and assume that at lower income levels these might prove to be hardships, making people less happy. But those on lower incomes may be working fewer hours or hold jobs which pay lower salaries but are also enjoyable or give them time for other things. The desire for money may sometimes require an individual to continue on an unsatisfying path in order to maintain a significant lifestyle.

MONEY MAY BUY HAPPINESS BUT NOT FRIENDSHIPS

Diener (2009) analyzed Gallup poll data of 136,000 people from 132 countries and found that people with larger incomes reported a higher level of happiness with their lives, but that income was not related to stronger social relationships, feelings of respect, or daily reports of positive feelings.

MONEY CAN BUY HAPPINESS IF SPENT ON EXPERIENCES

Howell and Hill (2009) reported, in a study of 154 adults, that spending money on *things* does not yield as much happiness as spending money on *experiences*. Once basic needs are met (shelter, food, a job), going to a ball game, theater or on vacation provides more happiness that buying a 60-inch flat-screen television. The television purchase happiness soon wears off. The experiences typically involve others (sociability) and provide rich memories. As Humphrey Bogart said to Lauren Bacall in *Casablanca*, "We'll always have Paris." Material things do not bring as much happiness.

In a national survey of more than 12,000 adults in the US, respondents were asked to think of an experiential and a material purchase they had made with the aim of increasing their happiness (Van Boven and Gilovich, 2003). More respondents said that their experiential investment made them happier than did their material investment. Why should experiences (doing) bring more happiness than material possessions (having)? Van Boven and Gilovich (2003) suggest several possibilities. First, experiences are more open to positive reinterpretations and are more closely connected to who one is, whereas material possessions are distinct from personal identity. Second, one can share stories about experiences since they are easier and more fun to talk about than material possessions. Third, experiences contribute to satisfying social relationships. Fourth, experiences more often involve a challenge and accomplishment. People think more about their experiences: their views of experiences improve over time; experiences seem to be resistant to unfavorable comparisons; and experiences tend to have more social value (Nicolao, Irwin, and Goodman, 2009; Solnick and Hemenway, 1998; Van Boven, 2005).

MONEY CAN BUY HAPPINESS BUT ONLY IF YOU GIVE IT AWAY

"I don't think it is a sin to be rich, it's a sin to die rich."
Rick Warren *(Sydney Morning Herald, July 4, 2006)*

Bill Gates, Paul Allen, and Warren Buffett are no fools. These billionaires have decided to give almost all of their money away. They have since invited several other very wealthy people to give away half of their money as well (Nichols, 2010). Dunn, Aknin, and Norton (2008) and Norton and Dunn (2008) suggest that how people spend money may be as important as how much money they have in contributing to their happiness. They suggest that spending money on others has a stronger positive impact on happiness than spending money on oneself. This hypothesis has been supported in three innovative studies. In the first study, happiness was more strongly correlated with spending on others than on oneself among respondents in a representative sample. In the second study, working men and women who received a profit-sharing bonus at work rated their happiness level before and after receiving the bonus and indicated how they planned to spend it. Respondents planning to spend their bonus on others rather than on themselves indicated higher levels of happiness. In the third study, participants in an experiment rated their happiness level before being given either US$5 or US$20 and being told to spend the money on themselves or on others. They then indicated their happiness level later that day. Again, individuals who spent the money on others reported greater happiness. It seems that giving reduces ties to materialism. In the same vein, Norton and Dunn (2008) suggest that employees share some of their bonus money to improve their own and others' morale.

WHY MONEY MOTIVES ARE CRITICAL

What you want and why you want it are important predictors of well-being (Carver and Baird, 1998; Kasser et al., 2004). Srivastava, Locke, and Bartol (2001) considered whether people's reasons for making money affected their psychological well-being. They developed a scale that measured people's motives for making money. The ten motives they identified were: security, family support, market worth, pride, leisure, freedom, ability to satisfy impulses, charity, social comparisons, and overcoming self-doubt. In their two studies of employed professionals and managers and employed entrepreneurs, after controlling for gender and actual income, they found that people who placed a higher importance on money in comparison to other goals, such as a satisfying family life or doing work one enjoys, were more likely to report lower subjective well-being. Only individuals who valued money but had negative motives for making it (e.g., social comparison, overcoming self-doubt) reported lower well-being, however. Those wanting to make money for positive reasons (e.g., supporting one's family) reported higher well-being. The association of materialistic values and reduced well-being have also been documented in two studies of business students (Kasser and Ahuvia, 2002; Vansteenkiste et al., 2006).

Reducing Greed

Greed has been with us for centuries. It cannot be stopped; the best we can do is to reduce its level and its dysfunctional aspects. If greed is to be reduced, it must be tackled at multiple levels: individual and family, organizational and societal. It is important to also state that the purpose of this chapter is not to criticize developed and developing countries or capitalism. Capitalism has improved the lives of countless millions of people worldwide. Unbridled capitalism, however, has sometimes produced negative consequences.

INDIVIDUAL FAMILY EFFORTS

Individuals and their families need to reduce the levels of their conspicuous consumption by making a commitment to living a simpler lifestyle (Segal, 1999). This involves emphasizing what is important to living a good life while avoiding the acquisition of things that cost a lot but add little to one's satisfaction (Kasser and Kanner, 2003; Needleman, 1991). Friends, family, recreation, and spirituality enrich one's life experiences (Izzo, 2005). Individuals need to monitor their use of time since time is finite (de Graaf, 2003; Honoré, 2004; Needleman, 1998).

In the developed world, materialism develops at a young age (Schor, 2004). Parents must be able to say "no" to their children and limit their access to media that push the latest products.

ORGANIZATIONAL EFFORTS

Organizations, too, need to move beyond selfishness (Mintzberg, Simons, and Basu, 2002). Organizations can downplay their use of financial rewards; they can still use them to reinforce excellence, but in a lower-profile way. Designing work spaces to minimize status or level distinctions would also help. Perks should be linked to performance deliverables and space assigned to those who need it rather than those at higher levels in the organization.

Mintzberg (2009) makes the radical case for scrapping executive bonuses entirely. He argues that executive bonuses, particularly in the form of stock and option grants, are a form of legal corruption that has hampered large organizations. Too many CEOs have become gamblers with other people's money: they are rewarded when it looks as if their organizations are doing well when they really aren't; they get paid even when their organizations are doing poorly; they get paid for signing merger agreements; and they get paid for staying with the company (through retention bonuses). These factors encourage CEOs to take great risks. They can't lose.

Mintzberg identifies several flaws in the notion of giving bonuses. These include the following:

- A company's health is reflected by financial measures alone.
- Financial measures reflect the true strength of a company.
- The CEO and his or her team are mainly responsible for company performance.

With reference to Mintzberg's last point, too many executives use bonuses for their own personal benefits; feeding their egos, meeting narcissistic needs, and satisfying greed. The CEO of a US$14 trillion economy (Barack Obama) receives US$400,000 a year. Why should the CEO of a much smaller organization get paid millions?

SOCIETAL EFFORTS

Societies need to understand the downside of unfettered greed. Fortunately, some steps are already being taken in this direction (Jackson, 2009). The current economic recession is forcing individuals, families and organizations to "cut back." New houses are being built smaller, and restaurants are reducing both their prices and the sizes of portions. As more individuals, families, and organizations make efforts to control greed, a greater number of societal-level changes will become evident.

Reducing levels of greed will prove difficult, however, and efforts must be made at several levels simultaneously. These efforts should prove worthwhile, since greed emerges as one of the major causes of crime and corruption in organizations.

References

Acharya, M. and Yew, T. (2009) "Drabinsky gets 7 years, bail," *Toronto Star*, August 10, at: http://www.thestar.com/news/gta/article/676447.

Aknin, L. B., Norton, M. I., and Dunn, E. W. (2009) "From wealth to well-being: Money matters, but less than people think," *Journal of Positive Psychology*, 4, 523–527.

Albrecht, C., Albrecht, C. C., and Dolan, S. (2007) "Financial fraud: The how and why," *European Business Forum*, 29, 34–39.

Arvedlund, E. (2009) *Too Good To Be True: The Rise and Fall of Bernie Madoff*, New York: Portfolio.

Bebchuk, L. A., Cohen, A., and Spamann, H. (2010) *The Wages of Failure: Executive Compensation at Bear Stearns and Lehman 2000–2008*, Discussion Paper 657, revised February 2010, Cambridge, MA: Harvard Law School. Available at: http://papers.ssrn.com/sol3/papers.cfm?abstract_id=1513522.

Belk, R. W. and Pollay, R. (1985) "Images of ourselves: The good life in twentieth century advertising," *Journal of Consumer Research*, 11, 887–897.

Brown, K. W. and Ryan, R. M. (2003) "The benefits of being present: Mindfulness and its role in well-being," *Journal of Personality and Social Psychology*, 84, 822–848.

Buettner, R. (2010) "Union's money fueled lavish lifestyle, prosecutors say," January 3, at: http://www.nytimes.com/2010/01/04/nyregion/04sandhog.html.

Burke, R. J. (2009) "Greed" in R. J. Burke and C. L. Cooper (eds) *Research Companion to Corruption in Organizations*, Cheltenham, UK: Edward Elgar, pp. 33–59.

Callahan, D. (2004) *The Cheating Culture: Why More Americans are Doing Wrong to Get Ahead*, Orlando, FL: Harcourt.

Carver, C. S. and Baird, E. (1998) "The American dream revisited: Is it what you want or why you want it that matters?" *Psychological Science*, 9, 289–292.

Cassell's Concise Dictionary (1997) London: Cassell.

CBC News (2009) "Ontario cleans house at OLG," August 31, at: http://www.cbc.ca/canada/toronto/story/2009/08/31/olg-shakeup.html.

CBC News (2010) "CEOs paid 174 times more than average worker: Report," January 4, at: http://www.cbc.ca/money/story/2010/01/04/executive-compensation-average-salary-ceo.html.

Center for Public Leadership (2009) *National Leadership Index 2009: A National Study of Confidence in Leadership*, Cambridge, MA: Harvard Kennedy School at Harvard University. Available at: http://content.ksg.harvard.edu/leadership/images/CPLpdf/cpl_nli_2009.pdf.

Chaplin, L. N. and John, D. R. (2007) "Growing up in a materialistic world: Age differences in materialism in children," *Journal of Consumer Research*, 34, 184–196.

Clark, A. (2009) "AIG boss starts new job—with Adriatic holiday overseeing grape harvest," *Guardian*, August 27, at: http://www.guardian.co.uk/business/2009/aug/27/aig-business-insurance-benmosche-croatia-grapes.

Colvin, G. (2004) "The verdict on business: Presumed guilty," *Fortune*, 150, 78.

Csikszcentmihalyi, M. (1999) "If we are so rich, why aren't we happy?" *American Psychologist*, 54, 821–827.

Dearing, S. (2009) "Kramer released from contract, Ontario's eHealth scandal blows up," June 8, at: http://www.digitaljournal.com/article/273828.

de Graaf, J. (2003) *Take Back Your Time: Fighting Overwork and Time Poverty in America*, San Francisco, CA: Berrett-Koehler.

Diener, E. (2009) "Summary of research presented at the 2009 annual convention of the American Psychological Association," *Monitor on Psychology*, October, 20.

Diener, E. and Seligman, M. E. P. (2004) "Beyond money: Towards an economy of well-being," *Psychology in the Public Interest*, 5, 1–31.

Diener, E., Diener, M., and Diener, C. (1995) "Factors predicting the subjective well-being of nations," *Journal of Personality and Social Psychology*, 69, 851–864.

Diener, E., Suh, E. M., Lucas, R. E. and Smith, H. L. (1999) "Subjective well-being: Three decades of progress," *Psychological Bulletin*, 125, 276–302.

Dunn, E. W., Aknin, L. B. and Norton, M. I. (2008) "Spending money on others promotes happiness," *Science*, 319, 1687–1688.

Easterbrook, G. (2004) *The Progress Paradox: How Life Gets Better While People Feel Worse*, New York: Random House.

Evans, M. (2009a) "While Rome burns, more bonuses for execs," November 26, at: http://www.allaboutnortel.com/2009/11/26/while-rome-burns-more-bonuses-for-execs/.

Evans, M. (2009b) "Mike Z. wants his dough," October 8, at: http://www.allaboutnortel.com/2009/10/08/mike-z-wants-his-dough/.

Financial Times (2009) "Court papers lift lid on Stanford's lifestyle." Available at: http://www.ft.com/cms/s/0/40e8847e-ff81-11dd-b3f8-00007.

Frank, R. H. (1999) *Luxury Fever: Why Money Fails to Satisfy in an Era of Excess*, New York: The Free Press.

Frank, R. H. and Cook, P. J. (1995) *The Winner-Take-All Society*, New York: The Free Press.

Fromm. E. (1976) *To Have or To Be?* New York: Harper & Row.

Furnham, A. and Argyle, M. (1998) *The Psychology of Money*, London, UK: Routledge.

George, D. (1997) "Working longer hours: Pressure from the boss or pressure from the marketers?" *Review of Social Economy*, 60, 33–65.

Guner, A. B., Malmendier, U., and Tate, G. (2008) "Financial expertise of directors," *Journal of Financial Economics*, 88, 323–354.

Honoré, C. (2004) *In Praise of Slow*, Toronto: Alfred Knopf.

Howell, R. and Hill, G. (2009) " The mediators of experiential purchases: determining the impact of psychological needs satisfaction and social comparison," paper presented at the Annual Meeting of the Society for Personality and Social Psychology, Tampa, FL, February.

Huffington Post (2009) "Allen Stanford owes over $200 million in federal taxes," February 18, at: http://www.huffingtonpost.com/2009/02/18/allen-stanford-owes-over-_n_168067.html.

Izzo, J. (2005) *The Five Secrets You Must Discover Before You Die*, Lions Bay, BC: Fairwinds Press.

Jackson, T. (2009) *Prosperity without Growth: Economics for a Finite Planet*, London: Earthscan Publications Ltd.

Jagri, R., Sheets, N., Jankovic, A., Motomura, A. R, Amarnath, B.. S. and Abel, P. A. (2010) "Frequency, nature, effects, and correlates of conflicts of interest in published clinical cancer research," *Cancer*, 115, 2783–2791.

Johansmeyer, T. (2009) "Goldman Sachs to pay $20 billion bonuses in stock, not cash," December 11, at: http://www.bloggingstocks.com/2009/12/11/goldman-sachs-to-pay-20-billion-in-stock-mostly-bonuses/.

Johnson, L. A. (2009) "Merck to pay $671M settlement," February 8, at: http://www2.ljworld.com/news/2008/feb/08/merck_pay_671m_settlement/.

Kasser, T. (2002) *The High Price of Materialism*, Cambridge, MA: MIT Press.

Kasser, T. and Ahuvia, A. C. (2002) "Materialistic values and well-being in business students," *European Journal of Social Psychology*, 32, 137–146.

Kasser, T. and Kanner, A. D. (2003) *Psychology and Consumer Culture: The Struggle for a Good Life in a Materialistic World*, Washington, DC: APA Books.

Kasser, T. and Sheldon, K. M. (2009) "Material and time affluence as predictors of subjective well-being," *Journal of Business Ethics*, 84, 243–255.

Kasser, T., Sheldon, K. M., Ryan, R. M., and Deci, E. L. (2004) "The independent effects of goal contents and motives on well-being: It's both what you do and why you do it," *Personality and Social Psychology Bulletin*, 30, 475–486.

Kirtzman, A. (2009) *Betrayal: The Life and Lies of Bernie Madoff*, New York: HarperCollins.

Kramer, A. E. (2009) "Ikea plans to halt investment in Russia," *New York Times*, June 23, at: http://www.nytimes.com/2009/06/24/business/global/24ruble.html.

Landers, R. M., Rebitzer, J. B., and Taylor, L. J. (1996) "Rat race redux: Adverse selection in the determination on work hours in law firms," *American Economic Review*, 86, 329–348.

Larson (2009) "Con man Edward Okun gets 100 years for fraud scheme (update 2)," August 4, at: http://www.bloomberg.com/apps/news?pid=newsarchive&sid=agwI8EGWuHkg.

Leamer, L. (2009) *Madness under the Royal Palms: Love and Death behind the Gates of Palm Beach*, New York: Hyperion.

Leonard, T. (2009) "Brooke Astor's son found guilty of defrauding heiress of millions," *Daily Telegraph*, October 8, at: http://www.telegraph.co.uk/news/newstopics/celebritynews/6275581/Brooke-Astors-son-found-guilty-of-defrauding-heiress-of-millions-of-dollars.html.

Lyubomirsky, S., Sheldon, K. M., and Schkade, D. (2005) "Pursuing happiness: The architecture of sustainable change," *Review of General Psychology*, 9, 111–131.

Macau (2008) "Ao Macau's crooked former government official gets 27 years," January 30, at: http://a2zmacau.com/1245/ao-macaus-crooked-former-government-official-gets-27-years-jail-term/.

McCool, G. and Zuill, L. (2009) "15 AIG employees give back bonuses," *Insurance Journal*, March 24, at: http://www.insurancejournal.com/news/national/2009/03/24/98987.htm.

Mintzberg, H. (2009) "No more executive bonuses!" *Wall Street Journal*, November 30, 2009.

Mintzberg, H., Simons, R., and Basu, K. (2002) "Beyond selfishness," *MIT Sloan Management Review*, Fall, 67–74.

Naharnet.com (2009) "Army intelligence questions Ezzedine over mysterious investments, possible foreign 'ambush'," September 28, at: http://www.naharnet.com/domino/tn/NewsDesk.nsf/Lebanon/9DBC49D1BD7E9933C225763F001C11A1?OpenDocument.

National Post (2009a) Montreal's Madoff: Earl Jones has no shame," July 15, at: http://ghostsintheeyes.typepad.com/work_in_progress/2009/07/montreals-madoff-earl-jones-has-no-shame.html.

National Post (2009b) "Lax spending disclosed: Review tabled in parliament excludes concerns about ex-rights group chief," September 5, p. A8. Available at: http://ezralevant.com/Waste%20at%20R%26D.pdf.

Needleman, J. (1991) *Money and the Meaning of Life*, New York: Doubleday/Currency.

Needleman, J. (1998) *Time and the Soul: Where has all the Meaningful Time Gone—And Can We Get It Back?* San Francisco, CA: Berrett-Koehler.

Nichols, M. (2010) "Billionaires to give away half their fortune," *The Independent*, August 4, at: http://www.independent.co.uk/news/world/americas/billionaires-to-give-away-half-their-fortune-2043168.html.

Nicolao, L., Irwin, J. R., and Goodman, J. K. (2009) "Happiness for sale: Do experiential or material purchases lead to greater happiness?" *Journal of Consumer Research*, 36, 188–198.

Norton, M. I. and Dunn, E. W. (2008) "Help employees give away some of that bonus," *Harvard Business Review*, 86, 27.

NPR (2009), "Baseball's Alex Rodriguez admits steroid use," February 9, at: http://www.npr.org/templates/story/story.php?storyId=100479107.

Nunes, P. F. and Mulani, N. P. (2008) "Can knockoffs knock out your business?" *Harvard Business Review*, October, 41–50.

Oppenheimer, J. (2009) *Madoff with the Money*, New York: John Wiley.

Patel, R. (2010) *The Value of Nothing: Why Everything Costs So Much More Than We Think*, New York: HarperCollins.

Phillips, T. (2005) *Knockoff: The Deadly Trade in Counterfeit Goods*, London, UK: Kegan Paul.

Prynn, J. and Duncan, H. (2010) " My parents think I'm paid too much, says £10m RBS boss Stephen Hester," *London Evening Standard*, January 12, at: http://www.thisislondon.co.uk/standard/article-23794059-my-parents-think-im-paid-too-much-says-pound-10m-rbs-boss-stephen-hester.do.

Reuters (2009) "Court lets senior Nortel execs share in bonus pool," March 20, at: http://www.reuters.com/article/idUSN2050393120090320.

Richins, M. L. and Dawson, S. (1992) "A consumer value orientation for materialism and its measurement: Scale development and validation," *Journal of Consumer Research*, 19, 303–316.

Robinson, J. (2003) "The incredible shrinking vacation" in J. de Graaf (ed.) *Take Back Your Time: Fighting Overwork and Time Poverty in America*, San Francisco, CA: Berrett-Koehler, pp. 20–27.

Rosenkrantz, H. (2009) "Executives took $350 million in pay as pensions ended," November 19, at: http://forum.prisonplanet.com/index.php?topic=145052.0.

Ryan, N. (2009) "Never mind the death threats," *Report on Business*, November, 54–58.

Schor, J. (1991) *The Overworked American: The Unexpected Decline of Leisure*, New York: Basic Books.

Schor, J. (1998) *The Overspent American*, New York: Basic Books.

Schor, J. B. (2004) *Born to Buy: The Commercialized Child and the New Consumer Culture*, New York: Simon & Schuster.

Segal, J. M. (1999) *Graceful Simplicity: The Philosophy and Politics of the Alternative American Dream*, Berkeley, CA: University of California Press.

Seskus, T., Cryderman, K., and Massinon, S. (2009) "Alleged mastermind in $100 million Canadian Ponzi scheme taken into custody," *Calgary Herald*, September 29, at: http://fwix.com/calgary/share/8fe16b4ff6/suspect_in_canadas_largest_ponzi_scheme_arrested_in_calgary.

Sharrock, D. (2009) "Irish parliamentary Speaker resigns over expense claims allegations," *The Sunday Times*, October 14, at: http://www.timesonline.co.uk/tol/news/world/ireland/article6873600.ece.

Sirgy, M. J. (1998) "Materialism and quality of life," *Social Indicators Research*, 43, 227–260.

Solnick, S. J. and Hemenway, D. (1998) "Is more always better? A survey on positional concerns," *Journal of Economic Behavior and Organization*, 37, 373–383.

Story, L. and Dash, E. (2009) "Bankers reaped lavish bonuses during bailouts," *New York Times*, July 30, at: http://www.nytimes.com/2009/07/31/business/31pay.html.

Stratton, A. (2009) "Defiant MPs challenge call to repay expenses," October 12, at: http://www.guardian.co.uk/politics/2009/oct/12/mps-expenses-concern.

Srivastava, A., Locke, E. A., and Bartol, K. M. (2001) "Money and subjective well-being: It's not the money, it's the motives," *Journal of Personality and Social Psychology*, 80, 959–971.

Telegraph.co.uk (2009) "MPs' expenses: Full list of MPs investigated by the Telegraph," May 8, at: http://www.telegraph.co.uk/news/newstopics/mps-expenses/5297606/MPs-expenses-Full-list-of-MPs-investigated-by-the-Telegraph.html.

The Independent (2009) "Michael Missick: The king of sleaze in the colonies," March 25, at: http://www.independent.co.uk/news/world/americas/michael-misick-the-king-of-sleaze-in-the-colonies-1653311.html.

Torstar Network (2010) "Lotto cheat sentenced," June 15, at: http://www.mississauga.com/news/article/833791--lotto-cheat-sentenced.

Towers Watson (2009) "CEO stock ownership value plunged in 2008 study finds—November 2009," press release, November 12, at: http://www.watsonwyatt.com/render.asp?catid=1&id=22682.

Van Boven, L. (2005) "Experientialism, materialism, and the pursuit of happiness," *Review of General Psychology*, 9, 134–142.

Van Boven, L. and Gilovich, T. (2003) "To do or to have? That is the question," *Journal of Personality and Social Psychology*, 85, 1193–1202.

Vansteenkiste, M., Duriez, B., Simons, H. J., and Soenens, B. (2006) "Materialistic values and well-being among business students: Further evidence of their detrimental effect," *Journal of Applied Social Psychology*, 36, 2892–2908.

Whybrow, P. C. (2005) *American Mania: When More is not Enough*, New York: W. W. Norton & Company.

Wikipedia (2010a) "Forbes list of billionaires," at: http://en.wikipedia.org/wiki/Forbes_list_of_billionaires.

Wikipedia (2010b) "List of countries by the number of US dollar billionaires," at: http://en.wikipedia.org/wiki/List_of_countries_by_the_number_of_US_dollar_billionaires.

Winnett, R. (2009) "MPs' expenses: £12,500 payback time for Gordon Brown," *Daily Telegraph*, October 12, at: http://www.telegraph.co.uk/news/newstopics/mps-expenses/6311388/MPs-expenses-12500-payback-time-for-Gordon-Brown.html.

3

Predicting Workplace Misconduct Using Personality and Academic Behaviors

Thomas H. Stone, I. M. Jawahar, and Jennifer L. Kisamore

Reports of corporate crimes have become commonplace in the media. Names such as Adelphia, Enron, Tyco, WorldCom, Northern Rock, Parmalat, and Halliburton have become synonymous with scandals and corporate misdeeds. Corporate crime is not a recent phenomenon, however, as is evident from Clinard's and Yeager's (2006) mid-1970s data which showed many incidents of serious crimes, particularly in large corporations. The website http://corporatecrimereporter.com illustrates the magnitude, cost and pervasiveness of corporate crimes.

Corporate crime raises obvious questions, such as what are the causes of these behaviors and how can they be reduced or eliminated? Despite more than 30 years of research using a variety of approaches, there are no clear answers. One of the best explanations to date may be found in a recent meta-analysis by Kish-Gephart et al. (2010), which examines the effects of individual characteristics ("apples"), moral issue characteristics ("cases"), and organizational environments ("barrels"). The authors conclude:

> ... our findings reveal a high degree of underlying complexity in unethical choices. That is, such choices cannot be explained by one or two dominant antecedents. Rather, they are multidetermined, with substrates spread widely, even within the distinct realms of individual, moral issue, and organizational environment characteristics. (Kish-Gephart et al., 2010, p. 17)

Kish-Gephart et al.'s meta-analysis shows that "bad apples," people characterized by self-interest, as indicated by low cognitive moral development (Kohlberg, 1969), high Machiavellianism, and external locus of control (Rotter, 1966) are more likely to hold unethical intentions and engage in unethical work behavior. Regarding "cases" or the conditions of decisions, support was found for four of Jones's (1991) six moral intensity dimensions. Specifically, the four dimensions of concentration of effect, probability of effect, proximity or familiarity with the victim, and social consensus (behavioral norms) had significant negative relationships with unethical intentions. Of these four, social consensus that a behavior was unethical had the largest effect on reducing unethical intentions. Results for characteristics of the organizational environment show that while climates of "everyone for themselves" encourage unethical behaviors, those emphasizing the well-being of all stakeholders and those with clear communication of acceptable and unacceptable behaviors combined with a "properly enforced code of conduct can have a powerful influence on unethical choices" (Kish-Gephart et al., 2010, p. 21). Generally, results of this meta-analysis support earlier theories of unethical behavior (McCabe, Butterfield, and Treviño, 1996; Treviño, 1986; Treviño and Youngblood, 1990). Kish-Gephart et al. (2010), however, note a surprising finding that many antecedents were more highly correlated with behavior than intention. This is surprising because it runs counter to established models including Rest's (1986) model of ethical decision-making and Ajzen's (1991) Theory of Planned Behavior (TPB) in which intention precedes behavior. Kish-Gephart et al. (2010) suggest an "ethical impulse perspective" explanation similar to Reynolds's (2006) theory contending that people make "reflexive judgments" using "prototypes to match ethical situations to actions" (p. 22).

While unethical and illegal behaviors are far too common in business, a logical question is: when or where does such behavior begin? There is considerable evidence that cheating and unethical behaviors are prevalent in high school (Josephson Institute of Ethics, 2010; Williams, 2001) and possibly earlier. Also, there is ample evidence of unethical behavior and violation of academic integrity in colleges and universities in the US (Davis et al., 1992; McCabe and Treviño, 1993, 1997; Whitley, 1998), Canada (Christensen-Hughes and McCabe, 2006; Genereux and McLeod, 1995), Australia (Brimble and Stevenson-Clarke, 2005), the UK (Newstead, Franklyn-Stokes, and Armstead, 1996), and many other countries (Grimes, 2004, Koljatic, Silva, and Ardiles, 2003; Magnus et al., 2002). Data collected from over 18,000 students in 61 schools in the US and Canada reveal that cheating and plagiarism rates are as high as 71 percent and 70 percent, respectively (McCabe, 2005). These data also indicate that cheating is especially prevalent in business programs: students are engaging in cheating earlier in their academic careers, and cheating is becoming a habit for a growing number of students. Recent work by McCabe, Butterfield, and Treviño (2006) reveals that not even graduate programs are immune from academic integrity violations. Their study of 5,331 graduate students found academic misconduct is on the rise among graduate students and that graduate students in business are again the worst offenders in terms of academic integrity policies.

Some research (Harding et al., 2004; McCabe, Treviño, and Butterfield, 1996; Nonis and Swift, 2001; Sims, 1993; Treviño, Weaver, and Reynolds, 2006) suggests associations between engaging in academic misconduct and both endorsing and committing unethical behaviors at work. These studies, however, did not use recognized measures of illegal or unethical work behavior and were not grounded in established theory and research related to deviant and counterproductive work behavior (CWB). The study reported here uses well-established measures of academic misconduct (see McCabe, 2005; McCabe and Treviño, 1993, 1997) and CWB (see Spector et al., 2006).

Recent conceptualization of unethical and illegal work behaviors argues that they are one of three broad classes of job performance which includes task performance, organizational citizenship behavior (OCB) and counterproductive work behavior (CWB) (Rotundo and Sackett, 2002; Sackett, 2002). That is, job performance is composed of prescribed role behaviors and extra-role behaviors including extra-role behaviors that are both positive and negative. OCB is employee behavior and activities that contribute "to the maintenance and enhancement of the social and psychological context that supports task performance" (Organ, 1997, p. 91). These include activities that support organizational objectives and conform to rules and procedures even when doing so is not convenient. Organ's (1997) conceptualization of OCB is similar to Borman's and Motowidlo's (1997) definition of contextual performance in that both constructs embody interpersonal facilitation and dedication to one's job. For the purpose of the current study, we consider them to be essentially equivalent. CWB or "workplace deviance," on the other hand, consists of "voluntary behavior of organizational members that violates significant organizational norms, and in so doing, threatens the well-being of the organization and/or its members" (Robinson and Bennett, 1995, p. 556). These behaviors include, but are not limited to, theft, excessive absence, production deviance, sabotage, interpersonal abuse, and rule violations (Miles et al., 2002; Spector et al., 2006). Such misconduct in organizational settings violates organizational norms and jeopardizes the welfare of organizations and their constituents (Gruys and Sackett, 2003; Robinson and Bennett, 1995).

As argued above, both misconduct and pro-social behaviors occur in academic settings and may be behavioral signs of similar behaviors at work. For instance, the reporting of acts of cheating by other students helps maintain the integrity of the educational process (McCabe and Treviño, 1993) and is analogous to OCB in work organizations. On the other hand, academic misconduct, including cheating and plagiarism, is intentional behavior that violates university policies and undermines the educational process, and thus is akin to CWB. In fact, research suggests that behavior is congruent between the academic setting and the workplace and specifically suggests that those who cheat in school are also likely to engage in unethical work behaviors (e.g., Harding et al., 2004; McCabe, Treviño, and Butterfield, 1996; Nonis and Swift, 2001; Sims, 1993; Treviño, Weaver, and Reynolds, 2006).

While a substantial body of research, to be reviewed later in this chapter, has investigated personality and other variables, such as attitudes and perceptions, as antecedents to OCB and to CWB, relatively little research exists on the use of behavioral samples to predict OCB and CWB. Personality scales and ability tests are examples of signs, while records of or ratings of actual behavior are types of behavioral samples. Reporting cheating by others may be viewed as a sample of OCB while a sample relevant to CWB is cheating behavior in academic settings. In this study, we use both personality and samples to examine how each relates to OCB and CWB.

The chapter is organized as follows. First, we review research on CWB with a focus on identifying antecedents. Second, we review research on academic integrity that has focused on personality variables as antecedents of academic misconduct. Third, we integrate these streams of research to argue that personality variables (adjustment, prudence, and sociability) and behavior (reporting cheating, and cheating behavior) from one domain (the academic world) could be useful predictors of undesirable (CWB) behaviors in another domain (the workplace). Fourth, we describe a study conducted to investigate our predictions. Finally, we discuss the implications of the study's results for theory and practice, and offer suggestions for future research.

The Relationship Between CWB and OCB

Although the focus of this chapter is CWB, both theory and research have established a significant, albeit negative, relationship between CWB and OCB (see, for example, Bennett and Stamper, 2001; Dalal, 2005; Miles et al., 2002; Sackett and DeVore, 2001; Sackett et al., 2006; Salgado, 2002; and Spector and Fox, 2002). While studies have generally shown a negative relationship between the two constructs, the magnitude of the relationship has varied across studies from a strong relationship (Bennett and Stamper, 2001; Berry, Ones and Sackett, 2007; Sackett and DeVore, 2001) to a weaker one (Dalal, 2005; Kelloway et al., 2002; Sackett et al., 2006). For example, Dalal's (2005) meta-analysis of 49 samples from 38 studies found a sample-size-weighted mean correlation, corrected for unreliability in both OCB and CWB, of -0.32.

Personality as an Antecedent of OCB and CWB

Antecedents of CWB and OCB have been explored in studies examining both variables (Berry, Ones, and Sackett, 2007; Cohen-Charash and Spector, 2001; Colquitt et al., 2001; Dalal, 2005) and those examining either OCB (LePine, Erez, and Johnson, 2002; Meyer et al., 2002; Organ and Ryan, 1995; Riketta, 2002) or CWB separately (Barrick and Mount, 1991; Mount, Ilies, and Johnson, 2006; Robinson and Greenberg, 1998; Salgado, 2002). Dalal's (2005) meta-analysis found that conscientiousness has a similar magnitude of relationship to OCB ($\hat{r}$ = 0.34) as to CWB ($\hat{r}$ = -0.36). His meta-analysis shows negative affectivity is much more strongly related to CWB, $\hat{r}$ = 0.41, than to OCB, $\hat{r}$ = -0.10, but results for positive affectivity, though positive for OCB and negative for CWB, were "less clear" (Dalal, 2005, p. 1248).

Prior meta-analyses (Cohen-Charash and Spector, 2001; Colquitt et al., 2001; LePine, Erez, and Johnson, 2002; Meyer et al., 2002; Organ and Ryan, 1995; Riketta, 2002) of the dimensionality and antecedents of OCB found similar results to those of Dalal (2005). Borman et al. (2001) identified 20 studies conducted since Organ's and Ryan's (1995) meta-analysis of the relationship between OCB and personality variables. They found significant, uncorrected correlation coefficients between OCB and various personality constructs, including other-oriented empathy (r = 0.28), conscientiousness (r = 0.24), helpfulness (r = 0.22), positive affectivity (PA; r = 0.18), negative affectivity (NA; r = 0.14), and agreeableness (r = 0.13). Although only conscientiousness and agreeableness are Big Five personality factors, other-oriented empathy and helpfulness appear to be related to emotional stability and agreeableness, respectively.

Major reviews (e.g., Barrick and Mount, 1991; Berry, Ones, and Sackett, 2007; Cullen and Sackett, 2003; Ones, Viswesvaran, and Schmidt, 1993, 2003; Salgado, 2002) of personality and CWB conclude that, of the Big Five personality constructs, conscientiousness, emotional stability, and agreeableness best predict CWB. Salgado (2002) found that conscientiousness (mean corrected correlation of -0.26) was the best predictor of a composite measure of CWB that includes behaviors such as theft, rule violations, substance abuse, disciplinary problems, property damage, and other irresponsible behaviors. Using items assessing the Big Five factors of conscientiousness, emotional stability and agreeableness, Hogan and Hogan (1989) developed the Reliability Scale from items of the Hogan Personality Inventory (HPI). This scale, often called an integrity test, predicts "organizational delinquency," including behaviors such as theft, substance abuse, insubordination, and other behaviors associated with CWB. The HPI is based on the Big Five personality model. Ones, Viswesvaran, and Schmidt (1993), in a study of integrity tests, found that the average criterion-related validity between scores on the Hogan Reliability Scale and CWB was 0.45. In summary, this stream of research has clearly established that personality variables are useful predictors of OCB and CWB.

Academic Integrity and Misconduct

Although a voluminous body of research exists on academic integrity, relatively few studies of academic misconduct have relied on personality as an antecedent. In a number of studies, locus of control has been related to cheating behavior in academic settings (Houston, 1983; Karabenick and Srull, 1978; Forsyth, Pope, and McMillan, 1985). The Kish-Gephart et al. (2010) meta-analysis found eight published studies using locus of control and six of Machiavellianism with mean correlations of 0.13 and 0.12, respectively, for measures of unethical behavior, although most did not assess academic integrity. At least two studies (Stone, Kisamore, and Jawahar, 2008; Stone, Jawahar, and Kisamore, 2010) relied on a measure of Big Five personality factors to predict academic misconduct. In a sample of 217 business students, Stone, Kisamore, and Jawahar (2008) reported correlations of -0.21 between HPI Reliability and intentions to cheat in college and 0.18 with the likelihood of reporting cheating. The HPI Reliability Scale is a composite measure of items typically used to measure adjustment, prudence and sociability (Hogan and Hogan, 1995, 1989). Stone, Jawahar, and Kisamore (2010) found that adjustment correlated -0.14 with cheating behaviors but was not significant for intent to cheat, and that prudence correlated -0.25 with cheating and -0.19 with intent in a sample of business students.

Personality, Academic Integrity, OCB and CWB

Personality is related to pro-social behaviors, such as reporting cheating by others, and to academic misconduct, such as cheating and plagiarism (e.g., Stone, Kisamore, and Jawahar, 2008; Stone, Kisamore, and Jawahar, 2010). Likewise, personality factors, including conscientiousness (e.g., Borman et al., 2001; Dalal, 2005) and agreeableness (e.g., Berry, Ones, and Sackett, 2007), are related to OCB and to CWB. Although Kish-Gephart et al. (2010) define unethical behavior as "any organizational member action that violates widely accepted (societal) moral norms" (p. 2), their meta-analysis excluded the substantial body of CWB research examining personality.

While Berry, Ones, and Sackett (2007), Dalal (2005) and other meta-analyses examined both personality and perceptions and attitudes toward work experiences, such as job satisfaction and organization commitment, as antecedents to OCB and CWB, a unique aspect of this study is a comparison of personality antecedents with behavioral samples obtained in an academic setting. That is, instead of attitudes and perceptions of job experiences such as job satisfaction and organizational commitment, in this study, self-reports of behavior reflecting OCB and CWB are used in conjunction with measures of prudence, adjustment, and sociability.

Academic misconduct appears to be related to attitudes toward CWB. Indeed, some research suggests that people who cheat in school are more likely to engage in unethical behavior at work (McCabe, Treviño, and Butterfield, 1996; Nonis and Swift, 2001; Sims, 1993). Cheating in school might well be a precursor to engaging in unethical behaviors at work. We argue that such cheating is a relevant behavior that predicts illegal, unethical, and counterproductive behavior at work.

Both theory and research suggest that academic misconduct is likely to be correlated with deviant work behavior (Gottfredson and Hirschi, 1990; Marcus and Schuler, 2004; Sackett and DeVore, 2001). A study by Marcus and Schuler (2004) demonstrated both the comparative strength of personality variables to predict CWB and the generality of these variables across a variety of CWBs. Their study tested Hirschi's and Gottfredson's (1994) construct of self-control against 23 other personality and situational predictors of a wide spectrum of CWBs. Based on their General Theory of Crime, Gottfredson and Hirschi (1990) argued that self-control, "the tendency to avoid acts whose long-term costs exceed momentary advantages" (Hirschi and Gottfredson, 1994, p. 4), is the core explanation for crime. Results of Marcus's and Schuler's (2004) study showed strong support for self-control that contained subcomponents of conscientiousness and emotional stability over other categories, including triggers (perceived injustice and job satisfaction) and opportunities that inhibit or facilitate CWB, such as group norms and sanctions.

Several studies (Harding et al., 2004; McCabe, Treviño, and Butterfield, 1996; Nonis and Swift, 2001; Sims, 1993) examined the relationship between academic misconduct and OCB and/or unethical behavior at work. None of these studies, however, used established CWB measures and none examined personality as an antecedent of CWB or OCB. Sims (1993) found, in a sample of 60 MBAs, a correlation of 0.48 between frequency ratings of cheating in school and work behaviors such as theft of materials and time and lying. In a much larger sample that included 1,051 students, Nonis and Swift (2001) found a stronger correlation between frequency of cheating at school and at work for both undergraduates ($r = 0.66$) and graduate ($r = 0.61$) students. Work behaviors rated in Nonis's and Swift's study were similar to those used in Sims (1993) with the addition of substance abuse and additional reasons for lying. The study presented here is the first to address the relationship between academic misconduct, counterproductive work behavior and personality using established measures of both cheating behavior and CWB.

As suggested earlier, employee performance can be viewed as including task performance, OCB and CWB (Rotundo and Sackett, 2002; Sackett, 2002; Viswesvaran and Ones, 2000). Therefore, it is appropriate to examine indicators of OCB and CWB in both the classroom and work contexts. We contend that just as misconduct in organizational settings violates organizational norms and jeopardizes the welfare of organizations and members (Gruys and Sackett, 2003; Robinson and Bennett, 1995; Sackett and DeVore, 2001), academic misconduct, including offenses such as cheating and plagiarism, violates university policies and undermines the educational process and is, therefore, a form of counterproductive behavior. Similarly, we argue that reporting instances of cheating by other students helps maintain the integrity of the educational process (McCabe and Treviño, 1993). Indeed, reporting cheating can be conceptualized as a form of extra-role behavior (Van Dyne and LePine, 1998), specifically, whistleblowing (Miceli and Near, 1988) as it goes beyond students' role requirements, especially at institutions without traditional honor codes, and is meant to benefit the institution. Thus, reporting cheating is an example of an OCB in an academic setting, given that such behavior contributes "to the maintenance and enhancement of the social and psychological context that supports task performance" (Organ, 1997, p. 91). Therefore, we argue that students who would report cheating or plagiarism in school are more likely to demonstrate OCB at work and less likely to engage in CWB.

The Current Study

The present study extends previous OCB and CWB research in several ways. First, the efficacy of three Big Five personality dimensions to predict measures of CWB, as well as academic cheating and reporting cheating, is examined in a structural equation model. Second, the efficacy of cheating behavior and intent to report cheating in school to predict CWB is examined using structural equation modeling. The vast majority of CWB and OCB research (Berry, Ones, and Sackett, 2007; Dalal, 2005) has relied on self, peer or supervisor responses to personality or perceptual measures. In this study we use behavior, as well as personality measures, from one organizational setting—school—to predict CWB in a work setting. Finally, this research responds to Dalal's (2005) contention that there is a "pressing need" for research on the antecedents of CWB.

This study examined two structural equation models—a full and a partial mediation model. In the full mediation model, three personality factors with demonstrated relations with CWB have paths to both cheating behavior and reporting cheating, and each of these behaviors has a direct path to four CWB measures. Acceptance of this model suggests that samples of behavior in school mediate the effects of the well-established personality predictors of CWB and OCB. The second model tested differs from the first as it also includes direct paths from each of the personality measures to each of the CWB measures. If this model is a significantly better fit to the data, this suggests that personality variables can account for variance in CWB not accounted for by cheating behaviors and report of cheating intentions.

METHOD

Sample and procedure Undergraduate business students in seven marketing, management, and economics classes at a large, mid-western public university in the US were recruited for participation in the current study. Based on class rosters, 438 students were included in the recruitment pool. Extra credit points were offered as an incentive for participation; an alternative opportunity for extra-credit was offered for students who did not choose to participate in the research study. A total of 207 participants provided usable responses yielding a response rate of 47 percent. The study was conducted near the end of the term, and some students had already earned their maximum extra credit and thus would not gain any credit for participation.

Participants completed both the HPI and the integrity survey online outside of class. They were given a log-on code and an individual password plus an assurance that their responses would be confidential.

Approximately 21 percent of participants were between the ages of 18 and 20, 43 percent between the ages of 21 and 23, and the rest were 24 or more years old. Forty-nine percent of the sample was male. Almost 75 percent of the participants were full-time students. Forty-nine percent of the participants had earned 90 or more hours of college credit, 21 percent between 60 and 90 hours of college credit, and the rest had earned less than 60 hours of college credit toward their degrees. Of the participants, 3.6 percent worked less than 10 hours per week, 30.2 percent worked between 11 and 20 hours per week, 28.8 percent worked between 21 and 30 hours per week, 18 percent worked between 31 and 40 hours per week, and 19.4 percent reported working over 40 hours per week.

MEASURES

All measures included in this study were self-report measures that were administered online.

Hogan personality inventory (HPI) The HPI is a measure of normal personality based on the socio-analytic theory of personality and was designed to parallel the Big Five personality factors (Hogan and Hogan, 1995). The HPI consists of seven personality scales: adjustment, ambition, school success, intellectance [sic], prudence, and sociability. For the current study, the HPI was used to measure adjustment, prudence, and sociability. The HPI manual lists the internal consistency reliability values for these three scales as 0.89, 0.78, and 0.71, respectively (Hogan and Hogan, 1995). Adjustment is highly correlated with the Big Five factor emotional stability ($r = 0.70$), prudence is correlated with conscientiousness ($r = 0.36$), and sociability is correlated with agreeableness ($r = 0.56$) (Hogan and Hogan, 1995).

Cheating behavior Academic misconduct was measured using ten items ($\alpha = 0.89$) asking how often respondents engaged in behaviors, such as cheating on a test themselves, or helped others cheat, engaged in unauthorized collaboration on an assignment, plagiarism and others. These questions were identical to those used in US and Canadian surveys of academic misconduct by McCabe and his co-authors (see McCabe, 2005; McCabe and Treviño, 1993, 1997). Responses were made on a five-point Likert-type scale with response options ranging from "never" to "many times." Higher scores indicate greater levels of academic misconduct than lower scores. Items used to measure the constructs of cheating behaviors, report cheating, organizational citizenship behaviors and counterproductive work behaviors are reported in the first column of the Appendix.

Reporting cheating The intent to report cheating was measured with four items ($\alpha = 0.85$). Questions asked how likely respondents were to report cheating by others. Responses were made on a five-point Likert-type scale with response options ranging from "very unlikely" to "very likely." Higher scores indicate a stronger intent to report academic misconduct by others. Intent to report cheating was measured instead of actual frequency of reporting cheating behavior, given that such behavior is relatively uncommon at this and most other universities. Donald McCabe (personal communication, February 1, 2010) stated, on the basis of his surveys of over 90,000 US undergraduates since 2002:

> *Of the 44 percent who have [observed cheating], only 9 percent indicate they have ever reported. Assuming many have observed more than one incident and have likely not reported all of them, the percentage of incidents reported is probably much lower.*

Counterproductive work behaviors Counterproductive work behaviors were measured using items on the Counterproductive Work Behavior Checklist (CWB-C) developed by Spector et al. (2006). On a five-point scale, respondents indicated how often, ranging from "never" to "every day," that they engaged in various counterproductive behaviors. The four types of counterproductive behaviors measured were sabotage ($\alpha = 0.62$), production deviance ($\alpha = 0.60$), withdrawal ($\alpha = 0.70$) and theft ($\alpha = 0.81$).

RESULTS

Confirmatory Factor Analysis (CFA) A survey was used to measure cheating behavior, report cheating, and four forms of counterproductive behaviors. Anderson and Gerbing (1988) recommend specifying and testing the measurement model prior to introducing the structural model. To examine the factor structure, a CFA was conducted using LISREL 8.5 (Jöreskog and Sörbom, 1993). Sample co-variances served as input for all LISREL estimates. The maximum likelihood approach was used as it is regarded as the most appropriate approach for theory testing and development (Anderson and Gerbing, 1988; Jöreskog and Wold, 1982). As recommended by Hu and Bentler (1999), root mean square error of approximation (RMSEA), comparative fit index (CFI) and standardized root mean square residual (SRMR) were used to evaluate model fit.

Factor structures of three different models were compared. The first was a one-factor model (Model 1) comprising all the items used to measure the six constructs. This model did not fit the data [$\chi^2(349, N = 207) = 3495.32$, RMSEA =

0.21, RMSEA 90 percent confidence interval (0.20, 0.21), CFI = 0.44, and SRMR = 0.29]. The second model was a two-factor model (Model 2) with all the items used to measure cheating behavior and report cheating as one factor and items used to measure the four forms of counterproductive work behaviors as the second factor. Fit statistics indicated poor fit for this model [χ^2(348, N = 207) = 1780.84, RMSEA = 0.14, RMSEA 90 percent confidence interval (0.14, 0.15), CFI = 0.80, SRMR = 0.14]. The third (Model 3) was the hypothesized model in which items used to measure each of the six constructs were specified to load on their respective constructs. The hypothesized model was supported; fit statistics indicated acceptable fit for the model [χ^2(334, N = 207) = 936.35, RMSEA = 0.09, RMSEA 90 percent confidence interval (0.087, 0.10), CFI = 0.91, and SRMR = 0.09]. The paths from the latent constructs to individual indicators were all statistically significant ($p < 0.05$), and completely standardized factor loadings ranged in values from 0.31 to 0.94. Means, standard deviations, and correlations between study variables are reported in Table 3.1.

Structural model As previously described, we tested two models, a full mediation model and a partial mediation model. In the full mediation structural model, we had paths from adjustment, prudence and sociability to cheating behavior and report cheating. These two variables, in turn, had direct paths to the counterproductive behaviors of sabotage, production deviance, withdrawal, and theft. This full mediation structural model had the same indicator structure as the measurement model and was fit to the data.

The full mediation model (see Figure 3.1) provided an acceptable fit to the data, χ^2(413, N = 207) = 1008.74, RMSEA = 0.084, RMSEA 90 percent confidence interval (0.077, 0.090), CFI = 0.90, and SRMR = 0.089). A second, less restrictive model was tested that also included direct paths from adjustment, prudence and sociability to the four forms of counterproductive work behaviors. This partial mediation model also fitted the data, χ^2(401, N = 207) = 993.13, RMSEA = 0.085, RMSEA 90 percent confidence interval (0.078, 0.092), CFI = 0.90, and SRMR = 0.088). The chi-square difference test was conducted between the full mediation and the partial mediation model. The obtained chi-square difference of 15.61 for 12 degrees of freedom was smaller than the critical chi-square value of 19.75, indicating that the less restrictive partial mediation model should be rejected and the more restrictive full mediation model should be retained.

In the full mediation model, adjustment ($\beta = -0.46$, $p < 0.01$) and prudence ($\beta = -0.28$, $p < 0.05$), but not sociability ($\beta = 0.44$, ns), were related to cheating behavior and collectively explained 18 percent of the variance in cheating behavior at school. Adjustment ($\beta = 0.12$, ns), prudence ($\beta = -0.08$, ns) and sociability

Table 3.1 Means, standard deviations, and correlations between study variables

	M	SD	1	2	3	4	5	6	7	8	9
1. Adjustment	22.28	6.99	(.89[a])								
2. Prudence	17.86	4.04	.25**	(.78[a])							
3. Sociability	18.42	2.86	.47**	.17*	(.71[a])						
4. Report Cheating	2.30	0.91	.04	.08	.07	(.85)					
5. Cheating Behavior	1.75	0.67	−.19**	−.23**	−.01	−.27**	(.89)				
6. Theft	1.12	0.25	−.16*	−.13	−.02	.10	.38**	(.81)			
7. Production Deviance	1.19	0.33	−.19**	−.13	.00	.04	.33**	.51**	(.60)		
8. Sabotage	1.17	0.31	−.20**	−.16*	−.01	.13	.32**	.69**	.55**	(.62)	
9. Withdrawal	1.53	0.51	−.14*	−.10	.04	.11	.28**	.47**	.46**	.42**	(.70)

Notes: ** $p < .01$, * $p < .05$; scale reliabilities are reported on the diagonal.
[a] Scale reliabilities are based on those reported in the HPI manual (Hogan and Hogan, 1995, p. 17).

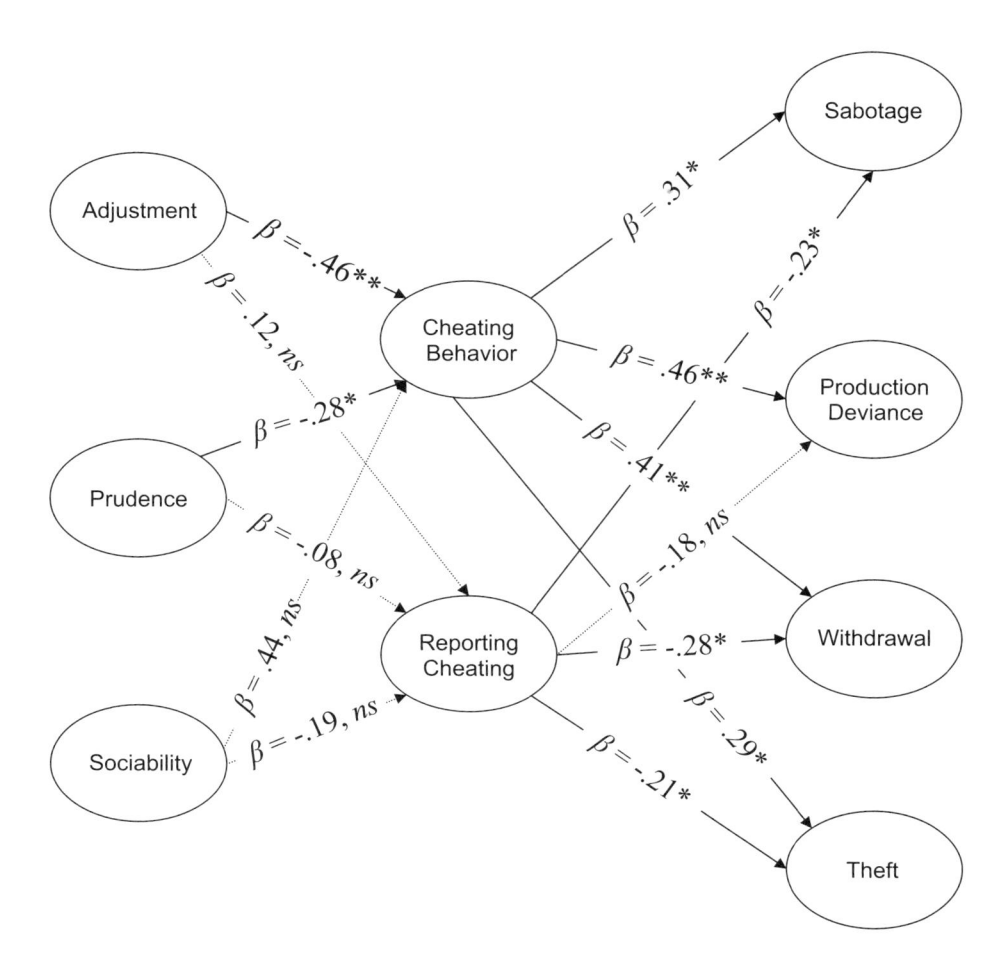

Figure 3.1 Results of structural equation model — full mediation model

Notes: *p <.05, **p <.01. Non-significant relationships are depicted by dotted arrows. Completely standardized factor loadings of indicators on latent variables are reported in the Appendix and are not shown here.

(β = – 0.19, ns) were not significantly related to reporting cheating behaviors by others. Cheating in school was positively related to counterproductive work behaviors of sabotage (β = 0.31, p < 0.05), production deviance (β = 0.46, p< 0.01), withdrawal (β = 0.41, p < 0.01) and theft (β = 0.29, p < 0.05). Reporting cheating by others at school was negatively related to sabotage (β = -0.23, p < 0.05), withdrawal (β = -0.28, p < 0.05), and theft (β = -0.21, p < 0.05) but not to production deviance (β = -0.18, ns). Collectively, the entire full mediation model explained 18 percent of the variance in cheating behavior in school, 2 percent of the variance in report cheating, 11 percent in sabotage, 20 percent in production deviance, 18 percent in withdrawal and 9 percent in theft.

DISCUSSION

Generally, results from both the full and partial mediation models support the efficacy of behavioral samples of cheating behavior and report cheating as useful predictors CWB behaviors. The better fit of the full mediation model means that none of the personality variables accounted for unique variance in CWB, beyond that of cheating and reporting cheating. The lack of direct effects between prudence and any components of CWB are likely due to mediation by cheating. Therefore, these results suggest that samples of dysfunctional cheating behavior mediate the relationship between prudence and all four CWB components. There are no significant direct effects from any personality variables to any CWB components. With respect to CWB, our results suggest that samples of an OCB behavior, reporting cheating, and particularly cheating behavior in school bear out established personality measures.

Limitations and Future Research

The generality of these findings are limited by several factors. First, although no strong causal attributions were made, the cross-sectional nature of the study renders causal attributions speculative. Second, the sample of primarily young, college students, many working less than full-time, may not represent the larger universe of older, non-college, full-time workers. It is possible, however, that the effect sizes observed in this sample underestimate what might be observed in samples of full-time, non-college workers.

Another potential limitation is that parts of Spector et al.'s (2006) CWB-C measures were omitted—specifically, the "abuse" dimension because it assessed deviance directed at individuals rather than at the organization (Berry et al., 2007). In addition, while reporting cheating by other students is a viable operationalization of OCB in an academic context, it is not the only form of OCB that could be considered. Other student behaviors such as joining student associations, especially those that deal with ethical issues and student governance, may be possible mediators of the relationships examined. And, although we argue that reporting cheating is related to whistleblowing, clearly, the stakes for whistleblowers in the work environment are much higher than in school. Finally, while self-ratings of actual cheating yielded a distribution, student reports of cheating are rare, and intention to report was used as a surrogate measure.

Ideally, future research would undertake a longitudinal examination of the relationship between Big Five personality factors, relevant behavior samples, and work behaviors, including task, OCB and CWB. A shortcoming of both this study and many other CWB studies is reliance on CWB behaviors rather than on actual job/task performance. Future research should seek objective measures of these behaviors in addition to behavior intentions. If OCB actually has claimed positive benefits, they should be reflected in some dimensions of objective work outcomes and, similarly, for negative consequences of CWB.

Research and Practical Implications

Clearly, one major implication of this study is that OCB and CWB research may benefit from an examination of samples of OCB and CWB in non-work contexts. For example, while past research shows conscientiousness is the best predictor of CWB, cheating behavior completely mediated personality. Indeed, the concept of "past behavior as a valid predictor of future behavior" is well established in selection (Hunter and Hunter, 1984). The methods of behavior description interviews, reference checks (Gatewood, Field, and Barrick, 2007), biographical inventory blanks (Shaffer, Saunders, and Owens, 1986), and reference checks are all examples of samples of past behavior used to predict work behaviors. Although Kish-Gephart et al. (2010) suggest that tests of conscientiousness and integrity may be useful to avoid hiring "bad apples", they fail to suggest the use of well-established samples of behavior suggested in this study. Future CWB research may benefit from use of behavioral measures or objective indices of behavior, such as school attendance, video rental records, driving records, and awards in sports and social groups. Results of this study suggest that examination of samples of past behavior may contribute to future research of pro-social and unethical behaviors.

Appendix: Scale Content and Completely Standardized Factor Loadings

CHEATING BEHAVIOR

Copied a few sentences from a source but not give credit	0.56
Copied from another student and turned in as own	0.63
Helped someone cheat on a test	0.69
Collaborated on assignment that was supposed to be individual work	0.66
Turned in work done by others	0.55

Copied from another student on test	0.76
Used notes on test without instructor permission	0.73
Received substantial help on assignment without permission	0.58
Cheated on test in any way	0.81
Used unfair methods to learn about a test	0.79

REPORTING CHEATING

I would report an incidence of cheating by a student whom I do not know	0.94
I would report an incidence of cheating by a student whom I consider to be a friend	0.82
It is important to report observations of academic dishonesty by other students	0.67
Reporting instances of cheating is necessary to be fair to honest students	0.60

COUNTERPRODUCTIVE WORK BEHAVIORS—SABOTAGE

Purposely wasted your employer's material/supplies	0.31
Purposely damaged a piece of equipment or property	0.92
Purposely dirtied or littered your place of work	0.44

COUNTERPRODUCTIVE WORK BEHAVIORS—PRODUCTION DEVIANCE

Purposely did your work incorrectly	0.62
Purposely worked slowly when things needed to get done	0.53
Purposely failed to follow instructions	0.59

COUNTERPRODUCTIVE WORK BEHAVIORS—WITHDRAWAL

Came to work late without permission	0.56
Stayed home from work and said you were sick when you weren't	0.68
Taken a longer break than you were allowed to take	0.71
Left work earlier than you were allowed to	0.48

COUNTERPRODUCTIVE WORK BEHAVIORS—THEFT

Stolen something belonging to your employer	0.56
Took supplies or tools home without permission	0.31
Put in to be paid for more hours than you worked	0.49

Took money from your employer without permission 0.96
Stole something belonging to someone at work 0.93

References

Ajzen, I. (1991) "The theory of planned behavior," *Organizational Behavior and Human Decision Processes*, 50, 179–211.

Anderson, J. C. and Gerbing, D. W. (1988) "Structural equation modeling in practice: A review and recommended two-step approach," *Psychological Bulletin*, 103, 411–423.

Barrick, M. R. and Mount, M. K. (1991) "The 'Big Five' personality dimensions and job performance: A meta-analysis," *Personnel Psychology*, 44, 1–26.

Bennett, R. J. and Stamper, C. L. (2001) "Corporate citizenship and deviancy: A study of work behavior" in C. Galbraith and M. Ryan (eds) *International Research in the Business Disciplines: Strategies and Organizations in Transition*, Amsterdam: Elsevier Science, pp. 265–284.

Berry, C. M., Ones, D. S., and Sackett, P. R. (2007) "Interpersonal deviance, organizational deviance, and their common correlates: A review and meta-analysis," *Journal of Applied Psychology*, 92, 410–424.

Borman, W. C. and Motowidlo, S. J. (1997) "Task performance and contextual performance: The meaning for personnel selection research," *Human Performance*, 10, 99–109.

Borman, W. C., Penner, L. A., Allen, T. D., and Motowidlo, S. J. (2001) "Personality predictors of citizenship performance," *International Journal of Selection and Assessment*, 9, 52–69.

Brimble, M. and Stevenson-Clarke, P. (2005) "Perceptions of the prevalence and seriousness of academic dishonesty in Australian universities," *Australian Educational Researcher*, 32, 19–44.

Christensen-Hughes, J. M. and McCabe, D. L. (2006) "Academic misconduct within higher education in Canada," *The Canadian Journal of Higher Education*, 36, 1–21.

Clinard, M. B. and Yeager, P. C. (2006) *Corporate Crime*, Transaction, New Brunswick, NJ.

Cohen-Charash, Y. and Spector, P. E. (2001) "The role of justice in organizations: A meta-analysis," *Organizational Behavior and Human Decision Processes*, 86, 278–321.

Colquitt, J. A., Conlon, D. E., Wesson, M. J., Porter, C. O., and Ng, K. Y. (2001) "Justice at the millennium: A meta-analytic review of 25 years of organizational justice research," *Journal of Applied Psychology*, 86, 425–445.

Cullen M. J. and Sackett, P. R. (2003) "Personality and counterproductive behavior workplace behavior" in M. Barrick, M. and A. M. Ryan (eds) *Personality and Work*, New York: Jossey-Bass-Pfeiffer.

Dalal, R. S. (2005) "A meta-analysis of the relationship between organizational citizenship behavior and counterproductive work behavior," *Journal of Applied Psychology*, 90, 1241–1255.

Davis, S. F., Grover, C. A., Becker, A. H., and McGregor, L. N. (1992) "Academic dishonesty: Prevalence, determinants, techniques, and punishments," *Teaching of Psychology*, 19, 16–20.

Forsyth, D. R., Pope, W. R., and McMillan, J. H. (1985) "Students' reactions after cheating: An attributional analysis," *Contemporary Educational Psychology*, 10, 72–82.

Gatewood, R. D., Field, H. S., and Barrick, M. R. (2007) *Human Resource Selection*, Dallas, TX: Southwestern.

Genereux, R. L. and McLeod, B. A. (1995) "Circumstances surrounding cheating: A questionnaire study of college students," *Research in Higher Education*, 36, 687–704.

Gottfredson, M. R. and Hirschi, T. (1990) *A General Theory of Crime*, Stanford, CA: Stanford University Press.

Grimes, P. (2004) "Dishonesty in academics and business: A cross-cultural evaluation of student attitudes," *Journal of Business Ethics*, 49, 273–290.

Gruys, M. L. and Sackett, P. R. (2003) "The dimensionality of counterproductive work behavior," *International Journal of Selection and Assessment*, 11, 30–42.

Harding, T. S., Carpenter, D.D., Finelli, J. C., and Passow, H. J. (2004) "Does academic dishonesty relate to unethical behavior in professional practice? An exploratory study," *Science and Engineering Ethics*, 10, 311–324.

Hirschi, T. and Gottfredson, M. R. (1994) "The generality of deviance" in T. Hirschi and M. R. Gottfredson (eds) *The Generality of Deviance*, New Brunswick, NJ: Transaction Publishers, pp. 1–22.

Hogan, J. and Hogan, R. (1989) "How to measure employee reliability," *Journal of Applied Psychology*, 74, 273–279.

Hogan, R. and Hogan, J. (1995) *Hogan Personality Inventory Manual* (2nd ed.), Tulsa, OK: Hogan Assessment Systems.

Houston, J. P. (1983) "College classroom cheating, threat, sex, and prior performance," *College Student Journal*, 17, 196–204.

Hu, L. and Bentler, P. M. (1999) "Cutoff criteria for fit indexes in covariance structure analysis: Conventional criteria versus new alternatives," *Structural Equation Modeling*, 6, 1–55.

Hunter, J. E. and Hunter, R. F. (1984) "Validity and utility of alternative predictors of job performance," *Psychological Bulletin*, 96, 72–98.

Jones, T. M. (1991) "Ethical decision making by individuals in organizations: An issue-contingent model," *Academy of Management Review*, 16, 366–395.

Jöreskog, K. G. and Sörbom, D. (1993) *LISREL 8: Structural Equation Modeling with the SIMPLIS Command Language*, Hillsdale, NJ: Scientific Software International.

Jöreskog, K. G. and Wold, H. (1982) "The ML and PLS techniques for modeling with latent variables: Historical and comparative aspects" in K. G. Jöreskog and H. Wold (eds) Systems under Indirect Observation: Causality, Structure, and Prediction Amsterdam: North-Holland, Part I, pp. 263–270.

Josephson Institute of Ethics (2010) "The ethics of American youth—2008 summary," at: http://charactercounts.org/programs/reportcard/index.html (accessed February 2010).

Karabenick, S. A. and Srull, T. K. (1978) "Effects of personality and situational variations in locus of control on cheating: Determinants of the congruence effect," *Journal of Personality*, 46, 72–95.

Kelloway, E. K., Loughlin, C., Barling, J. and Nault, A. (2002) "Self-reported counterproductive behaviors and organizational citizenship behaviors: Separate but related constructs," *International Journal of Selection and Assessment*, 10, 143–151.

Kish-Gephart, J. J., Harrison, D. A., and Treviño, L. K. (2010) "Bad apples, bad cases, and bad barrels: Meta-analytic evidence about sources of unethical decisions at work," *Journal of Applied Psychology*, 95, 1–31.

Kohlberg, L. (1969) "Stage and sequence: The cognitive-developmental approach to socialization" in D. A. Goslin (ed.) *Handbook of Socialization Theory and Research*, Chicago, IL: Rand McNally.

Koljatic, M., Silva, M., and Ardiles, J. (2003) "Are student perceptions of parent acceptance of academic dishonesty associated with its occurrence?" *Psychological Reports*, 93, 93–97.

LePine, J. A., Erez, A., and Johnson, D. E. (2002) "The nature and dimensionality of organizational citizenship behavior: A critical review and meta-analysis," *Journal of Applied Psychology*, 87, 52–65.

Magnus, J. R., Polterovich, V. M., Danilov, D. L., and Savvateev, A.V. (2002) "Tolerance of cheating: An analysis across countries," *Journal of Economic Education*, 33, 125–135.

Marcus, B. and Schuler, H. (2004) "Antecedents of counterproductive behavior at work: A general perspective," *Journal of Applied Psychology*, 89, 647–660.

McCabe, D. L. (2005) "Promoting academic integrity in business schools, Professional development workshop," paper presented at the Annual Meeting of the Academy of Management, Honolulu, HI.

McCabe, D. L. and Treviño, L. K. (1993) "Academic dishonesty: Honor codes and other contextual influences," *Journal of Higher Education*, 64, 522–538.

McCabe, D. L. and Treviño, L. K. (1997) "Individual and contextual influences on academic dishonesty: A multi-campus investigation," *Research in Higher Education*, 38, 379–396.

McCabe, D. L., Treviño, L. K., and Butterfield, K. D. (1996) "The influence of collegiate and corporate codes of conduct on ethics-related behavior in the workplace," *Business Ethics Quarterly*, 6, 461–476.

McCabe, D. L., Butterfield, K. D., and Treviño, L. K. (2006) "Academic dishonesty in graduate business programs: Prevalence, causes and proposed action," *Academy of Management Learning and Education*, 5, 294–306.

Meyer, J. P., Stanley, D. J., Herscovitch, L., and Topolnytsky, L. (2002) "Affective, continuance, and normative commitment to the organization: A meta-analysis of antecedents, correlates, and consequences," *Journal of Vocational Behavior*, 61, 20–52.

Miles, D. E., Borman, W. E., Spector, P. E., and Fox, S. (2002) "Building an integrative model of extra role work behaviors: A comparison of counterproductive work behavior with organizational citizenship behavior," *International Journal of Selection and Assessment*, 10, 51–57.

Mount, M., Ilies, R., and Johnson, E. (2006) "Relationship of personality traits and counterproductive work behaviors: The mediating effects of job satisfaction," *Personnel Psychology*, 59, 591–622.

Miceli, M. P. and Near, J. P. (1988) "Individual and situational correlates of whistle-blowing," *Personnel Psychology*, 41, 267–281.

Newstead, S. E., Franklin-Stokes, A., and Armstead, P. (1996) "Individual differences in student cheating," *Journal of Educational Psychology*, 88, 229–41.

Nonis, S. and Swift, C. O. (2001) "An examination of the relationship between academic dishonesty and workplace dishonesty: A multi-campus investigation," *Journal of Education for Business*, 77, 69–77.

Ones, D. S., Viswesvaran, C., and Schmidt, F. L. (1993) "Comprehensive meta-analysis of integrity test validities: Findings and implications for personnel selection and theories of job performance," *Journal of Applied Psychology*, 78, 679–703.

Ones, D. S., Viswesvaran, C., and Schmidt, F. L. (2003) "Personality and absenteeism: A meta-analysis of integrity tests," *European Journal of Personality*, 17, S19–S38.

Organ, D. W. (1988) *Organizational Citizenship Behavior: The Good Soldier Syndrome*, Lexington, MA: Lexington Books.

Organ, D. W. (1997) "Organizational citizenship behavior: It's construct clean-up time," *Human Performance*, 10, 85–97.

Organ, D. W. and Ryan, K. (1995) "A meta-analytic review of attitudinal and dispositional predictors of organizational citizenship behavior," *Personnel Psychology*, 48, 775–802.

Rest, J. (1986) *Development in Judging Moral Issues*, Minneapolis, MN: University of Minnesota Press.

Reynolds, S. J. (2006) "A neurocognitive model of the ethical decisionmaking process: Implications for study and practice," *Journal of Applied Psychology*, 91, 737–748.

Riketta, M. (2002) "Attitudinal organizational commitment and job performance: A meta-analysis," Journal of Organizational Behavior, 23, 257–266.

Robinson, S. L. and Bennett, R. J. (1995) "A typology of deviant workplace behaviors: A multidimensional scaling study," *Academy of Management Journal*, 38, 555–572.

Robinson S. L. and Greenberg, J. (1998) "Employees behaving badly: Dimensions, determinants and dilemmas in the study of workplace deviance" in D. M. Rousseau and C. Cooper (eds) Trends in Organizational Behavior, Vol. 5, New York: Wiley, pp. 1–23.

Rotter, J. (1966) "Generalized expectancies for internal versus external control of reinforcement," *Psychological Monographs*, 80, 1–28.

Rotundo, M. and Sackett, P. R. (2002) "The relative importance of task, citizenship, and counterproductive performance to global ratings of job performance: A policy capturing approach," *Journal of Applied Psychology*, 87, 66–80.

Sackett, P. R. (2002) "The structure of counterproductive work behaviors: Dimensionality and relationships with facets of job performance," *International Journal of Selection and Assessment*, 10, 5–11.

Sackett, P. R. and DeVore, C. J. (2001) "Counterproductive behaviors at work" in N. Anderson, D. Ones, H. Sinangil, and C. Viswesvaran (eds) *Handbook of Industrial, Work, and Organizational Psychology*, Vol. 1, London: Sage, pp. 145–164.

Sackett, P. R., Berry, C. M., Wiemann, S., and Laczo, R. M. (2006) "Citizenship and counterproductive work behavior: Clarifying relationship between the two domains," *Human Performance*, 19, 441–464.

Salgado, J. F. (2002) "The big five personality dimensions and counterproductive behaviors," *International Journal of Selection and Assessment*, 10, 117–125.

Shaffer, G. S., Saunders, V., and Owens, W. A. (1986) "Additional evidence for the accuracy of biographical data: Long-term retest and observer ratings," *Personnel Psychology*, 39, 791–809.

Sims, R. L. (1993) "The relationship between academic dishonesty and unethical business practices," *Journal of Education for Business*, 68, 207–212.

Spector, P. E. and Fox, S. (2002) "An emotion-centered model of voluntary work behavior: Some parallels between counterproductive work behavior and organizational citizenship behavior," *Human Resource Management Review*, 12, 269–292.

Spector, P. E., Fox, S., Penney, L. M., Bruursema, K., Goh, A., and Kessler, S. (2006) "The dimensionality of counterproductivity: Are all counterproductive behaviors created equal?" *Journal of Vocational Behavior*, 68, 446–460.

Stone, T. H., Jawahar, I. M. and Kisamore, J. L. (2010) "Predicting academic misconduct intentions and behavior using the Theory of Planned Behavior and personality," *Basic and Applied Psychology*, 32, 35–45.

Stone, T. H., Kisamore, J. L., and Jawahar, I. M. (2008) "Predicting students' perceptions of academic misconduct on the Hogan Personality Inventory Reliability Scale," *Psychological Reports*, 102, 495–508.

Treviño, L. K. (1986) "Ethical decision making in organizations: A person-situation interactionist model," *Academy of Management Review*, 11, 601–617.

Treviño, L. K. and Youngblood, S. A. (1990) "Bad apples in bad barrels: A causal analysis of ethical decision-making behavior," *Journal of Applied Psychology*, 75, 378–385.

Treviño, L. K., Weaver, G. R., and Reynolds, S. J. (2006) "Behavioral ethics in organizations: A review," *Journal of Management*, 32, 951–990.

Van Dyne, L. and LePine, J. A. (1998) "Helping and voice extra-role behavior: Evidence of construct and predictive validity," *Academy of Management Journal*, 41, 108–119.

Viswesvaran, C. and Ones, D. S. (2000) "Perspectives on models of job performance," *International Journal of Selection and Assessment*, 8, 216–226.

Whitley, B. E. Jr (1998) "Factors associated with cheating among college students," *Research in Higher Education*, 39, 235–274.

Williams, J. (2001) "Analysis: Cheating in America's high schools and colleges," *Talk of the Nation*, National Public Radio, May 21, at: http://www.encyclopedia.com/doc/1P1-44539946.html (accessed June 2009).

4

The Role of Trust in Employee Theft[1]

Edward C. Tomlinson

The Role of Trust in Employee Theft

At the time of writing, the global economy is undergoing a painful and seemingly intractable recession. While the causes of economic downturns are often complex and multifaceted, it is beyond general dispute that one key contributing factor has been unsound business practices fueled by greed (see Chapter 5, this volume). In the US, when the federal government responded with unprecedented "stimulus" funding to bail out particularly troubled companies, and then entire industries, populist angst exploded into anger upon the discovery that even these funds were used improperly (to fund executive junkets, to pay enormous executive bonuses, etc.). Moreover, in the midst of this crisis, with many losing (or fearful of losing) their livelihoods, employee theft appears to be rising. This "unauthorized appropriation of company property by employees either for one's own use or for sale to another" (Greenberg, 1995, p. 154) has taken a staggering toll on enterprise even in good economic times—for example, recent estimates place the annual loss in the US at US$994 billion (AFCE, 2008). Now that human resource and security professionals are indicating the growing threat of employees stealing sensitive company data in response to the recession (Friedman, 2009; Koster, 2009; Needleman, 2008; Roberts, 2009) there may be even more of a threat to the survival of many organizations and, ultimately, to economic recovery.

Against this backdrop, the role of trust in relation to employee theft is increasingly salient: if employees do not trust the executives who manage their organizations to behave responsibly with company assets, they may be less likely

---

[1] I thank Roger Mayer for his helpful comments during the preparation of this chapter. Any errors are my own.

to resist such temptations themselves. Similarly, the degree to which employers monitor their employees may be construed as the extent to which those employees are trusted (e.g., Dunn and Schweitzer, 2005), with implications for employee theft. Of course, both researchers (Cressey, 1953; Litsky, Eddleston, and Kidder, 2006; Niehoff and Paul, 2000) and practitioners (e.g., Abcede, 1994; Balmer, 2009; Banks, 2007; Davies, 2003; Sennewald, 1986) have invoked the concept of trust throughout the years in discussing employee theft. The unusually troubling economic hardships we are enduring at the moment only serve to accentuate the notion that theft from employees may be related to the level of trust in the employment relationship. Unfortunately, despite the vast literature on trust in organizations, until now there has been no systematic theoretical treatment of trust in relation to employee theft. Accordingly, this chapter endeavors to fill this gap by drawing from extant trust theory to posit connections between trust and theft. To accomplish this goal, the following sections will (1) review a prominent model of organizational trust, (2) situate the role of trust within existing approaches to studying employee theft, (3) invoke this trust model to posit how trust among employees and employers relates to employee theft, and (4) derive practical applications resulting from this analysis.

Understanding Trust in Organizations

Trust refers to "a psychological state comprising the intention to accept vulnerability based upon positive expectations of the intentions or behavior of another" (Rousseau et al., 1998, p. 395). As an area of academic inquiry for over 50 years (Deutsch, 1958), the concept of trust has generated an enduring interest, given its pivotal relation to organizational effectiveness. Trust has been associated with beneficial outcomes ranging from individual-level attitudes (such as job satisfaction and organizational commitment) and behaviors (such as job performance and organizational citizenship) to organizational-level operational metrics (such as revenue and profit) (for a review, see Lewicki, Tomlinson, and Gillespie, 2006). Due to the impracticalities of relying on legalistic, control-based mechanisms to formalize all aspects of professional interaction (Arrow, 1973; Parkhe, 1998), trust offers an alternative mechanism to enable and facilitate interdependence.

This chapter will rely on Mayer's, Davis's and Schoorman's (1995) integrative model of organizational trust to explicate how trust and employee theft might be related. The integrative model clarifies how trust differs from its antecedents and consequences, and allows for more sophisticated insights based on this precision. According to this theory, trust in another is a result of, first, the trustor's own *propensity to trust* and, second, the trustee's *trustworthiness*. Propensity to trust refers to a relatively stable trait describing the degree to which other people in general are deemed trustworthy (Rotter, 1967). Among other factors, salient life experiences can provide the basis for such expectations, and this predisposition is more heavily relied on in situations where the trustworthiness of a specific trustee is not yet known. With respect to the characteristics of a specific trustee, trustworthiness is reflected in one's level of *ability* (competence within a specific domain), *benevolence* (goodwill toward the trustor), and *integrity* (adherence to values accepted by the trustor). Integrity may be evident in several forms, including the trustee's "sense of justice" (Mayer, Davis, and Schoorman, 1995, p. 719); while justice has been extensively studied in relation to employee theft (Greenberg, 1990, 1993, 2002; Greenberg and Scott, 1996; Greenberg and Tomlinson, 2004; Tomlinson and Greenberg, 2005, 2007), other aspects of this model have not been previously investigated in this context. At any rate, both the trustor's propensity to trust and his or her perception of the trustee's trustworthiness lead to the degree of trust (i.e., willingness to accept vulnerability) given to the trustee.

Mayer and his colleagues (1995) stress that trust, as the willingness to accept vulnerability, is separate from the behavioral manifestation of actually taking a risk (referred to as "risk taking in the relationship" in their model). Relevant to the current context of employee theft, monitoring and surveillance would indicate a lack of risk-taking in the relationship. The effect of trust on risk-taking in relationships is also moderated by the perceived degree of risk in a given situation, where risk refers to the "likelihoods of gains or losses outside of considerations that involve the relationship with the particular trustee" (Mayer, Davis, and Schoorman, 1995, p. 726). These distinctions lead to two important observations: first, trust itself does not involve taking any risk, only an attitudinal willingness to do so; and, second, one can trust another very highly yet still not engage in risk-taking due to a high degree of perceived risk.

Finally, depending on the outcome (i.e., positive or negative) of this risk-taking, trustworthiness perceptions are updated for the next interaction with the trustee; this process is likely to be strongly influenced by attributional processes (Tomlinson and Mayer, 2009). Drawing from this model of trust, we may now proceed to consider how trust relates to existing perspectives on the causes of employee theft.

Perspectives on Employee Theft

Given the pervasive and insidious nature of employee theft, investigators from a diverse array of disciplinary backgrounds have emerged to examine this phenomenon. The resulting perspectives on the nature and causes of employee theft can be generally categorized into the security orientation, the individual differences orientation, and the social orientation (Greenberg, 1997a; Gross-Schaefer et al., 2000; Kidder, 2005; Niehoff and Paul, 2000; Tomlinson, 2009a; Tomlinson and Greenberg, 2005, 2007).

The *security orientation* views employee theft primarily as a matter of individuals acting opportunistically when they believe they can do so without detection (Greenberg, 1997a; Tomlinson and Greenberg, 2005, 2007). Espoused primarily by loss prevention experts, this perspective emphasizes the reduction of employee theft through processes and technologies that enhance detection capability, such as sophisticated auditing systems, surveillance cameras, and security clearance policies and procedures (Sennewald, 1996). This approach embodies a twofold strategy to reducing employee theft: the enhanced security may deter many employees from even attempting theft, and even if some employees do choose to steal, they are much more likely to be identified and held accountable.

The *individual differences orientation* contends that only certain individuals (i.e., those with a propensity toward dishonesty and/or who experience pressures that may exacerbate the temptation to steal) will engage in theft from their employers (Greenberg, 1997a; Tomlinson and Greenberg, 2005, 2007). Consequently, criminologists and industrial-organizational psychologists strive to develop profiles of those likely to engage in theft in order to prevent them from ever becoming employees in the first place. This perspective explains the frequent use of pre-employment honesty or integrity tests (Sackett, 1994) and background checks (Buss, 1993).

Whereas the previous perspectives have represented more traditional approaches to employee theft, a more recently developed view known as the *social orientation* has emerged (Greenberg, 1997a, 1997b; Tomlinson and Greenberg, 2005, 2007). This perspective is based on research indicating that stealing at work is often embedded in, or enabled by, social dynamics. That is, employee theft can be attributed to "a variety of social motives" (Greenberg, 1997b, p. 88). Drawing upon social exchange theory (Blau, 1964) as a framework for understanding the dynamics that result in the give-and-take of social resources from one party to another, researchers have previously elaborated on two specific factors that motivate employee theft: perceptions of unfair treatment and social norms (Greenberg, 1997a, 1997b; Greenberg and Scott, 1996; Tomlinson and Greenberg, 2005, 2007).

The concept of trust has surfaced in descriptive accounts (Greenberg and Tomlinson, 2004) of employee theft behavior (e.g., Cressey, 1953), and has also been invoked in prescriptive advice for managers from researchers (Litsky,

Eddleston, and Kidder, 2006) and in practitioner outlets (e.g., Abcede, 1994; Banks, 2007). The level of trust between employees and employers is relevant to each of these orientations. Specifically, (1) in relation to the *security orientation*, higher trust may entail less monitoring and control, and thus enable theft to occur (e.g., Cressey, 1953); (2) in relation to the *individual differences orientation*, screening applicants for trustworthiness can reduce theft by restricting access to the organization's assets to those who are least inclined to behave dishonestly (e.g., Sackett, 1994; Sackett and Wanek, 1996); and (3) in relation to the *social orientation*, trust is a social resource exchanged between employees and employers (Blau, 1964), and the trust one party has toward another has implications for employee theft (e.g., Litsky, Eddleston, and Kidder, 2006).

Nonetheless, despite their intuitive appeal, the connections between trust and employee theft have remained glib assertions rather than rigorously developed and demonstrated relationships (with the exception of integrity testing). Drawing on the vast literature on trust and its development (for reviews, see Kramer, 1999; Lewicki, Tomlinson, and Gillespie, 2006) can provide much needed insight for positing how trust and employee theft may be related, and lay the necessary foundation for empirical testing. This is the subject of the next section.

The Relationship Between Trust and Employee Theft

Given the bilateral nature of trust, it is important to acknowledge that both employers and employees are confronted with decisions regarding how much (if at all) to trust the other. Having reviewed the Mayer et al. (1995) model, I will now apply it to each party's perspective in turn.

THE EMPLOYER'S TRUST IN ITS EMPLOYEES

In the context of employee theft, employers regard employees to be trustworthy insofar as they are perceived to have the capacity to refrain from stealing (ability), that they desire to protect and safeguard the organization's welfare (benevolence), and that they behave honestly in carrying out their job responsibilities (integrity). Note that, in most cases, an employee's ability to refrain from theft is not brought into question, although an exception might arise due to some type of psychopathic disorder (see Greenberg, 1997a; Tomlinson and Greenberg, 2005). After all, even a hardened criminal is likely to obey the law under some conditions (Tomlinson, 2009b). At any rate, these perceptions of trustworthiness affect the degree of trust employers will place in their employees.

Notwithstanding this process, advocates of the social and security orientations have given managers conflicting prescriptive advice regarding the degree of trust to place in their employees. On the one hand, managers are urged to trust their employees because if workers receive signals of distrust, they will be more motivated to steal (Litsky, Eddleston, and Kidder, 2006; Murphy, 1993). This suggests that trust and theft are negatively related. On the other hand, managers are cautioned against granting too much trust, out of fear that it will enable employee-thieves the opportunity to inflict catastrophic damage through their nefarious activities (e.g., Abcede, 1994). This suggests that trust and theft are positively related. A closer look at each perspective is warranted.

Trust and theft are negatively related Some writers have explicitly advocated that employers "treat employees with ... trust" (Taylor, 1986, p. 24) out of the notion that it is harder to steal from someone who has worked to establish a personal and caring relationship. As discussed in the previous section, when employers trust their employees this primarily presupposes that those employees will be benevolent and act with integrity (i.e., honesty). Furthermore, conveying trust as a social resource invites its reciprocation (Serva, Fuller, and Mayer, 2005; Zand, 1972). Das and Teng (1998) assert, "When a trustee realizes that a trustor has taken considerable risk in trusting her, she tends to be motivated to behave in a trustworthy manner" (p. 503). Ultimately, the prediction is that, all else equal, higher trust is associated with lower theft—in other words, trust is honored.

In fact, some researchers (e.g., Dunn and Schweitzer, 2005; Kruglanski, 1970) have suggested that screening, monitoring, and enforcement of employees' behavior is taken as a signal by these employees that they are not trusted and that this is the true root cause of employee theft (Gross-Schaefer et al., 2000). This lack of trust leads employees to be dissatisfied (Murphy, 1993) and offended, and prompt theft, or another form of deviance, out of retaliation (Kruglanski, 1970; Litsky, Eddleston, and Kidder, 2006). Essentially, distrust from management arguably has the potential to create a self-fulfilling prophecy where employees do, in fact, resort to theft (Litsky, Eddleston, and Kidder, 2006). If this occurs, it may confirm the employer's suspicions of untrustworthiness, with the lowered degree of trust leading to even more monitoring or surveillance—in other words, less risk-taking in the relationship (Strickland, 1958). Furthermore, research has suggested that when trustors fail to take substantial risk, trustees are much less likely to perceive that trust has been granted and sense the obligation to reciprocate by behaving in a trustworthy manner (Malhotra, 2004).

Trust and theft are positively related   Under this view, when employers trust their employees (presumably due to perceptions of benevolence and integrity), they are by definition, willing to become vulnerable. This leads to risk-taking in the relationship, where they forego monitoring and control in the belief that it is unnecessary. Ironically, it is this very trust (when placed in an untrustworthy individual) that has the potential to enable the very theft it is intended to avoid (Christopher, 2003; Cressey, 1953). In fact, one of the oldest recorded instances of theft involved scribes and priests pilfering fabric, grain, and other valuables from ancient Egyptian temples (Peet, 1924). Such concerns linger today, as some contend that religious and non-profit organizations are highly vulnerable to employee theft due to the high degree of trust placed in their workers (who are often unpaid volunteers) and low controls (Balmer, 2009). Indeed, practitioners across a wide range of industries have been appalled to discover that it was often their most trusted employees who were committing heinous acts of theft (Koster, 2009; Needleman, 2008; Roberts, 2009). Trust can blind employers to the possibility that their employees would steal, and heighten the sense of betrayal they experience if and when this is unequivocally confirmed (Abcede, 1994). Unfortunately, some employees are literally 'con artists' who employ elaborate schemes to steal, such as faking robberies (Abcede, 1994) or creating phantom vendors (Balmer, 2009). Obviously, such incidents can damage whatever trust an employer had in its employees (Christopher, 2003). Furthermore, discovery of employee theft might negatively affect the employer's propensity to trust and/or perceptions of aggregate employee trustworthiness (even if not all employees are involved in theft).

Recent surveys of data theft in organizations reveal alarming statistics that speak to employee trustworthiness. One survey found that 59 percent of respondents admitted they would preemptively steal corporate data if they sensed that job loss was imminent (Cyber-Ark, 2008). Another recent survey of 945 US workers who left their jobs in 2008 found that:

- 59 percent of respondents admitted taking confidential data with them when they left their jobs
- 70 percent admitted that company policy prohibited them from doing so
- Only 15 percent indicated that their company performed a data audit before their departure

- 89 percent indicated that their data storage devices were not scanned before leaving
- 24 percent indicated that they still had network access after they left (Ponemon Institute, 2009).

While it is unclear exactly how much their employers trusted these employees, many of them certainly do not appear to be trustworthy in terms of their integrity. It also appears that whatever trust was conveyed to these employees entailed the lack of controls to prevent data theft (50 percent of respondents justified their theft by saying the company did nothing to prevent it).

In summary, managers have received conflicting prescriptive advice, leaving them with a "darned if you do, darned if you don't" dilemma. To the extent that such a decision can be made strategically to begin with, rigorous empirical research is needed to clarify which of these positions is correct and/or what boundary conditions should govern these choices.

Fortunately, in the meantime, we are left with some potentially valuable clues from extant research that may suggest possible reconciliation of these divergent views. One of the earliest research studies on employee theft was a descriptive effort by Cressey (1953) to explain the distinction between those who embezzle and those who do not. These findings are consistent with the view that increasing one's risk-taking in a relationship due to trust can indeed result in trust being exploited. Furthermore, his interviews with convicted embezzlers suggested that the relationship between trust and theft is more complex:

Trusted persons become trust violators when they conceive of themselves as having a financial problem which is non-sharable, are aware that this problem can be secretly resolved by violation of the position of financial trust, and are able to apply to their own conduct in that situation verbalizations which enable them to adjust their conceptualizations of themselves as trusted persons with their conceptions of themselves as users of the entrusted funds or property. (Cressy, 1953, p. 30)

In other words, the relationship between trust and employee theft appears to be moderated by other factors such that trust in employees is not inappropriate per se, yet under specific conditions (e.g., certain pressures and temptations), higher trust in employees can lead to increases in theft because of the opportunity it gives them to steal without detection. To the extent that employees succumb to this combination of temptation and opportunity, their benevolence and/or integrity decline. The result is that, despite the trust bestowed upon them, they have become less trustworthy. Another troubling finding is that the embezzlers in this study relied extensively on complex rationalizations that enabled them to preserve their self-image as trustworthy individuals whose behavior was well justified (see also Greenberg, 1993). Indeed, these individuals expressed dismay at the notion that they were crooks and viewed themselves as wrongfully imprisoned. Ostensibly, the extent to which individuals take offense at the lack of others' trust in them (Gross-Schaefer et al., 2000; Litsky, Eddleston, and Kidder, 2006) cannot be taken as a reliable indicator that they are indeed trustworthy and would not act in dishonest ways. Furthermore, given the complex rationalizations that employee-thieves use to maintain a positive self-concept (Anand, Ashforth, and Joshi, 2004; Greenberg and Scott, 1996; Sykes and Matza, 1957), these individuals inoculate themselves from perceiving the damage to their trustworthiness that would be so evident to managers or outside observers.

It is also interesting to note that, in both cases, the employee with high integrity and benevolence would be expected to refrain from stealing (i.e., behave in a trustworthy manner). In other words, a truly trustworthy person will not steal regardless of how much the employer trusts him or her. Indeed, not everyone who has an opportunity to steal will engage in this behavior (Greenberg, 1997a; Murphy, 1993). In fact, it is this logic that led to the development and use of honesty or integrity tests for pre-employment screening (Murphy, 1993; Sackett, 1994; Tomlinson and Greenberg, 2005, 2007), and this tool can be valuable in helping employers understand which applicants are trustworthy. Taken together, the security orientation (which prescribes lower trust) and the social orientation (which prescribes higher trust) are in direct conflict with each other; a possible reconciliation of these views involves the individual differences orientation (which allows for more trust once some acceptable level of trustworthiness has been established). This issue clearly warrants empirical research.

Finally, most of the advice given to managers on trust neglects the role of risk. Mayer, Davis and Schoorman (1995) stress how important it is to jointly consider both trust and risk in risk-taking in a relationship. Some situational risks are so high that they outweigh one's trust in a highly trustworthy employee, making it unwise to engage in risk-taking. For example, I may have a very highly trusted employee (who is in fact extremely trustworthy) to whom I have granted exclusive access to sensitive company data. This does not protect me from that employee's (less trustworthy) co-workers finding a way to steal that information without the trusted employee's detection. Nor would I be protected if there is a flaw in the information system, beyond that employee's control, that fails to properly secure the data. According to the Mayer, Davis and Schoorman model, safeguards enacted to mitigate this risk need not be based on, or even signal a lack of trust in, a particular employee. Yet when situational risks are high—e.g., a company database contains personal information for thousands of employees that could be used to facilitate identity theft—it seems fully prudent to not rely on trust (e.g., in a single database administrator) alone in making a risk-taking decision.

THE EMPLOYEE'S TRUST IN THE EMPLOYER

Employees regard employers to be trustworthy insofar as they are perceived to competently manage all aspects of the organization's performance, which might include the adequate safeguarding of organizational assets and resources (ability), demonstrating care and consideration of employee needs (benevolence), and enacting the values they espouse (integrity). Collectively, these trustworthiness perceptions influence the employee's ultimate trust for his or her employer, which in turn predicts a variety of outcomes. Some researchers have also proposed that employee trust is related to their theft behaviors (Murphy, 1993; Niehoff and Paul, 2000).

When employees have high trust in their employers, they may be more likely to value the relationship and desire to be trusted in return—which prompts greater trustworthiness on their part (Davies, 2003; Serva et al., 2005; Zand, 1972). Referring back to the 2009 Ponemon Institute survey on data theft, perhaps the only encouraging statistic was the finding that the most important factor in whether ex-employees will steal is whether they view the organization as having integrity or not. Only 13 percent of respondents reported stealing when they had a favorable view of their prior employer's integrity (Ponemon Institute, 2009).

When employees' trust in their employers is damaged, they may become more willing to steal. Specifically, perceiving a trust violation by the employer may incite a desire to retaliate by engaging in deviant behavior (Litsky, Eddleston, and Kidder, 2006). This lowered degree of trust might be due to damaged perceptions of ability (e.g., employees do not believe that management can sustain the organization's viability), which might influence them to steal to realize gains that would help them "land on their feet" should they become laid off (Ponemon Institute, 2009). Perceptions of low benevolence from the employer (e.g., abuse of power that exploits employees) may motivate retaliation in the form of theft (Greenberg and Scott, 1996). Perceptions of low integrity may signal that unethical norms are accepted in the organization. Some security professionals have asserted a link between recent business scandals and increased employee temptation to steal (IOMA, 2002). A recent survey by Watson Wyatt found that only 49 percent of employees trust their senior management, and only 55 percent believe that their top managers behave consistently with company values (Watson Wyatt, 2007).

Aside from an employees' perceptions of their specific employer's trustworthiness, there are also signs suggesting that the prevalence of major business scandals has eroded their overall sense of trust in organizations in general. A survey of individuals across 20 countries found that 62 percent of respondents say they have less trust in corporations now than they did just a year ago (Edelman, 2009). An article in *Business Week* entitled, "Can you trust anybody anymore?" expressed the following commentary in the wake of the Enron collapse:

> *There are business scandals that are so vast and so penetrating that they profoundly shock our most deeply held beliefs about the honesty and integrity of our corporate culture ... This financial disaster goes far beyond the failure of one big company. This is corruption on a massive scale.* (Nussbaum, 2002, p. 30)

Taken together, this suggests that many individuals' propensity to trust has been negatively affected.

It is also possible that an employee's level of trust in the employer affects the risks they take in the relationship insofar as higher trust leads them to forego opportunities to steal. The employee theft literature has repeatedly demonstrated how pilfering has become so widespread that it represents an invisible wage structure (often referred to as "fiddles") that partially compensates for low wages (Ditton, 1977; Mars, 1973). Perhaps high trust in the employer leads an employee to accept more risk inherent in compensation without "fiddles". Yet, such risk-taking might also be affected by situational risk. In this case, an employee might accept less risk (i.e., steal more) from even a highly trusted employer during a period of high economic instability (e.g., when there is fear of layoffs, etc.). These propositions are speculative and await future research.

At any rate, once again, it is likely that employees who are very trustworthy will be more likely to refrain from stealing, in any case. While such employees may not be as likely to exhibit high benevolence toward an employer who conveys low benevolence to them, their integrity should remain high, given the stability of this characteristic (Tomlinson and Mayer, 2009).

Current Empirical Assessment of Predicted Relationships

In light of the many passionate and conflicting claims being made regarding the nature, causes, and cures for employee theft, it is critical to carefully evaluate the available empirical evidence at hand (Tomlinson, 2009a). The many assertions regarding the connection between trust and employee theft still beg for rigorous research to provide support, refutation, or clarification. Despite the intuitive appeal for the relevance of trust, recent meta-analyses on deviant behavior do not specifically examine trust or trustworthiness (Berry, Ones, and Sackett, 2007; Lau, Au, and Ho, 2003). Only one published meta-analysis demonstrates a relationship between employee trust and counterproductive behavior (Colquitt, Scott, and LePine, 2007), and they found a corrected correlation of -0.33. However, the specific counterproductive behaviors in their sample of studies included variables such as tardiness and absenteeism or more general measures of deviance, but not employee theft in particular. A study by Dineen, Lewicki, and Tomlinson (2006) found that employee perceptions of their managers' behavioral integrity were not a significant predictor of organizational deviance (which included theft) among employees at two separate banking organizations (although it was a significant predictor of interpersonal deviance). With the exception of the relationship between integrity testing and employee theft (Tomlinson, 2009a), the connections between perceptions of trustworthiness, trust, and employee theft should be viewed cautiously until future research confirms their presence. Nonetheless, given the descriptive data at hand (Cressey, 1953), it would be worthwhile for researchers to proceed to the analytical phase (Greenberg and Tomlinson, 2004) to determine if, and to what extent, trust is actually related to employee theft.

Practical Applications

While every attempt has been made to carefully explicate the relationships between trust and employee theft, it must be reiterated that much of this analysis awaits careful empirical confirmation. That said, given the current state of the trust literature and how this foundation has contributed valuable insights in so many other domains, I offer the following considerations of how the present work may be beneficial to managers dealing with employee theft.

MANAGERIAL PRESCRIPTIONS TO TRUST EMPLOYEES

This chapter has highlighted the relevance of trust to all three primary perspectives on employee theft. In doing so, it has pointed out the divergent prescriptions for managerial trust in employees: the social orientation exhorts high trust in employees, yet the security orientation contends that this approach only enables and facilitates the very theft managers seek to avoid. Clearly, simple admonitions to trust or not trust one's employees are not sound advice; despite the apparent competition among perspectives on employee trust, it is arguably more effective to understand how they are interrelated and can be jointly leveraged for maximum impact (Murphy, 1993; Tomlinson and Greenberg, 2007). In this regard, the individual differences orientation's focus on placing trust only in those who are deemed trustworthy appears to offer one plausible, and much needed, reconciliation to these contrasting views. This leads me to the next point.

RATIONAL ASSESSMENT OF TRUST BY EVALUATING TRUSTWORTHINESS

The decision to trust is arguably best determined by your own evaluation of each trustee's trustworthiness, rather than by a blanket prescription by others who do not even know your employees on a personal level. In this regard, this analysis on employee theft emphasizes that managers should take special care to evaluate employee integrity and benevolence. After all, employees who have the highest trustworthiness should be the least likely to steal in any event. The extant literature supports the efficacy of integrity tests to screen out applicants who are more likely to steal (Tomlinson, 2009a), and also suggests that there are ways of administering these tests without creating problems with distrust (cf. Tomlinson and Greenberg, 2007). Other selection tests, such as background checks, may also be relevant to assessing an applicant's integrity. While benevolence is conceptualized as a relationship-specific trustworthiness factor in the Mayer, Davis, and Schoorman (1995) model and may not be directly evaluated until after an applicant is hired, there may be proxies that can be considered, such as the degree to which the applicant can demonstrate a record of pro-social behaviors (Brief and Motowidlo, 1986). It might also be useful to assess integrity, as well as benevolence, during the employment relationship (e.g., Murphy, 1993).

PROMOTE EMPLOYEE BENEVOLENCE AND INTEGRITY

Employers should strive to foster an environment that maintains and nurtures benevolence and integrity among employees. Perhaps the literature on organizational citizenship (Organ, 1988) can be used to generate more insight into cultivating employee benevolence toward the employer. With respect to integrity, research has shown that ethics training can enhance cognitive moral development over time (Izzo, Langford, and Vitell, 2006; Loe and Weeks, 2000;

Penn and Collier, 1985). Indeed, introducing a comprehensive ethics program that included ethics training as one component led to reduced theft in a financial services company (Greenberg, 2002), even though all the participants were underpaid (considered a violation of distributive justice in that study, yet also arguably describing a lack of employer integrity). The ethics program may have served to reinforce employee integrity, even when they were not treated with integrity themselves. Periodic integrity-testing of employees has been suggested as a way of tracking this factor over time (Murphy, 1993), and regular attitude surveys could measure employee benevolence.

BALANCE TRUST AND CONTROL

There appears to be some basis for arguing that employees should be both trusted more and trusted less. Until researchers have brought more clarity to this issue, managers should certainly take steps to carefully evaluate employee trustworthiness, and respond with the appropriate level of trust based on that process. Too much control may preclude the development of employer trust in employees at all, as employees have little opportunity to demonstrate trustworthiness (Strickland, 1958). However, even in the case of high employee trustworthiness (and hence trust), it is prudent to still maintain some balance between trust and control (Dunn and Schweitzer, 2005). In other words, some degree of control is likely to always be appropriate (Banks, 2007). The reality is that managers owe a fiduciary duty to stakeholders to safeguard organizational assets. As one executive in the loss prevention industry has stated, "If nothing else, employers should remember that 'trust is not a security policy'" (cited in Koster, 2009, p. 13). Managers also arguably have a moral obligation—as well as practical reasons—for trusting employees deserving of this privilege. Yet trust should not be conveyed without any controls at all, as this neglects the types of situational factors (e.g., ethics monitoring mechanisms such as confidential hotlines, ethics enforcement) that are also a powerful influence on ethical behavior (Greenberg, 2002; Murphy, 1993; Treviño, 1986). In fact, some professionals suggest calibrating trust such that those with greater access to theft opportunities be monitored more carefully due to the greater risk (Koster, 2009; Roberts, 2009).

ATTRIBUTE CONTROL TO ISSUES OF RISK, NOT TRUST

Even a highly trusted employee might not lead to employer risk-taking (i.e., less monitoring/control) when situational risk is extremely high (Mayer, Davis, and Schoorman, 1995). In this regard, a control system (as a manifestation of less risk-taking) per se does not necessarily indicate low employer trust in employees; it may simply hedge against situational risk (although the employees themselves may or may not see it this way). Employees who work for certain types of employer (e.g., banks, casinos) are quite accustomed to extensive monitoring, and may be less likely to perceive such monitoring as a lack of trust in them personally; they may simply view it as a prudent step to take in managing a high degree of risk (Kidwell and Kidwell, 1997). To the extent that employers explain how control systems are aimed at protecting the entire enterprise (up to and including the ability to provide competitive salaries and benefits to its employees) from many potentially costly forms of loss (including employee theft as well as other forms of shrink), these systems might be framed as a friend instead of a foe. In other words, there may be little to gain from explicitly framing a control system as a "cloak and daggers," "us versus them" endeavor. However, employers could simply point out how costly shrink and other forms of loss are in their organization, and this makes it necessary to engage in some type of controls. For example, if I am a convenience store clerk, I might possibly resent the security camera that is aimed at me all day while I operate the cash register, if I am led to perceive this monitoring as specifically impugning my trustworthiness. However, if the purpose of the monitoring is positioned more broadly, I may come to appreciate the presence of the camera (e.g., when it helps to identify and apprehend a robber who threatened me with a weapon). And it is worth reiterating that if the employee is truly trustworthy, he or she probably has little reason to fear or take offense at a monitoring system. Furthermore, it is possible that legislation requiring certain types of control may reduce or eliminate employee perceptions that their employers lack trust in them, as the cause of such controls would neither be due to the managers' initiative nor controllable by them (Weiner, 1986).

ELICIT EMPLOYEE TRUST BY BEING A TRUSTWORTHY EMPLOYER

If it is true that employee trust in employers is negatively related to their theft behaviors, then employers can influence this trust by behaving in a manner that leads their employees to view them as having high ability, benevolence, and integrity. This is easier said than accomplished, as a variety of factors can lead to damaged perceptions of employer trustworthiness (Simons, 2002). In addition, in the context of employee theft, the range of relevant trustworthiness perceptions is likely broader for employees evaluating their employer than vice versa. Whereas employers are more likely to focus on employee benevolence and honesty (a part of integrity), employees may be more sensitive to a more holistic evaluation of their employer: ability to both run a successful company and adequately safeguard organizational assets; benevolence as reflected in their degree of comprehensive care and consideration for employees; and integrity in a fuller sense of the term, encompassing fair treatment, enacting espoused values, and credible communication.

One potentially valuable mechanism for enabling trustworthy perceptions would be for the organization to voluntarily institute some sort of internal standards and controls that hold top managers to the same standards as front-line employees. Such consistent standards help reinforce an organization's ethical culture and speak to the integrity of top management insofar as they are willingly "putting their own money where their mouth is" (Nakayachi and Watabe, 2005; Treviño and Nelson, 2007).

Conclusion

It appears that while the notion of trust has been frequently invoked in discussions of employee theft, this has mostly been done in a casual manner that neglects the vast, extant body of research on trust, and has even led to contradictory claims. The Mayer, Davis, and Schoorman (1995) model applied here offers more sophistication and potential diagnostic capability to understand not only how trust might impact theft, but also how trust perceptions are formed through trustworthiness factors (i.e., ability, benevolence, and integrity). Furthermore, it distinguishes trust from risk-taking in a relationship (which would reflect the degree of monitoring to deter and detect employee theft), and explicitly incorporates the role of situational risk in moderating the trust-risk-taking relationship. Accordingly, it provides a sound theoretical platform for empirical testing of posited relationships.

References

Abcede, A. (1994) "Trust remains barrier in spotting employee theft," *National Petroleum News*, 86, 30–33.
AFCE (2008) *Report to the Nation on Occupational Fraud and Abuse*, Austin, TX: Association of Certified Fraud Examiners.
Anand, V., Ashforth, B. E., and Joshi, M. (2004) "Business as usual: The acceptance and perpetuation of corruption in organizations," *Academy of Management Executive*, 18, 39–53.
Arrow, K. J. (1973) *Information and Economic Behavior*, Stockholm: Federation of Swedish Industries.

Balmer, S. (2009) "Theft prevails in some sectors," *National Underwriter/Property & Casualty Risk & Benefits Management*, 113, 32.

Banks, C. (2007) "'Trust but verify': Protect store from employee theft," *Ward's Dealer Business*, 41, 4.

Berry, C. M., Ones, D. S., and Sackett, P. R. (2007) "Interpersonal deviance, organizational deviance, and their common correlates: A review and meta-analysis," *Journal of Applied Psychology*, 92, 410–424.

Blau, P. (1964) *Exchange and Power in Social Life*, New York: Wiley.

Brief, A. P. and Motowidlo, S. J. (1986) "Prosocial organizational behaviors," *Academy of Management Review*, 11, 710–725.

Buss, D. (1993) "Ways to curtail employee theft," Nation's Business, 81, April, 36–37.

Christopher, D. A. (2003) "Small business pilfering: The 'trusted' employee," *Business Ethics: A European Review*, 12, 284–297.

Colquitt, J. A., Scott, B. A., and LePine, J. A. (2007) "Trust, trustworthiness, and trust propensity: A meta-analytic test of their unique relationships with risk taking and job performance," *Journal of Applied Psychology*, 92, 909–927.

Cressey, D. (1953) *Other People's Money: A Study in the Social Psychology of Embezzlement*, Belmont, CA: Wadsworth.

Cyber-Ark (2008) "The global recession and its effect on work ethics," December, at: http://www.complianceweek.com/s/documents/CyberArk.pdf.

Das, T. K. and Teng, B. S. (1998) "Between trust and control: Developing confidence in partner cooperation in alliances," *Academy of Management Review*, 23, 491–512.

Davies, K. R. (2003) "Broken trust: Employee stealing," *Dealernews*, 39, 22–24.

Deutsch, M. (1958) "Trust and suspicion," *Journal of Conflict Resolution*, 2, 265–279.

Dineen, B. R., Lewicki, R. J., and Tomlinson, E. C. (2006) "Supervisory guidance and behavioral integrity: Relationships with employee citizenship and deviant behavior," *Journal of Applied Psychology*, 91, 622–635.

Ditton, J. (1977) "Perks, pilferage, and the fiddle: The historical structure of invisible wages," *Theory and Society*, 4, 39–71.

Dunn, J. and Schweitzer, M. E. (2005) "Why good employees make unethical decisions: The role of reward systems, organizational culture, and managerial oversight," in R. E. Kidwell, Jr and C. L. Martin (eds) *Managing Organizational Deviance*, Thousand Oaks, CA: Sage, pp. 39–60.

Edelman (2009) *2009 Edelman Trust Barometer Executive Summary*, at: http://www.edelman.co.uk/files/trust-barometer-2009-summary.pdf.

Friedman, S. (2009) "Tough times prompt spike in employee theft, Chubb warns." *National Underwriter/Property & Casual Risk & Benefits Management*, 113, 10.

Greenberg, J. (1990) "Employee theft as a reaction to underpayment inequity: The hidden cost of pay cuts," *Journal of Applied Psychology*, 75, 561–568.

Greenberg, J. (1993) "Stealing in the name of justice: Informational and interpersonal moderators of theft reactions to underpayment inequity," *Organizational Behavior and Human Decision Processes*, 54, 81–103.

Greenberg, J. (1995) "Employee theft" in N. Nicholson (ed.) *The Blackwell Encyclopaedic Dictionary of Organizational Behaviour*, Oxford, UK: Blackwell, pp. 154–155.

Greenberg, J. (1997a) "A social influence model of employee theft: Beyond the fraud triangle" in R. J. Lewicki, B. H. Sheppard, and R. J. Bies (eds) *Research on Negotiation in Organizations*, Vol. 5, Greenwich, CT: JAI Press, pp. 22–49.

Greenberg, J. (1997b) "The STEAL motive: Managing the social determinants of employee theft" in R. Giacalone and J. Greenberg (eds) *Antisocial Behavior in Organizations*, Thousand Oaks, CA: Sage, pp. 85–108.

Greenberg, J. (2002) "Who stole the money, and when? Individual and situational determinants of employee theft," *Organizational Behavior and Human Decision Processes*, 89, 985–1003.

Greenberg, J. and Scott, K. S. (1996) "Why do workers bite the hands that feed them? Employee theft as a social exchange process," *Research in Organizational Behavior*, 18, 111–156.

Greenberg, J. and Tomlinson, E. C. (2004) "The methodological evolution of employee theft research: The DATA cycle" in R. W. Griffith and A. M. O'Leary-Kelly (eds) *The Dark Side of Organizational Behavior*, San Francisco, CA: Jossey-Bass, pp. 426–461.

Gross-Schaefer, A., Trigilio, J., Negus, J., and Ro, C. (2000) "Ethics education in the workplace: An effective tool to combat employee theft," *Journal of Business Ethics*, 26, 89–100.

IOMA (2002) "Do corporate scandals give staff 'permission to steal'?" *Security Director's Report*, October. Available at: http://www.ioma.com/issues/SDR/2002_10/491697-1.html.

Izzo, G. M., Langford, B. E., and Vitell, S. (2006) "Investigating the efficacy of interactive ethics education: A difference in pedagogical emphasis," *Journal of Marketing Theory and Practice*, 14, 239–248.

Kidder, D. L. (2005) "Is it 'who I am', 'what I can get away with', or 'what you've done to me'? A multi-theory examination of employee misconduct," *Journal of Business Ethics*, 57, 389–398.

Kidwell, L. A. and Kidwell, R. E., Jr (1997) "Toward a multilevel framework for studying electronic control systems," *Journal of Accounting and Public Policy*, 16, 89–109.

Koster, K. (2009) "Could your employees be corporate thieves? Increased layoffs heighten risk of information theft," *Employee Benefit News*, 23, 12–14.

Kramer, R. M. (1999) "Trust and distrust in organizations: Emerging perspectives, enduring questions," *Annual Review of Psychology*, 50, 569–598.

Kruglanski, A. W. (1970) "Attributing trustworthiness in supervisor-worker relations," *Journal of Experimental Social Psychology*, 6, 214–232.

Lau, V. C. S., Au, W. T., and Ho, J. M. C. (2003) "A qualitative and quantitative review of antecedents of counterproductive behavior in organizations," *Journal of Business and Psychology*, 18, 73–99.

Lewicki, R. J., Tomlinson, E. C., and Gillespie, N. (2006) "Models of interpersonal trust development: Theoretical approaches, empirical evidence, and future directions," *Journal of Management*, 32, 991–1022.

Litsky, B. E., Eddleston, K. A., and Kidder, D. L. (2006) "The good, the bad, and the misguided: How managers inadvertently encourage deviant behaviors," *Academy of Management Perspectives*, 20, 91–103.

Loe, T. W. and Weeks, W. A. (2000) "An experimental investigation of efforts to improve sales students' moral reasoning," *Journal of Personal Selling & Sales Management*, 20, 243–251.

Malhotra, D. (2004) "Trust and reciprocity decisions: The differing perspectives of trustors and trusted parties," *Organizational Behavior and Human Decision Processes*, 94, 61–73.

Mars, G. (1973) "Hotel pilferage: A case study in occupational theft" in M. Warner (ed) *The Sociology of the Workplace*, New York: Halsted, pp. 200–210.

Mayer, R. C., Davis, J. H., and Schoorman, F. D. (1995) "An integrative model of organizational trust," *Academy of Management Review*, 20, 709–734.

Murphy, K. R. (1993) *Honesty in the Workplace*, Pacific Grove, CA: Brooks/Cole Publishing.

Nakayachi, K. and Watabe, M. (2005) "Restoring trustworthiness after adverse events: The signaling effects of voluntary 'hostage posting' on trust," *Organizational Behavior and Human Decision Processes*, 97, 1–17.

Needleman, S. E. (2008) "Businesses say theft by their workers is up," Wall Street Journal—Eastern Edition, December 11, p. B8.

Niehoff, B. P. and Paul, R. J. (2000) "Causes of employee theft and strategies that HR managers can use for prevention," *Human Resource Management*, 39, 51–64.

Nussbaum, B. (2002) "Can you trust anybody anymore?" *Business Week*, January 28, 30–32.

Organ, D. W. (1988) *Organizational Citizenship Behavior: The Good Soldier Syndrome*, Lexington, MA: Lexington Books.

Parkhe, A. (1998) "Understanding trust in international alliances," *Journal of World Business*, 33, 219–240.

Peet, T. E. (1924) "A historical document of Ramesside Age," *Journal of Egyptian Archaeology*, 10, 116–127.

Penn, W. Y. and Collier, B. D. (1985) "Current research in moral development as a decision support system," *Journal of Business Ethics*, 4, 131–136.

Ponemon Institute (2009) "Data loss risks during downsizing—As employees exit so does the corporate data." Available at: http://whitepapers.techrepublic.com.com/abstract.aspx?docid=1109069.

Roberts, B. (2009) "Protect data during layoffs," *HR Magazine*, 54.

Rotter, J. B. (1967) "A new scale for the measurement of interpersonal trust," *Journal of Personality*, 35, 651–665.

Rousseau, D. M., Sitkin, S. B., Burt, R. S., and Camerer, C. (1998) "Not so different after all: A cross-discipline view of trust," *Academy of Management Review*, 23, 393–404.

Sackett, P. R. (1994) "Integrity testing for personnel selection," *Current Directions in Psychological Science*, 3, 73–76.

Sackett, P. R. and Wanek, J. E. (1996) "New developments in the use of measures of honesty, integrity, conscientiousness, dependability, trustworthiness, and reliability for personnel selection," *Personnel Psychology*, 49, 787–829.

Sennewald, C. (1986) "Theft maxims," *Security Management*, 30, 85.

Sennewald, C. (1996) *Security Consulting* (2nd ed.), Boston, MA: Butterworth-Heinemann.

Serva, M. A., Fuller, M. A., and Mayer, R. C. (2005) "The reciprocal nature of trust: A longitudinal study of interacting teams," *Journal of Organizational Behavior*, 26, 625–648.

Simons, T. (2002) "Behavioral integrity: The perceived alignment between managers' words and deeds as a research focus," *Organization Science*, 13, 18–35.

Strickland, L. H. (1958) "Surveillance and trust," *Journal of Personality*, 26, 200–215.

Sykes, G. M. and Matza, D. (1957) "Techniques of neutralization: A theory of delinquency," *American Journal of Sociology*, 22, 664–670.

Taylor, R. R. (1986) "Your role in the prevention of employee theft," *Management Solutions*, 31, 20–25.

Tomlinson, E. C. (2009a) "Reducing employee theft: Weighing the evidence on intervention effectiveness" in R. Burke and C. D. Cooper (eds) *Research*

Companion to Corruption in Organizations, Cheltenham, UK: Edward Elgar, pp. 231–250.

Tomlinson, E. C. (2009b) "Teaching the interactionist model of ethics: Two brief case studies," *Journal of Management Education*, 33, 142–165.

Tomlinson, E. C. and Greenberg, J. (2005) "Discouraging employee theft by managing social norms and organizational justice" in R. E. Kidwell, Jr and C. L. Martin (eds) *Managing Organizational Deviance*, Thousand Oaks, CA: Sage, pp. 211–232.

Tomlinson, E. C. and Greenberg, J. (2007) "Understanding and deterring employee theft with organizational justice" in J. Langan-Fox, C. L. Cooper, and R. J. Klimoski (eds) *Research Companion to the Dysfunctional Workplace*, Cheltenham, UK: Edward Elgar, pp. 285–301.

Tomlinson, E. C. and Mayer, R. C. (2009) "The role of causal attribution dimensions in trust repair," *Academy of Management Review*, 34, 85–104.

Treviño, L. K. (1986) "Ethical decision making in organizations: A person-situation interactionist model." *Academy of Management Review*, 11, 601–617.

Treviño, L. K. and Nelson, K. A. (2007) *Managing Business Ethics: Straight Talk About How To Do It Right*, Hoboken, NJ: John Wiley & Sons.

Watson Wyatt (2007) *Debunking the Myth of Employee Engagement, 2006/2007 WorkUSA® Survey Report*, at: http://au.hudson.com/documents/Debunking-the-Myths-of-Employee-Engagement.pdf.

Weiner, B. (1986) *An Attributional Model of Motivation and Emotion*, New York: Springer-Verlag.

Zand, D. (1972) "Trust and managerial problem solving," *Administrative Science Quarterly*, 17, 229–239.

5

The Influence of National Culture on the Rationalization of Corruption

Amy Guerber, Aparna Rajagoplan, and Vikas Anand

One needs only to peruse current business headlines to realize that corruption has become embedded in numerous modern business organizations. In fact, within a few years Enron and WorldCom have become distant memories as scandals continue to break out in businesses around the globe. A notable characteristic of the numerous scandals that have broken out is that these frauds are typically perpetrated by individuals who are not social deviants, but average, morally-developed people. So how is it that otherwise moral individuals come to engage in corrupt behaviors in the workplace? The simple answer is that in business organizations, corrupt practices that start as deliberate choices at the individual level can become mindless activities that are performed routinely. This process of routinizing corruption and taking it for granted is called *normalization*. Normalization of corruption is underpinned by three forces:

1. *Rationalization*—the process by which justifications or excuses are created to neutralize or project corrupt practices in a positive light;
2. *Socialization*—the process by which newcomers are introduced and made to accept the existing corrupt practices; and
3. *Institutionalization*—the process by which corrupt practices are embedded in organizational practices (Ashforth and Anand, 2003).

Once corruption has become a normal part of organizational activities, the three forces of rationalization, socialization, and institutionalization serve to complement and reinforce one another, perpetuating the corrupt behaviors.

The process by which corruption becomes normalized in an organization takes place over time. Just as the term "erosion" means that a once more substantial mass of land or rock has been worn away, the term "corruption" connotes that a once estimable organization has suffered moral or ethical decay. A key component of normalization is the rationalization process which allows individuals to "refram[e] the meaning of the [corrupt] acts so as to preserve a salutary social identity" (Ashforth and Anand, 2003, p. 16). Because rationalization has a fundamental role in the normalization of corruption, it is important to understand the factors that influence it (Anand, Ashforth, and Joshi, 2004).

Previous research regarding the normalization of corruption has focused on describing the various types of rationalization technique an individual might adopt in order to justify or excuse unethical behaviors (Ashforth and Anand, 2003). This chapter builds on earlier descriptive work by exploring the factors that could predispose individuals to favor some rationalizations over others. Specifically, we explore the ways in which cultural values may influence which types of rationalization technique are likely to be adopted or accepted. Studies show that, around the world, people's ways of thinking, interpreting events, and making sense of the world around them is very much influenced by their cultural values (Hofstede, 1980; Schwartz, 1994).

National culture is likely to influence the rationalizations adopted by employees indulging in corrupt acts, for a number of reasons. First, culture is an important factor in determining what behaviors one views as acceptable or unacceptable (Licht, Goldschmidt, and Schwartz, 2007). Second, culture plays a key role in determining what justifications are viewed as acceptable for various behaviors (Cullen, Parboteeah, and Hoegl, 2004). Third, the values and characteristics which an individual views as part of a desirable social identity are shaped by the culture to which that individual belongs (Mosquera, Manstead, and Fischer, 2002; Schwartz, 2006). For these reasons, it is likely that individuals will differ in the rationalization techniques they adopt, based on the cultural values they hold (Gollan and Witte, 2008; Licht, Goldschmidt, and Schwartz, 2007). Examining these differences will enhance our understanding of organizational corruption and the processes by which corruption can become a normal part of organizational activities. With this chapter we hope to set the stage for future research regarding the effects of culture and other factors on the different stages of the process which allow corruption to become embedded in organizations.

Understanding cultural factors that are likely to influence corruption is especially important today because increased globalization has led to greater cross-national interdependence between and within organizations and to an increasingly mobile labor market. Understanding the influence of culture on processes by which corruption becomes a part of organizational life is important for practitioners because it allows companies to tailor training programs that help workers with specific cultural backgrounds to be cognizant of specific rationalization techniques that they may use. Research in this area is also important for business scholars because it can help develop an understanding of the influence of contextual factors on our models of the process by which corruption becomes endemic to certain organizations.

In the following sections we explain the different rationalization techniques described in previous literature, develop a typology of these techniques based on common underlying motives, and describe the dimensions of cultural values based on a well-established framework. Finally, we examine the underlying assumptions of each rationalization strategy and offer predictions regarding cultural differences in preferring one strategy over the other.

Rationalization

Rationalizations are mental tactics employed by individuals that explain why specific acts of corruption "… are justifiable or excusable exceptions to the general normative rules" (Ashforth and Anand, 2003, p. 16). Individuals use rationalizations in order to mitigate any perceived stigma that may be associated with engaging in corrupt acts. For example, employees who pad their expense accounts may rationalize the act by saying that the firm wasn't hurt just by this relatively insignificant act. Or they may compare themselves with other colleagues and conclude that they are better than others who inflated their expense statements to a greater degree.

Several different rationalization techniques have been identified in previous research. Here we focus on the rationalization techniques reviewed and summarized by Ashforth and Anand (2003). These techniques are listed in Table 5.1 and described below.

In a general sense, these rationalizations can be classified into two primary types—justifications and excuses (Scott and Lyman, 1968; Shaw, Wild, and Colquitt, 2003). Justifications and excuses are both "socially approved vocabularies which neutralize an act or its consequences when one or both are called into question" (Scott and Lyman, 1968, p. 46). These justifications and excuses are self-serving statements that can be used for internal consumption or to justify or explain misconduct to outsiders (Elsbach, 1994; Goodrick and Salancik, 1996). The primary distinction between these two categories is that justifications involve accepting responsibility for the act in question, but denying

Table 5.1 Rationalization techniques: description and summary

Category	Rationalization Technique	Description	Examples
Justifications			
	Appeal to higher loyalties	The actors argue that their violation of norms is due to their attempt to realize a higher-order value.	"We answered to a more important cause." "I would not report it because of loyalty to my boss."
	Denial of injury	The actors are convinced that no one is harmed by their actions; hence the actions are not really corrupt.	"No one was really harmed." "It could have been worse."
Social excuses			
	Denial of victim	The actors counter any blame for their actions by arguing that the violated party deserved whatever happened.	"They deserved it." "They chose to participate."
	Social weighting	The actors assume one of two practices that moderate the salience of corrupt behaviors: (1) condemn the condemner, (2) selective social comparison.	"You have no right to criticize us." "Others are worse than we are."
Contextual excuses			
	Denial of responsibility	The actors engaged in corrupt behaviors perceive that they have no other choice than to participate in such activities.	"What can I do? My arm is being twisted." "It is none of my business what the corporation does overseas."
	Denial of illegality	Actors excuse corrupt practices on the basis that their actions are not illegal.	"There's no law against it."
	Metaphor of the ledger	The actors rationalize that they are entitled to indulge in deviant behaviors because of their accrued credits (time and effort) in their jobs.	"We've earned the right." "It's all right for me to use the Internet for personal reasons at work because I do work overtime."

Source: Adapted from Anand, Ashforth, and Joshi (2004).

the negative quality of the act. Excuses, on the other hand, involve admitting that the act was bad, but denying or displacing full responsibility for the act (Scott and Lyman, 1968). In this chapter we distinguish between two categories of excuses. The first category is social excuses which rely on displacing blame on to some aspect of the perpetrator's social environment. The second category is contextual excuses which involve blaming other, inanimate elements in the perpetrator's environment.

JUSTIFICATION

When justifying their actions, people deny that their actions were wrong or harmful. This type of rationalization has the advantage of redeeming the actors in their own eyes from guilty perpetrators to innocent actors. One form of justification is when an actor justifies committing a corrupt act as a means of safeguarding a more valuable moral value or of achieving a more important goal. This type of rationalization is referred to as an *appeal to higher loyalties*. An appeal to higher loyalties is likely to be based on values and moral principles that are salient to the individuals or the group. For example, an individual may lie in order to cover for a co-worker who misses work regularly out of loyalty to that co-worker. The implicit assumption here is that loyalty to a co-worker is a more valued, and thus higher, principle than being honest with one's superiors or customers.

The other rationalization strategy in the justification category is the *denial of injury*. The use of denial of injury involves convincing oneself that a corrupt act is acceptable because no one is really hurt by the act in question. For example, an employee at a retail store might justify taking merchandise by reasoning that the organization will easily be able to write off the loss and that the loss is too small to materially impact on the organization.

SOCIAL EXCUSES

The second category of rationalizations is social excuses. By definition, all excuses involve attributing, or displacing, full or partial blame on to some externality. When using excuses, individuals rationalize their behavior by citing pressures in their environment that caused or contributed to their behavior. Individuals may perceive pressures that arise from their social environment as well as pressures from the more general contextual environment. Because the social and contextual environments may exert different pressures on individuals, we differentiate between social excuses and contextual excuses. Social excuses are excuses made by shifting blame on to another person or by viewing one's own acts in relation to the acts of others. Contextual excuses are excuses made by placing blame on other environmental elements such as circumstances, policies, or past experiences.

When using social excuses, individuals refuse to acknowledge full responsibility for their actions by attributing blame to elements in their social environment. Social excuses focus on the relational factors that contributed to the actor's decision to engage in, and ability to rationalize, corrupt behaviors. In a broad sense, actors indulging in this type of rationalization refuse to give credence to the beliefs, opinions, or moral rights of other people (Ashforth and Kreiner, 2002). Actors using social excuses view themselves in a positive light in comparison to others, or they deny the injured parties the right to claim any harm.

Two rationalization strategies are categorized as social excuses. These strategies are *denial of victim* and *social weighting*. When actors adopt one of these rationalization techniques, they either displace blame on to the victims or discount the integrity of the accusers or other social actors. Denial of the victim can involve adopting the belief that the victims deserved what they got, that the victims were responsible for what happened to them, or that the victims do not share the same moral rights as others (Anand, Ashforth, and Joshi, 2004). Social weighting can be accomplished either by condemning the condemner or by making a selective social comparison. Condemning the condemner involves casting accusations at, or questioning the credibility of, the accuser. Selective social comparisons involve viewing one's own actions relative to the actions of someone who is doing, or has done, worse. For example, employees at a firm producing defective products may reason that they are better than their competitors who sell similar quality products, but at a much higher rate.

CONTEXTUAL EXCUSES

The last category of rationalizations is contextual excuses. When using contextual excuses, individuals don't take responsibility for their own actions. Instead, they blame circumstances (including coercion, normative pressure, lack of laws, and past actions) for causing or allowing them to commit the unethical act. Thus, the actors accept that they committed a damaging act, but deny accountability for their actions. For example, an employee who embezzles money may rationalize the act by citing dire financial needs.

Three rationalization techniques are categorized as contextual excuses. These strategies are *denial of responsibility, denial of illegality*, and *the metaphor of the ledger*. Denial of responsibility involves believing that one had no choice but to engage in the corrupt act. A perpetrator who denies responsibility may instead blame a coercive system or pressure from peers or authorities. Individuals who use the denial of illegality rationalization technique excuse their corrupt behaviors on the basis that what they did was not against the law. Thus, they reason that they shouldn't be blamed for a defective legal system. Using the metaphor of the ledger as a rationalization technique involves excusing one's misconduct on the basis of the belief that past good deeds or successes can be used as credit to offset the negativity of engaging in corrupt actions. For example, an employee stealing from the company may reason that she was entitled as she had saved the company a lot of money in previous instances.

Individuals may adopt any of these types of rationalization to neutralize their corrupt acts. A variety of factors will dictate which rationalization a person may adopt. These include personality differences, situational demands, and cultural values. In this chapter we explore the effects of national culture in determining which rationalization type an individual or group will choose to adopt. The next section elaborates more on key aspects of cultural value systems. Then, the final section explores relationships between rationalization strategies and cultural values.

Cultural Dimensions

Culture can be defined as "... the collective programming of the mind that distinguishes the members of one group or category of people from others." (Hofstede, 2001, p. 9). A number of frameworks for studying cultural values have been developed by various researchers (Hofstede, 1980; Inglehart, 1997; Schwartz, 1994). Here, we use Schwartz's cultural dimensions for a number of reasons. Schwartz's framework was developed with sound theoretical reasoning and has been validated through methodologically rigorous studies using samples of students and teachers in numerous societies. Also, the dimensions of cultural values included in Schwartz's framework are specifically designed to be orthogonal, with each dimension relating to a different fundamental social question. This reduces the amount of overlap between the values in different dimensions and makes the Schwartz framework intuitively appealing and easy to interpret.

Schwartz (1994) developed his cultural value dimensions by reflecting on the ways in which societies can answer three fundamental social questions, or issues. The first of these questions determines how a society views the "nature of the relation or the boundaries between the person and the group" (Schwartz, 2006, p. 140). The second social question addresses how to "guarantee that people behave in a responsible manner that preserves the social fabric" (ibid.).

This essentially determines the system by which a society ensures that its members engage in productive work that furthers the ends of the group. The third social question that all societies must address is "how people manage their relations to the natural and social world" (Schwartz, 2006, p. 141).

AUTONOMY/EMBEDDEDNESS

In response to the first question, as to the way a society views the nature of the relationship between the individual and the group, societies will adopt values somewhere along the *autonomy* to *embeddedness* continuum. Autonomy refers to the extent individuals' freedom of thought and affect is valued by the collectivity. Schwartz (1994, 2006) distinguished two types of autonomy that might be valued in a society. One is *affective autonomy* which refers to the freedom to pursue positive affective experiences. In societies that value affective autonomy, importance is placed on pleasure and on being able to lead an exciting and varied life. The other type of autonomy is *intellectual autonomy* which refers to the freedom to pursue one's own ideas independently. Societies characterized by intellectual autonomy value broadmindedness, curiosity, and creativity (Schwartz, 2006).

Embeddedness, on the other hand, refers to the extent to which people are viewed as being integrated with the larger collectivity and is the polar opposite of autonomy. In cultures characterized by embeddedness, importance is given to social relationships through identification with the group, a shared way of life, and striving toward shared goals. Such cultures value social order, respect for tradition, security, obedience, and wisdom (Schwartz, 2006).

For example, in countries that are high on the embeddedness dimension individuals may be considered wise for their knowledge of social norms, whereas in highly autonomous countries individuals may be considered wise for their rich and varied experiences.

EGALITARIANISM/HIERARCHY

In response to the second social question, regarding how to ensure responsible and productive behavior from members of society, societies adopt values on a second dimension which ranges from *egalitarianism* at one end to *hierarchy* at the other end. Egalitarianism means that people view and treat others as moral equals who share the same basic interests. In egalitarian societies important values are equality, social justice, responsibility, help, and honesty (Schwartz, 2006).

Hierarchy, on the other hand, refers to a society in which roles are ascribed in order to ensure responsible behavior. A hierarchical social structure includes an unequal distribution of power, roles, and resources. People are socialized to accept the rules and obligations that come with their roles. Important values in a hierarchical society are social power, authority, humility, and wealth (Schwartz, 2006).

Thus, countries high on the hierarchy dimension may value the usage of deferential words like "sir" or "madam" for those in positions of power, whereas countries high on the egalitarianism dimension may frown on the usage of such language.

HARMONY/MASTERY

In response to the third social question which addresses the way in which people should order their relationships with the social and natural environment, societies adopt values from a third dimension with *harmony* at one end and *mastery* at the other. Harmony refers to the extent to which people try to fit into the world as it is without trying to change or exploit it. In societies that are oriented toward harmony, important values are world at peace, unity with nature, and protecting the environment (Schwartz, 2006).

At the other extreme, mastery refers to the extent to which people assert effort to change, direct, or exploit their natural and social environments. In societies that are oriented toward mastery important values are ambition, success, daring, and competence.

Figure 5.1 (from Schwartz, 2006) provides a visual representation of the cultural value dimensions and the specific values that are most important in each of the cultural value orientations. It should be noted that cultural value orientations that are depicted adjacent to one another, such as hierarchy and mastery, are generally compatible with one another. Value orientations that are depicted across from one another, such as hierarchy and egalitarianism, represent polar opposites for that dimension of cultural values. A society is characterized by its configuration of cultural values rather than by its place along only one of the dimensions. For example, West European countries, such as Sweden, France, and Spain, are characterized by intellectual autonomy, egalitarianism, and values near the mid-point between harmony and mastery. At the opposite side of the spectrum are Eastern cultures, such as Hong Kong, Thailand, and Nepal, which are characterized by both hierarchy and embeddedness.

Culture and Rationalization

In order to understand which rationalization techniques are more likely to be utilized in various cultures, it is important to first consider the definitions

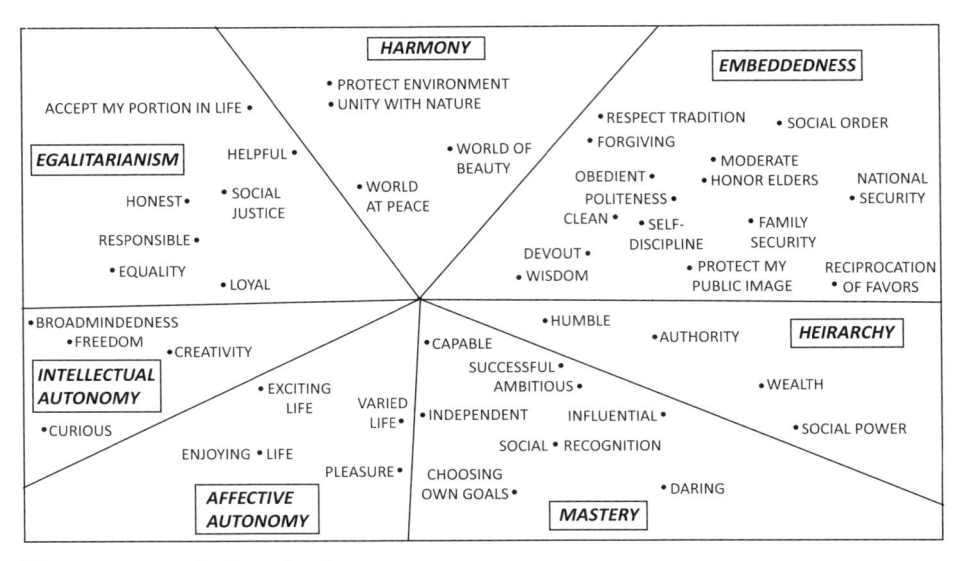

Figure 5.1 Cultural values
Source: Schwartz (2006).

and underlying assumptions that go with each of them. After considering these implicit assumptions, one can begin to make predictions about which rationalization techniques will be conducive to particular cultural values. In the this section we discuss the assumptions that go with each of the rationalization techniques and the ways in which each of these assumptions may correspond or clash with certain cultural values.

JUSTIFICATION

The rationalization techniques in the justification category are somewhat complex because they could work through different mechanisms in different cultures. For instance, one of the rationalization techniques in the self-justification categories is to appeal to higher loyalties. It is likely that individuals in any culture could use this technique for rationalizing corrupt behaviors, but the specific loyalties to which they appeal are likely to change from culture to culture. The second justification technique is the denial of injury. This rationalization technique is commonly used to justify stealing from one's employer or engaging in other acts that harm larger organizations, and is based on the belief that no one was really harmed or that the victim can easily recover from the damages.

Appeal to higher loyalties The first rationalization technique in the justification category is making an appeal to higher loyalties. When rationalizing corrupt acts using this technique, individuals "argue that some ethical norms need to be breached to fulfill more important goals" (Anand, Ashforth, and Joshi, 2004, p. 13). As mentioned earlier, this rationalization technique is very flexible, and could fit with any cultural value system. The loyalties to which individuals appeal are likely to vary from culture to culture. Specifically, individuals should be most likely to appeal to higher-order values that are important in their own cultures. For example, individuals in a culture characterized by embeddedness would be more likely to rationalize engaging in corrupt acts on the basis that these acts were necessary in order to protect their families or to pay back favors that had been done to them in the past because family security and reciprocation of favors are accepted as important values in such cultures. Individuals in cultures characterized by egalitarianism might be likely to justify engaging in corrupt acts by appealing to values such as loyalty and social justice.

Denial of injury Denial of injury is also likely to work by different mechanisms in different cultures. In an autonomous society individuals will be more likely to view themselves as separate from the victim. The perpetrator may feel that the victim has more resources than needed, and may feel that they should have the freedom or right to enjoy those resources for themselves. Also in an autonomous society individuals may feel that, as long as their actions are not directly impinging on the freedoms of others, they are not doing any harm. In a society characterized by embeddedness, on the other hand, individuals are likely to view themselves as one with the organization or group. In such a society individuals may feel entitled to the resources of the organization or group because the distinction between "yours" and "mine" may be less clear when the sense of belongingness is strong.

Summary To summarize, justifications include two rationalization techniques: appeal to higher loyalties and denial of injury. Because justifications allow perpetrators to reframe their corrupt acts in a way that casts these acts in a favorable light, the ways in which these rationalization techniques are going to be used will vary from culture to culture. In each case, individuals involved in corrupt acts will rely on the values that are important in their own cultures to serve as justifications for their actions.

SOCIAL EXCUSES

The rationalization techniques in this category come with the implicit notion of comparing others negatively with the self. This comparison could be in the form of denying victimhood to the injured party or selectively comparing the corrupt act with those actions that appear even more egregious. It is probable that such rationalizations would be less effective in an egalitarian society where justice and equality of rights are valued. These excuses may be more acceptable in hierarchical societies which are characterized by unequal rights and implicit notions of entitlement.

Denial of victim The first rationalization technique in the category of social excuses is denial of the victim. Individuals who use this technique are able to convince themselves that the victim deserved what they got. Denial of the victim can take a few different forms. In one variation the perpetrator may believe that whatever happened to the victim constituted just revenge for the victim's past actions. In another variation the perpetrator may believe that the victim was responsible for whatever happened to him simply because he chose to be in the wrong place at the wrong time. A third variety of denial of the victim involves a perpetrator actually denying the moral rights of the victims. This is the most severe form of denial of victim because the victim is actually dehumanized in the perpetrator's mind (Bandura, 1999).

The assumption that underlies all variations of the denial of victim rationalization technique is that different people deserve different outcomes. This rationalization technique should be less likely to be utilized in an egalitarian society because the underlying assumption clashes with the concepts of social justice and equality which are valued in such cultures. Conversely, denial of victim should be relatively more likely to be utilized in a hierarchical society because of the value placed on social power and authority.

Denial of the victim is also likely to fit well in cultures characterized by embeddedness because the value placed on social order and respect for tradition in such cultures could allow members of such societies to accept the idea that certain individuals are ascribed different rights than others. This rationalization technique would be likely to clash with the values of an autonomous culture because, as a cultural value, autonomy means that members of such societies value not only their own freedoms and rights, but also the freedoms and rights of other members of society.

Social weighting The second rationalization technique in the social excuses category is social weighting. Social weighting involves two distinct techniques. One of these techniques is to rationalize one's own actions by comparing oneself to someone worse. This technique is referred to as "selective social comparison" (Anand, Ashforth, and Joshi, 2004, p. 13). Selective social comparisons allow individuals to feel better about their own behavior by viewing their actions relative to the actions of someone who has done worse (or who they perceive to have done worse).

The underlying assumption of selective social comparison is that it is acceptable to evaluate your own actions by comparing yourself to others rather than to some universal standard. It is also based on the assumption that only the very worst actions are really wrong. This technique and the assumptions on which it relies are matched with cultural values of embeddedness because embeddedness implies that one's identity is defined, through social comparison, by one's relative position within the group.

The second type of social weighting is to condemn the condemner. When using this rationalization technique, an alleged perpetrator retaliates by calling into question the legitimacy or credibility of the accusers and their accusations (Anand, Ashforth, and Joshi, 2004). This technique could actually be considered more of a response to an accusation than a rationalization technique because it implies that someone has made a condemnatory statement of some sort. It is likely that the grounds on which one would condemn a condemner would vary by culture. For instance, in an egalitarian society it might be quite condemning to say that an accuser is showing a lack of loyalty. In a hierarchical society one might criticize a condemner for showing a lack of respect for authority, while in an intellectually autonomous society one might criticize a condemner for blindly following rules or orders.

Summary To summarize, social excuses include denial of victim and social weighting. We predict that denial of victim would be most likely to be utilized in cultures characterized by hierarchical and embeddedness values. Social weighting can be achieved through either selective social comparison or condemning the condemner. We predict that selective social comparisons will be most likely to be utilized in societies characterized by embeddedness. We also predict that condemning the condemner will be likely to be used across different cultures based on different condemnations.

CONTEXTUAL EXCUSES

In this category of rationalizations, the blame for one's corrupt acts is attributed outwards to circumstances, normative and coercive pressures felt, or the social order and systems. Another form of contextual excuse is to conjure a list of past good deeds and metaphorically balance the ledger by engaging in the corrupt act. As these attributions are mostly external, individuals from cultures in which one views oneself as in control of what happens in one's life, may not value such rationalizations. In contrast, individuals who attach importance to the external world and social systems may find comfort in contextual excuses.

Denial of responsibility   The first rationalization technique in the contextual excuses category is denial of responsibility. Individuals who use this technique believe, or convince themselves, that they have no choice in whether or not they engage in the corrupt behavior. Instead, individuals who use the denial of responsibility rationalization technique view their actions as being compelled by circumstances outside of their own control (Anand, Ashforth, and Joshi, 2004). People often cite this type of rationalization for engaging in corrupt acts when pressure from top-management to meet objective targets is high.

Underlying the denial of responsibility rationalization technique is the assumption that one is powerless over one's actions. This technique also relates to an external locus of control. Denial of responsibility also implies acceptance of the idea that situational factors or powerful others may dictate one's actions. The assumptions underlying denial of responsibility are more likely to be accepted by members of a culture characterized by embeddedness because of the emphasis placed on such values as social order, obedience, and respect for tradition in such societies. At the opposite pole from embeddedness are cultures characterized by autonomy. The assumptions underlying denial of responsibility are likely to be especially unacceptable to individuals in cultures high on intellectual autonomy due to the emphasis placed on freedom, creativity, and broadmindedness. The value placed on social power and authority in hierarchical cultures also makes denial of responsibility likely to be utilized and accepted in these cultures.

Denial of illegality   The second rationalization technique that relies on contextual excuses involves rationalizing corrupt behaviors on the grounds that the behavior is legal, or at least not illegal. This rationalization technique could be viewed as a specific variety of denial of responsibility. While denial of responsibility involves blaming various circumstances for one's actions, denial of illegality focuses on circumstances involving the legal system. When using denial of illegality as a rationalization technique a perpetrator views oversights in the legal system as adequate justification for corrupt actions.

Rationalization by denying illegality is based on the assumption that it is up to someone else to decide, and to state, what is right and wrong. Like denial of responsibility, denial of illegality implies that one is willing to accept rules and orders, without the need to question or think critically about one's own behaviors, as long as they are not illegal. As a rationalization technique, denial of illegality is well-matched with cultures characterized by embeddedness because these cultures value social order, security, and obedience. It also fits with the value placed on social power and authority in hierarchical cultures.

Metaphor of the ledger   The final rationalization technique in the category of contextual excuses is the metaphor of the ledger, also known as balancing the ledger. This rationalization technique involves the belief that one is entitled to engage in corrupt practices due to accrued credit for past efforts or due to having incurred past damages. An example of this rationalization technique is when employees justify spending time on Facebook or checking personal e-mails at work by claiming that they have earned the right to do so because of the time and effort they have put into their jobs.

The assumption that underlies the metaphor of the ledger is that one's actions are weighed together, as if "good" acts could be piled on to one side of a scale and "bad" acts on the other. So long as the bad acts do not outweigh the good, perpetrators can continue to feel as if they are alright in an ethical, or at least a karmic, sense. The metaphor of the ledger should be conducive to the value placed on social justice and equality in egalitarian societies.

Summary   To summarize, contextual excuses include denial of responsibility, denial of illegality, and the metaphor of the ledger. We predict that both denial of responsibility and denial of illegality will be most likely in cultures characterized by embeddedness and hierarchical values. The metaphor of the ledger is predicted to fit well with egalitarian cultural values.

Conclusion

This chapter represents an initial step in understanding the ways in which cultural values are likely to influence the techniques individuals choose for rationalizing corrupt behavior. We examined the different types of rationalizations adopted when individuals try to neutralize or recast their corrupt actions in a positive light. We classified these rationalizations into three categories:

1. *Justifications*—where responsibility is accepted for the act in question but no pernicious quality is attached;
2. *Social excuses*—where the harm done by the act is accepted, but responsibility is denied by comparing the self more positively than others; and
3. *Contextual excuses*—where the harm done by the act is accepted but responsibility is attributed to externalities.

Adopting a particular form of rationalization may be affected by numerous factors. One important factor is the national culture of the actors. To study culture, we adopted the Schwartz framework of describing a particular national culture along three polar dimensions: *embeddedness-autonomy, hierarchy-egalitarianism* and *harmony-mastery*. Finally, we examined the underlying assumption(s) of each rationalization technique and discussed which cultural values would be most likely to predict adoption of a particular technique. For example, we predicted that the adoption of the "denial of illegality" rationalization technique may be more likely in societies high on embeddedness because the technique contains an implicit assumption that one's actions are determined by the external world.

References

Anand, V., Ashforth, B. E., and Joshi, M. (2004) "Business as usual: The acceptance and perpetuation of corruption in organizations," *Academy of Management Executive*, 18(2), 39–53.

Ashforth, B. E. and Anand, V. (2003) "The normalization of corruption in organizations," *Research in Organizational Behavior*, 25, 1–52.

Ashforth, B. E. and Kreiner, G. E. (2002) "Normalizing emotion in organizations: Making the extraordinary seem ordinary," *Human Resource Management Review*, 12, 215–235.

Bandura, A. (1999) "Moral disengagement in the perpetration of inhumanities," *Personality and Social Psychology Review*, 3(3), 193–209.

Cullen, J. B., Parboteeah, K. P., and Hoegl, M. (2004) "Cross-national differences in managers' willingness to justify ethically suspect behaviors: A test of institutional anomie theory," *Academy of Management Journal*, 47(3), 411–421.

Elsbach, K. D. (1994) "Managing organizational legitimacy in the California cattle industry: The construction and effectiveness of verbal accounts," *Administrative Science Quarterly*, 39(1), 57–88.

Gollan, T. and Witte, E. H. (2008) "'It was right to do it because' — Understanding justifications of actions as prescriptive attributions," *Social Psychology*, 39(3), 189–196.

Goodrick, E. and Salancik, G. R. (1996) "Organizational discretion in responding to institutional practices: Hospitals and caesarian births," *Administrative Science Quarterly*, 41(1), 1–28.

Hofstede, G. (1980) *Culture's Consequences: International Differences in Work-related Values*, Beverly Hills, CA: Sage.

Hofstede, G. (2001) *Culture's Consequences: Comparing Values, Behaviors, Institutions, and Organizations across Nations*, Thousand Oaks, CA: Sage.

Inglehart, R. (1997) *Modernization and Postmodernization: Cultural, Economic and Political Change in 43 Societies*, Princeton, NJ: Princeton University Press.

Licht, A. N., Goldschmidt, C., and Schwartz, S. H. (2007) "Culture rules: The foundations of the rule of law and other norms of governance," *Journal of Comparative Economics*, 35(4), 659–688.

Mosquera, P. M. R., Manstead, A. S. R., and Fischer, A. H. (2002) "Honor in the Mediterranean and northern Europe," *Journal of Cross-Cultural Psychology*, 33(1), 16–36.

Schwartz, S. H. (1994) "Beyond individualism/collectivism: new cultural dimensions of values" in U. Kim, H. C. Trandis, C. Kagitcibasi, S. C. Choi, and G. Yoon (eds) *Individualism and Collectivism: Theory, Method, and Applications*, Thousand Oaks, CA: Sage, pp. 85–119.

Schwartz, S. H. (2006) "A theory of cultural value orientations: Explication and applications," *Comparative Sociology*, 5(2), 137–182.

Scott, M. B. and Lyman, S. M. (1968) "Accounts," *American Sociological Review*, 33(1), 46–62.

Shaw, J. C., Wild, E., and Colquitt, J. A. (2003) "To justify or excuse? A meta-analytic review of the effects of explanations," *Journal of Applied Psychology*, 88(3), 444–458.

PART III
Costs of Crime and Corruption in Organizations

6

The Debilitating Effects of Fraud in Organizations

Conan C. Albrecht, Matthew L. Sanders, Daniel V. Holland, and Chad Albrecht

Fraud is a topic of marked interest to investors, analysts, regulators, auditors, and the general public. Major financial statement frauds at Satyam, Enron, WorldCom, Xerox, Qwest, Tyco, HealthSouth, Cendant, Parmalat, Harris Scarfe and HIH, SKGlobal, YGX, Livedoor Co., Royal Ahold, and Vivendi resulted in a significant loss of confidence in the integrity of business (Carson, 2004) and contributed to a severe decline in stock markets worldwide. New and increasingly complex business environments have led to multifarious corporate corruption schemes such as that seen at Enron, while more traditional fraud schemes like that seen at WorldCom have continued. On an individual level, people today are inundated with fraud in the form of e-mail spam (e.g., the Nigerian 419 letter), phishing scams, online auction fraud, viruses that lead to identity theft and loss of productivity, mail fraud, etc. Although fraud and corruption have always been a part of society, modern technological advances have allowed fraudsters to contact potential victims at increasing distances and on a far greater scale.

Types of Fraud

There are two primary ways of illegally taking assets from an individual. The first is by robbing the individual using physical force; the second is through trickery. In the first case, the individual unwillingly gives the assets; in the second, the individual willingly provides access because of deception. In its broadest sense, fraud is an illegal act characterized by deceit, concealment, or violation of trust—and usually with the goal of achieving gain (CERN, 2009).

One of the most classic frauds is the Ponzi scheme. While Ponzi schemes have undoubtedly been used throughout history, the name references Carlo "Charles" Ponzi's scams in the early 1900s whereby he provided earlier investors with "returns" that actually came from later investors. In this scheme, the pyramid continues to grow because each successive level requires a larger number of investors. The scheme eventually breaks down as the pyramid grows to an unmanageable size.

The Ponzi scheme is a good example of fraud because it illustrates its deceptive nature: investors are led to believe that returns are coming from clever investing when the returns are actually coming from the outlays of new investors. It also illustrates the greed involved by both the perpetrator and the victims, as both are seeking something for nothing. Finally, the Ponzi scheme illustrates the trust involved in all fraud: investors give their money to a person who they feel is trustworthy. Because Ponzi schemes provide early returns, investors often become lured into a false sense of confidence in the abilities of the perpetrator. For example, Ponzi often told investors that he could provide a 40 percent return in just 90 days—an unbelievable return in any economy (SEC, 2009). In fact, those who claim to have "unbelievable" deals are often providing exactly that.

Fraud can be classified as (1) fraud committed *on behalf* of organizations, and (2) fraud committed *against* organizations or people. In fraud committed on behalf of organizations, the fraud is perpetrated in an effort to make the organization look better than it really is, which may end up benefiting all who are associated with the organization, at least in the short term. This can occur in governments, corporations, and non-profit organizations. For example, in the Satyam case—India's most publicized large-scale fraud—Chairman B. Ramalinga Raju explained that the fraud was committed only to make the company look more competitive and to further its business interests. "Neither me, nor the Managing Director took even one rupee/dollar from the company and have not benefited in financial terms on account of the inflated results" (Raju, 2009). In fraud committed against organizations, the goal is usually personal gain through theft perpetrated by employees, vendors, customers, or other parties. These frauds usually involve actual changing of assets, whereas fraud on behalf of organizations often involves false amounts on the books only. Within these two classifications, several types of fraud are most prominent. Table 6.1 provides descriptions of each.

How Fraud Affects Organizations

Perhaps the best way to illustrate how fraud affects organizations is to review two fraud cases. The first is a derivatives fraud case committed by an employee

Table 6.1   Types of fraud

Type of Fraud	Perpetrator	Victim	Comments
Employee embezzlement	Employees of an organization	The employer	Employees use their positions to take or divert assets belonging to their employer. This is the most common type of fraud.
Vendor fraud	Vendors of an organization	The organization to which the vendors sell goods or services	Vendors either overbill or provide lower-quality or fewer goods than agreed.
Customer fraud	Customers of an organization	The organization which sells to the customers	Customers don't pay, pay too little, or get too much from the organization through deception.
Management fraud (financial statement fraud)	Management of a company	Shareholders and/or debt-holders and regulators	Management manipulates the financial statements to make the company look better than it is. This is the most expensive type of fraud.
Investment scams and other consumer frauds	Fraud perpetrators —all kinds	Unwary investors	These types of fraud are committed on the Internet and in person and involve gaining people's confidence in order to get them to invest money in worthless schemes.
Other types of fraud	All kinds—depends on the situation	All kinds—depends on the situation	Any time anyone takes advantage of the confidence of another person to deceive him or her.

Source: Albrecht, Albrecht, and Albrecht (2006).

who became a rogue trader at his company (Albrecht, 2005a). Over the nine years the fraud was committed, the amount taken from the company exceeded US$2.6 billion. Figure 6.1 summarizes the amount of the fraud at odd-year intervals

In years 8 and 9, several of the world's largest financial institutions became involved because they thought the employee was acting in the best interests of the companies. Because of their associations, these financial institutions were drawn into significant litigation that cost them several hundred million dollars each.

In the second example (a fictitious one), assume a company has $100 in revenue (it could be $100 million, $100,000, etc.). Also, assume that it has operating expenses of $90 and operating profit of $10, resulting in a 10 percent profit margin. If a person commits a fraud worth $1, operating profit is reduced

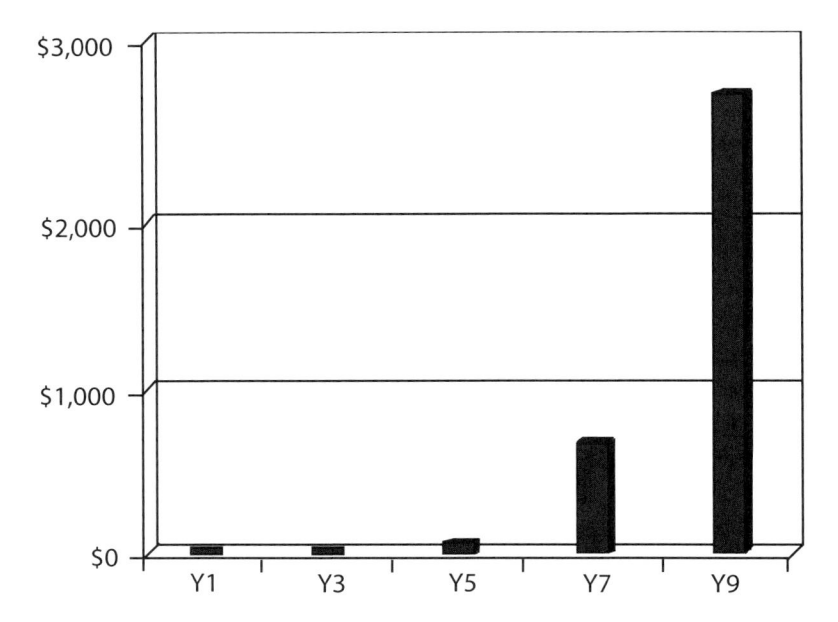

Figure 6.1 Amount embezzled at odd-year intervals

to $9. Because this company's profit margin is 10 percent, the company must generate approximately ten times the amount of the fraud or an additional $10 of revenue to restore net income to $10. These figures do not include litigation costs, loss of additional future sales due to a decrease in resources available, damage to the company image, or other negative effects of the fraud. Table 6.2 shows the income statement for this company.

To understand how dramatic this multiplier effect can be, consider the real case of a large General Motors. The company experienced a US$436 million dealer fraud in the 1980s. At the time, the company's profit margin was about 10 percent. At this profit margin, the company needed to generate US$4.36 billion in additional revenues to restore net income to its pre-fraud level. If you assume that the average automobile made by this company sold for US$20,000, this company would have to make and sell an additional 218,000 automobiles just to return to the profitability level it would have been at without the fraud.

Now, consider how much this fraud—and another US$70 million fraud later that same year—put this automobile company behind its competitors. While this automobile company was spinning its wheels to restore stolen profit, its competitors, who had not experienced significant frauds, were boosting their profits and investing in increased capacity. A similar problem occurs in countries with high rates of corruption—especially in the developing world. Because of the high cost of fraud and corruption, in many ways, high-corruption countries

Table 6.2   Income statement

Income Statement	Amount ($)	Explanation
Revenues	100	
Operating expenses	90	
Operating income	10	Profit margin is 10% or $10/$100
Amount of fraud	1	Fraud is 1% of revenues
Profit after fraud	9	Operating profit less fraud
Additional revenues needed to restore income to $10	10	Since profit margin is 10%, for every $10 of revenues, only $1 becomes profit

spin their wheels while other countries with lower amounts of fraud and corruption increase their per capita incomes, reduce poverty and hunger, and become more prominent members of the world economy (Albrecht, 2005b). For corrupt countries, the problem is exacerbated because investors will not want to place capital in economies with high rates of corruption (Wei, 2000). These examples show how costly fraud and corruption are and why good research to combat these problems is necessary. If society can gain a better understanding of why people commit fraud and what types of environment contribute to corruption, it can reduce fraud and corruption in its various forms.

Fraud Perpetrators—Who They Are

When fraud research gained momentum nearly four decades ago, the first thing researchers studied was perpetrator characteristics. This early research showed that there is no universal profile for those who commit fraud (Albrecht et al., 1981). Fraud perpetrators cannot usually be distinguished from other people using demographic or other characteristics. Some fraudsters are dishonest shortly after being hired, while others are honest for decades before stealing. This early research on fraud perpetrators found them to be college-educated, optimistic with high self-esteem, and socially conforming. In short, they were like most employees, customers, vendors, and business associates. Consequently, it can be very difficult to do any kind of profiling for fraud potential. This lack of clear perpetrator characteristics suggests that it would be prudent for all individuals to be on guard for fraud and corruption.

The Fraud Triangle

It can be argued that a certain percentage of society lacks moral guidance and moves from one fraud to another. However, often it is those with a fairly honest past who commit fraud. In fact, individuals who hold positions of significant trust commit most large frauds. For example, Bernie Madoff was a leader for decades in the financial market, and yet he committed the largest stock investment scam in history. How otherwise "normal" individuals get caught up in fraud can be explained with the fraud triangle which is based on criminological and psychological research and describes how perceived pressures, perceived opportunities, and rationalizations come together to enable individuals to commit fraud (see Figure 6.2).

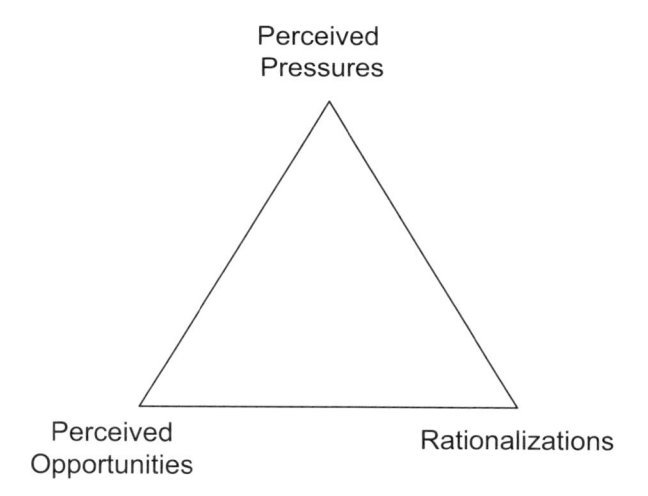

The fraud triangle is often compared with the fire triangle. Fire requires heat, fuel, and oxygen to be present for fire to occur. If any one of these elements is removed, the fire goes out. A fire with little fuel but significant heat and oxygen will burn strongly, signaling that one particularly strong element may compensate for a weaker element. Likewise, the three parts of the fraud triangle must be present for fraud to occur, but they do not all have to be significant. A person with considerable rationalization needs little pressure or opportunity to commit fraud. A person with substantial pressure may work to create opportunities despite a strong control environment or may develop elaborate rationalizations in the face of a longstanding personal ethic.

Figure 6.2 The fraud triangle

PERCEIVED PRESSURES

Fraud perpetrators feel some kind of perceived pressure that prompts them to commit fraud. These pressures do not need to be real; investigators often cannot understand how a pressure was strong enough to motivate fraud. A source of pressure may be very strong for one person, but not for another. Most pressure involves a financial need, but other pressures include the need to report strong performance, frustration with work, a challenge to beat the system, ill-feelings toward a person's work, or various vices that require funding.

For example, consider Susan Jones. Susan had worked at the same company for over 32 years. Her integrity had never been questioned. At age 63, she became a grandmother—and immediately thereafter, a "spendaholic." She bought everything she could get her hands on for her two grandchildren. She even became addicted to the Home Shopping Network. During the three years prior to her retirement, Susan stole over US$650,000 from her employer. When caught, she was sentenced and served one year in prison. She also deeded everything she and her husband owned to her former employer in an attempt to pay the employer back. By giving her employer her home, her retirement account, and her cars, she repaid approximately US$400,000 of the US$650,000 she stole. She also entered into a restitution agreement to pay back the remaining US$250,000 she still owed. And, because she had not paid income taxes on the remaining US$250,000 of fraudulent "income," the IRS required her to make monthly tax payments after she got out of prison (Albrecht, Albrecht, and Albrecht, 2006).

Of course, many other pressures exist, such as addictions to gambling, drugs, or alcohol; greed and selfishness; or an attempt to keep up with others who have more money. Still other perpetrators are lured by the simple act of "beating the system" or have an insatiable need to be successful and will do whatever it takes to achieve their goals. Many pressures are work-related, including recognition for job performance, job dissatisfaction, fear of being laid off, a desire to impress others at work, or anger toward a boss or a business.

PERCEIVED OPPORTUNITIES

Perceived opportunities are an individual's belief in the ability to commit fraud. Within an extremely strong control environment, even the most dishonest person may not be able to commit fraud. In permissive environments with poor fraud controls, honest people may need little pressure to make the wrong decision. The old adage, "locks on doors help the honest people stay honest," speaks to the opportunity portion of the triangle.

Prime opportunities typically have three primary facets: the opportunity to commit fraud, the opportunity to conceal fraud, and the opportunity to avoid punishment. Individuals generally perceive that all three facets of the opportunity are in place before perpetrating a fraudulent act. While organizations can often do little to alleviate personal pressures, they can do much to decrease opportunities through a strong control environment.

Specific control activities include segregation of duties, system of authorizations, independent checks, physical safeguards, and documents and records (COSO, 2002). Within each of these groups, specific controls can be placed that help prevent fraud. Fraud prevention planners should always understand that frauds are intentional and are committed by intelligent, active human beings. They are very different than anomalies or mistakes. Even in strong control environments, creative individuals may still circumvent the controls and commit fraud. The control environment certainly decreases opportunities for fraudsters, but it can never fully prevent fraud.

Several factors can be detrimental to a strong control environment. First, the inability to judge the quality of work can increase opportunities. In these circumstances, it becomes easy for perpetrators to overcharge for a service, add additional hours to a timecard, perform work that is not necessary, provide substandard products or services, or charge for work not performed. Workers can submit more overtime than necessary or can even clock into work, leave the organization for non-work purposes, and come back later to clock back out. Some people find it easy to rationalize less work than necessary or lower than expected quality in products and services because they do not see it as direct dishonesty but rather as simple exaggeration.

Failure to discipline fraud perpetrators can also negatively affect the control environment and the corporate culture of honesty. While fraud perpetrators may be honest for 30 years before committing their first fraud, most repeat the behavior soon afterward. Fraud perpetrators have a high rate of recidivism. As individuals commit fraud and are not punished (or are merely terminated), others see that fraud is not taken seriously in an organization. Many companies want to process fraud cases quietly because of fears of bad press, stock decreases, or other negative results. Unfortunately, this attitude simply encourages more fraud and exacerbates the problem.

Victims who lack access to information are at a disadvantage because they may be unable to see the larger picture that potential fraudsters see. This lack of transparency allows those "in the know" to make businesses look much better than they really are, and it allows scammers to take advantage of individuals. In the security field, a common strategy adopted by managers is to make information obscure and difficult to find in an effort to keep hackers and others out of systems. This "security through obscurity" is a misnomer and is rejected by most security experts. In fact, this strategy can even encourage hackers by raising the challenge. Effective security is achieved through transparent, tried-and-true methods that involve encryption, firewalls, and other well-accepted security measures. Likewise, limiting transparency in an effort to keep potentially fraudulent individuals in the dark usually only harms the victims and allows fraudsters to literally work in the dark. Individuals and organizations should insist on full disclosure, transparent dealings, and arms-length transactions to force fraudsters out into the open.

Ignorance, apathy, and incapacity can also lead to fraud opportunities. Victims often include older individuals who may not understand technology or newer business types, individuals with language difficulty, or other "vulnerable" citizens. E-mail scammers often target these groups by scaring or tricking individuals into revealing passwords or sensitive financial information.

Finally, the lack of an audit trail can provide opportunities for fraud. Bribery, for example, is almost always done off-book, with little audit trail. Other frauds involve cash payments or manipulation of records or existing audit trails that cannot be followed. These frauds are difficult to discover with records, so investigators often focus on tips or conversion activities.

RATIONALIZATIONS

Rationalization has been defined as "a defense mechanism by which your true motivation is concealed by explaining your actions and feelings in a way that is not threatening" (Wordnet, 2009). It is important to recognize that there are very few people, if any, who do not rationalize. We like to feel good about ourselves and thus we rationalize away our shortcomings (Festinger, 1957). We rationalize being overweight. We rationalize not exercising enough. We rationalize spending more than we should. We rationalize taking small things from an organization. We rationalize why we need to spend more, or less, time at work. It has been said that we judge ourselves by our intentions, and we judge others by their actions. If we were truly as good as we think we are, and if we were only half as bad as others think we might be, the world would be a better place.

Although all people rationalize behavior to some degree, fraud perpetrators seem to do so in a more severe and detrimental way. Remember, the types of people who commit fraud are not normally hardened criminals. Rather, they are educated, often religious, optimistic people. Many are first-time offenders who would not commit other crimes. It is common to hear co-workers make remarks like "I can't believe it was him," or "She was one of our most trusted workers." In the mind of the perpetrator, the act must be rationalized and brought in line with personal ethics.

Common rationalizations used by fraud perpetrators include the following:

- The organization owes it to me.
- I am only borrowing the money—I will pay it back.
- Nobody will get hurt.
- I deserve more.
- It's for a good purpose.
- We'll fix the books as soon as we get over this financial difficulty.

Countless other rationalizations exist. Some may not make sense or hold up logically to a third party but, whatever the rationalization, it need only resolve the ethical dissonance in the perpetrator's mind.

To understand the extent of income tax fraud, for example, consider that in 1988, for the first time, the IRS required taxpayers who claimed dependents to list social security numbers for their dependents. In 1987, 77 million dependents were claimed on federal tax returns. In 1988 the number of dependents claimed dropped to 70 million. Fully 10 percent of the dependents claimed—7 million dependents—disappeared. The IRS determined that, in 1987 and probably in previous years, over 60,000 households had claimed four or more dependents who did not exist, and several million more had claimed one or more non-existent dependents (Albrecht, Albrecht, and Albrecht, 2006). Claiming for non-existent dependents is one of the easiest-to-catch income tax frauds. Yet, rationalizations were strong enough to drive millions of citizens to blatantly cheat on their tax returns. When the opportunity was closed by the IRS, the amount of rationalization occurring was evident.

The three elements of the fraud triangle, perceived pressure, perceived opportunity, and rationalization, are useful in understanding why people commit fraud. Organizations should do everything possible to address each part of the triangle. While pressures are often difficult for organizations to affect, much can be done to decrease opportunities and rationalizations. Effective controls are the usual tactic in decreasing opportunities, but other methods exist as well. Rationalizations can be targeted through effective training programs and a clear "tone at the top" in organizations.

Fraud Recruitment

The fraud triangle is useful in understanding how individuals become involved in fraud, but many frauds are often committed in groups. Although most people understand the dishonesty of one or two people, how is it possible that several individuals, even dozens, compromise their ethics and allow fraud to occur? Fraud recruitment research explains some of this group behavior through the concept of power (French and Raven, 1959). Research highlights five types of power an individual may exert over another:

1. *Reward power* is the ability of a fraud perpetrator to convince a potential victim that he or she will receive benefits, such as bonuses, a share of the fraudulent income, or job promotions.
2. *Coercive power* is the ability of a fraud perpetrator to dole out punishment to individuals if they do not agree to participate in frauds.
3. *Expert power* is the ability of a fraud perpetrator to convince others that he or she has expert knowledge. While the deviant behavior may look like fraud, he or she convinces others that it is not.
4. *Legitimate power* is the true or fiat power of a fraud perpetrator. This may be exerted by a manager who might come to a subordinate to ask for a fraudulent entry into the system. The subordinate may simply feel that "I'm just doing my job."
5. *Referent power* is the ability of a fraud perpetrator to relate to others and influence people.

Perpetrators often use some combination of these five types of power to convince others that they should participate in fraudulent activity. Many cases of financial statement fraud involve not only a CEO, but also a recruited CFO and others in the organization.

Fraud Prevention

Fraud may be a costly, difficult problem, but organizations can take proven and effective measures to minimize the chance of being a victim to fraud. While they cannot always be prevented, many frauds can be avoided through proper training, organizational structure, and corporate policies. In fact, preventing fraud is generally the most cost-effective way to reduce losses from fraud.

It is difficult to place an exact value on fraud prevention activities. Although costs associated with investigating and prosecuting a fraud can be calculated, organizations cannot know how many frauds might have been avoided through prevention. However, it is clear from research that organizations which implement fraud prevention measures experience far less fraud than others. Even though a fraud might be insignificant financially, loss of customer trust and adverse public opinion resulting in stock price drops are often the most significant effects. Listed below are six steps that all organizations should take to minimize the risk of fraud. Many of these items could be classified simply as "good business" and have positive effects on organizations as a whole.

1. *"Tone at the top" and sound governance*
   First, create a culture of honesty and high ethics. In today's business world, this is termed as "tone at the top." In other words, it is essential that top management label and model appropriate ethical behavior. Labeling refers to letting individuals within the organizations understand the types of behavior that will and will not be acceptable within the organization. If top management communicates a "no tolerance" policy towards fraudulent behavior within the organization, then individuals who are faced with the temptation of participating in unethical behavior will be less likely to rationalize their dishonest acts. Furthermore, management should communicate exactly what constitutes fraudulent behavior. To the typical manager, this statement may seem extremely basic; however, many employees may not know where to draw the line. For example, is taking office supplies, such as pencils and paper, home considered to be stealing from the organization? Modeling refers to showing employees appropriate ethical behavior. When management is engaged in unethical or fraudulent acts themselves, the likelihood that other members of the organization will participate in similar actions is quite high. It is absolutely critical that expectations be clearly conveyed to all stakeholders of the company.

2. *Hiring, education, and training*
   Make every effort to hire honest employees. Conduct background checks as part of the hiring process. Although there is no perfect way of knowing whether or not an individual will participate in fraudulent behavior, the most basic and sound measure for identifying unethical employees is to conduct thorough background checks. Try to discover whether individuals may have previously participated in fraud or other similar activities. Psychological tools have often been used to assess an individual's level of honesty, but recent research has shown mixed results as to their effectiveness. Investigate potential employees using web searches. Check Facebook and MySpace pages, read through blog posts, and discover any other online presence potential employees might have.

3. Utilize effective employee training programs so that employees know the line between honest and dishonest behavior. Ensure

that management—at all levels—understands the costs and risks of fraud. If appropriate, train vendors, customers, and other interested external parties to work together to root out deception and corruption. Training programs have been shown to have a strong effect on decreasing fraudulent behavior.

4. *Integrity risk and control assessments*
Sponsor meetings in which managers and employees brainstorm potential risks in their respective areas. Have these individuals identify appropriate controls to mitigate the specified risks, and then evaluate whether existing controls are sufficient and appropriate. Constantly review and update risk assessment and control assessment documents and policies.

5. *Reporting and monitoring*
Create an effective whistleblowing system. Fraud is most commonly detected through tips. In one large company, for example, 33 percent of all frauds were detected through tips while auditors detected only 18 percent of the frauds. In another company that experienced more than 1,000 frauds in one year, 42 percent were discovered through tips and complaints from employees and customers. When employees know that colleagues have an easy, non-obligatory way to report suspected fraud, they are more reluctant to become involved in dishonest acts. Effective whistleblowing systems come in many forms and can be as simple as a toll-free telephone number. What is important is that the system provides anonymity for respondents, is independent of the organization, and is easily accessible for employees.

6. *Proactive fraud auditing*
Do not wait for fraud to come to you; instead, proactively seek it. Although whistleblowing lines are still the single most effective tool that organizations can use to prevent and discover fraud, many organizations are now employing data-driven techniques for this purpose. Normally, this involves searching through databases for known patterns of fraud, red flags, and other symptoms.

7. *Rigorous investigation and follow up*
A strong prosecution policy that lets employees know that dishonest acts will be punished and that unauthorized borrowing from the company will not be tolerated is essential in reducing fraud. Even though prosecution is often expensive and time consuming, and even though it stimulates concerns about unfavorable press coverage, failing to prosecute is a cost-efficient strategy only in the

short term. In the long run, avoiding prosecution sends a message to other employees that fraud may be worth the risk because the worst thing that happens to perpetrators is termination.

THE ETHICS DEVELOPMENT MODEL

Ethics research has produced the Ethics Development Model (EDM) (Albrecht, Hil, and Albrecht, 2006), which describes the levels individuals proceed through in the development of personal ethics. The model presents four progressive levels of development. These are depicted in Figure 6.3.

The most basic level of the diagram describes one's personal understanding of ethics. It involves knowing the differences between right and wrong, the sense of fair play, learning to care for and empathize with others, the respect one has for others, and basic principles of integrity and reality. A quote from Karl G. Maeser exemplifies this most basic level of ethics. When asked what was meant by personal honor, he stated, "I will tell you. Place me behind prison walls—walls of stone ever so high, ever so thick, reaching ever so far into the ground—there is the possibility that in some way or another I may escape; but stand me on the floor and draw a chalk line around me and have me give my word of honor never to cross it. Can I get out of the circle? No. Never! I'd die first!" (cited in Burton, 1953). An individual's personal ethical code is applied to all aspects of life, including how he or she works with others, conducts business transactions, rationalizes, and conducts his or her life.

Ethical Leadership

Ethical Courage

Application of Ethics
to Business Situations

Personal Ethical Understanding
Right and Wrong, Fairness, Honesty, Personal Integrity, Respect for Others

Figure 6.3 The Ethics Development Model
Source: Albrecht, Hil, and Albrecht (2006).

The second level of the EDM involves translating one's ethical understanding to professional employment activities. Such translation is not always easy. For example, individuals may have strong ethics in the way in which they treat family and friends, but not understand how closing a plant or how failure to submit tax withholdings to the government affects people's lives or constitutes unethical or fraudulent behavior. Many of the people involved in the financial abuses of the past few years considered themselves to be honest, ethical people. Yet, when faced with decisions about whether to go along with requests to "cook the books" or to reveal observed inappropriate behavior, they made the wrong choices. They did not know how to translate their personal ethical values to business settings. This second level should be a primary target for teaching at business schools.

The third level of the EDM is ethical courage. Ethical courage is the strength and conviction to act appropriately in questionable situations. Someone can have a personal ethical understanding and be able to translate that understanding to business settings, but may not have the courage to take a stand when necessary. Organizations can help develop courage in their employees through training and education, clear policies, and a strong tone at the top.

Ethical leadership is at the highest level of the EDM. It involves providing leadership to others in difficult ethical situations and instilling ethical courage in co-workers. This higher form of ethical behavior requires a person to inspire others through labeling, modeling, persuasion, and good management. In most organizations there is a small group of employees who have well-defined personal codes of conduct and who have learned how to translate those ethical values to business settings. They also have the courage to do what is right. These employees will almost always do the right thing. There is another small group that lacks strong personal codes of conduct. This group will be dishonest anytime it benefits them. The largest group is the "swing group" comprising individuals with situational ethics. This group knows right from wrong, knows how to translate their ethical values to the business world, and at times even has the courage to do what is right. Yet, they may be somewhat unpredictable, and their ethical choices may depend on the pressure they feel and the opportunities presented. Generally, this group will follow their leaders and can be influenced by organizational structure and culture. When there is a strong, positive tone at the top, a strong code of conduct, and strong ethical leadership in the company, this large group will usually make the right decisions. The labeling and modeling of the leaders send powerful messages that keeps employees honest and making the right decisions.

Fraud Detection

Fraud detection includes all the activities of discovering fraud within companies, against individuals, in governments, and in financial statements. This includes a wide variety of methods that are often best planned by those most familiar with the processes of each organization. In its *Report to the Nation* (2008), the Association of Certified Fraud Examiners (ACFE) finds that occupational frauds are most often found by tips and informers. According to the ACFE, the discovery method breakdown is as shown in Figure 6.4.

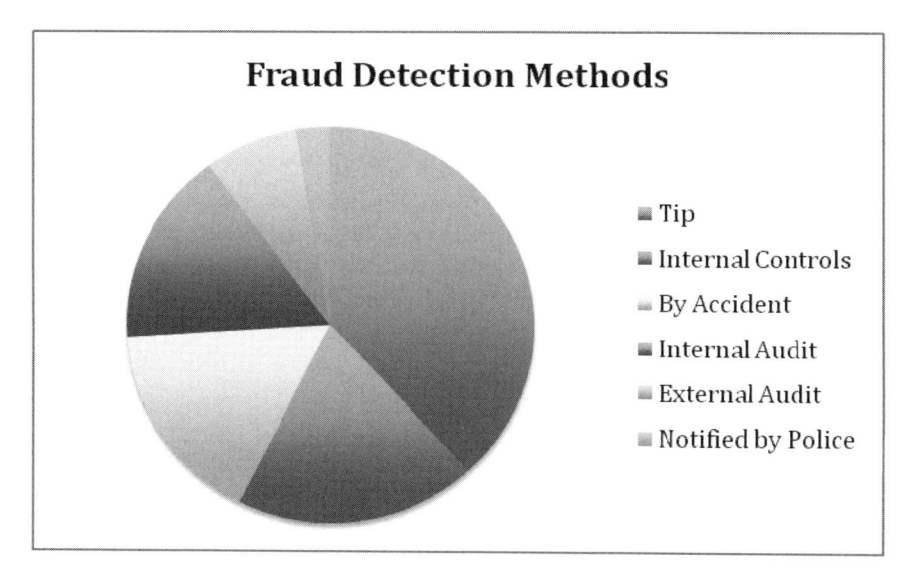

Figure 6.4   Fraud detection method breakdown
Source: AFCE (2008).

Note that tips are the most common fraud detection method by a large margin. This statistic supports the traditional view that anonymous tip lines are one of the most important fraud detection methods. All organizations should have a way for employees and others to report fraud anonymously, whether it is by a web form submission, phone line, or other method. The chart also highlights the need for new, proactive methods of fraud detection. When tips and accidental discovery are combined, the chart shows that over half of occupational frauds are uncovered by factors outside investigator control. With both of these methods, investigators must wait for fraud detection to come to them.

Recently, the use of proactive methods has become more common. These methods generally focus on the discovery of fraud symptoms, and they can be either people- or transaction-focused. When investigators focus on people, they use online information, public records, and other information about those who might commit fraud to look for common indicators. When investigators focus on transactions, they run queries in corporate databases to discover patterns of fraudulent behavior. Regardless of the focus, the foundation of this type of fraud detection is the focus on indicators of fraud. Fraud examiners often call these indicators "red flags."

FRAUD SYMPTOMS

Fraud symptoms, or red flags, are often the first indication of fraud. Unlike traditional crime where investigators often have direct evidence such as discharged firearms, damaged goods, or even direct witnesses, fraud examiners often work with indirect evidence. Fraud is usually committed behind closed doors, and perpetrators make great efforts to hide their actions. Fraud often exists on paper only, and it is hidden within a significant number of transactions. Therefore, fraud examiners often focus on red flags and the side-effects of fraudulent behavior. Red flags can be viewed within the following groupings:

- *Items that should match, but do not.* For example, invoices for purchases that have no receiving reports in a warehouse may be indicative of fraudulent behavior. Travel expenses for restaurants in an area other than the one in which an individual traveled should be investigated.
- *Items that should not match, but do.* The classic example of this type of fraud symptom is a vendor address that matches an employee address. The vendor may be a non-existent firm set up by the employee. Suspicious meetings between individuals in government and lobby groups (who should not normally have a reason to meet) may be indicative of some type of corruption.
- *Outliers and extremes.* Individuals who travel much more than others in their same work group or people with significantly more overtime than others are examples of this type of red flag.
- *Suspicious trends.* This type of red flag can be fairly simple, such as invoice amounts that do not match Benford's distribution of natural numbers, or it can include complex time analysis of purchasing trends of company purchasers paired with individual vendors. Purchasers with significantly different trends may be involved in some type of kickback scheme, especially if prices are rising, quantities purchased are rising, and quality is decreasing.

- *Accounting anomalies* resulting from unusual processes or procedures in the accounting system. Because the perpetrators are manipulating the systems to commit fraud, unusual processes may be followed. This may be as simple as a manager asking a subordinate to process a transaction outside the normal systems and controls.
- *Internal control weaknesses* that allow the fraud to occur. Even within well-defined internal control environments, fraud perpetrators can be very creative in working around the controls.
- *Analytical symptoms* within the financial and non-financial data. These may include unreasonable changes in volume, mix, or price of products. They may also be found through vertical and horizontal analysis of the financial statements across multiple periods.
- *Extravagant lifestyles* that perpetrators often lead. A fraud perpetrator very rarely saves what he or she steals. Because fraud is almost always motivated by a pressure (usually financial), perpetrators spend what they steal, and, within a short time, start to lead extravagant lifestyles. Employees may suddenly start wearing more expensive clothes or jewelry, or drive a car that would seem to be out of their price range.
- *Unusual behavior* by those that are committing fraud. Because of the rationalizations individuals create, they can unexpectedly flip between pleasant and angry behavior, may spend long hours at work, may never take vacations, may become paranoid about those around them, or may exhibit other eccentric behaviors.

As with all fraud symptoms, red flags do not necessarily mean fraudulent behavior. Documents may have been legitimately lost. Lifestyles may have changed because of inherited money. Trends may be different with a given purchaser and vendor because of a special relationship the company has with that vendor.

Red flags should be approached the same way a medical doctor might approach a diagnosis of a patient. Suppose a patient came into a doctor's office with abdominal pain. A negligent doctor might immediately tell the patient that he or she has stomach ulcers. A more experienced doctor would hold off the diagnosis until he or she completed additional scans, asked questions to pinpoint the source, and ruled out common ailments. Similarly, fraud examiners should not obsess about a single red flag. Instead, they should view red flags as a signal for additional observation, testing, and investigation.

DATA-DRIVEN FRAUD DETECTION

It could be argued that tips are the most common type of fraud detection simply because investigators are not effective using other methods, especially in proactive, data-driven methods. The six-step method to data-driven fraud detection is a method of targeting fraud within large datasets, *with no prior predication that fraud might exist*. The steps are described below (Albrecht, Albrecht, and Dunn, 2001).

Step 1: Understand the business The same fraud detection procedures cannot be applied generically to all businesses or even to different units of the same organization. Rather than rely on generic fraud detection methods or generic queries, examiners must gain intimate knowledge of each specific organization and its processes. Having a detailed understanding underlies the entire strategic fraud detection process. Understanding processes in an organization or unit is similar to the activities undertaken when performing business process re-engineering.

The following are several potential methods of gathering information about a business:

- Tour the business, department or plant.
- Become familiar with competitor processes.
- Interview key personnel.
- Analyze financial statements and other information.
- Review process documentation.
- Work with auditors and security personnel.
- Watch employees perform their duties.

Step 2: Identify the possible frauds that could exist Once a fraud examiner is confident about his or her understanding of the business, the next step is to determine what possible frauds might exist or could occur in the operation being examined. This risk assessment step requires an understanding of the nature of different frauds, how they occur, and what symptoms they exhibit. The fraud identification process begins by conceptually dividing the business unit into its individual functions. Most businesses or even sub-units are simply too large and diverse for examiners to consider simultaneously. Dividing the business into its individual functions helps focus the detection process. For example, an examiner might decide to focus directly on the manufacturing plant, the collections department, or the purchasing function.

In this step, people involved in the business functions are interviewed. Fraud examiners should ask such questions as:

- Who are the key players in the business?
- What types of employee, vendor, or contractor are involved in the business transactions?
- How do insiders and outsiders interact with each another?
- What types of fraud have occurred or been suspected in the past?
- What types of fraud could be committed against the company or on behalf of the company?
- How could employees or management acting alone commit fraud?
- How could vendors or customers acting alone commit fraud?
- How could vendors or customers working in collusion with employees commit fraud?

Also during this stage, the fraud detection team should brainstorm potential frauds by type and player. The likely occurrence of the various frauds should be considered, and, in the end, a laundry list of frauds that will be studied should be developed.

Step 3: Catalogue possible fraud symptoms   Fraud itself is never seen; rather, only its symptoms are observed. And what appears to be a fraud symptom often ends up being explained by other, non-fraud factors, creating confusion, delay, and additional expense for the fraud team. For example, a company's accounts receivable balance might be increasing at a rate that appears to be unrealistically high. The increasing receivables balance could be the result of fraud, or it could just be the result of major customers having financial difficulties, or a change in credit terms. In addition there is no empirical evidence that the presence of more suspected red flags increases the probability of fraud (although the more confirmed red flags there are, the higher the probability of fraud), or that certain red flags have greater predictive ability than other red flags.

Even with these weaknesses, identifying red flags or fraud symptoms is the best, and often the only, practical method of proactive fraud detection. All auditing fraud standards recommend the red-flag approach for detecting fraud. Tips usually occur late in the process, after the fraud has grown to the stage at which the tipster overcomes his or her natural reluctance to report it. And for every fraud that is eventually reported, perhaps ten or more are never detected or disclosed.

Note that up to and including this step the strategic or proactive method of fraud detection is purely analytical. The first three steps are generic and can be applied in any type of organization or sub-unit. This strategic approach produces a comprehensive analysis of the specific types of fraud that might be found in various business entities.

Step 4: Use technology to gather data about symptoms   Once symptoms are defined and correlated with specific frauds, supporting data is extracted from corporate databases and other sources. Although the technology expert performs this step, the fraud examiner should have working knowledge of how databases are organized. Such knowledge empowers the fraud examiner to correctly direct the work of the technology expert.

Step 5: Analyze the results   Once the relevant data is retrieved, it should be compared against expectations and models. Since very large datasets—normally composed of thousands of smaller subsets—are often analyzed, computer programs should be written to perform automated analyses. These algorithms examine records and highlight anomalies, unknown values, suggestive trends, or "outliers" that can then be analyzed directly by examiners.

Step 6: Investigate the symptoms   Once anomalies are highlighted and determined by the examiners to be indications of fraud, they are investigated either using traditional or technology-based methods. As computer-based analysis is often the most efficient method of investigation, every effort should be made to screen results using computer algorithms. Investigation of leads should only be done on anomalies that cannot be explained through continued analysis. Examiners normally work with auditors and security personnel to identify reasons for anomalies. They talk with co-workers, investigate paper documents, and contact outside individuals. Often traditional investigation into symptoms provides new insights that allow further refinement of algorithms and queries. Information about one anomaly often clears up other highlighted results. These serve to improve the computer-based methods and provide increasingly meaningful results.

Conclusion

Fraud and corruption have always been problems in societies. There will always be individuals who succumb to significant pressures, recognize tempting opportunities, and rationalize their way through fraudulent actions. Recent developments in technology, the rapidly shrinking world, the convergence of cultures, and the complexity of today's businesses have provided new opportunities for fraudsters. Individuals and organizations must employ a combination of time-tested methods and cutting-edge techniques of protecting against fraud and discovering existing corruption.

In many ways, fraud and corruption hold organizations and even countries back from needed development. Yet, fraud can be both prevented and discovered. Societies, organizations, and individuals must take a strong stand against it, or fraud will continue to eat away vital resources that could be used much more productively. Although perpetrators have new tools and opportunities available to them, fraud examiners also have new tools and methods. The availability of information on the Internet, the computation power of today's computers, the availability of data in companies, and the wealth of training available all play to the examiner's advantage. Now is the time for countries, organizations, and especially individuals to provide the ethical leadership necessary to root out deception at its source.

References

ACFE (2008) *Report to the Nation on Fraud and Occupational Abuse*, Austin, TX: Association of Certified Fraud Examiners.

Albrecht, W. S. (2005a) Author's interview with expert witness on the case. [The name of the company cannot be revealed because of a protective order that is in place.]

Albrecht, W. S. (2005b) "How fraud perpetuates world hunger and prevents economic growth," presentation to the Center for Strategic and International Studies, Senators, and Think Tanks. Washington, DC.

Albrecht, C. C., Albrecht, W. S., and Dunn, J. G. (2001) "Conducting a pro-active fraud audit: A case study," *Journal of Forensic Accounting*, 2, 3–16.

Albrecht, W. S., Albrecht, C. C., and Albrecht, C. O. (2006) *Fraud Examination*, Mason, OH: Thompson Publishing.

Albrecht, W. S., Cherrington, D., Payne, R., Roe, A., and Romney, M. (1981) *How to Detect and Prevent Business Fraud*, Englewood Cliffs, NJ: Prentice-Hall.

Albrecht, W. S., Hil, N. C., and Albrecht, C. C. (2006) "The ethics development model applied to declining ethics in accounting," *Australian Accounting Review*, 38.

Burton, P. A. (1953) *Karl G. Maeser: Mormon Educator*, Salt Lake City, UT: Deseret Book Co.

CERN (2009) "Glossary," at: http://internal-audit.web.cern.ch/internal-audit/method/glossary.html (accessed October 2009).

COSO (2002) *Fraudulent Financial Reporting: 1987–1997 An Analysis of U.S. Public Companies*, at: http://www.coso.org/publications/ffr_1987_1997.pdf (accessed July 2010).

Carson, T. (2004) "Self-interest and business ethics: Some lessons of the recent corporate scandals," *Journal of Business Ethics*, 43, 389–394.

French, J. R. P. and Raven, B. (1959) *The Basis of Social Power*, Ann Arbor, MI: University of Michigan Press.

Festinger, L. (1957) *A Theory of Cognitive Dissonance*, Evanston, IL: Row Peterson.

Raju, B. R. (2009) "Statement to the Board of Directors," *The Hindu Business Times*, January 7, at: http://www.thehindubusinessline.com/businessline/stocks/announcements/satyam_computer_services_ltd_070109.pdf.

Wei, S-J . (2000) "Local corruption and global capital flows," *Brookings Papers on Economic Activity*, 2, 303–355.

SEC (2009) "Ponzi Schemes," at: http://www.sec.gov/answers/ponzi.htm (accessed October 2009).

Wordnet (2009) Definition of "rationalization", at: http://wordnetweb.princeton.edu/perl/webwn (accessed September 2009).

7

A Re-examination of the Withdrawal Syndrome vis-à-vis Organizational Ethics in Schools

Zehava Rosenblatt and Orly Shapira-Lishchinsky

Withdrawal behaviors, namely employees staying on the job but reducing their participation (Kaplan et al., 2009), constitute a major problem for human resource management. In this chapter we focus on three key potential withdrawal symptoms out of the wide array: lateness, absence, and intent to leave. Each of these is related to a different behavioral aspect of work. *Lateness* usually refers to arriving late at work or leaving before the end of the day (Koslowsky, 2000); *absence* is missing work for the entire day (Johns, 2003); and *intent to leave* is an employee's inclination to voluntarily remove him or herself from the organization as a whole (Carmeli, 2005).

Grouped together, these three withdrawal symptoms give rise to the question of whether withdrawal symptoms relate to each other in any systematic way, forming a "syndrome." This question has been asked in several studies (Johns, 2003; Koslowsky, 2000; Koslowsky et al., 1997) in which researchers looked at the internal structure of relationships in the withdrawal syndrome. A leading idea in this line of research is that withdrawal symptoms may be ranked according to some external criterion related to organizational well-being. We follow up this idea using a conceptual framework focused on organizational ethics as a potent criterion of organizational well-being. We will examine whether the above three withdrawal symptoms (lateness, absence, and tendency to leave) are related to organizational ethics, and whether these relationships are consistent with a theoretical conceptualization of the withdrawal syndrome. The theoretical conceptualization tested in this study is the progressive model, which views withdrawal behaviors as manifested in a predetermined sequence (Koslowsky et al., 1997). In other words, we will try to identify a withdrawal model that best describes progressive relationships between the different withdrawal behaviors and organizational ethics.

The importance of studying employees' withdrawal behaviors cannot be overstated. Withdrawing employees with such behaviors are likely directly or indirectly to reduce their effort at work (Kaplan et al., 2009), which will probably lower work productivity and prove detrimental to organizational effectiveness (Shaw, Gupta, and Delery, 2005). Because of the voluntary element in withdrawal symptoms they may represent unethical work behavior, with preferences for self-interest over organizational interests; hence the relevance of examining them through the lens of organizational ethics.

This study examines the pattern of relationships between withdrawal behaviors and organizational ethics in schoolteachers. Schools seem to be an ideal scene for the study of organizational ethics because they constitute ethical environments (Starratt, 1991) and, accordingly, a key mission of schools is to stress the importance of ethical conduct by students and staff. Also, the complex nature of teaching, due to its diversified boundaries of time, place, content and tasks, invites numerous situations in which ethical dilemmas may arise (Van Maanen, 1995). Teachers are often seen as moral agents in the school environment (Delattre and Russell, 1993); they are expected to be role models and educate their students while transmitting individual and social values (Starratt, 1991). This ethical framework is highly relevant to teacher withdrawal behavior in schools.

For the teaching profession, withdrawal behaviors are particularly salient. Studies show repeatedly that withdrawal behaviors often represent reactions to adverse working conditions, and relate to interpersonal relationships, peer relations, support, and school climate (Kwantes, 2003). Teachers who experience sub-optimal working conditions may be expected to develop motivation to withdraw from work in various ways.

This context led to our choice of schools as our study scene, and teachers as our population, in order to probe the relationship between organizational ethics and withdrawal behaviors. We will start with an overview of the withdrawal syndrome and the nature of its relationships to organizational-ethics variables. This will be followed by an illustration of empirical results drawn from three studies on withdrawal symptoms and organizational ethics, in an attempt to test the progressive model. We conclude with an integrative discussion.

Theoretical Background

THE WITHDRAWAL SYNDROME

The withdrawal syndrome describes an array of organizational behaviors whereby employees contribute sub-optimally, or not at all, while still on the organizational payroll (Kaplan et al., 2009; Vardi and Weitz, 2004). A wide range of possible behaviors is included, such as reduced effort at work, lateness, absence, intent to leave, and actual leaving. These behaviors have been referred to as a "syndrome" because they share a key common characteristic: their detrimental yet obscure effect on the organization. We focus now on three withdrawal behaviors: lateness, absence, and intent to leave.

Lateness behavior is described as arriving late at work or leaving before the end of the day (Koslowsky, 2000). In schools, it refers to teachers' lack of punctual arrival at their classes. Theoretically, lateness is classified into three dimensions: chronic, unavoidable, and avoidable. Chronic lateness is often a response to bad working conditions, disliked by the employee. Relevant antecedents to chronic lateness will be, for example, low organizational commitment and low job satisfaction. Avoidable lateness (stable periodic lateness) occurs when employees have better or more important things to do than arrive on time. Leisure-income trade-off and work-family conflict may be frequent antecedents to this type of lateness. Unavoidable lateness is due to factors beyond the employee's control, such as transport problems, bad weather, illness, and accident (Blau, 1995). One of the major reasons for teacher lateness concerns the school's organizational justice (Shapira-Lishchinsky, 2007).

Whatever its causes, lateness is universally considered a dysfunctional behavior, interfering with work rhythm, working norms, and production (Koslowsky, 2000). Showing up late for class requires organizational last-minute solutions to keep students busy. Lessons given by teachers who are consistently late are shorter than normal, and, because these teachers may not have time to cover all the material needed for final exams, students may be left to make it up on their own (Shapira-Lishchinsky, 2007). Teachers who are late often try to make up for lost time by continuing to teach into the break, which detracts from much needed downtime. Lateness, then—particularly a consistent tendency to be late—greatly interferes with schoolwork.

Work absence is "the lack of physical presence at a behavior setting when and where one is expected to be" (Harrison and Price, 2003). Sagie (1998) distinguished two basic types: *voluntary absence*, which is normally under the direct control of the employee and is frequently utilized for personal issues, such as testing the market for alternative prospects of employment; and *involuntary absence*, which is usually beyond the employee's immediate control.

Typical reasons for teachers' work absence include work stress (Myburgh and Poggenpoel, 2002) and principals' restrictive behavior (Gaziel, 2004). Recent reviews of the literature emphasize absence as a variable related not only to individuals' demographic characteristics, but also to organizational environment and social context (Felfe and Schyns, 2004; Martocchio and

Jimeno, 2003). In educational research, teacher absenteeism proved related to a culture consisting of attendance norms (Myburgh and Poggenpoel, 2002) and principals' supportive leadership style (Scott-Norton, 1998). These studies showed that teachers react to undesired social elements in their workplace context by staying away from work. Again, regardless of whether absence results from voluntary or involuntary triggers, it may be detrimental to organizational effectiveness because it implies production loss. Teacher absence reduces student motivation to attend school and thus may increase the students' own absenteeism (Imants and Van Zoelen, 1995). More directly, studies (Miller, Murnane, and Willett, 2008; Woods, and Montagno, 1997) show that interruptions in the daily continuity of students' instruction tend to lower their achievements. Financially, teacher absence can easily translate into direct extra costs to school management. Rosenblatt and Shirom (2003) estimated net annual expenditure on substitute teachers at public-sector elementary and middle schools in Israel at US$14,285,714 (for a teacher population of about 60,000).

Intent to leave work, often considered a potent predictor of voluntary turnover (Carmeli, 2005; Lambert and Hogan, 2009), is a key concern for management interested in securing and maintaining a qualified workforce in schools (Smylie and Miretzky, 2004). Teachers who intend to leave their school are likely to reduce their efforts at work. A typical reason for intent to leave is pay level, particularly one's perception of being underpaid. For teachers, whose starting salaries often fall below those of other professionals in business and industry (Grissmer and Kirby, 1997), low salary is a significant predictor of withdrawal behaviors (see, e.g., Liu and Meyer, 2005). Other frequent reasons for teachers' voluntary turnover include classroom relations and working conditions (Ingersoll, 2001).

Intent to leave may have negative pedagogical implications. First, the literature shows that intent to leave strongly predicts actual leaving (Ladebo, 2005). Often, teachers who consider leaving are the more qualified ones, which jeopardizes schools' teaching standards (Ingersoll, 2001). Second, because teacher quality depends, among other things, on experience, intent to leave, followed by actual leaving, can damage school reputation and faculty cohesion, and hence school effectiveness (Ingersoll, 2004). Like other employees, teachers with intent to leave are likely to reduce their effort at work (Maertz and Campion, 1998), which in turn lowers their productivity and may affect their colleagues' motivation and efforts (Albion et al., 2008).

Research on the withdrawal syndrome as a whole has been mainly concerned with the internal relationships among the behaviors constituting it (Johns, 2003; Koslowsky et al., 1997). The underlying assumption behind this concern is that withdrawal behaviors are not merely a collection of random behaviors but constitute a behavioral "syndrome," with consistent links among them. Of the various models describing the internal relationships among withdrawal behaviors, the progressive model has received the most attention. This model posits that withdrawal manifestations occur in sequence, starting with relatively mild forms, then moving to more severe symptoms, and ending with most severe manifestations such as intent to leave and turnover (Koslowsky et al., 1997).

This progression may be triggered by organizational events and circumstances that employees perceive as harming their well-being or quality of working life. Such events and circumstances (a cut in benefits, loss of managerial support, sour relationships with colleagues) may lead to reactions that start with mild behavior such as occasional late arrival at work, then escalate to full-day absences and advance to intent to leave, and actual quitting. We will describe how this progressive sequence may be initiated by organizational ethics.

ORGANIZATIONAL ETHICS

Three organization-ethics notions are investigated in the present study: ethical climate, organizational justice, and tendency to misbehave. These were selected because of pervasive research interest in them in recent years, and because each represents a different aspect of organizational ethics.

Ethical climate means organizational norms of behavior and decisions that bear ethical content, as perceived by employees (Victor and Cullen, 1988). In schools, ethical climate may have a significant influence on the manner in which teachers behave and may influence the students' ethical environment (Robinson and Bennett, 1995).

Victor and Cullen (1988) proposed a two-dimensional model of ethical climate. One dimension represents three basic ethical approaches: egoism (maximizing self-interest), benevolence (maximizing joint interests), and principle (adherence to ethical principles). The second dimension represents levels of analysis: individual, local, and cosmopolitan. Numerous studies have tested these authors' original theory (e.g., Appelbaum, Deguire, and Lay, 2005; Kelly and Dorsch, 1991; Peterson, 2002; Upchurch and Ruhland, 1996; Vardi, 2001; Wimbush and Shepard, 1994) and the ethical factors that follow from their model. In a study conducted in Israel, Rosenblatt and Peled (2002) identified two factors that emerged as the most powerful and valid predictors of school outcomes: "caring" and "formal." Because of their relevance to the Israeli educational system, the site of the present study, we adopt Rosenblatt's and Peled's (2002) constructs in our study.

A caring climate is characterized by employees' genuine interest in each other's welfare inside and outside the organization. At work, a caring climate reflects concern for all organizational stakeholders. A formal climate emphasizes organizational rules and professional codes, and encourages respect for them. In such a climate employees are expected to follow the organization's rules and to adhere to their profession's codes and regulations. Because a formal ethical climate is based on fair resource distribution and transparent procedures, it is perceived as protecting employees from abusive treatment by management and others. Both types of ethical climate—in particular, the way in which it is perceived by employees—may predict employees' behavior on the job (Peterson, 2002).

Organizational justice is another concept of organizational ethics used to describe equity in the workplace (Greenberg, 1995). It taps into how employees' perceptions of equity are determined, and how these perceptions influence organizational outcomes. Organizational justice research has focused on two key dimensions: first, distributive justice, which refers to the fairness of the outcomes an employee receives (Adams, 1965); and, second, procedural justice, which describes the fairness of the procedures used to determine organizational outcomes (Pillai, Williams, and Tan, 2001). Employees will perceive work procedures as fair if they feel they have control over the process of implementing and administering organizational decisions pertaining to them. Whether the focus is on distributive or procedural justice, studies show that employees expect fairness in the workplace (Greenberg, 1995), and their perceptions of such fairness affect their work attitudes and behaviors; accordingly, perceptions of organizational justice have a predictive role regarding employees' outcomes at work.

The third aspect of organizational ethics is *tendency to misbehave*, which represents employees' perceptions of acceptability of engaging in misbehaviors at work (e.g., deliberate lateness, voluntary absence). Misbehavior is defined as a voluntary act of violating organizational norms, core societal values and standards of proper conduct (Vardi and Wiener, 1996). As such, misbehavior may also be measured in terms of employee perception, namely the degree to which employees view their workplace as characterized by work misbehavior. In organizational behavior literature, misbehavior is closely related to concepts such as "workplace deviance" (Diefendorff and Mehta, 2007) and "counterproductive behavior" (Miles et al., 2002). Largely, organizational misbehavior embraces a wide range of work-related types of misconduct that are presumably perpetrated by organization members.

THE ETHICAL ELEMENT IN WITHDRAWAL BEHAVIORS

One of the common characteristics of the withdrawal symptoms discussed in the present study is that they are largely under the employee's control. In many cases, even when external circumstances lead employees to consider arriving late for work (e.g., a child's illness), being absent (e.g., personal errands) or leaving the organization (e.g., a spouse's move), proper time management could reduce the occurrence of these withdrawal behaviors or their harmful effect (Blau, 1994). Because it is frequently up to the employee to withdraw or not, the organizational-ethics perspective has a key role in explaining decisions to withdraw from work. Next, we discuss the ethical element in the three withdrawal symptoms, using schoolteachers as a case in point.

Employee lateness, absence, and intent to leave adversely affect students, who are entitled to the full value of every teaching hour (Shapira-Lishchinsky, 2007; Shapira-Lishchinsky and Rosenblatt, 2009, 2010). Lost time in the case of lateness is often not paid back. In the case of teacher absence, time loss is made up by substitutes, who are normally not entirely suitable to cover for the absent teachers. As regards intent to leave, teachers who entertain thoughts of leaving, although present on the job, are very likely to invest less effort in their work because of diminished motivation or time needed to search for an alternative job. These withdrawal behaviors are likely to adversely affect student achievements (Rosenblatt, Shapira-Lishchinsky, and Shirom, 2010). Thus students' interests are compromised due to the personal interests of the withdrawing teachers.

Latecomers and absent teachers negatively affect their colleagues' well-being, too. Teachers who do arrive on time are required to supervise the latecomers' classes to prevent them from disturbing other classes, adding to their normal workload. Often, teachers who are present at school are asked to fill in for a missing teacher. From colleagues' perspective, lateness and absence may therefore represent social-loafing behavior (Comer, 1995) and potentially disturb the equilibrium between the inputs and outputs of school faculty (Adams, 1965). The two withdrawal behaviors also burden school management which needs to find administrative solutions for late and absent teachers, drawing from limited school resources and administrative time. Lateness and absence also adversely affect school norms regarding presence behaviors. These norms normally protect the quality of working life for most employees, and establish law and order in the workplace. Late and absent teachers may introduce negative norms, which sow chaos and resentment among school personnel.

Unlike lateness and absence, intent to leave and actual voluntary leaving are perfectly legitimate behaviors. However, according to social exchange theory (Montes and Zweig, 2009) they may involve certain unethical behaviors. Social exchange theory proposes that the parties in any given relationship seek balance and fairness in it. This theory has served as the foundation of the notion of psychological contract, where both organization and individual offer inputs and expect outcomes from each other (Robinson and Rousseau, 1994; Rousseau, 1995). The organization expects that, in exchange for a decent salary, acceptable working conditions and generous organizational benefits, employees will display loyalty and dependability. So intent to leave, when not triggered by adverse managerial treatment, may be viewed as a breach of the psychological contract on the employee's part, and hence as an unethical behavioral intention.

In sum, while withdrawal behaviors may be motivated by various personal and work-related reasons, they all share elements of unethical behavior at work. The next question is: what might explain the presumed link between withdrawal behaviors and organizational ethics? On the basis of widespread literature on organizational behavior, where organizational commitment emerges as a powerful explicator of employees' work behaviors (Cohen, 2003), we suggest that organizational commitment may best explain the relationship of withdrawal behaviors and organization ethics, thus constituting a mediating variable.

ORGANIZATIONAL COMMITMENT AS A MEDIATOR BETWEEN WITHDRAWAL BEHAVIORS AND ORGANIZATIONAL ETHICS

Meyer and Allen (1997) identified three types of organizational commitment: affective, normative, and continuous. *Affective commitment* refers to employees' emotional attachment to the organization, and their identification and involvement with it. *Normative commitment* reflects a sense of obligation to continue working for the organization. *Continuous commitment* refers to people's external reasons for staying with the organization, such as the cost associated with leaving it.

The general consensus is that organizational commitment is strongly related to work outcomes and job performance (Kwantes, 2003; Luchak and Gellatly, 2007; Meyer et al., 2002). Nevertheless, the relationship between organizational commitment and work outcomes may not be universal for all types of commitment. Studies have demonstrated that affective and normative commitment positively affect work outcomes, including withdrawal behaviors, whereas continuous commitment show little or negligible relationships of this type (Luchak and Gallatly, 2007; Mathieu and Zajac; 1990 Meyer et al., 2002). These conclusions were reiterated by Cohen (2003), who pointed out that in organizational behavior literature affective and normative commitment are more dominant than continuous commitment. On the basis of these arguments we chose to investigate only affective and normative commitment as potential mediators in our study model.

The relationship between organizational commitment and withdrawal behaviors may very well be explained by social exchange theory, mentioned earlier. Employees who perceive their organization as treating them well will reciprocally increase their positive perceptions of it. Conversely, employees who feel they have been mistreated by the organization are likely to intensify their negative perceptions (Kickul, 2001) and may seek ways to retrieve the benefits they feel entitled to, in order to protect themselves from future mistreatment (Turnley et al., 2004).

Consistent with this theory, we argue that organizational ethics is one of the organizational inputs into the social exchange to which teachers react. Organizational ethics reflects values that guide teachers' behavior (Schein, 1990). When employees do not feel at ease with organizationally endorsed values they reciprocate by lowering their level of commitment, which in turn generates unfavorable work attitudes and behaviors such as tendencies to be late to work, frequent absences, and leaving (Kwantes, 2003; Lo and Aryee, 2003). Organizational commitment acts as a partial mediator in the relationships between perceived organizational ethics and withdrawal behaviors.

Empirical Test of the Progressive Model: Predicting Withdrawal Behaviors by Organizational Ethics, Mediated by Organizational Commitment

The study's theoretical model posits that the three withdrawal behaviors investigated will be negatively related to organizational ethics, as conceptualized by ethical climate (caring and formal), organizational justice (distributive, procedural) and tendency to misbehave. These relationships will be mediated by organizational commitment. The strength of these relationships will be determined by the degree of severity of the withdrawal symptoms for organizational well-being. Intent to leave, which is relatively more harmful to the organization than the other two symptoms, will be most strongly related to organizational ethics. Lateness, which is relatively the least severe symptom, will be least strongly related to organizational ethics, and work absence will be in-between. Because of the exploratory nature of these arguments, no formal hypotheses are advanced. We test our theoretical model through a research program comprising a series of empirical studies we conducted in an Israeli school system.

POPULATION AND SAMPLE

The study population consisted of teachers in the largest private high-school network in Israel (over 50 schools). Participants were 1,016 teachers (response rate of 67.7 percent) from 35 schools. The average number of teachers at each school was 54.74 (SD = 25.54). Teachers filled out questionnaires related to their lateness in the previous month and absences in the previous five months, their tendency to leave work, their organizational commitment, and their background characteristics.

The sample consisted of 68 percent women. Participants' average age was 43.19 years (SD = 9.42). Average school tenure was 12.6 years (SD = 8.48) and average job tenure was 17.9 years (SD = 9.39); 86.1 percent of the teachers had tenure and the others were engaged through temporary contracts. The majority of teachers (53.7 percent) had a Bachelor's degree and 35.7 percent had a Master's degree; the rest had technical, rather than academic, degrees. These background characteristics are typical of Israeli high-school teachers (Shapira-Lishchinsky, 2009), indicating that respondents closely represented the Israeli teacher population.

VARIABLES AND MEASURES

Lateness Lateness was measured by a single item measuring the number of times a given teacher arrived six or more minutes after the bell rang in the course of the previous 30 days. It was adapted from Blau (1994) and Neal et al. (1993). The choice of a 30-day period to report lateness was based on a pilot study in which teachers were asked about a reasonable timespan in which lateness could be remembered. The rationale for defining lateness as six minutes or more draws on previous studies showing that this timespan is normatively unacceptable in various organizations, including schools.

Work absence Teachers were asked how many work-days they had missed in each of the previous five months, and to report each occasion separately. We attached calendars to all the questionnaires to refresh respondents' memories.

The measure used was absence frequency (not duration)—that is, the number of times a teacher was absent during the reported period, regardless of the number of days lost. It is generally believed that absence frequency is the best measure of voluntary absence, whereas absence duration (total number of days lost) is the best reflection of involuntary absences. Studies show that an absence of 1-2 days is considered voluntary, whereas an extended period of days of absence is considered involuntary regardless of the reason given for the absence (Blau, Tatum, and Ward-Cook, 2004; Gellatly, 1995; Sagie, 1998).

We chose absence frequency as our dependent variable because our purpose was to investigate the relationship between ethical perceptions and absenteeism in the context of the teachers' social exchange, which reflects their choice to attend or not to attend (voluntary absence).

A five-month timespan was chosen so as to produce a valid picture of teacher absence, because it represents half a school year in Israel (one semester), and because it is reasonable to expect teachers to be able to recall their absences during this period (Johns, 1994).

Intent to leave This measure tapped into teachers' tendency to leave their work. It was adopted from Walsh, Ashford, and Hill (1985). Rosenblatt and Inbal (1999), who used this scale in studies of Israeli teachers, reported a reliability rate of a = .90.

Ethical climate This variable elicited teachers' perceptions of what is ethically correct behavior and how ethical issues should be handled. We used Victor's and Cullen's (1988) original 27-item ethical climate scale, translated into Hebrew by Rosenblatt and Peled (2002). Because our model called for only two dimensions (caring and formal), we performed a factor analysis (principal components, Varimax rotation) of the Hebrew version of the scale. Our analysis yielded six factors, the first two of which corresponded to the two dimensions selected a priori for the study. These factors were: (a) "caring" climate, defined as a climate of concern for the welfare of all school members (corresponding to the "friendship" and "social responsibility" dimensions of the original index; 15.87 percent explained variance); and (b) "formal" climate, defined as a climate of compliance with both professional and social codes and the school's rules and regulations (corresponding to both "rules and procedures", "law and order" and "efficiency" dimensions of the original index; 15.68 percent explained variance). All the other factors proved negligible (6.85–9.61 percent explained variance).

Organizational justice This 21-item measure was based on Moorman (1991) and was translated into Hebrew by Rosenblatt and Hijazi (2004). A factor analysis (principal components, Varimax rotation) yielded three factors, of which the first two, representing the dominant types of justice (distributive and procedural), were selected for the present study. Distributive justice assessed the fairness of various school outcomes, including pay level, work schedule, and workload (20.33 percent explained variance). Procedural justice assessed the degree to which job decisions included mechanisms that ensured the acquisition of accurate and unbiased information, a voice for teachers in school matters, and an appeal process (37.08 percent explained variance).

Tendency to misbehave The measure containing behavioral descriptions was derived from previous work by Robinson and Bennett (1995), Fimbel and Burstein (1990), and Vardi (2001). Teachers were asked to rate their endorsement of a wide range of work-related types of misconduct, such as lateness without permission or absence without true justification. To minimize the potential "social desirability" bias, teachers were not asked whether they themselves tended to misbehave, but whether they were willing to accept misconduct of others (Vardi, 2001). Respondents were asked to indicate whether certain behaviors in their school were acceptable to them.

Organizational commitment Two of Meyer's and Allen's (1997) original measures were adopted. Affective commitment addressed teachers' perceptions of the reasons for wanting to remain at their school. Normative commitment addressed teachers' perceptions of the reasons why they ought to remain in their school.

Control variables We used a set of control background variables that were likely to be related to withdrawal behaviors (Rosenblatt and Shirom, 2005, 2006). These include personal variables such as gender (0 = men, 1 = women), seniority (1 to 44 years, SD = 8.48), holding an administrative position, and age. Background organizational variables included school size and school policy (regarding lateness and absence).

DATA ANALYSIS

Multi-level analysis The study's analysis is on the individual level, aiming to capture teachers' perceptions and subjective experiences regarding their intent to leave and school ethics. However, the data's hierarchical nature (teachers nested within schools) made the usual assumption of independence of all observations inapplicable. We applied the SAS mixed-model procedure. All variables entered into the model were on the individual level, and the group (school) level was included in the model as a random effect. Consistent with Chan's (1998) direct consensus model, we assumed that the import of the higher-level construct (schools) lay in the consensus of the lower-level units (individuals).

Mediation analysis The aim of the mediation analysis was to test whether the relationship between organizational ethics and withdrawal behaviors was partly due to a mediation effect of organizational commitment. To test this hypothesis we adopted Kenny's, Kashy's, and Bolger's (1998) causal step approach, which is one of the most commonly used procedures to test mediation effect (MacKinnon, Lockwood, and Williams, 2004).

RESULTS

We employed a general optimal prediction model, based on the mixed-model procedure. For each withdrawal variable we entered all relevant organizational ethics variables, as well as the relevant control variables. The results, reflecting the optimal prediction model for each withdrawal variable, using stepwise regression and backward deletion procedures, are presented next.

Lateness and organizational ethics Lateness was significantly related to one indicator of organizational ethics, namely distributive justice. No mediation effect was found, although organizational affective commitment was found to moderate—not mediate—the relationship between lateness and distributive justice. All five levels of affective commitment (1 through 5) were used in the analysis. Findings (see Figure 7.1) showed that, with a high level of affective commitment, the relationship between distributive justice and lateness was negative. With moderate levels of affective commitment, change in the relationship was negligible. With a low level of affective commitment, a significant positive relationship existed between distributive justice and lateness. In other words, only with high levels of affective organizational commitment is the perception of distributive justice in school negatively related to teachers' low tendency to be late. With low levels of affective organizational commitment this relationship is unexpectedly reversed (more details are given in Shapira-Lishchinsky, 2007). These findings support the study's argument for a presumed relationship between lateness and organizational ethics only for highly committed teachers.

Work absence and organizational ethics The only ethics variable related to absence and mediated by commitment (affective) was formal ethical climate (more details appear in Shapira-Lishchinsky and Rosenblatt, 2010). Figure 7.2 summarizes results pertaining to work absence.

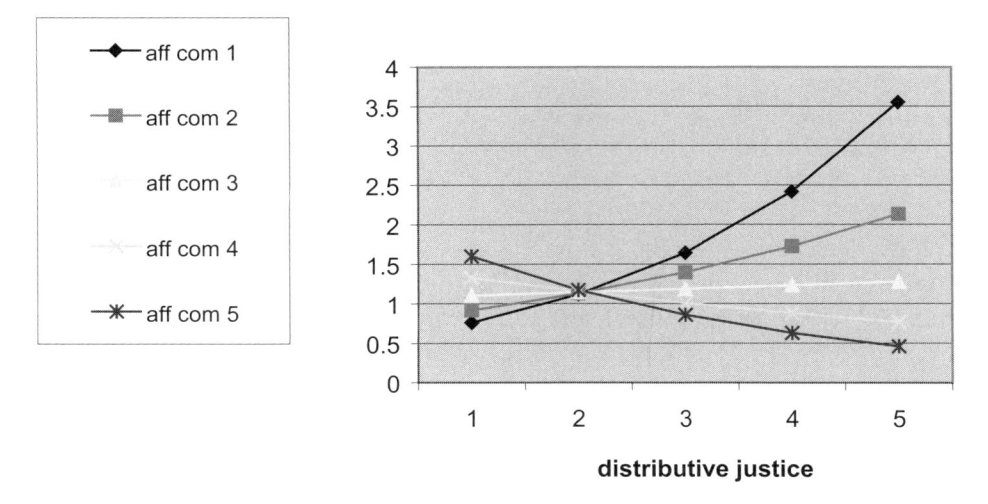

Figure 7.1 The interaction effect of distributive justice and affective commitment on lateness

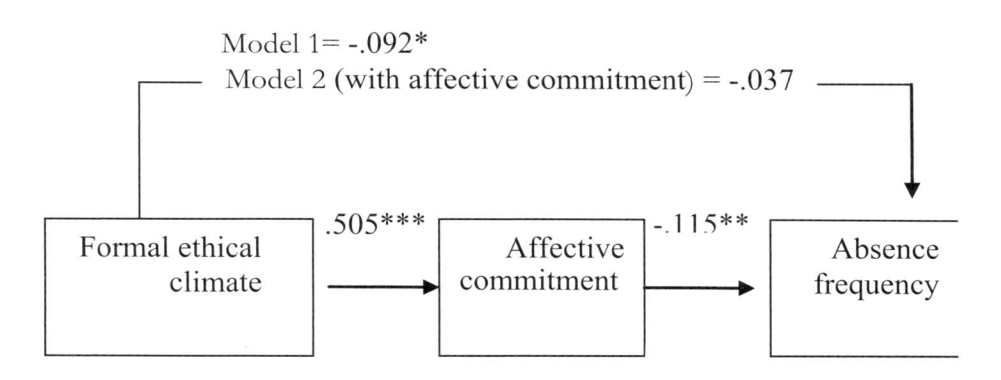

Figure 7.2 Summary of coefficient modeling results of the relationship between teachers' perceptions of formal ethical climate and absence frequency, mediated by affective commitment

$N = 1.016$; * $p<0.05$; ** $p<0.01$; *** $p<0.001$ (GENMOD procedure)
Source: Shapira-Lishchinsky and Rosenblatt (2010).

Intent to leave and organizational ethics Intent to leave was significantly related to all three variables of organizational ethics. The relation to caring (but not formal) ethical climate was fully mediated by affective and normative commitment; the relation to procedural (but not distributive) justice was partially mediated by affective and procedural justice; the relation to tendency to misbehave was partially mediated by affective (but not normative) commitment (see more details in Shapira-Lishchinsky and Rosenblatt, 2009). These results are summarized in Figure 7.3.

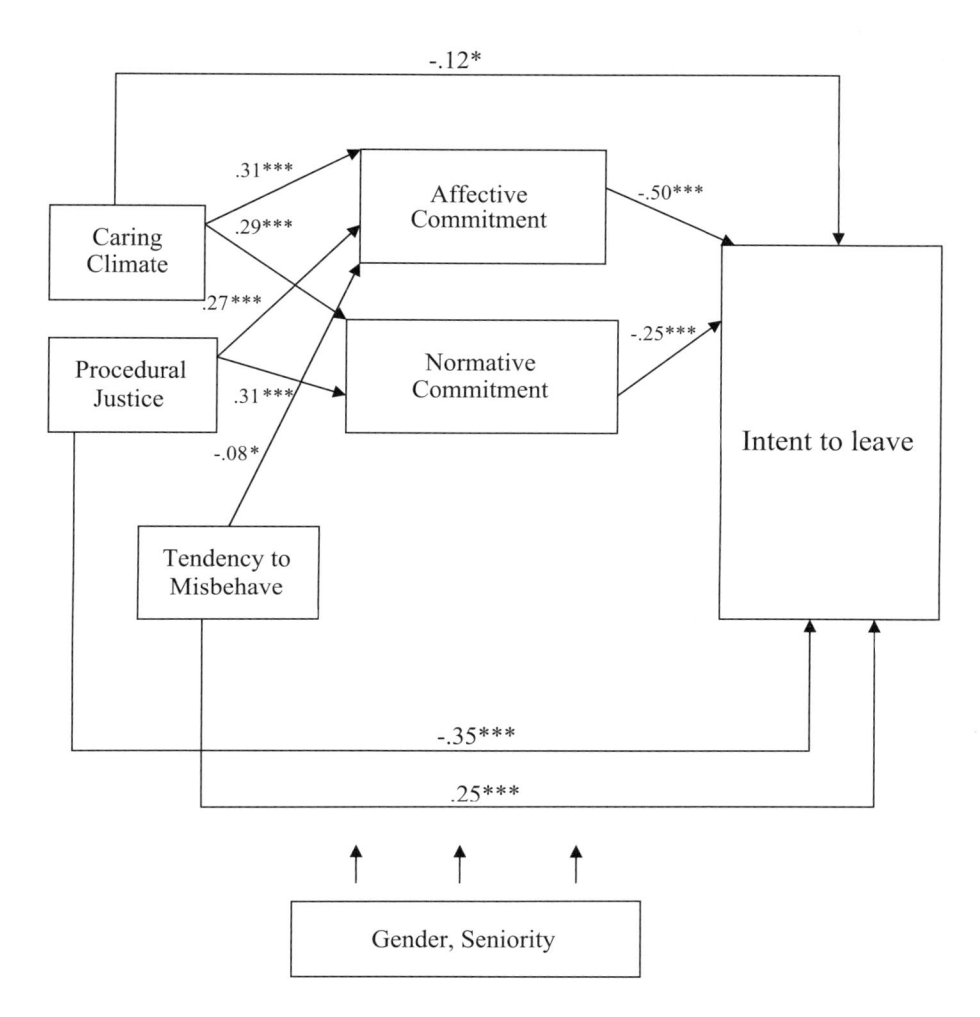

Figure 7.3 **Summary of the results of the relationship of ethical variables with intent to leave, mediated by affective and normative commitment**

Note: The figure is based on several analyses
N = 1,016; * $p<0.05$; ** $p<0.01$; *** $p<0.001$ (the mixed procedure)
Source: Shapira-Lishchinsky and Rosenblatt (2009).

Discussion

The purpose of the study was to investigate the relationship of teachers' withdrawal syndrome and organizational ethics, and explain it through organizational commitment. In particular, we explored the progressive nature of the relationship. To this end we considered simultaneously three withdrawal behaviors (lateness, absence, and intent to leave) and three organizational ethics indicators (ethical climate-caring and formal, organizational justice-distributive and procedural, and tendency to misbehave). Each withdrawal behavior addressed in this study was found to be related to at least one indicator of organizational ethics. Organizational commitment proved a factor that helps explain these relationships, either as a mediator (in regard to absence and intent to leave) or as a moderator (in regard to lateness).

Although researchers tend to group withdrawal behaviors as an overall syndrome, our findings show that each retains its unique characteristics, as attested by each withdrawal symptom being related to a different indicator (or set of indicators) of organizational ethics. Judging by these findings, the withdrawal behaviors explored in this study were relatively independent in regard to their relationship with organizational ethics, as described next.

Lateness was related to distributive justice, and only for highly-committed teachers. When highly- committed teachers feel that their school administration does not distribute awards fairly, they possibly try to re-establish justice by "stealing" working time for personal purposes. Alternatively, highly committed teachers who tend to be late for any reason may develop the perception that their behavior is legitimate, given the unjust distribution of organizational outcomes. Because lateness is often not recorded, and disciplinary procedures for it are rare, it is easier to adopt lateness than any other withdrawal behavior to redress the perceived inequity.

For low-committed teachers the above relationship between lateness and distributive justice was reversed. This finding is puzzling. Apparently, teachers who were not affectively committed to their schools, and perceived their schools as allocating outcomes in a just way, tended to be late for work. It is possible that those low-committed teachers did not view school distributive justice as relevant to them (believing that the low commitment was mutual: the school was equally not committed to them), and that distributive justice was only relevant to teachers other than themselves, or to students. So they reciprocated (to distributive justice targeted toward others) by allowing themselves to be late. This speculative interpretation needs to be tested directly in future studies.

Work absence was related to formal justice, mediated by affective commitment. This relationship may be explained in the setting of organizational administrative policy. Of all withdrawal behaviors, work absence is the most regulated and monitored by both organizational policy and, when relevant, union rules (Imants and Van Zoelen, 1995; Rosenblatt, Shapira-Lishchinsky, and Shirom, 2010). Therefore, teachers in this study may have associated their absence behavior to formal ethical climate more than to any other ethical manifestations. When teachers perceived their work climate as characterized by clear rules, they became more affectively committed to their schools, and their commitment led to their tendency to refrain from being absent. This relation may also work in reverse: a tendency to be absent from work triggers low organization affective commitment, which in turn leads to a tendency to view formal work rules as unethical.

Intent to leave was related to all three ethical variables (the caring dimension of ethical climate, the procedural dimension of organizational justice, and tendency to misbehave). In contrast to both lateness and absence, which reflect actual work behaviors, intent to leave represents an inner psychological state where teachers experience behavioral intentions directed to their workplace. Earlier we mentioned Rousseau's (1995) psychological contract as a theoretical framework, explaining the relationship of organizational characteristics and employee behaviors. On this basis it is conceivable that intent to leave, which represents intention to misbehave, will be more firmly related to *perceived* inputs by the organization (ethics) than to lateness and absence, which represent actual behaviors. It is noteworthy that the ethical dimensions associated with intent to leave (caring climate, procedural justice) are all characterized by a greater focus on the *process* aspect of organizational ethics than on its formal aspect (distributive justice and formal ethical climate).

Despite the clear differences between the withdrawal symptoms investigated in this study, as evinced by the findings, closer examination of the results pertaining to the three study analyses shows a consistent pattern of relationships between them and organizational ethics. The most severe withdrawal behavior from the organizational standpoint—intent to leave—was most strongly related to organizational ethics (three predictors: caring ethical climate, procedural justice and tendency to misbehave), explained by both affective and normative commitment. The next most severe behavior, absence, was related to formal climate through one dimension of organizational commitment (affective); the least severe behavior, lateness, was only related to one ethical concept—distributive justice, mediated by affective commitment. These results may lend some support to the *progressive* model, showing that the relationships of withdrawal behaviors to organizational ethics may grow stronger as the withdrawal behavior becomes more severe.

Also, as reflected in the findings, the level on which organizational commitment explains the relationship between withdrawal behaviors and organizational ethics seems also to rise as the withdrawal behavior becomes more severe: the least severe behavior (lateness) is most weakly explained by organizational commitment (only in the case of highly-committed teachers), while the most severe behavior (intent to leave) is most strongly explained by organizational commitment (both affective and normative commitment explain the relationships between intent to leave and two ethical indicators—procedural justice and tendency to misbehave—and affective commitment explains the relationship to caring climate).

While these interpretations are highly speculative, they call for further investigation into the internal structure of the three withdrawal behaviors vis-à-vis organizational ethics. We also recommend that more rigorous methods be introduced to examine the progressive model vis-à-vis other theoretical structures of the withdrawal syndrome. For example, the *spillover* model posits that individuals are likely to react to certain antecedents with a set of withdrawal behaviors rather than with just one (Beehr and Gupta, 1978; Koslowsky et al., 1997). On the other hand, *compensatory forms* postulates that when a certain withdrawal behavior cannot be executed, another will kick in (Nicholson and Goodge, 1976). A test of these models will necessitate a qualitative study in which teachers report on their specific motives and constraints. Also, other organizational antecedents of withdrawal behaviors should be added, so that the results pertaining to the influence of organizational ethics will be viewed in proportion.

THEORETICAL IMPLICATIONS

The present study makes three theoretical contributions. The first is some support for the progressive model in its relationship with organizational ethics. The second is the focus on the role of organizational commitment as a consistent link explaining the relationship of various ethics perceptions to teachers' withdrawal behaviors. The consistent explanatory role of organizational commitment strengthens the study model beyond mere correlation. Third, the study shapes our understanding of individual-level predictors of teachers' withdrawal behaviors, while also considering school potential effects (e.g., collective ethical norms).

PRACTICAL IMPLICATIONS FOR SCHOOL LEADERS

Practically, the results imply that school leadership policies aiming at maintaining teachers' work presence and loyalty should focus on organizational ethics. In particular, schools should promote high standards of caring and formal climate, as well as distributive and procedural justice, and reduce tolerance of organizational misbehavior. Educational leaders should understand their ethical and moral obligation to create and promote ethics-oriented schools, and should be particularly aware of possible inequities in their schools' operations (Scheurich and Skrla, 2003; Skrla et al., 2004). Such awareness may be achieved through leaders' and teachers' workshops. These may help educational leaders develop their sensitivity to issues of need and fairness, and act more ethically and effectively. Although the importance of this emphasis is independent of any organizational gains, our results point to the significant link between a higher level of ethics and a lower level of teachers' withdrawal behavior.

LIMITATIONS AND FUTURE RESEARCH

The self-reported study instrument was vulnerable to a same-source bias. Also, with self-reports the results may be influenced by "social desirability" responses, endangering the "truth" of the findings. There was likewise a risk of compromising validity and of inaccuracy due to memory decrement and systematic bias (Blau et al., 2005; Nicholson and Payne, 1987) in the questions regarding lateness and absence. We recommend that future studies apply a social desirability measure, or some other guard against self-report bias. Another limitation concerns the generalizability of the results. The sample was limited to teachers at high schools in Israel, and this might have affected external validity. However, as our main results proved consistent with those of other studies on school ethics and withdrawal behaviors (Ingersoll, 2001, 2004; Rosenblatt and Peled, 2002; Koslowsky, 2000), they may reasonably be expected to apply to other organizations in Israel and elsewhere. Finally, we recommend that the results pertaining to the progressive nature of the relationship of withdrawal behaviors and organizational ethics be more rigorously investigated in future studies; statistical methods that simultaneously examine relationship of various withdrawal symptoms to the same organizational outcomes may be used.

References

Adams, J. S. (1965) "Inequity in social exchange" in L. Berkowitz (ed.) *Advances in Experimental Social Psychology*, Vol. 2, New York: Academic Press, pp. 267–299.

Albion, J. A., Fogarty, G. J., Machin, M. A., and Patrick, J. (2008) "Predicting absenteeism and turnover intentions in the health professions," *Australian Health Review*, 32(2), 271–281.

Appelbaum, S. H. Deguire K. J., and Lay, M. (2005) "The relationship of ethical climate to deviant workplace behaviour," *Corporate Governance*, 5(4), 43–55.

Beehr, T. A. and Gupta, N. (1978) "A note on the structure of employee withdrawal," *Organizational Behavior and Human Performance*, 21, 73–79.

Blau, G. (1994) "Developing and testing a taxonomy of lateness," *Journal of Applied Psychology*, 79, 959–970.

Blau, G. (1995) "Influence of group lateness on individual lateness: A cross-level examination," *Academy of Management Journal*, 38, 1483–1496.

Blau, G, Tatum, D. S., and Ward-Cook, K. W. (2004) "Comparing correlates for different types of absence versus lateness behaviors," *Journal of Allied Health*, 33(4), 238–246.

Blau, G., Tatum, D. S., Ward-Cook, K., Doberia, L., and McCoy, K. (2005) "Testing for time based correlates of perceived gender discrimination," *Journal of Allied Health*, 34(3), 130–137.

Carmeli, A. (2005) "The relationship between organizational culture and withdrawal intentions and behavior," *International Journal of Manpower*, 26(2), 177–195.

Chan, D. (1998) "Functional relationships among constructs in the same content domain at different levels of analysis: A typology of composition models," *Journal of Applied Psychology*, 83, 234–246.

Cohen, A. (2003) *Multiple Commitments in the Workplace: An Integrative Approach*, London: Erlbaum.

Comer, D. R. (1995) "A model of social loafing in real work groups," *Human Relations*, 4(86), 647–667.

Delattre, E. and Russell, W. (1993) "Schooling, moral principles, and the formation of character," *Journal of Education*, 175(2), 23–43.

Diefendorff, J. M. and Mehta, K. (2007) "The relations of motivational traits with workplace deviance," *Journal of Applied Psychology*, 92, 967–977.

Felfe, J. and Schyns, B. (2004) "Is similarity in leadership related to organizational outcomes? The case of transformational leadership," *Journal of Leadership & Organizational Studies*, 10(4), 92–102.

Fimbel, N. and Burstein, J. S. (1990) "Defining the ethical standards of the high-technology industry," *Journal of Business Ethics*, 9, 929–948.

Gaziel, H. (2004) "Predictors of absenteeism among primary school teachers," *Social Psychology of Education*, 7, 421–434.

Gellatly, I. R. (1995) "Individual and group determinants of employee absenteeism: Test of a causal model," *Journal of Organizational Behavior*, 16, 469–485.

Greenberg, J. (1995) *The Quest for Justice on the Job: Essays and Experiments*, Thousand Oaks, CA: Sage.

Grissmer, D. W. and Kirby, S. (1992) *Patterns of Attrition among Indian Teachers*, Santa Monica, CA: Rand.

Harrison, D. A. and Price, K. H. (2003) "Context and consistency in absenteeism: Studying social and dispositional influences across multiple settings," *Human Resource Management Review*, 13, 203–25.

Imants, J. and Van Zoelen, A. V. (1995) "Teachers' sickness absence in primary schools, school climate and teachers' sense of efficacy," *School Organization*, 15(1), 77–86.

Ingersoll, R. M. (2001) "Teacher turnover and teacher shortages: An organizational analysis," *American Educational Research Journal*, 38(3), 499–534.

Ingersoll, R. M. (2004) "Four myths about America's teacher quality problem" in M. A. Smylie and D. Miretzky (eds) *Developing the Teacher Workforce*, Chicago, IL: University of Chicago Press, pp. 1–33.

Johns, G. (1994) "How often were you absent? A review of the use of self-reported absence data," *Journal of Applied Psychology*, 79(4), 574–591.

Johns, G. (2003) "How methodological diversity has improved our understanding of absenteeism from work," *Human Resource Management Review*, 13, 157–184.

Kaplan, S., Bradley, J. C., Lachman, J. N., and Hayness, D. (2009) "On the role of positive and negative affectivity in job performance: A meta-analytic investigation," *Journal of Applied Psychology*, 94(1), 162–176.

Kelly, S. W. and Dorsch, M. J. (1991) "Ethical climate, organizational commitment, and indebtedness among purchasing executives," *The Journal of Personal Selling & Sales Management*, 11(4), 55–66.

Kenny, D. A., Kashy, D. A., and Bolger, N. (1998) "Data analysis in social psychology" in D. T. Gilbert, S. T. Fiske, and G. Lindzey (eds) *The Handbook of Social Psychology* (4th ed.), Boston, MA: McGraw-Hill, pp. 236–265.

Kickul, J. (2001) "Promises made, promises broken: An exploration of small business attraction and retention practices," *Journal of Small Business Management*, 39, 320–335.

Koslowsky, M. (2000) "A new perspective on employee lateness," *Applied Psychology: An International Review*, 49, 390–407.

Koslowsky, M., Sagie, A., Krausz, M., and Singer, A. D. (1997) "Correlates of employee lateness: Some theoretical considerations," *Journal of Applied Psychology*, 82(1), 79–88.

Kwantes, C. T. (2003) "Organizational citizenship and withdrawal behaviors in the USA and India. Does commitment make a difference?" *International Cultural Management*, 3(1), 5–26.

Ladebo, O. J. (2005) "Effects of work related attitudes on the intention to leave the profession," *Educational Management Administration & Leadership*, 33(3), 355–369.

Lambert, E. and Hogan, N. (2009) "The importance of job satisfaction and organizational commitment in shaping turnover intent," *Criminal Justice Review*, 34(1), 96–118.

Liu, X. S. and Meyer, J. P. (2005) "Teachers' perceptions of their jobs: A multilevel analysis of the teacher follow-up survey for 1994–95," *Teacher College Record*, 107(5), 985–1003.

Lo, S. and Aryee, S. (2003) "Psychological contract breach in a Chinese context: An integrative approach," *Journal of Management Studies*, 40(4), 1005–1020.

Luchak, A. A. and Gellatly, I. R. (2007) "A comparison of linear and nonlinear relations between organizational commitment and work outcomes," *Journal of Applied Psychology*, 92(3), 786–793.

MacKinnon, D. P., Lockwood, C. M., and Williams, J. (2004) "Confidence limits for the indirect effect: Distribution of the product and resampling methods," *Multivariate Behavioral Research*, 39(1), 99–128.

Maertz, C. P. and Campion, M. A. (1998) "25 years of voluntary turnover research: A review and critique," *International Review of Industrial and Organizational Psychology*, 13, 49–81.

Martocchio, J. J. and Jimeno, D. I. (2003) "Employee absenteeism as an affective event," *Human Resource Management Review*, 12, 227–241.

Mathieu, J. E. and Zajac, D. M. (1990) "A review and meta-analysis of the antecedents, correlates and consequences of organizational commitment," *Psychological Bulletin*, 108, 171–94.

Meyer, J. P. and Allen, N. J. (1997) *Commitment in the Workplace: Theory, Practice, and Application*, Thousand Oaks, CA: Sage.

Meyer, J. P., Stanley, D. J., Herscovitch, L., and Topolnytsky, L. (2002) "Affective, continuance, and normative commitment to the organization: A meta-analysis of antecedents, correlates, and consequences," *Journal of Vocational Behavior*, 61, 20–52.

Miles, D. E., Borman, W. E., Spector, P. E., and Fox, S. (2002) "Building an integrative model of extra role work behaviors: A comparison of counterproductive work behavior with organizational citizenship behavior," *International Journal of Selection and Assessment*, 10, 51–57.

Miller, R. T., Murnane, R. J., and Willett, J. B. (2008) "Do teacher absences impact student achievement? Longitudinal evidence from one urban school district," *Educational Evaluation and Policy Analysis*, 30(2), 181–200.

Montes, S. D. and Zweig, D. (2009) "Do promises matter? An exploration of the role of promises in psychological contract breach," *Journal of Applied Psychology*, 94(5), 1243–1260.

Moorman, R. H. (1991) "Relationship between organizational justice and organizational citizenship behaviors: Do fairness perceptions influence employee citizenship?" *Journal of Applied Psychology*, 76, 845–855.

Myburgh, C. P. H. and Poggenpoel, M. (2002) "Teachers' experience of their school environment: Implications for health promotion," *Education*, 123(2), 260–268.

Neal, M. B., Chapman, N. J., Ingersoll-Dayton, B., and Emlen, A. C. (1993) *Balancing Work and Caregiving for Children, Adults, and Elders*, Newbury Park, CA: Sage.

Nicolson, N. and Goodge, P. (1976) "The influence of social, organizational, and biographical factors on female absence," *Journal of Management Studies*, 13, 234–254.

Nicholson, N. and Payne, R. (1987) "Absence from work: Explanation and attributions," *Applied Psychology: An International Review*, 36, 121–132.

Peterson, D. K. (2002) "Deviant workplace behavior and the organization's ethical climate," *Journal of Business and Psychology*, 17(1), 47–61.

Pillai, R., Williams, E. S., and Tan, J. J. (2001) "Are the scales tipped in favor of procedural or distributive justice? An investigation of the U.S., India, Germany, and Hong Kong (China)," *The International Journal of Conflict Management*, 12(4), 312–332.

Robinson, S. L. and Bennett, R. J. (1995) "A typology of deviant workplace behaviors: A multi-dimensional scaling study," *Academy of Management Journal*, 38, 555–572.

Robinson, S. L. and Rousseau, D. M. (1994), "Violating the psychological construct: Not the exception but the norm," *Journal of Organizational Behavior*, 15, 145–259.

Rosenblatt, Z. and Hijazi, H. (2004) "Organizational justice in teacher promotions: Cultural differences," paper presented at the biannual conference of the International Society for the Study of Work and School Organizational Values, New Orleans, August.

Rosenblatt, Z. and Inbal, B. (1999) "Skill flexibility among school teachers: Operationalization and organizational implications," *Journal of Educational Administration*, 37(4), 345–365.

Rosenblatt, Z. and Peled, D. (2002) "School ethical climate and parental involvement," *Journal of Educational Administration*, 40(4), 349–367.

Rosenblatt, Z. and Shirom, A. (2003) "Teachers' absenteeism in Israel," paper submitted to the Chief Scientist in the Department of Education, State of Israel, Jerusalem (in Hebrew).

Rosenblatt, Z. and Shirom, A. (2005) "Predicting teacher absenteeism by personal background factors," *Journal of Educational Administration*, 43(2), 209–225.

Rosenblatt. Z. and Shirom, A. (2006) "The effects of organizational-level characteristics on the absence behavior of school administrators: A multi-level analysis," *Educational Administration Quarterly*, 42, 3, 361–384.

Rosenblatt, Z., Shapira-Lishchinsky, O., and Shirom, A. (2010) "An organizational ethics perspective of work absence in Israel: The case of school teachers," *Human Resource Management Review*, 20, 247–259.

Rousseau, D. M. (1995) *Pyschological Contracts in Organizations:Understanding Written and Unwritten Agreements*, Thousand Oaks, CA: Sage.

Sagie, A. (1998) "Employee absenteeism, organizational commitment and job satisfaction: Another look," *Journal of Vocational Behavior*, 52, 156–171.

Schein, E. H. (1990) "Organizational culture," *American Psychologist*, 2(45), 109–119.

Scheurich, J. J. and Skrla, L. (2003) *Leadership for Equity and Excellence: Creating High Achievement Classrooms, Schools, and Districts*, Thousand Oaks, CA: Corwin Press.

Scott-Norton, M. S. (1998) "Teacher absenteeism: A growing dilemma in education," *Contemporary Education*, 69(2), 95–99.

Shapira-Lishchinsky, O. (2007) "Israeli teachers' perceptions of lateness: A gender comparison," *Sex Roles*, 57, 3, 4, 187–199

Shapira-Lishchinsky, O. (2009) "Towards professionalism: Israeli teachers' ethical dilemmas," *European Journal of Teacher Education*, 32(4), 469–483.

Shapira-Lishchinsky, O. and Rosenblatt, Z. (2009) "The relationship between teachers' perceptions of organizational ethics and their intent to leave: An integrative approach," *Educational Administration Quarterly*, 5(45), 1–34.

Shapira-Lishchinsky, O. and Rosenblatt, Z. (2010) "School formal ethical climate and teachers' voluntary absence," *Journal of Educational Administration*, 48, 161–181.

Shaw, J. D., Gupta, N., and Delery, J. E. (2005) "Alternative conceptualizations of the relationship between voluntary turnover and organizational performance," *Academy of Management Journal*, 48(1), 50–68.

Skrla, L., Scheurich, J. J., Garcia, J., and Nolly, G. (2004) "Equity audits: A practical leadership tool for developing equitable and excellent schools," *Educational Administration Quarterly*, 40(1), 135–163.

Smylie, M. and Miretzky, D. (2004) *Developing the Teacher Workforce*, Chicago, IL: University of Chicago Press.

Starratt, R. J. (1991) "Building an ethical school: A theory for practice in educational leadership," *Educational Administration Quarterly*, 27(2), 185–202.

Turnley, W. H., Bolino, M. C., Lester, S. W., and Bloodgood, J. M. (2004) "The effects of psychological contract breach on union commitment," *Journal of Occupational Psychology*, 77, 421–428.

Upchurch., R. S. and Ruhland, S. K. (1996) "The organizational bases of ethical work climates in lodging operations as perceived by general managers," *Journal of Business Ethics*, 15(10), 1083–1093.

Van Maanen, M. (1995) "On the epistemology of reflective practice," *Teachers and Teaching: Theory and Practice*, 1(1), 33–50.

Vardi, Y. (2001) "The effects of organizational and ethical climates on misconduct at work," *Journal of Business Ethics*, 29, 325–337.

Vardi, Y. and Weitz, E. (2004) *Misbehavior in Organizations: Theory, Research, and Management*, Mahwah, NJ: Erlbaum.

Vardi, Y. and Wiener, Y. (1996) "Misbehavior in organizations: A motivational framework," *Organization Science*, 7, 151–165.

Victor, B. and Cullen, J. B. (1988) "The organizational bases of ethical work climates," *Administrative Science Quarterly*, 33, 101–125.

Walsh, J. P., Ashford, S. J., and Hill, T. E. (1985) "Feedback obstruction: The influence of the information environment on employee turnover intentions," *Human Relations*, 38, 23–46.

Wimbush, J. C. and Shepard, J. M. (1994) "Toward an understanding of ethical climate: Its relationship to ethical behavior and supervisory influence," *Journal of Business Ethics*, 13, 637–647.

Woods, R. C. and Montagno, R. V. (1997) "Determining the negative effect of teacher attendance on student achievement," *Education*, 112, 307–316.

PART IV
Corruption in the Professions

8

Making Sense of Academic Misconduct[1]

Alison L. Antes and Michael D. Mumford

Stories of fraud and corruption among professionals surfaced with increasing frequency in the later part of the past century, and the pace remained unchanged during the first decade of the twenty-first century. Thus, we find the misbehavior of professionals at the forefront of our minds and the subject of many discussions. Corporate and government corruption often seem most salient, but misconduct is a concern across all professions. In recent years, the misconduct of academics—individuals working as teachers and researchers at institutions of higher education—has received a great deal of attention. A number of high-profile cases exposing egregious behavior among academics and scientists account for this increased attention, at least in part. In one such case, South Korean researcher Hwang Woo-Suk fabricated data and results from human stem-cell cloning experiments and published his fraudulent findings in top scientific journals (Cyranoski, 2006). This incident derailed progress in stem cell research and wasted untold sums of money. In another case, American researcher Eric Poehlman declared the therapeutic effects of hormone replacement for menopausal women, a statement based entirely on falsified data (Dalton, 2005). This incident led to millions of wasted research dollars and landed Poehlman in prison, serving a one-year sentence for reporting fraudulent information in federal grant proposals.

---

[1] We sincerely thank all of our colleagues who contributed to this work. We would like to especially thank Jay Caughron, Cheryl Beeler, Ryan Brown, Shane Connelly, Lynn Devenport, Stephen Murphy, and Cheryl Stenmark. The work presented in this chapter was partly supported by the National Institutes of Health, National Center for Research Resources, General Clinical Research Center Grant (#M01 RR-14467) and a grant from the National Institutes of Health/Office of Research Integrity (#5R01-NS049535-02), Michael D. Mumford, Principal Investigator.

As outlandish as these accounts of misconduct may seem, it appears that they represent only the tip of the iceberg. Although estimates of serious violations, such as outright fabrication of findings, are typically rather low (roughly about 1 or 2 percent of scientists), when a broader definition of misconduct is applied, it is apparent that ethically questionable behavior is not uncommon (Fanelli, 2009; Marshall, 2000; Resnik, 2003; Steneck, 2007). These less severe forms of misconduct include inappropriately assigning authorship, unfairly reviewing other's work, and omitting details of study limitations, to name a few. Approximately 30 percent of scientists admit to taking part in activities of this nature (Martinson, Anderson, and DeVries, 2005). These figures, however, are based on reported incidents or self-reported misbehavior and are thus likely to be underestimates. When individuals reported observed misconduct among others, an estimate less subject to self-report bias, frequency estimates were 14 percent for serious misconduct and up to 72 percent for questionable behaviors (Fanelli, 2009). Estimates of less severe, yet commonplace, misconduct especially concern the scholarly community, as they suggest that many, if not most, academics encounter issues of misconduct in their work (DeVries, Anderson, and Martinson, 2006).

At least one other factor has stimulated increased interest in academic misconduct: academic ties to industry are strengthening as business success increasingly depends on science and engineering (Zellner, 2003). Therefore, academic misconduct poses a threat to economic growth. Likewise, each year funding agencies around the world allocate billions of dollars to academics for research purposes. Not only does misconduct squander these resources, but it also misleads decision-makers as to where to allocate additional funds.

For individuals working in the academic realm, these comments indicating that academia is not free from corruption may not be all that surprising. However, they may startle those not working in academia, as they challenge the idealistic image of academics objectively pursing truth. As in many professions, academia is composed of imperfect people working in high-pressure, complex environments on high-stakes projects where they must work with others who sometimes have complementary goals but often have competing agendas. As a result, academics are unlikely to escape temptation, poor judgment, or unscrupulous decision-making. In this chapter we seek to make sense of this phenomenon. Rather than being unsettled by the reality of academic misconduct, this is an ideal time to take stock of what we know about academic misconduct, what might be done to overcome it, and where we might go from here. Before delving into our discussion of academic misconduct, we first put the discussion into context by considering the unique characteristics of academic work.

The Nature of Academic Work

First and foremost, the purpose of academic work is rather unique. Generally speaking, academic work seeks to generate and disseminate knowledge about the world, apply knowledge to solve real-world problems, and/or contribute to the quality of human life. Academics gather and apply knowledge by describing, predicting, and/or manipulating phenomena of interest within their particular domain (Cook and Campbell, 1979). For example, meteorologists use instruments to take measurements from the physical world and predict weather patterns. Engineers apply scientific principles—for instance, mathematics and physics—to develop innovative solutions to practical problems, and microbiologists study the nature, consequences, and uses of microscopic organisms. Psychologists study human behavior and interaction, and historians describe and interpret past events. Painters, musicians, and dancers use different media to express ideas, invoke thought and emotion, and entertain others. Taken as a whole, academic work seeks to understand and improve human (and often non-human) life, health, and well-being. However, field-specific differences exist with respect to the specific purpose and nature of academic work.

One key field-specific difference pertains to the extent to which the work is applied to address real-world issues. For instance, engineering and medical fields are particularly applied in nature—engineers design technical solutions and products, and medical researchers and doctors work directly with patients to treat them. Philosophers, on the other hand, typically work less directly with the public, producing ideas and basic knowledge rather than concrete products. The applied nature of many academic and scientific fields implies greater public, political, and economic connection and, typically, more significant consequences for the work (Tordoir, 1995; Weingart, 2002). As the world economy becomes increasingly knowledge-, research- and innovation-based, many academic fields are likely to become more applied.

Perhaps the most significant general characteristic of academic work is its complexity. Academics work in ambiguous, complex domains where knowledge continually advances and new problems must be solved. Thus, success in academic work depends on expertise along with critical and creative thinking skills (Mumford et al., 2005; Weisberg, 2006). Given the need for expertise, academic work requires advanced educational training (Lajoie, 2009). Thus, early career academics work, typically for many years, as mentees under the guidance of an expert in their field. This apprentice model creates a natural hierarchy in academia based on expertise and represents another central characteristic of academic work. In addition to expertise, achievement in complex, demanding work such as academia requires innate intellectual ability and personal drive (Hunter and Schmidt, 1996; Steele-Johnson et al., 2000).

In addition to the mentor-mentee relationship, academic work involves other significant social elements, including collaborations, teacher-student relationships, and peer review. First and foremost, academic work typically requires collaboration (Dunbar, 1995). Working collaboratively allows groups to capitalize on the knowledge, skills, and resources of others to jointly solve problems and carry out the work (Bordons and Gómez, 2000; Gibson, 2001). Thus, academics must develop effective working relationships with other scholars in their field. In addition, academics are likely to form close ties with exceptional students as they impart their knowledge in the classroom (Janssen and Van Yperen, 2004).

Another social feature of academic work is the heavy reliance on the peer review system. In this process, other scholars judge the merit of one's work, whether for publication, funding, promotion, or awards. Objective judgments of other's work are considered optimal (Crigger, 1998; Wennerås and Wold, 1997). That is, judgments of a colleague's paper, proposal, performance, or product should be based on its inherent value rather than personal or professional preferences. However, this ideal proves unfeasible as human judgment always involves some degree of bias (Pronin, 2007). As a result, the peer review process generates a number of issues relevant to appropriate and ethical conduct.

Finally, academic work tends to be competitive and high-pressure, and is thus characterized by high stress. Generally speaking, it takes place under conditions of limited resources where the basis of promotion and success is the production of complex ideas, solutions, performances, and products that must be recognized and desired by those within, and even beyond, one's field. This work requires months or years of effort. Thus, when one's work is not recognized or respected by others, it is likely to be a significant setback (Schweitzer, Ordóñez, and Douma, 2004). Along this same line, success in academic and scientific work typically requires disproving or discounting the theories, ideas, and approaches of others. This aspect of the work can obviously put academics and scientists as odds with others in their field. With this background as the context for our remaining discussion, we turn to what constitutes academic misconduct.

What is Academic Misconduct?

Academic misconduct refers to the violation of standard codes of scholarly conduct and ethical behavior in the course of conducting scholarly work.

Conduct with respect to research activities is typically most scrutinized, primarily due to the significant consequences of research and the money invested in it. In fact, ethical principles—for example, protection of research participants and balancing risk and benefit—were first applied to research aspects of academic work. In discussing academic misconduct, three specific behaviors are considered the most serious violations; these include fabrication, falsification, and plagiarism (collectively referred to as FFP). In fact, institutional and federal policies typically define academic and research misconduct as fabrication, falsification, or plagiarism in the course of proposing, performing, reviewing, or reporting research (Resnik, 2003; Steneck, 2007). Reflection on the key purpose and foundation of academic work sheds some light on why the academic community considers fabrication, falsification, and plagiarism so severe.

Knowledge acquisition serves as the basis of academic work, and fabrication (making up data and results and presenting them as true) and falsification (altering or omitting data or aspects of research findings or methods) disrupt progress towards the accumulation of a body of knowledge (Gerber, 2006; Sox and Rennie, 2006). Moreover, these acts waste resources when scholars unknowingly seek to build upon others' fraudulent work. Although plagiarism (copying the ideas, processes, data, results, or words of others without giving them credit) does not directly distort knowledge, it undermines scholarly work, given the importance of sharing ideas, techniques, and findings. Stealing the intellectual contributions of others ultimately undermines trust and communication among scholars.

Although FFP clearly represent serious acts, the FFP model of academic misconduct proves incomplete. This model does not take into account the manner in which the work was conducted; instead it focuses on outcomes of the work (Mumford, Antes, Beeler, and Caughron, 2009). Clearly, the way in which academic work is carried out—for instance, how one interacts with study participants, mentees, and colleagues—involves dimensions of professional and ethical conduct. Indeed, many research ethics principles emphasize the fair and considerate treatment of research participants. Furthermore, FFP represent rather isolated concerns, but issues of appropriate conduct in the course of day-to-day work affect all academics (DeVries, Anderson, and Martinson, 2006; Resnik, 2003). Thus, the frequency of more commonplace instances of misbehavior, relative to more severe instances, makes them a significant threat to the integrity of the academic endeavor. Moreover, instances of misconduct may create a climate in which more serious forms of misconduct are likely to occur, and misconduct observed by younger academics and researchers is likely to be adopted and implemented as ordinary aspects of their work.

In an effort to address the limitations of the FFP model, Helton-Fauth et al. (2003) examined professional codes of conduct across different scientific fields. Professional societies create codes of conduct to elaborate appropriate and inappropriate behavior in the course of conducting work in a particular field. Helton-Fauth et al. (2003) systematically reviewed biological, health, and social science codes and developed a comprehensive taxonomy of the general behavioral dimensions constituting misconduct. As presented in Table 8.1, they obtained 17 dimensions common to misconduct across fields that could be categorized under four broader dimensions, including data management, study conduct, professional practices, and business practices.

To provide evidence for the validity of this taxonomy, Helton-Fauth et al. (2003) reviewed professional codes of conduct in 60 fields and found that the taxonomy covered 82 percent of the behaviors covered by theses codes. Behaviors not covered by the taxonomy were highly field-specific. Further evidence for the validity of this taxonomy was provided by a study conducted by Kligyte, Marcy, Sevier, et al. (2008) examining the applicability of the taxonomy to work in engineering, computer science, and meteorology. Using an interview technique of experts in these fields, the authors found that, although some dimensions were not relevant, such as the treatment of animal subjects, the remaining dimensions covered over 90 percent of the ethical issues in these fields.

A similar investigation conducted by Stenmark et al. (under review) addressed whether this taxonomy might extend to the work of scholars in the humanities (e.g., historians and philosophers) and the performing and fine arts (e.g., poets, dancers, painters, and musicians). Although some dimensions specific to human and animal research did not always apply, they found that these dimensions covered the primary ethical issues in these disciplines. The specific nature of some dimensions differed from science and engineering—for instance, the nature of data and publication—but the key aspects of the work remained similar. In fact, business dimensions in these fields, particularly in the performing arts, were especially salient. For these fields, an addition was made to the broad professional practices dimension—specifically, a teaching sub-dimension to reflect the strong teaching emphasis and the corresponding ethical issues with respect to this aspect of the work.

This taxonomy and those generated on the basis of it are significant for a number of reasons. First, they take into account processes and relationships involved in academic work in addition to the business aspects of academic work. Furthermore, the professional practices dimension takes into account professional norms in academic work. Clearly, these taxonomies represent a more comprehensive framework of the ethical dimensions of academic work than

Table 8.1 Taxonomy of ethical dimensions of academic work

Broad dimension	Sub-dimensions
Data management	
	Data massaging, fabrication, and interpretation
	Publication practices (e.g., reporting data and assigning authorship)
Study conduct	
	Institutional review board practices
	Informed consent and debriefing
	Confidentiality
	Treatment of human subjects
	Treatment of animal subjects
Professional practices	
	Objectivity in evaluating work
	Recognition of expertise
	Protection of intellectual property
	Adherence to professional commitments
	Protection of public welfare and environment
	Exploitation of staff and/or collaborators
Business practices	
	Conflicts of interest
	Deceptive bid/contract practices
	Inappropriate use of physical resources
	Inappropriate management/supervisory practices

Source: Helton-Fauth et al. (2003).

the FFP model. This approach to capturing dimensions of academic misconduct is also significant because it implies that issues of academic misconduct may not always be black-and-white. Although fabrication and plagiarism, and to a lesser extent falsification, are rather clear actions, other behaviors, such as maintaining objectivity in evaluating work and appropriateness in management practices, are more debatable. In fact, these dimensions of ethical conduct, and what constitutes ethical or appropriate behavior, may differ across individuals, work groups, institutions, and fields.

Although defining academic and research misconduct in terms of FFP may be appropriate for the purposes of policy-making and investigations, ultimately, an overly limited definition of academic misconduct proves problematic. If only severe violations such as FFP are considered as misbehavior, then a whole host of issues are overlooked in studying misconduct, teaching about it, and in people's reflections upon their own behavior at work. Notably, when DeVries et al. (2006) asked scientists to describe the issues they were most worried about, it was the "gray" issues that were of most concern. Before turning to a discussion of what might be the source of academic misconduct, we first consider its consequences.

Consequences of Academic Misconduct

It may be fairly obvious why corporate and political misconduct is detrimental, but why is academic misconduct such a concern? First and foremost, academic endeavors, particularly research, use billions of dollars of public and private funds each year (Nova, 2009; Pear, 2009). Moreover, instituting regulation mechanisms and investigating misconduct cases requires considerable amounts of money and resources (Steneck, 2000). Simply put, academic misconduct wastes money and resources. Of course, monetary consequences are not the only significant consequences of concern. For instance, serious consequences may result when flawed research guides product development, medical decisions, educational techniques, or public policy. In worst-case scenarios, violated research procedures, faulty products, and medical treatments may result in physical harm and even death. Ultimately, public distrust of science and research constitutes one rather serious social consequence of academic misconduct (Haerlin and Parr, 1999; Friedman, 2002). Although research should inform people's decisions, it often merely creates doubt and confusion.

In addition to these broad consequences, academic misconduct produces significant consequences within the workplace. Even when a specific person or work group engages in misconduct, the consequences span far beyond this person or group (Biaggio, Duffy, and Staffelbach, 1998). Other individuals may be drawn into the issue because they observe the misconduct and must wrestle with how to respond, if at all. Instances of misconduct also damage reputations. Beyond these concerns, unprofessional and unethical conduct creates negative work environments characterized by poor communication, distrust, and tension (Schminke, Arnaud, and Kuenzi, 2007). Overall, misconduct simply distracts people from their work and undermines productivity.

Considerable consequences also result for individuals—typically known as whistleblowers—who report serious misconduct. Although institutional policies include provisions for the protection of whistleblowers, they are commonly persecuted as much or more as individuals accused of misconduct (Miethe, 1999). Specifically, the community and investigative panels question the whistleblower's motivations and intentions, and require him or her to provide substantiating evidence. Whistleblowers may be tagged as troublemakers and encounter obstacles when pursuing future employment.

Finally, although it may be difficult for some individuals to sympathize with perpetrators of misconduct, consequences for these individuals are quite significant (Odling-Smee et al., 2007). In reality, pure maliciousness rarely motivates academic misconduct; rather, other motivations, pressures, and faulty judgments lead to unexpected behavior. In many cases, even after penalty for misconduct or a finding of no fault, people's reputations and careers are permanently damaged (McCook, 2009). Given this background, the key question becomes: what causes academic misconduct?

Searching for the Source of Academic Misconduct

A number of explanatory systems accounting for ethical behavior have been suggested over the years. For instance, moral development theory suggests that moral reasoning serves as the basis for ethical conduct and proceeds in six discernible stages, with each stage using different systems for justifying a particular behavior in response to an ethical dilemma (Kohlberg, 1969). Moral identity theory suggests that when people construct their sense of self around moral values, they are more likely to engage in moral behavior (Reynolds and Ceranic, 2007). Other models emphasize factors such as social appraisal (Haidt, 2001), environmental conditions (Hegarty and Sims, 1979), leadership (Brown and Treviño, 2006), and intuition (Reynolds, 2006) in accounting for ethical behavior. These theories provide a basis for understanding certain aspects of ethical behavior, but a sense-making model seems to best illustrate the mechanisms involved in ethical behavior among academics (Mumford, Connelly et al., 2008; Sonenshein, 2007). Specifically, sense-making accounts for how academics might recognize and respond to ethical problems within the course of their dynamic, complex work—work in which ethical implications may not always be readily obvious.

THE SENSE-MAKING FRAMEWORK

Mumford, Connelly, and colleagues (2008) proposed a sense-making model of ethical decisions among scholars (see Figure 8.1). According to this model, personal and professional experiences continually inform the interpretation and processing of workplace events. In addition, workplace events activate relevant professional principles, perceptions of causes of the situation, key goals, and requirements for goal attainment. In turn, these elements stimulate framing, or appraisal, of the situation and problem based on one's mental model. As the individual recognizes potential outcomes for self and others, emotions are evoked. In turn, the individual begins to forecast the potential outcomes of various actions. Self-reflection about goals, past experiences, and self-conceptions informs this forecasting, and ultimately gives rise to sense-making where the individual has interpreted the situation, integrated its components, and arrived at an understanding for acting with the situation. It is this sense-making that yields a decision and, ultimately, an action.

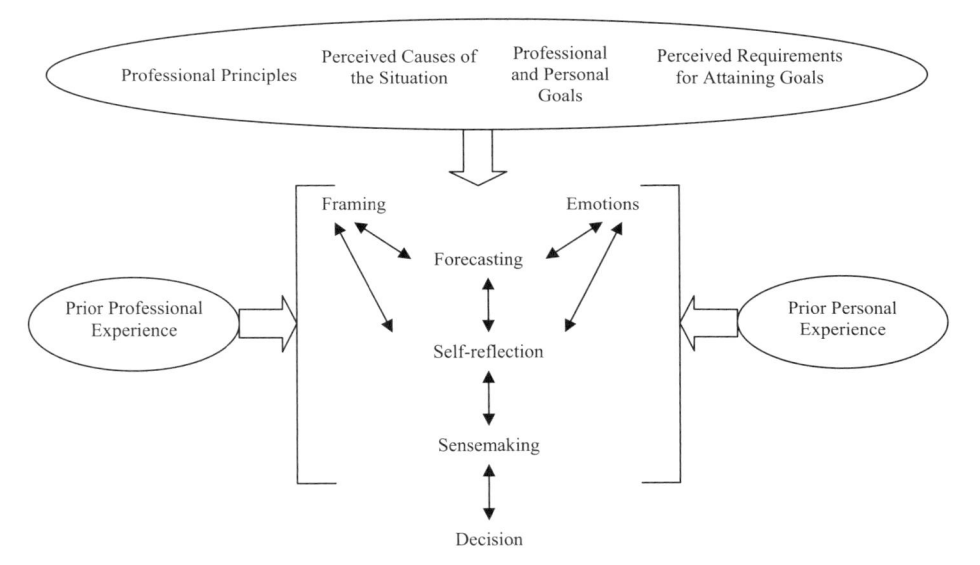

Figure 8.1   Sense-making model of ethical decision-making

This model of ethical decision-making among academics implies several social-cognitive strategies likely to facilitate this sense-making process and thus improve ethical decision-making. These strategies involve deliberative, active processing about the situation and reflection on the thought process itself. Mumford and colleagues (2006) identified seven core strategies that might underlie effective engagement in this sense-making process yielding ethical decisions. These strategies include recognizing circumstances, seeking help, questioning one's judgment, anticipating consequences, dealing with emotions, analyzing personal motivations, and considering others. Table 8.2 presents more detailed definitions of these strategies.

To provide initial evidence for this model and further test propositions arising from this line of reasoning, Mumford and his colleagues (2006) first developed and provided validity evidence for a measure of ethical decision-making requiring participants to respond to complex scenarios like those likely to be encountered in their work. In this measure, participants received 12 scenarios relevant to their field, with three ethical problems following from each of the broader original scenarios that provided the background context, making a total of 36 ethical problems. These problems mapped to the 17-dimension taxonomy constructed by Helton-Fauth et al. (2003), with two to three problems for each sub-dimension in the taxonomy. Intermixed with these ethical problems were issues that pertained to technical problems to avoid demand characteristics. For each ethical problem, participants were asked to select two preferred options for responding to the problem. They were provided with eight options, reflecting low, moderate, and high ethicality as scored by field experts using relevant norms and guidelines. By aggregating ethicality

Table 8.2   Strategies facilitating sense-making

Sense-making strategies	Description
Recognizing circumstances	Awareness of relevant principles, individuals involved, key goals, and critical causes of the problem.
Seeking help	Asking for advice from an objective individual, seeking institutional resources, or considering what others have done in similar situations.
Questioning one's judgment	Considering that one's interpretation of the problem and potential decisions might be biased or based on faulty assumptions.
Anticipating consequences	Considering possible outcomes, including the likely short- and long-term consequences of possible decision alternatives.
Managing emotions	Assessing and regulating emotional responses to the problem that can hinder objectivity.
Analyzing personal motivations	Considering deeply-rooted personal motivations, values, and goals, and how they might affect decision-making in the situation.
Considering others	Recognizing and being mindful of others' perceptions and concerns and the likely impact of one's actions on others.

scores associated with each response option and then averaging scores for questions pertaining to each of the four dimensions of ethical behavior, the measure yielded four decision-making scores. Specifically, a score was obtained for the ethicality of decision-making with respect to data management, study conduct, professional practices, and business practices.

Embedded within this measure were measures of sense-making strategies based on the responses endorsed by participants. Expert judges familiar with social-cognitive mechanisms and ethical decision making rated the response options. They assigned scores to each of the response options according to the extent to which each of the seven sense-making strategies (shown in Table 8.2) would give rise to the response. Participants' strategy scores were obtained by averaging the scores from the two responses endorsed on each problem and then averaging across all problems.

To provide initial evidence indicating that sense-making might underlie ethical decision-making, Mumford and his colleagues (2006) examined the relationship between sense-making strategies and ethical decision-making. Graduate students in the biological, health, and social sciences completed the ethical decision-making measure. It was found that the sense-making strategies were indeed related to ethical decision-making in data management, study conduct, professional practices, and business practices, with positive correlations generally between 0.25 and 0.45. The three strategies most strongly related to ethical decision-making were recognizing circumstances, anticipating consequences, and considering others, with correlations ranging from 0.45 to 0.52. Additional evidence for the plausibility of this sense-making model of ethical decision-making was obtained in studies using the sense-making framework as the basis for an instructional program (Kligyte, Marcy, Waples, et al., 2008; Mumford, Connelly, et al., 2008). The program provided participants with practice applying the seven strategies. Training in these strategies significantly improved pre- to post-training performance on the measure of ethical decision-making.

With this initial evidence of the plausibility of this model in place, Mumford and his colleagues asked a number of questions about potential influences—specifically, field socialization, work environment, experiential learning, and personality—on sense-making, and conducted a series of investigations to test these influences (Antes et al., 2007; Mumford et al., 2007, Mumford, Connelly, et al., 2009; Mumford, Waples, et al., 2009). In these investigations, a sample of graduate students working in the biological, health, and social sciences completed the ethical decision-making criterion measure and psychological measures of the predictors of interest. We now turn to a discussion of the key findings emerging from these investigations.

INFLUENCES ON ETHICAL DECISION-MAKING

Field socialization Mumford, Connelly, et al. (2009) asked whether socialization into a field might account for differences in ethical decision-making. Different fields address different problems, use different approaches to solve these problems, and develop different patterns of social interaction and normative expectations (Feldman, 1999; Morrison, 1993; Simonton, 2005). Thus, Mumford, Connelly, and colleagues (2009) expected that socialization into different fields might influence the ethicality of decisions and sense-making with respect to ethical problems. To provide initial evidence for this proposition, after controlling for the effects of individual differences, the authors examined differences between individuals more and less socialized into three different scientific fields (i.e., the biological, health, or social sciences) in ethicality of decisions and the application of sense-making strategies. Degree of socialization into one's field was operationalized as the number of years students had been working in their field. Thus, students in their first year of graduate school were compared to students in their third or fourth years.

The results generally indicated that, with socialization into the social and biological sciences, ethical decision-making scores either did not change or improved, while ethical decision-making decreased with socialization in the health sciences. Next, Mumford, Connelly, et al. (2009) asked whether these changes in ethical decision-making might be accounted for by changes in sense-making strategies applied by those in different fields. Here, it was found that the use of sense-making strategies remained similar or improved with socialization into social and biological sciences, while sense-making strategies decreased in the health sciences with socialization into the field. Moreover, these differences were not accounted for by differential exposure to unethical behaviors across these fields.

These findings raise the question of why socialization into different fields results in differences in sense-making and ethical decision-making. Less effective, or even declining, sense-making in the health sciences may be accounted for by the highly significant consequences associated with the health sciences. This characteristic of the work might encourage different approaches to thinking about, and coping with, these consequences, which could actually serve to undermine sense-making and ethical decision-making. For instance, in the health sciences, individuals might deal with exposure to life-and-death issues and even suffering by turning inward to emotionally self-protect and focus more on the technical treatment aspects of their work rather than the social elements (Mumford, Antes, Beeler, and Caughron, 2009). While this study provides initial evidence that field socialization might influence ethical decision-making, additional studies must examine specific mechanisms for these differences along with other fields.

Work environment Workplace conditions have been shown to influence individuals' ethical conduct (Agarwal and Malloy, 1999; Barnett and Vaicys, 2000; Gelman and Gibelman, 2002). Therefore, Mumford and colleagues (2007) asked how the work environment of scientists might influence their ethical decision-making. In this investigation, students in their first year of graduate school were examined, as they are especially likely to be sensitive to environmental conditions. Graduate students completed a workplace climate measure assessing their perceptions of their work environment, including their perceptions of equity, interpersonal conflict, occupational engagement, and work commitment within their work. People base their perceptions of their work environment on the patterns of behaviors and attitudes demonstrated by those in that environment.

In addition to perceptions of their work environment, Mumford et al. (2007) proposed that specific environmental experiences with respect to social interactions, adjustment to the environment, and leadership experienced by graduate students would be likely to influence their ethical decision-making, perhaps even more so than their perceptions of the work environment. Therefore, participants also completed a measure of environmental experiences in which they reported the frequency of exposure to specific experiences with respect to professional leadership, poor coping, lack of rewards, limited competitive pressure, and poor career direction.

When climate perceptions were correlated with ethical decision-making, perceptions of interpersonal conflict were negatively related to the ethicality of decisions made with respect to professional practices ($r = -0.26$) and business practices ($r = -0.24$). On the other hand, perceptions that the work environment was characterized by occupational engagement were positively related to ethical decision-making with respect to professional practices ($r = 0.21$), and perceptions of work commitment in one's workplace were positively related to ethical decision-making regarding study conduct ($r = 0.22$).

The findings with respect to the specific environmental experiences revealed that poor coping was negatively related to ethical decision-making with respect to data management ($r = -0.27$), professional practices ($r = -0.20$), and business practices ($r = -0.20$). Therefore, it appears that individuals struggling to adjust to their work environment may be more likely to make poor decisions. Moreover, graduate students experiencing a lack of rewards may also make poor decisions, as lack of rewards was negatively related to ethical decisions with respect to data management ($r = -0.21$) and professional practices ($r = -.36$).

On the other hand, reporting experiencing limited competitive pressure within the work environment was positively related to ethical decisions across all decision-making dimensions (i.e., data management, $r = 0.19$; study conduct, $r = 0.21$; professional practices, $r = 0.24$; and business practices, $r = 0.22$).

Clearly, these findings suggest that the work environment does influence ethical decision-making. It appears that conflict, competitive pressure, lack of rewards, and poor coping are particularly likely to create a dysfunctional work environment, breeding poor ethical decision-making. These findings lead Mumford, Antes, Beeler, and Caughron (2009) to ask whether these variables influence the application of sense-making strategies. Interestingly, with the exception of lack of rewards, which was negatively related to all of the sense-making strategies (average $r = -0.38$), the other climate perceptions and environmental experiences were not strongly related to the use of sense-making strategies. Lack of rewards in one's work might undermine the use of sense-making strategies and produce unethical decision-making because appropriate practices are circumvented to obtain rewards. The other environmental variables may indirectly influence sense-making to produce unethical decision-making. For instance, a dysfunctional work environment may operate to produce unethical decision-making by creating justification for misconduct (Mumford, Antes, Beeler, and Caughron, 2009).

Experiential learning Given the importance of workplace experiences in accounting for ethical conduct, Mumford, Waples, et al. (2009) asked specifically how exposure to unethical practices in one's work might influence ethical decision-making. It was expected that exposure to unethical work practices might also influence perceptions of the work climate and judgments of the acceptability of unethical practices. Thus, participants' ratings of the frequency of their exposure to unethical practices were correlated with their ethical decision-making scores, in addition to climate perceptions and judgments of the acceptability of unethical practices. These relationships were examined across experience levels, but also separately for more and less experienced students, as it was expected that the influence of exposure to unethical practices might differ according to experience level.

The findings indicated that exposure to unethical practices was negatively related to ethical decision making (average $r = -0.20$), with stronger correlations among less experienced (average $r = -0.28$) students compared to more experienced (average $r = -0.12$) students. Exposure to unethical practices was less strongly and consistently related to climate perceptions and judgments of the acceptability of unethical practices than to ethical decision-making. Thus, it appears that exposure to unethical work practices may influence the development of professional expertise and sense-making processes, such that unethical practices are adopted as an understanding of how the work is done. These experiences seem to be especially central to less experienced students' understanding of how work is conducted. Unethical practices may serve as case models for conduct within one's work and thus become part of one's professional knowledge (Kolodner, 1997). However, with experience, more incidents will be encountered, and additional learning may include exposure to positive case models, thus accounting for why exposure to misconduct may have a more pronounced effect on ethical decision-making in less experienced individuals.

Personality In addition to environmental factors, characteristics of individuals are also likely to account for misconduct (Ones, Viswesvaran, and Schmidt, 1993; Murphy, 2000). In an investigation examining personality—characteristic ways of thinking, feeling, and behaving (Myers, 2007)—Antes et al. (2007) examined personality characteristics influencing how one views oneself and others. Given the uncertainty involved in scientific work and the collaborative nature of the work, Antes et al. (2007) expected that narcissism—the inflated, grandiose perception of oneself (Penney and Spector, 2002)—and cynicism—negative perceptions of others (Kanter and Mirvis, 1989)—might prove especially important to ethical decision-making among scientists. The authors also explored the relationship of general personality characteristics, including extroversion, neuroticism, openness, conscientiousness, and agreeableness (John and Srivastava, 1999), as these variables are commonly believed to influence workplace behavior (Barrick and Mount, 1991).

When measures of these personality characteristics were correlated with ethical decision-making, narcissism—in particular the arrogance (average $r = -0.16$) and entitlement (average $r = -0.22$) scales—were negatively related to ethical decision-making, as was cynicism (average $r = -0.16$). Given these relationships with ethical decision-making, Antes and colleagues (2007) next asked whether these personality characteristics might influence the application of sense-making strategies and thus provide some explanation for why these personality characteristics might undermine ethical decision-making. They therefore examined the relationship of these personality characteristics with sense-making strategies.

Given that narcissistic individuals experience a sense of entitlement, lack of empathy, and desire for power, it was not surprising that narcissism was negatively related to the application of all sense-making strategies. Moreover, cynicism was also negatively related to the use of sense-making strategies. Apparently, the view that others are driven by selfish motives undermines sense-making and ethical decision-making, perhaps because it encourages little social justification for ethical behavior and may even stimulate the desire to protect oneself (Tyson, 1990). The general personality characteristics exerted some influence on sense-making strategies (e.g., openness was positively related to anticipating consequences, and neuroticism was negatively related to dealing with emotions), but these general personality variables did not demonstrate strong relationships with ethical decision-making among researchers. Before turning from these findings with respect to personality, it is noteworthy that individuals who seek high-pressure, high-status careers are likely to be narcissistic (Wallace and Baumeister, 2002), and successful scientists have been found to be rather arrogant and cynical, and perhaps even exploitive (Feist, 1998). Therefore, determining how to manage these personality-related influences on ethical decision-making may prove not only critical, but also challenging.

Overall, these findings emerging from the work of Mumford and his colleagues provides initial evidence that sense-making may be a plausible model for understanding ethical decision-making in academic work. Mumford et al.'s research has provided some initial guidance with respect to environmental and individual-level factors influencing sense-making and ethical decision-making, but more work along these lines must extend these findings to other fields, institutions, and more experienced professionals, in addition to investigating the causal mechanisms behind these relationships. Furthermore, as the findings reported here are based on one measure of sense-making and ethical decision-making, future work must utilize additional measures of these and other constructs. Of course, given that the research described here examines precursors to behavior (i.e., sense-making and ethical decision-making), research providing evidence of the link between sense-making and decision-making and concrete workplace behavior would be particularly valuable. Moreover, complex interactions are likely to exist between environmental and individual factors, jointly influencing ethical decisions and behavior (Treviño, 1986; Treviño, Weaver, and Reynolds, 2006). As we continue to pursue a sense-making model of academic misconduct and investigate environmental and individual factors influencing it, this research will allow us to develop more effective interventions, such as organizational policy changes and ethics instruction. Next we consider the current status of common approaches to overcoming misconduct.

Overcoming Academic Misconduct

For many years, self-regulation was thought to be sufficient for managing the integrity of academic work. However, this notion has been challenged by the increasing visibility of instances of misbehavior, along with increased awareness of its prevalence and significant consequences. As a result, the academic community has adopted a number of external mechanisms to manage misconduct in response to this concern. Primary mechanisms include professional codes of conduct and institutional policies and oversight. More recently, instruction in the ethical and responsible conduct of scholarly work, in particular research aspects of this work, has been implemented.

CODES OF CONDUCT, POLICIES, AND OVERSIGHT

The codes of conduct supported by different professional fields vary widely in terms of their content and their depth and breadth, and the value of codes of conduct as a mechanism for managing misconduct is debatable (Iverson, Frankel, and Siang, 2003; Lere and Gaumnitz, 2003). Codes of conduct do appear to be an effective tool for communicating formal norms and expectations within a field. However, they are limited because they tend to overemphasize key outcomes in a field and overlook processes. Therefore, they typically provide little guidance regarding procedures for properly carrying out day-to-day work. Furthermore, codes of conduct present idealized views of the work, emphasizing general principles such as beneficence, honesty, and integrity. Idealized images of work provide best-case scenarios, but do not provide guidance concerning how to make real-world decisions in one's work.

The creation of agencies and committees at the international, national, and institutional levels has also provided external regulation. These entities implement policies, review proposed research, investigate allegations of misconduct, and support education in the responsible and ethical conduct of scholarly work. For example, institutional review boards and institutional animal care and use committees review, approve, and monitor biomedical and behavioral research involving human and animal participants. The US Office of Research Integrity (ORI) oversees and directs activities with respect to biomedical and behavioral research supported by the Public Health Service (Pascal, 2000; Stenek, 2007). Although the ORI's policies and procedures pertain primarily to major violations, this office was instrumental in raising awareness of the importance of more day-to-day research activities, such as publication practices, mentor-mentee relationships, collaboration, and training in these domains. Overall, codes of conduct, policies, and oversight play some role in overcoming academic misconduct, but these mechanisms represent only surface remedies.

ETHICS INSTRUCTION

Ethics instruction has been proposed as a key approach to managing academic misconduct; however, effective approaches for such instruction are still largely unknown (Antes et al., 2009; Kalichman, 2007; Steneck and Bulger, 2007). The significance of this issue increases substantially as ethics instruction becomes an expected component of academic training and funding agencies mandate it (Basken, 2009; Dalton, 2000). Before turning to a discussion of approaches to ethics instruction, a critical question must first be considered: is instruction capable of enhancing ethical behavior and professional conduct? An answer to this question must take several points into consideration.

First, instruction is unlikely to induce morality in otherwise immoral persons (Chen, 2003). Second, instruction is likely to be ineffective if individuals are not at least somewhat motivated to behave according to accepted norms, although, of course, instruction might stimulate some degree of this requisite motivation (Tannenbaum et al., 1991). Third, whether ethics instruction is deemed effective depends on its intended instructional outcomes (Alliger et al., 1997; Kraiger, Ford, and Salas, 1993). Clearly, the likelihood of effectiveness differs when morality is the expected outcome, as against knowledge and skills for understanding and addressing ethical issues. The answer, then, to whether instruction can enhance ethical behavior is: it depends. When the objective of instruction is to improve knowledge and skills, and participants are relatively moral and motivated, then the answer becomes a more solid "probably." Nonetheless, we remain somewhat uncertain about what such effective instruction might look like.

Meta-analysis of existing approaches Approaches to ethics instruction vary widely in content and format. Perhaps most notably, underlying frameworks applied for the construction of instruction vary from moral development models to philosophical theory to problem-solving models. These different frameworks yield markedly different approaches to instruction. For example, moral development models might imply courses of much longer length than problem-solving models (Bebeau and Thoma, 1994; Duckett et al., 1997; Gawthrop and Uhlemann, 1992). Moreover, problem-solving approaches might suggest face-to-face instruction, as opposed to less interactive online instruction. The variation in approaches makes comprehensive, coherent conclusions about the most effective instructional approaches challenging. In an effort to provide some direction in this regard, Antes et al. (2009) conducted a meta-analysis of ethics instruction in the sciences.

In their study Antes et al. (2009) examined the effects of instructional content and methods along with participant characteristics. Taken as a whole, the results were rather sobering. The overall Cohen's d effect size was 0.42, indicating that instruction was only marginally effective. However, the effectiveness of instruction was moderated by several factors, with effect sizes ranging from 0.50 to 0.80, depending on various instructional characteristics.

The pattern of largest effect sizes yielded the conclusion that more effective instruction focuses on a cognitive problem-solving approach, with instruction focused on social-interactional elements of ethical problems proving the next most effective approach. In terms of specific instructional content, instruction regarding potential reasoning biases and errors, such as thinking in black-and-white terms or acting too hastily, was associated with more effective instruction. Moreover, covering thinking strategies, such as considering other's perspectives and anticipating consequences, which facilitate thinking through problems resulted in more effective instruction. In addition to covering reasoning errors and strategies, effective instruction explicitly outlined the dimensions of academic work that might involve ethical problems—for instance, peer review, mentor-mentee relationships, and data-sharing. Covering dimensions of work that involve ethical concerns probably serve as a basis for framing what constitutes professional ethics and issues that require ethical decision-making. This framing, in turn, activates sense-making, and when strategies for working through problems are available, ethical decision-making is enhanced (Gick and Holyoak, 1983; Mumford, Connelly, et al., 2008).

Antes and colleagues' (2009) meta-analysis also revealed that older participants benefited most from instruction. Some base-level knowledge in the field may be needed before adding to this knowledge complex information about ethical issues relevant to the work (Daley, 1999; Ericsson and Charness, 1994). A motivational explanation may also apply. It could be that experience in one's field creates awareness about ethical problems and motivates learning about these issues (Klein, Noe, and Wang, 2006; Salas and Cannon-Bowers, 2001). Experience may also provide valuable case models that one can draw upon during learning (VanLehn, 1998). In fact, the meta-analysis demonstrated that instruction using cases and case analysis were more effective than other approaches, such as lecture-based instruction. Case analysis facilitates practice with new knowledge and skills, and provides learners with contextualized exemplars that can be drawn upon in future problem-solving (Kolodner et al., 2003). Case-based instruction also tends to be more interactive and social, if case analysis is accompanied by discussion. Indeed, courses that were more interactive proved more effective than those with limited social interaction.

Finally, shorter, seminar-type courses were more effective compared to longer, semester-length courses. It may be that shorter courses also tend to be interactive and case-based. However, it is also possible that learners find shorter courses more salient because they exist outside of the regular curriculum, which enhances course effectiveness. Shorter courses may also prove more engaging because they might assume base knowledge and focus more heavily on skills development. These observations lead us to an important point. Some instructional characteristics, such as length, may seem less critical than others, but, in fact, they prove rather significant in terms of influencing learning outcomes (Goldstein and Ford, 2002). Overall, the findings from this meta-analysis provided additional evidence for the importance of sense-making, as it appears that more effective instruction facilitated individuals' understanding of what constitutes ethical problems and how to think through them.

It is important to note that the conclusions emerging Antes et al.'s (2009) meta-analysis were not without limitations. Most significantly, only a limited number of instructional evaluation studies could be included in the investigation, and the limited sample size may have jeopardized the stability of effect size estimates, and prevented analysis of effects at the level of individual instructional outcomes. Many studies could not be included in the meta-analysis because inadequate details were reported about the instruction and/or statistical analyses. This observation led Antes et al. (2009) to emphasize the need for rigor in future evaluation efforts. Indeed, the nature of the evaluation studies and the criterion measures applied produced differences in effects observed in the meta-analysis. Antes and colleagues (2009) specifically observed an overreliance on the Defining Issues Test (DIT) for measuring instructional outcomes (Rest, 1976). Although the DIT may measure some aspect of ethical reasoning, it is unlikely to measure all the possible or desired instructional outcomes (Kraiger and Jung, 1996).

Sense-making instruction The course designed by Mumford, Connelly, and colleagues (2008) around their sense-making framework incorporates many of the elements found effective in the meta-analysis. Their course has met with relative success across a number of academic fields where the primary course participants were graduate students. This course takes place over two days, including about 12 hours of face-to-face instruction and four hours' out-of-class work. The emphasis of this training program is to provide instruction in the strategies that facilitate sense-making and to provide practice applying them to realistic, complex problems.

Before learning the strategies, students learn about basic research principles and guidelines. They learn that although guidelines provide a general foundation for conduct, they do not take context into account, nor do they provide concrete guidance about how to go about making real-world decisions. Next, students learn about the tendency for people to discount situational influences on their behavior and to assume that their values, although highly idealized, will provide a solid foundation for making ethical decisions. Students then brainstorm additional internal and external constraints (e.g., time pressure, poor communication, black-and-white thinking, and hasty decision-making) that create ethical problems in their work and limit effective decision-making.

In the next segment of the course, students are presented with the seven sense-making strategies (see Table 8.2). These strategies are described as tools that facilitate identifying, understanding, and responding to complex ethical problems in one's work. Next, students apply these strategies to a number of complex cases. The second day of instruction further emphasizes the use of these strategies for analyzing elements of ethical problems and arriving at decisions. For instance, on the second day, students participate in a role-play. Specifically, each student takes on and acts out the role of a character within a complex scenario. They then discuss how characters might apply the strategies in working through their role in the case.

A sample of 60 graduate students in the biological and social sciences evaluated this course. Participants completed a pre-post version of Mumford et al.'s (2006) ethical decision-making measure. The effect sizes obtained in the evaluation were quite sizable, especially in comparison to the 0.42 effect size obtained in the meta-analysis. The Cohen's d effect size gains from the pre- to post-test for the ethicality of decisions made with respect to data management (0.66), study conduct (1.46), professional practices (0.61), and business practices (0.49) were moderate to large. Pre- to post-test improvements for the use of sense-making strategies were also sizable: recognizing circumstances (1.24), seeking help (0.84), questioning one's judgment (1.27), dealing with emotions (0.90), anticipating consequences (0.77), analyzing personal motivations (1.36), and considering others (0.45). Follow-up evaluation, six months later, revealed that these effects largely held over time. This same instructional program was also provided to graduate students working in computer science, meteorology, and engineering (Kligyte, Marcy, Waples, et al., 2008). The results revealed large gains in ethical decision-making and strategy use, and a follow-up study provided evidence for the maintenance of these effects over time (Brock et al., 2008).

Taken as a whole, these studies provide rather compelling evidence that sense-making instruction—instruction focused on providing strategies that facilitate analysis and understanding of complex, ambiguous ethical problems—proves a rather promising approach to ethics instruction. Strategy-based training has been shown to be effective for improving performance on other complex, cognitively demanding tasks, such as creative problem-solving (Scott, Leritz, and Mumford, 2004). The sense-making framework presented in this chapter maintains that ethical decision-making is, indeed, a complex, multifaceted cognitive activity. Thus, it is only fitting that enhancing this complex phenomenon requires dynamic, multifaceted instruction.

The potential dark side of ethics instruction Instruction seems to be the most celebrated approach to managing professional and ethical conduct, perhaps because academics view education as an endeavor promoting universal benefit. The findings of a study conducted by Antes et al. (2010), however, call this assumption into question. This study examined the effects of existing semester-long responsible conduct of research courses for biomedical students at a number of US universities. The method applied to test the effects of these courses was online completion of the pre-post version of Mumford et al.'s (2006) ethical decision-making measure.

The results showed that the ethicality of decisions generally did not improve or decline following instruction, but ethicality decreased with respect to decisions concerning business practices. The pattern of responses endorsed by participants revealed mixed effects of instruction on sense-making strategies. Participants improved in their analysis of situational elements and reflection on personal motivations and biases, but declined in their consideration of others and acceptance of personal responsibility. Overall, the findings suggested that ethics instruction may not necessarily be beneficial, and, in fact, may produce detrimental effects.

Antes and colleagues (2010) suggested some potential explanations for why ethics instruction may produce no, or negative, effects. It may be that ethics instruction encourages self-protective behaviors by overemphasizing severe negative outcomes of incidents of misconduct. Hence, instruction would reduce active processing about effects on others and induce avoidance of personal responsibility. Instruction might also induce overconfidence and self-enhancement. Overconfidence might result if courses present ethics as a closed system where a delimited set of knowledge is sufficient to produce ethical behavior. Such a focus might lead students to assume that completing an ethics course has provided them with this requisite knowledge. Thus, responses to future problems might be shallow and too automatic. To mitigate this concern, instruction must promote the understanding that ethical decision-making is an ongoing, dynamic process. Instruction might encourage self-enhancement, or even moral credentialing, if students perceive their likely behavior in comparison to extreme case examples as especially ethical (Brown et al., in press). In turn, students are less likely to actively analyze situations and the effects of their actions on others. Overall, Antes et al. (2010) concluded that the complexities inherent in designing and delivering effective ethics instruction must not be taken for granted.

FIELD AND ORGANIZATIONAL INTERVENTIONS

Of course, it is likely that interventions other than training might be effective for managing the integrity of academic work. Field- and organizational-level interventions that manage the demands placed on academics, improve fairness and transparency in recognition and reward systems, and monitor work environments may prove of particular value. Given that sense-making is a cognitively resource-intensive activity, it should not be surprising that excessive environmental stressors, such as time pressure, excessive production demands, and uncertainty about resources might undermine the process of making sense of complex, ambiguous situations and, in turn, make ethical decision-making more difficult (Fiedler and Garcia, 1987). Therefore, ensuring fairness and transparency in promotion requirements and procedures for obtaining resources may help overcome such stressors and thereby improve conduct. As an example, the academic community should make certain that expectations for tenure, such as publishing requirements, are reasonable. Moreover, reward systems in academia must reward other aspects of academic work, such as mentoring practices that are valued.

Another management strategy might involve professions and organizations, particularly those including high-risk, high-pressure fields, should implement procedures for monitoring indicators of professional and organizational well-being, such as intensity of competition and conflict, perceptions of fairness and objectivity, and cynicism (Martinson et al., 2006; Mumford, Antes, Beeler, and Caughron, 2009). Monitoring systems allow for the active management of root causes of academic misconduct, instead of managing the outcomes after misbehavior has occurred. Fields, particularly high-risk fields, should specifically monitor socialization processes and develop strategies for effective field socialization. For instance, peer mentoring might be used to facilitate information-sharing and reduce role uncertainty. Peer mentor relationships might also facilitate the development of viable collaborations. Moreover, existing regulatory policies and oversight mechanisms, such as institutional review boards, should be examined for their contributions to environments conducive to ethical conduct (DeVries et al., 2006; Franzen, Rödder, and Weingart, 2007).

Where Do We Go From Here?

Although much more work remains to be done, as we look ahead, we can be confident in our strides toward understanding academic misconduct.

Without question, one of the most essential steps has been a reframing of what constitutes academic and research misconduct. Although major violations do occur, we are now conscious of the significant impact of more common, day-to-day workplace issues. This more comprehensive, practical understanding of academic misconduct has brought to light the reality that this issue concerns all individuals, not just a select few. Additionally, this framing of academic misconduct led Mumford, Connelly, and colleagues (2008) to apply a sense-making framework to account for the process by which academics analyze and respond to the complexities of their work. Ultimately, these developments will make more effective interventions for minimizing misconduct possible.

Future work must continue to investigate sense-making among academics. In this chapter we have reviewed some influences on sense-making—for instance, socialization and cynicism—and seven key strategies for facilitating sense-making processes, but additional research is needed to examine factors that influence sense-making and strategies that facilitate sense-making processes. For example, in a study along these lines, Stenmark et al. (2010) examined the effects of analyzing causes of the ethical problem on ethical decision-making. They found that considering the most critical causes of the problem facilitated the anticipation of potential outcomes and led to more ethical decisions. In another recent study Caughron et al. (under review) found that emphasis of organizational-level consequences, as opposed to personal consequences, facilitated sense-making and, in turn, ethical decision-making.

The findings presented in this chapter imply other essential investigations. Future research might examine organizational and work variables inducing situation-based cynicism. Additional work might explore differences in the development of sense-making across various academic fields over time. This understanding would provide insight into changing instructional needs over the course of an academic's career. Aspects of academic work involving social dimensions, specifically teaching, mentorship, and collaboration, also require additional research. For instance, research might examine the influence of mentorship, particularly early in one's career, on sense-making about one's work and ethical problems. This work would support the preparation of academics for their mentoring role. Importantly, these investigations must examine fields beyond science and engineering as academic misconduct is a concern across fields (Stenmark et al., under review).

As we move forward, we must continue to determine what constitutes effective ethics instruction specifically and academic training in general. It appears that ethics instruction emphasizing the complex, social nature of the work and imparting cognitive strategies for analyzing and understanding these complexities proves particularly effective. Future research might examine other training interventions facilitating the navigation of the complexities of academic work. For example, although academic training traditionally emphasizes only technical aspects of the work, perhaps instruction in communication and conflict management skills would prove of value. Enhanced interaction with others would lead not only to greater productivity, but also to improved worker well-being.

In addition, future research should pursue advanced needs for ethics instruction. For example, mentors and organizational leaders might benefit from instruction pertaining to the identification and management of emerging issues symptomatic of an environment conducive to misconduct (Mumford, Friedrich, Caughron, and Byrne, 2007). Other work might examine variables within the workplace (e.g., peer groups and production pressure) that influence the application of learning from ethics instruction to the work context (Tracey, Tannenbaum, and Kavanagh, 1995). Finally, the finding that individual differences influence sense-making and ethical decision-making suggests another issue worthy of investigation (Antes et al., 2007), namely the interaction of individual difference variables with ethics instruction and its resulting effectiveness (Colquitt, LePine, and Noe, 2000; Herold et al., 2002). It is likely, for example, that narcissism and cynicism interact with instructional efforts to reduce their effects.

Conclusion

Academic misconduct is a matter of day-to-day workplace problems and people's interpretations of, and responses to, these problems. As a result, the scholarly community has begun to recognize that academic work can no longer be viewed only according to its technical aspects. Instead, we must take into account its social and ethical dimensions. This new understanding raises a major implication—specifically, that the expertise necessary for success in science and academia includes knowledge and skills for understanding and handling the social and ethical elements of the work. Therefore, as we seek to educate young scholars, educational experiences, both formal (e.g., ethics instruction) and informal (e.g., mentorship), must provide for the development of this expertise. We hope that this chapter provides a shared framework for understanding academic misconduct that promotes future research and also provides a common language encouraging open discussion of ethical issues as a normal, day-to-day aspect of academic life.

References

Agarwal, J. and Malloy, D. C. (1999) "Ethical work climate dimensions in a not-for-profit: An empirical study," *Journal of Business Ethics*, 20, 2–13.

Alliger, G. M., Tannenbaum, S. I., Bennett, W., Traver, H., and Shotland, A. (1997) "A meta-analysis of the relations among training criteria," *Personnel Psychology*, 50, 341–358.

Antes, A. L., Brown, R. P., Murphy, S. T., Waples, E. P., Mumford, M. D., Connelly, S., and Devenport, L. D. (2007) "Personality and ethical decision-making in research: The role of perceptions of self and others," *Journal of Empirical Research on Human Research Ethics*, 2, 15–34.

Antes, A. L., Murphy, S. T., Waples, E. P., Mumford, M. D., Brown, R. P., Connelly, S., and Devenport, L. D. (2009) "A meta-analysis of ethics instruction effectiveness in the sciences," *Ethics and Behavior*, 19, 379–402.

Antes, A. L., Wang, X., Mumford, M. D., Brown, R. P., Connelly, S., and Devenport, L. D. (2010) "Evaluating the effects that existing instruction on responsible conduct of research has on ethical decision making," *Academic Medicine*, 85, 519–525.

Barnett, T. and Vaicys, C. (2000) "The moderating effect of individuals' perceptions of ethical work climate on ethical judgment and behavioral intentions," *Journal of Business Ethics*, 27, 351–362.

Barrick, M. R. and Mount, M. K. (1991) "The Big Five personality dimensions and job performance: A meta-analysis," *Personnel Psychology*, 44, 1–26.

Basken, P. (2009) "NSF defers to universities on ethical standards," *The Chronicle of Higher Education*, August 20, at: http://chronicle.com/article/NSF-Defers-to-Universities-on/48095/.

Bebeau, M. J. and Thoma, S. J. (1994) "The impact of a dental ethics curriculum on moral reasoning," *Journal of Dental Education*, 58, 684–692.

Biaggio, M., Duffy, R., and Staffelbach, D. F. (1998) "Obstacles to addressing professional misconduct," *Clinical Psychology Review*, 18, 273–285.

Bordons, M. and Gómez, I. (2000) "Collaboration networks in science" in B. Cronin and H. B. Atkins (eds) *The Web of Knowledge: A Festschrift in Honor of Eugene Garfield*, Medford, NJ: Information Today, Inc., pp. 197–214.

Brock, M. E., Vert, A., Kligyte, V., Waples, E. P., Sevier, S. T., and Mumford, M. D. (2008) "Mental models: An alternative evaluation of a sensemaking approach to ethics instruction," *Science and Engineering Ethics*, 14, 449–472.

Brown, M. E. and Treviño, L. K. (2006) "Socialized charismatic leadership, values congruence, and deviance in work groups," *Journal of Applied Psychology*, 91, 954–962.

Brown, R. P., Tamborski, M., Wang, X., Barnes, C. D., Mumford, M. D., Connelly, S., and Devenport, L. D. (in press) "Moral credentialing and the rationalization of misconduct," *Ethics and Behavior*.

Caughron, J. J., Antes, A. L., Stenmark, C. K., Thiel, C. E., Wang, X., and Mumford, M. D. (under review) "Sense-making strategies for ethical decision-making," *Ethics and Behavior*.

Chen, D. T. (2003) "Curricular approaches to research ethics training for psychiatric investigators," *Psychopharmacology*, 171, 112–119.

Colquitt, J. A., LePine, J. A., and Noe, R. A. (2000) "Toward an integrative theory of training motivation: A meta-analytic path analysis of 20 years of research," *Journal of Applied Psychology*, 85, 678–707.

Cook, T. D. and Campbell, D. T. (1979) *Quasi-Experimentation: Design and Analysis Issues for Field Settings*, Boston, MA: Houghton Mifflin.

Crigger, N. J. (1998) "What we owe the author: Rethinking editorial peer review," *Nursing Ethics*, 5, 451–458.

Cyranoski, D. (2006) "Verdict: Hwang's human stem cells were all fakes," *Nature*, 439, 122–123.

Daley, B. J. (1999) "Novice to expert: An exploration of how professionals learn," *Adult Education Quarterly*, 49, 133–147.

Dalton, R. (2000) "NIH case tied to compulsory training in good behavior," *Nature*, 408, 629.

Dalton, R. (2005) "Obesity expert owns up to million-dollar crime," *Nature*, 434, 424.

DeVries, R., Anderson, M. S., and Martinson, B. C. (2006) "Normal misbehavior: Scientists talk about the ethics of research," *Journal of Empirical Research on Human Research Ethics*, 1, 43–50.

Duckett, L., Rowan, M., Ryden, M., Krichbaum, K., Miller, M., Wainwright, H., and Savik, K. (1997) "Progress in the moral reasoning of baccalaureate nursing students between program entry and exit," *Nursing Research*, 46, 222–229.

Dunbar, K. (1995) "How scientist really reason: Scientific reasoning in real world laboratories" in R. J. Sternberg and J. E. Davidson (eds) *The Nature of Insight*, Cambridge MA: MIT Press, pp. 365–396.

Ericsson, K. A. and Charness, N. (1994) "Expert performance: Its structure and acquisition," *American Psychologist*, 49, 725–747.

Fanelli, D. (2009) "How many scientists fabricate and falsify research? A systematic review and meta-analysis of survey data," *PLoS ONE* 4, e5788. doi: 10.1371/journal.pone.0005738. Available at: http://www.plosone.org/article/info:doi/10.1371/journal.pone.0005738.

Feist, G. J. (1998) "A meta-analysis of personality in scientific and artistic creativity," *Personality and Social Psychology Review*, 2, 290–309.

Feldman, D. H. (1999) "The development of creativity" in R. J. Sternberg (ed.) *Handbook of Creativity* Cambridge, UK: Cambridge University Press, pp. 169–188.

Fiedler, F. E. and Garcia, J. E. (1987) *New Approaches to Effective Leadership*, New York: Wiley.

Franzen, M., Rödder, S., and Weingart, P. (2007) "Fraud: Causes and culprits as perceived by science and the media," *European Molecular Biology Organization Reports*, 8, 3–7.

Friedman, P. J. (2002) "The impact of conflict of interest on trust in science," *Science and Engineering Ethics*, 8, 413–420.

Gawthrop, J. C. and Uhlemann, M. R. (1992) "Effects of the problem-solving approach in ethics training," *Professional Psychology: Research & Practice*, 23, 38–42.

Gelman, S. and Gibelman, M. (2002) "Plagiarism in academia: Are students emulating (bad) faculty role models?" paper presented at the ORI Research Conference on Research Integrity, Potomac, MD, November.

Gerber, P. (2006) "What can we learn from the Hwang and Sudbo affairs?" *Medical Journal of Australia*, 184, 632–635.

Gibson, C. B. (2001) "From knowledge accumulation to accommodation: Cycles of collective cognition in work groups," *Journal of Organizational Behavior*, 22, 121–134.

Gick, M. and Holyoak, K. (1983) "Schema induction and analogical transfer," *Cognitive Psychology*, 15, 1–38.

Goldstein, I. L. and Ford, J. K. (2002) *Training in Organizations: Need Assessment, Development, and Evaluation* (4th ed.), Belmont, CA: Wadsworth.

Haerlin, B. and Parr, D. (1999) "How to restore public trust in science," *Nature*, 400, 499.

Haidt, J. (2001) "The emotional dog and its rational tail: A social intuitionist approach to moral judgment," *Psychological Review*, 108, 814–834.

Hegarty, W. H. and Sims, H. P. (1979) "Organizational philosophy, policies, and objectives related to unethical decision behavior: A laboratory experiment," *Journal of Applied Psychology*, 64, 331–338.

Helton-Fauth, W., Gaddis, B., Scott, G., Mumford, M. D., Devenport, L. D., Connelly, S., and Brown, R. P. (2003) "A new approach to assessing ethical conduct in scientific work," *Accountability in Research*, 10, 205–228.

Herold, D. M., Davis, W., Fedor, D. B., and Parsons, C. K. (2002) "Dispositional influences on transfer of learning in multistage training programs," *Personnel Psychology*, 55, 851–869.

Hunter, J. E. and Schmidt, F. L. (1996) "Intelligence and job performance: Economic and social implications," *Psychology, Public Policy, and Law*, 2, 447–472.

Iverson, M., Frankel, M. S., and Siang, S. (2003) "Scientific societies and research integrity: What are they doing and how well are they doing it?" *Science and Engineering Ethics*, 9, 141–158.

Janssen, O. and Van Yperen, N. W. (2004) "Employees' goal orientations, the quality of leader-member exchange, and the outcomes of job performance and job satisfaction," *Academy of Management Journal*, 47, 368–384.

John, O. P. and Srivastava, S. (1999) "The Big Five Trait taxonomy: History, measurement, and theoretical perspectives" in L. A. Pervin and Oliver P. John (eds) *Handbook of Personality: Theory and Research* (2nd ed.), New York: Guilford Press, pp. 102–139.

Kalichman, M. W. (2007) "Responding to challenges in educating for the responsible conduct of research," *Academic Medicine*, 82, 870–875.

Kanter, D. L. and Mirvis, P. H. (1989) *The Cynical Americans: Living and Working in an Age of Discontent and Disillusion*, San Francisco, CA: Jossey-Bass.

Klein, H. J., Noe, R. A., and Wang, C. (2006) "Motivation to learn and course outcomes: The impact of delivery model, learning goal orientation, and perceived barriers and enablers," *Personnel Psychology*, 59, 665–702.

Kligyte, V., Marcy, R. T., Sevier, S. T., Godfrey, E. S., and Mumford, M. D. (2008) "A qualitative approach to responsible conduct of research (RCR) training development: Identification of metacognitive strategies," *Science and Engineering Ethics*, 14, 3–31.

Kligyte, V., Marcy, R. T., Waples, E. P., Sevier, S. T., Godfrey, E. S., Mumford, M. D., and Hougen, D. F. (2008) "Application of a sensemaking approach to ethics training for physical sciences and engineering," *Science and Engineering Ethics*, 14(2), 251–278.

Kohlberg, L. (1969) "Stage and sequence: The cognitive development approach to socialization" in D. A. Goslin (ed.) *Handbook of Socialization Theory* Chicago, IL: Rand McNally, pp. 347–480.

Kolodner, J. L. (1997) "Educational implications of analogy: A view from case-based reasoning," *American Psychologist*, 52, 57–66.

Kolodner, J., Camp, P., Crismond, D., Fasse, B., Gray, J., Holbrook, J., Puntambekar, S., and Ryan, M. (2003) "Problem-based learning meets case-based reasoning in the middle-school science classroom: Putting learning by design into practice," *The Journal of the Learning Sciences*, 12, 495–547.

Kraiger, K., Ford, J. K., and Salas, E. (1993) "Applications of cognitive, skill-based, and affective theories of learning outcomes to new methods of training evaluation," *Journal of Applied Psychology*, 311, 311–328.

Kraiger, K. and Jung, K. M. (1996) "Linking training objectives to evaluation criteria" in M. A. Quiñones and A. Ehrenstein (eds) *Training for a Rapidly Changing Workplace: Application of Psychological Research*, Washington, DC: American Psychological Association, pp. 151–175.

Lajoie, S. P. (2009) "Developing professional experience with a cognitive apprentice model: Examples from avionics and medicine" in K. A. Ericsson (ed.), *Development of Professional Expertise*, New York: Cambridge University Press, pp. 61–83.

Lere, J. C. and Gaumnitz, B. R. (2003) "The impact of codes of ethics on decision making: Some insights from information economics," *Journal of Business Ethics*, 48, 365–379.

Marshall, E. (2000) "How prevalent is fraud? That's the million-dollar question," *Science*, 290, 1662–1663.

Martinson, B. C., Anderson, M. S., Crain, A. L., and DeVries, R. (2006) "Scientists' perceptions of organizational justice and self-reported misbehaviors," *Journal of Empirical Research on Human Research Ethics*, 1, 51–66.

Martinson, B. C., Anderson, M. S., and DeVries, R. (2005), "Scientists behaving badly," *Nature*, 435, 737–738.

McCook, A. (2009) "Life after fraud," *The Scientist*, July, at: http://www.the-scientist.com/article/display/55772/.

Miethe, T. D. (1999) *Whistleblowing at Work: Tough Choices in Exposing Fraud, Waste, and Abuse on the Job*, Boulder, CO: Westview Press, Inc.

Morrison, E. W. (1993) "Newcomer information seeking: Exploring types, modes, sources, and outcomes," *The Academy of Management Journal*, 36, 557–589.

Mumford, M. D., Antes, A. L., Stenmark, C. K., and Caughron, J. (2009) "On the corruptions of scientists: The influence of field, environment, and personality" in R. J. Burke and C. L. Cooper (eds) *Research Companion to Corruption in Organizations*, Cheltenham, UK: Edward Elgar.

Mumford, M. D., Connelly, S., Brown, R. P., Murphy, S. T., Hill, J. H., Antes, A. L., Waples, E. P., and Devenport, L. D. (2008) "Sensemaking approach to ethics training for scientists: Preliminary evidence of training effectiveness," *Ethics and Behavior*, 18, 315–339.

Mumford, M. D., Connelly, S., Murphy, S. T., Devenport, L. D., Antes, A. L., Brown, R. P., Hill, J. H., and Waples, E. P. (2009) "Field and experience influences on ethical decision-making in the sciences," *Ethics and Behavior*, 19, 263–289.

Mumford, M. D., Connelly, S., Scott, G., Espejo, J., Sohl, L. M., Hunter, S. T., and Bedell, K. E. (2005) "Career experiences and scientific performance: A study of social, physical, life, and health sciences," *Creativity Research Journal*, 17, 105–129.

Mumford, M. D., Devenport, L. D., Brown, R. P., Connelly, S., Murphy, S. T., Hill, J. H., and Antes, A. L. (2006) "Validation of ethical decision-making measures: Evidence for a new set of measures," *Ethics and Behavior*, 16, 319–345.

Mumford, M. D., Friedrich, T. L., Caughron, J. J., and Byrne, C. L. (2007) "Leader cognition in real-world settings: How do leaders think about crises?" *The Leadership Quarterly*, 18, 515–543.

Mumford, M. D., Murphy, S. T., Connelly, S., Hill, J. H., Antes, A. L., Brown, R. P., and Devenport, L. D. (2007) "Environmental influences on ethical decision-making: Climate and environmental predictors of research integrity," *Ethics and Behavior*, 17, 337–366.

Mumford, M. D., Waples, E. P., Antes, A. L., Murphy, S. T., Connelly, S., Brown, R. P., and Devenport, L. D. (2009) "Exposure to unethical career events: Effects on decision-making, climate, and socialization," *Ethics and Behavior*, 19, 351–378.

Murphy, K. R. (2000) "What constructs underlie measures of honesty or integrity?" in R. Goffin and E. Helmes (eds) *Problems and Solutions in Human Assessment: Honoring Douglas N. Jackson at Seventy*, Boston, MA: Kluwer, pp. 265–284.

Myers, D. G. (2007) *Psychology* (8th ed.), New York: Worth Publishers.

Nova, J. (2009) *Climate Money: The Climate Industry: $79 Billion So Far—Trillions to Come*, Haymarket, VA: Science and Public Policy Institute.

Odling-Smee, L., Giles, J., Fuyuno, I., Cyranoski, D., and Marris, E. (2007) "Where are they now?" *Nature*, 445, 244–245.

Ones, D. S., Viswesvaran, C., and Schmidt, F. L. (1993) "Comprehensive meta-analysis of integrity test validities: Findings and implications for personnel selection and theories of job performance," *Journal of Applied Psychology*, 78, 679–703.

Pascal, C. B. (2000) "Scientific misconduct and research integrity for the bench scientist," *Proceedings for the Society for Experimental Biology and Medicine*, 224, 220–230.

Pear, R. (2009) "U.S. to compare medical treatments," *New York Times*, February 15, at: http://www.nytimes.com/2009/02/16/health/policy/16health.html.

Penney, L. M. and Spector, P. E. (2002) "Narcissism and counterproductive work behavior: Do bigger egos mean bigger problems?" *International Journal of Selection and Assessment*, 10, 126–134.

Pronin, E. (2007) "Perception and misperception of bias in human judgment," *Trends in Cognitive Science*, 11, 37–43.

Resnik, D. B. (2003) "From Baltimore to Bell Labs: Reflections on two decades of debate about scientific misconduct," *Accountability in Research*, 10, 123–135.

Rest, J. (1976) "New approaches in the assessment of moral judgment" in T. Lickona (ed.) *Moral Development and Behavior: Theory, Research, and Social Issues*, New York: Holt, Rinehart & Winston.

Reynolds, S. J. (2006) "A neurocognitive model of the ethical decision-making process: Implications for study and practice," *Journal of Applied Psychology*, 91, 737–748.

Reynolds, S. J. and Ceranic, T. L. (2007) "The effects of moral judgment and moral identity on moral behavior: An empirical examination of the moral individual," *Journal of Applied Psychology*, 92, 1610–1624.

Salas, E. and Cannon-Bowers, J. A. (2001) "The science of training: A decade of progress," *Annual Review of Psychology*, 52, 471–499.

Schminke, M., Arnaud, A., and Kuenzi, M. (2007) "The power of ethical work climates," *Organizational Dynamics*, 36, 171–186.

Schweitzer, M. E., Ordóñez, L., and Douma, B. (2004) "Goal setting as a motivator of unethical behavior," *Academy of Management Journal*, 47, 422–432.

Scott, G. M., Leritz, L. E., and Mumford M. D. (2004) "The effectiveness of creativity training: A meta-analysis," *Creativity Research Journal*, 16, 361–388.

Simonton, D. K. (2005) "Creativity and development," *American Journal of Psychology*, 118, 645–649.

Sonenshein, S. (2007) "The role of construction, intuition, and justification in response to ethical issues at work: The sensemaking-intuition model," *Academy of Management Review*, 32, 1022–1040.

Sox, H. C. and Rennie, D. (2006) "Research misconduct, retraction, and cleansing the medical literature: Lessons from the Poehlman case," *Annals of Internal Medicine*, 144, 609–613.

Steele-Johnson, D., Beauregard, R. S., Hoover, P. B., and Schmidt, A. M. (2000) "Goal orientation and task demand effects on motivation, affect, and performance," *Journal of Applied Psychology*, 85, 724–738.

Steneck, N. H. (2000) *Assessing the Integrity of Publicly Funded Research: A Background Report for the November 2000 ORI Research Conference on Research Integrity*, Washington DC: Office of Research Integrity.

Steneck, N. H. (2007) *ORI Introduction to the Responsible Conduct of Research*, Washington, DC: US Government Printing Office.

Steneck, N. H. and Bulger, R. E. (2007) "The history, purpose, and future of instruction in the responsible conduct of research," *Academic Medicine*, 82, 829–834.

Stenmark, C., Antes, A. L., Wang, X., Caughron, J. J., Thiel, C.E., and Mumford, M. D. (2010) "Strategies in forecasting outcomes in ethical decision-making:

Identifying and analyzing the causes of the problem," *Ethics and Behavior*, 20, 110–127.

Stenmark, C., Antes, A. L., Wang, X., Caughron, J., Thiel, C. E., and Mumford, M. D. (under review) "Forecasting outcomes in ethical decision-making: Identifying and analyzing the causes of the problem," *Ethics and Behavior*.

Tannenbaum, S. I., Mathieu, J. E., Salas, E., and Cannon-Bowers, J. A. (1991) "Meeting trainees' expectations: The influence of training fulfillment on the development of commitment, self-efficacy, and motivation," *Journal of Applied Psychology*, 76, 759–769.

Tordoir, P. P. (1995) *The Professional Knowledge Economy*, Dordrecht: Kluwer Academic Publishers.

Tracey, J. B., Tannenbaum, S. I., and Kavanagh, M. J. (1995) "Applying trained skills on the job: The importance of the work environment," *Journal of Applied Psychology*, 80, 239–252.

Treviño, L. K. (1986) "Ethical decision making in organizations: A person-situation interactionist model," *Academy of Management Review*, 11, 601–617.

Treviño, L. K., Weaver, G. R., and Reynolds, S. J. (2006) "Behavioral ethics in organizations: A review," *Journal of Management*, 32, 951–990.

Tyson, T. (1990) "Believing that everyone else is less ethical: Implications for work behavior and ethics instruction," *Journal of Business Ethics*, 9, 715–721.

VanLehn, K. (1998) "Analogy events: How examples are used during problem solving," *Cognitive Science*, 22, 347–388.

Wallace, H. M. and Baumeister, R. F. (2002) "The performance of narcissists rises and falls with perceived opportunity for glory," *Journal of Personality and Social Psychology*, 82, 819–834.

Weingart, P. (2002) "The moment of truth for science: The consequences of the 'knowledge society' for society and science," *European Molecular Biology Organization Reports*, 3, 703–706.

Weisberg, R. W. (2006) "Modes of expertise in creative thinking: Evidence from case studies" in K. A. Ericsson, N. Charness, P. J. Feltovich and R. R. Hoffman (eds) *The Cambridge Handbook of Expertise and Expert Performance*, New York: Cambridge University Press, pp. 761–787.

Wennerås, C. and Wold, A. (1997), "Nepotism and sexism in peer-review," *Nature*, 387, 341–343.

Zellner, C. (2003) "The economic effects of basic research: Evidence for embodied knowledge transfer via scientists' migration," *Research Policy*, 32, 1881–1895.

9

Medicines and Money: The Corruption of Clinical Information

Joel Lexchin

Introduction

In his 1984 book on the pharmaceutical industry, the Australian researcher John Braithwaite reported that two American pharmaceutical executives whom he interviewed had the job title of "vice-president responsible for going to jail" (Braithwaite, 1984). In other words, should the companies that these two people worked for ever be convicted in criminal court and a jail sentence imposed, they were the ones who would be imprisoned.

In the intervening 25 years no executives have ever had to serve time, but there are multiple instances where companies and their employees have appeared in court. To give just a small selection, in 2007 Purdue Pharma and three of its executives pleaded guilty in criminal court to having misled doctors and patients about the risk of addiction from one of the company's products. The company was fined US$600 million and the three executives had to pay US$34.5 million (Meier, 2007). Pfizer was charged, pleaded guilty, and paid US$430 million to resolve criminal and civil charges related to marketing practices around Neurontin (gabapentin) (Harris, 2004). GlaxoSmithKline was sued by the New York State Attorney-General for consumer fraud in respect of withholding the results of negative studies involving its antidepressant Paxil (paroxetine) (Bass, 2008). Most recently, Pfizer paid US$1.3 billion in criminal penalties and an additional US$1 billion in civil fines related to its marketing of a number of drugs including Bextra (valdecoxib) (Harris, 2009).

Court appearances are merely the tip of the iceberg when it comes to questionable undertakings by pharmaceutical companies. Companies can corrupt the generation of information about the clinical value of medicines without inevitably committing crimes or becoming the subject of civil lawsuits. This chapter will use concrete case studies to look at a range of these activities, including biasing the conduct of clinical research, the quality of communications between companies and drug regulators on safety issues, selective and misleading publication of research results, hiring ghostwriters to ensure that the published material reflects the spin that the companies want, promoting products for uses that have not been approved, ensuring that the content of continuing medical education (CME) courses and clinical guidelines is favorable and shutting down people and groups critical of industry practices or who propose to publish material that runs contrary to the industry's interests.

It would be a mistake to see these practices as isolated examples committed by companies operating outside the usual parameters adopted by industry. All the major drug companies are motivated to engage in these types of practice by the exigencies of the marketplace. Over the past couple of decades companies have moved into a "blockbuster" mentality—they need to have products sell US$1 billion or more worldwide on an annual basis in order to maintain the rates of return that their investors have become accustomed to. Any potential threats to sales that come from negative research findings or from unfavorable journal articles have to be either prevented or aggressively countered.

Biasing the Conduct of Clinical Research

The results of clinical research are the cornerstone for ensuring that patients get optimal pharmacotherapy when drug treatment is necessary. The results of studies on humans are used to determine the conditions for licensing products and are the basis for subsequent prescribing guidelines and other information that doctors use in deciding on how to treat their patients. Therefore, any threat to the integrity of clinical research strikes at the heart of pharmacotherapy.

In the US, pharmaceutical and biotechnology firms contributed almost half of the US$94 billion spent on biomedical research in 2004, with the bulk of industry spending going toward clinical research (Moses et al., 2005). In Norway most of the clinical trials approved by five regional medical research ethics committees were conducted by industry (Hole, Winther, and Straume, 2001). Over the period 1994 to 2003 the vast majority of the most cited randomized controlled trials received funding from industry, and the proportion increased significantly over time: 18 of the 32 most cited trials published after 1999 were funded by industry alone (Patsopoulos, Ioannidis, and Analatos, 2006).

Alongside the dominance of the pharmaceutical industry in funding clinical research there is accumulating evidence that research funded by companies is much more likely to yield positive results than research sponsored by any other source. A qualitative systematic review identified 17 studies published between 2003 and 2006 that demonstrated this point, with only two studies showing the opposite—that industry sponsorship did not systematically yield more positive outcomes (Sismondo, 2008). The degree of bias extended to the situation where if the same two second-generation antipsychotic drugs were being compared in separate studies by the different manufacturers, the drug that was found to be superior was the one made by the sponsor of the study (Heres et al., 2006). Not only does this finding of bias apply to clinical trials, but the same is true for meta-analyses (Yank, Rennie, and Bero, 2007) and pharmacoeconomic studies (Miners et al., 2005).

Various explanations have been advanced to account for this result. In some cases, the doses of the study and comparator drugs were not equivalent; the drug given at the higher dose was that of the sponsoring company, leading to its drug appearing more effective (Rochon et al., 1994); at other times, an inferior comparator was chosen (Johansen and Gotzsche, 1999). The increasing use of post-marketing studies—studies carried out once a drug is already on the market (Dembner, 2002)—offers another avenue for introducing bias into the research process. Many of these trials, referred to as "seeding" trials, have the sole purpose of getting doctors to start to use a product with the aim of establishing the drug as a regular part of the doctor's prescribing. The most widely publicized seeding trial was the ADVANTAGE study undertaken by Merck to promote the use of Vioxx (rofecoxib). Based on an analysis of Merck internal and external correspondence, reports, and presentations, Hill and colleagues showed that:

> ... the trial was designed by Merck's marketing division to fulfill a marketing objective; Merck's marketing division handled both the scientific and the marketing data, including collection, analysis, and dissemination; and Merck hid the marketing nature of the trial from participants, physician investigators, and institutional review board members. (Hill et al., 2008, p. 251)

Company Communication of Safety Issues to Regulators

Drugs are initially tested on carefully selected patient populations before they are marketed in order to make it relatively easy to identify whether or not they are efficacious. However, the fact that only a restricted range of patients receives the drug also means that safety problems in other groups of patients will remain hidden until the drug is marketed. In the US about one in ten new drugs either has to be withdrawn from the market because of safety concerns or requires a black-box warning because of serious safety issues (Lasser et al., 2002). In Canada, 3-4 percent of drugs approved in any five-year period are eventually withdrawn for safety reasons (Lexchin, 2009).

Aggressive marketing campaigns by pharmaceutical companies can mean that during the period between the initial marketing of drugs and the discovery of safety issues, millions of people may have been exposed to the products (Friedman et al., 1999). The Vioxx case is one such example. In the five years that it was on the US market 20 million people received a prescription for it and there were between 88,000 and 40,000 excess cases of serious coronary heart disease with a case-fatality rate of 44 percent (Graham et al., 2005). The large number of people taking these products also means large sales—sales that may suffer should significant safety issues come to light.

There have been no systematic studies looking into how pharmaceutical companies communicate safety issues to drug regulators, but there are case histories showing that, at least in some instances, firms have tried to manipulate the safety information in order to minimize safety concerns and maintain the profits they were making from their drugs.

In 1990 sales of the sedative Halcion (triazolam) accounted for 30 percent of Upjohn's overall healthcare sales. When confronted with reports that Halcion was associated with amnesia, aggressiveness, agitation, and other psychiatric side-effects, a spokeswoman for Upjohn defended her company saying "Upjohn puts nothing ahead of patients' health. We stand by the fact that our science is sound and that Halcion remains safe and effective medication when it is used as recommended in the labeling" (cited in Abraham and Sheppard, 1999, p. 110). The findings of a Food and Drug Administration (FDA) inspection report saw the situation differently. It stated that a key Upjohn study on the safety of the drug had represented a "gross and seminal failure to properly tabulate data" and that "the claim [made by Upjohn] that the overall incidence of subjects reporting adverse effects would not change is misleading. In fact, the overall incidence and other numbers did change because the report was roughly 30 per cent incomplete." The FDA report goes on to state that "the firm [Upjohn] attempted to gain approval for long-term use of the drug even though available evidence indicated that long-term use was both dangerous and medically untenable" (cited in Abraham and Sheppard, 1999, p. 109).

A second example of the same phenomenon comes from the actions that Wyeth took in trying to defend its diet pill Redux (dexfenfluramine). Market research indicated that sales of Redux would peak at about US$900 million in

1998. FDA regulations stated that if a company received an adverse drug event (ADE) report indicating a "serious, labeled" side-effect, the report had to be sent to the FDA within 15 days; however "serious, labeled, *foreign*" reports only had to be sent in periodically. Furthermore, if an ADE documented more than one side-effect the one listed first would determine how the FDA reviewed the report. Primary pulmonary hypertension (PPH) was already a recognized problem with Redux and therefore reports about this condition were expected, whereas heart valve damage was unknown and reports about this side-effect were unexpected. An analysis of company ADE reports showed that many of them listed PPH first and heart valve damage second in order to downplay the discovery of this new and significant problem. Furthermore, although it was known that PPH could occur, the number of cases recognized by the FDA was delayed because European reports about this condition were "foreign" and were not communicated in an expedited manner to the organization (Mundy, 2001).

Lurie and Wolfe (2005) have reported on GlaxoSmithKline's (GSK) attempt to mislead the FDA about the safety of its long-acting asthma drug Serevent (salmeterol). In 1996, following reports about possible increases in respiratory deaths associated with this type of drug, GSK initiated a placebo-controlled 28-week study to examine the situation. When the company submitted the final data from the trial to the FDA it included information not just for the 28-week study period, but also for the following six months, without alerting the FDA to this fact. Combining the two sets of data had the effect of diminishing the apparent danger associated with the use of Serevent and possibly of weakening the new warning about the drug that the FDA required GSK to add to the product's label.

Finally, internal data produced by Merck in April 2001 from two Vioxx trials identified a significant increase in total mortality compared to a placebo, when the drug was used in clinical trials in patients with either Alzheimer's disease or cognitive impairment. "These mortality analyses were neither provided to the FDA nor made public in a timely fashion." Instead, the information submitted to the FDA in July 2001 used a different type of analysis that minimized the appearance of any mortality risk. "In December 2001,when the FDA raised safety questions about the submitted safety data," Merck responded that the rofecoxib placebo findings are "small numeric differences, most consistent with chance fluctuations" (Psaty and Kronmal, 2008, p. 1815).

Selective and Misleading Publication

Medical information is transferred from research scientists to practicing clinicians largely through publications in journals. Even if doctors don't read the primary research, they will read the reviews about the drug or listen to the CME or use the clinical guidelines, all of which have their origin in the original research. A favorable study, especially one published in a high-impact journal, can have very positive effects on sales. In the case of the VIGOR study, which purported to show a significant safety advantage for Vioxx over traditional anti-inflammatories and was published in the New England Journal of Medicine, Merck purchased 900,000 copies of the article to distribute to doctors (Smith, 2006).

The evidence indicates that the significant bias in the published literature is widespread and systematic. It is becoming increasingly obvious that drug companies keep unfavorable results from being published and publish favorable results more prominently and often in multiple publications. Melander et al. (2003) compared published versions of trials for five selective serotonin reuptake inhibitors (SSRIs) with the versions of these studies submitted to the Swedish regulatory authority (Melander et al., 2003). They demonstrated that studies showing positive effects from these drugs were published as stand-alone publications more often than studies with non-significant results; many publications ignored the results of conservative intention to treat analyses and only reported the more favorable per protocol analyses; and 21 studies, out of 42 contributed to at least two publications each, and three studies contributed to five publications. The latter point echoes what Gøtzsche (1989) and Huston and Moher (1996) found for publications about non-steroidal anti-inflammatories and risperidone, respectively—favorable trials are frequently published more than once.

More recently, multiple analyses comparing FDA submissions to eventual publications have confirmed and extended Melander et al.'s (2008) findings. Out of 74 FDA-registered studies dealing with 12 antidepressants "a total of 37 studies viewed by the FDA as having positive results were published; 1 study viewed as positive was not published" (Turner et al., 2008, p. 252). An additional 11 studies that produced either negative or questionable results were published in a way that conveyed a positive outcome. According to the published literature, it appeared that 94 percent of the trials conducted were positive. By contrast, the FDA analysis showed that 51 percent were positive (Turner et al., 2008). Just as disturbing as this selective publication was the fact that, for all 12 drugs, the effect size in the published trials was greater than the effect size reported to the FDA by a mean of 32 percent, meaning that the drugs appeared much more effective to clinicians reading the medical literature. Wyeth attempted to dismiss its failure to publish two negative Effexor (venlafaxine) studies by claiming that they were "failed studies" rather than studies showing that the drug didn't work. Further, Wyeth maintained that it "strongly advocates publication transparency regardless of the trial outcome" (Ninan, Poole, and Stiles, 2008, p. 252). In reply, Turner and Tell noted that "publication transparency regardless of the trial outcome" does not equate with a decision not to publish a study based on how it turns out (Turner and Tell, 2008. p. 2181).

What Turner et al. (2008) found about antidepressant studies is also what occurs more generally. A second study looked at 164 efficacy trials submitted to the FDA in the 2001-2002 period in support of 33 new drug applications (NDA). Many trials had still not been published five years after FDA approval of the drug, and those that were published were much more likely to have positive results. In the 164 trials there were 43 primary outcomes that did not favor the drug and 20 of these 43 were excluded in the publications. The statistical significance of five of the remaining 23 outcomes was changed in the published literature and four of the five changes favored the drug in question. In total there were 99 conclusions that were present in both the NDA and the publications. Nine of these were changed from the former to the latter and all favored the companies' products (Rising, Bacchetti, and Bero, 2008).

Selective publication is not just of academic concern; it can have real clinical consequences. Although SSRIs were never approved for the treatment of depression in children or adolescents, they were frequently prescribed off-label to these groups of patients. A meta-analysis of the published literature indicated that there was a favorable risk-benefit profile for some SSRIs. However, the equation changed when the unpublished studies were added into the meta-analysis. When all the studies, both published and unpublished, were combined, the conclusion was that, except for Prozac (fluoxetine), the risks could outweigh the benefits (Whittington et al., 2004). In at least some cases the company involved made an active decision to withhold negative data from publication. Study 329 was undertaken by GSK to look at the effectiveness of Paxil (paroxetine) in a pediatric population. The results showed that Paxil was no better than placebo, and a second trial found that the placebo was actually more effective. A confidential document prepared by a unit of GSK advised that "[p]ositive data from Study 329 will be published in abstract form at the [European College of Neuropsychopharmacology] meeting" and that "[i]t would be commercially unacceptable to include a statement that efficacy had not been demonstrated, as this would undermine the profile of paroxetine" (Kondro and Sibbald, 2004, p. 783). Negative results from Paxil studies were known to researchers, but they were prohibited from revealing what they knew because of non-disclosure clauses (Garland, 2004).

Ghostwriting

An especially egregious form of biasing the publication record is the practice of employing ghostwriters. It is legitimate for people who have conducted research to seek help in writing up their results, especially when the researchers do not have English (the usual language of publication) as a first language or when their written skills are not adequate. Ghostwriting takes the use of "help" to a new level. Ghostwriters are men and women specifically recruited to take data from clinical trials and write an article with a "spin" favorable to the drug. The company making the drug, or someone working on its behalf, then recruits a well-known academic or doctor to sign the write-up and masquerade as the author. While there are multiple anecdotal reports of ghostwriting (Dunbar and Tallman, 2009; Fugh-Berman, 2005) once again, the evidence points to this practice as being widespread and systematic.

In 1994 Wyeth signed a US$180,000 contract with Excerpta Medica, a New Jersey medical publishing company, to generate positive medical literature about its diet drug Redux. Excerpta outlined a schedule of nine articles, each with a carefully crafted message aimed at a series of different audiences. The articles were written by a ghostwriter who was paid US$5,000 and then they were signed by a prominent researcher who was paid US$1,500 to review the work and assign his or her name to it for publication. Although Wyeth officials maintained that the academic authors had the final approval of the articles, company officials frequently tinkered with the text of the articles, removing unflattering references to Redux or deleting positive references to other drugs.

> *In one article, for example, an early draft read that a recent study "found that the use of anti-obesity drugs, including dexfenfluramine, was associated with an increased risk of primary pulmonary hypertension. The risk was especially great for long-term users." After Wyeth reviewed the draft, the reference to dexfenfluramine and the sentence about long-term use were crossed out. (Kauffman and Julien, 2000, p. A1)*

Wyeth also utilized ghostwriters to defend the US$2 billion in annual sales from Premarin and Prempro, its two hormone replacement therapy (HRT) products, before and after the publication of the Women's Health Initiative (WHI). WHI showed that HRT not only did not prevent cardiovascular events in postmenopausal women, but also that its use could actually result in an increase in cardiovascular disease in this population (Writing Group, 2002). Court documents show that ghostwriters played a major role in producing 26 scientific papers backing the use of HRT that were published between 1998 and 2005. These articles, some of which appeared in major journals such as the *American Journal of Obstetrics and Gynecology*, emphasized the benefits and played down the risks of taking hormones. They did not disclose Wyeth's role in initiating and paying for the work (Singer, 2009).

In the course of legal proceedings, a document outlining the involvement of the medical information company Current Medical Directions (CMD) in the preparation of 85 studies about Zoloft (sertraline), an SSRI made by Pfizer, was made available to Healy and Cattell (2003). The document suggested that there were a number of manuscripts which had originated within communication agencies, with the first draft of articles already written and the authors' names listed as "to be determined." Using a search of the medical literature, Healy and Cattell looked for evidence of publication of these papers. Out of the 55 that they found, only 13 appeared to have had no involvement with CMD. When articles with CMD involvement were compared to ones on Zoloft that had been independently produced, the former were cited more often and published in more prestigious medical journals. Since these articles were almost uniformly favorable to Zoloft there is a high likelihood that the overall literature regarding this drug was biased towards presenting a more positive view of the drug than was warranted.

Court documents have also been used to build up a picture of how Merck worked, either independently or with medical communication companies, to ensure a positive profile for Vioxx:

> *Merck employees work[ed] either independently or in collaboration with medical publishing companies to prepare manuscripts and subsequently [recruit] external, academically affiliated investigators to be authors. Recruited authors were frequently placed in the first and second positions of the authorship list. For the publication of scientific review papers, documents were found describing Merck marketing employees developing plans for manuscripts, contracting with medical publishing companies to ghostwrite manuscripts, and recruiting external, academically affiliated investigators to be authors. Recruited authors were commonly the sole author on the manuscript and offered honoraria for their participation. Among 96 relevant published articles ... 92% (22 of 24) of clinical trial articles published a disclosure of Merck's financial support, but only 50% (36 of 72) of review articles published either a disclosure of Merck sponsorship or a disclosure of whether the author had received any financial compensation from the company. (Ross et al., 2008, p. 1800)*

Merck has actually gone even further than ghostwriting, paying an undisclosed sum of money to the medical publishing company Elsevier to produce nine pseudo-journals that were distributed in Australia. (An additional 13 journals were in the process of being created.) These journals had the appearance of being peer-reviewed publications but were really marketing tools for Merck's products and did not disclose the fact that they were paid for by the company (Grant, 2009; Laidlaw, 2009).

Promoting Drugs for Unapproved Indications

Companies in developed countries are only legally allowed to promote their products for indications for which the drug has been approved by the regulatory authority. In usual practice that means that companies have to present convincing evidence from randomized controlled trials showing that the medicine is safe and efficacious for the particular use. However, it is sometimes economically advantageous to promote products for off-label uses—that is, uses that have not been approved. Clinical trials to establish a new indication can be expensive, ranging into hundreds of millions of dollars, and, especially if the remaining patent life on the product is short, it may not be in the company's interests to spend the money trying to prove that its product has additional uses.

Zyprexa (olanzapine) is an Eli Lilly product first marketed in the US in 1996 and is currently approved for the acute and long-term treatment of bipolar I disorder and Schizophrenia, as well as agitation associated with these conditions. Use of Zyprexa has been linked to the development of obesity and diabetes, so inappropriate use could cause significant morbidity without any benefits.

Although Lilly had high expectations for sales of this product, bipolar disorder and schizophrenia are conditions primarily treated by psychiatrists. However, Lilly saw an additional market of about US$350 million per year if it could also get primary care doctors to prescribe the drug. To that end, according to court documents, it developed an off-label promotion campaign designed to get general practitioners (GPs) and other primary care providers to prescribe the drug for symptoms of dementia and "'thought disturbances,' including ... disorganized thinking, as well as poor attention, poor judgment and lack of insight. Olanzapine was specifically marketed for 'mood, thought, and behavior disorders' in an 'intentionally broad and vague' manner, 'providing latitude to frame the discussion around symptoms and behaviors rather than specific indications'"(Spielmans, 2009, p. 17). Lilly continued to promote Zyprexa for dementia, despite abandoning its attempt to get FDA approval for this indication in 2003 primarily because by then it had seven studies showing that the drug was ineffective for Alzheimer's disease and other forms of dementia (Fisk, Lopatto, and Feeley, 2009).

In 2006 a Lilly spokeswoman denied that Lilly had ever promoted Zyprexa for off-label uses when documents about its marketing campaign first came to light (Berenson, 2006). By 2009 when the company agreed to pay a monetary settlement of US$1.415 billion, including a criminal fine of US$515 million, "John Lechleiter, chief executive officer of Lilly, said in a press release that 'we deeply regret the past actions covered by this misdemeanor plea'"(Spielmans, 2009, p. 14).

As was mentioned briefly in the introduction to this chapter, in 2004 Pfizer paid a fine of US$430 million for the illegal marketing of Neurontin. Neurontin was originally approved in 1994 as an "add on" drug for the treatment of certain types of seizure disorders. However, with its patent due to expire in 1998, "senior officials with Parke-Davis determined that it was not sufficiently profitable for Parke Davis [now part of Pfizer] to obtain FDA approval for Neurontin's alternative uses" (Lenzer, 2003, p. 620). At the same time, the company was not willing to let these markets go untapped. According to the *Boston Globe*:

> ... beginning in August 1994, the company recruited hundreds of physicians, particularly those who prescribed competing drugs to patients, to participate in teleconferences about Neurontin. One former Parke-Davis employee charged that in order to encourage doctors to prescribe Neurontin off-label, they were paid as "consultants" to attend lavish, all expenses paid trips to resorts. (Kowalczyk, 2002)

Not only was Pfizer illegally promoting Neurontin, but it was also distorting the findings of clinical trials on the product. Information to substantiate the practices of Pfizer comes from court documents:

> For 8 of ... 12 reported trials, the primary outcome defined in the published report differed from that described in the protocol ... Trials that presented findings that were not significant ... for the protocol-defined primary outcome in the internal documents either were not reported in full or were reported with a changed primary outcome. The primary outcome was changed in the case of 5 of 8 published trials for which statistically significant differences favoring gabapentin were reported. Of the 21 primary outcomes described in the protocols of

the published trials, 6 were not reported at all and 4 were reported as secondary outcomes. Of 28 primary outcomes described in the published reports, 12 were newly introduced. (Vedula et al., 2009, p. 1963)

Despite the ensuing fine, in 2009 Pfizer paid an even larger fine of US$2.3 billion for off-label promotion of Bextra and three other drugs.

Drug companies likely persist in these illegal practices of companies because the amounts of the fines do not come anywhere close to the profits that blockbuster drugs can generate. Between 2000 and 2008 Lilly earned US$36 billion in revenue from Zyprexa; in just one year, 2002, Pfizer made US$2.27 billion from Neurontin, 90 percent of which was from off-label sales, and between 2001 and 2008 sales of Bextra and the three other drugs that were illegally promoted were US$16.8 billion (Evans, 2009).

Biasing the Content of CME and Clinical Guidelines

As I mentioned earlier, doctors frequently learn about new clinical information either through CME courses or from clinical practice guidelines. The pharmaceutical industry is heavily involved in financing both of these sources of information. In the US there were over 100,000 CME courses in 2008, and the pharmaceutical industry provided more than 50 percent of the funding for these courses (ACCME, 2009). "*Nature* studied more than 200 guidelines from around the world that were deposited with the US National Guideline Clearinghouse in 2004." Out of 90 that "contained details about individual authors' conflicts of interest ... just 31 were free of industry influence" (Taylor and Giles, 2005, p. 1070).

The medical education campaign conducted by Wyeth, the company marketing the weight reduction medication Redux, consisted of pay-outs to academic physicians, lavish conferences, and generous grants to professional medical societies (Elliott, 2004). Once it became known that Redux was associated with heart valve damage, Wyeth put together a group of 30 doctors known as the Visiting Important Professor Program (VIPP) charged with getting out a positive message about the drug. The criteria for being part of the VIPP were: "Has national recognition. Will deliver an appropriate message. Is an advisor or consultant [to Wyeth]. Has credibility. Advocates pharmacotherapy" (Mundy, 2001, p. 123). Pfizer paid dozens of doctors tens of thousands of dollars each to speak to other physicians about how Neurontin could be prescribed for a variety of conditions that had not been approved by the FDA (Petersen, 2003).

In 2001 the FDA approved Eli Lilly's Xigris (drotrecogin alfa) for the treatment of sepsis (severe infections). To improve the sales of Xigris, in 2002 Lilly hired Belsito and Company, a public relations firm, to develop and help implement a three-pronged marketing strategy. One of the keys to the strategy was the Surviving Sepsis Campaign formed, according to Lilly, to raise awareness of severe sepsis and generate momentum toward the development of treatment guidelines for its management. Towards that end, in June 2003, international experts were convened to create these guidelines. Lilly provided more than 90 percent of the funding, and many participants had financial or other relationships with the company. Despite two trials that demonstrated serious risks with the drug, and led to a safety warning from the FDA, no mention of these trials was made in a supplement to the Surviving Sepsis Campaign guidelines. The guidelines also played down the magnitude of the risk of serious bleeding from Xigris and mention of the fact that the Infectious Diseases Society of America declined to endorse the guidelines was deleted from an editorial in the journal that published them. Finally, Lilly started awarding unrestricted grants for an "Implementing the Surviving Sepsis Campaign" program. The main goal of the program was the creation of performance bundles based on selected recommendations from the campaign guidelines. "Despite the persisting scientific controversy surrounding the safety and efficacy of [Xigris] ... the campaign's manual on bundle implementation [does not mention] ... the [two negative] trials or the [FDA] warnings they precipitated" (Eichacker, Natanson, and Danner, 2006, p. 1642).

Attempting to Silence its Critics

Science is supposed to work through a self-correcting process; research or hypotheses are presented, critiqued, refined, and eventually accepted or discarded. The essence of the process is the encouragement of a vigorous discussion and the free flow of scientific information. If part of the discussion is stifled, then the end result may be the propagation of a flawed piece of research and, in the field of medical science, that may result in harm, or worse, to patients. The pharmaceutical industry has a long history of attempting to silence its critics by threatening legal action against them or by complaining to their superiors. While the industry is often not successful in the long run, its actions can create a climate of fear that makes people reluctant to speak up in the future.

On a number of occasions Merck has tried to suppress criticism of its products. In the mid-1990s it tried to use the judicial system to stop the distribution of a newsletter critical of Fosamax (aledronate) by the Norwegian Medicines Control Authority (Hemminki, Hailey, and Koivusalo, 1999). About a decade later Merck took a Spanish pharmacologist to court over an article in a drugs and therapeutics bulletin he edited, in which he criticized the VIGOR study for allegedly minimizing the cardiovascular side-effects of Vioxx (Bosch, 2004). The same pharmacologist, Dr Joan-Ramon LaPorte, was scheduled to be a featured speaker at a 2004 annual Spanish conference for general practitioners that Merck had helped fund for the previous eight years. When the organizer of the conference refused Merck's request that Dr LaPorte be removed from the conference, Merck withdrew its funding (Mathews and Martinez, 2004). Merck also "went after" American academics who questioned Vioxx. Dr Gurkirpal Singh of Stanford University was giving lectures about Vioxx for Merck but when he asked the company for additional safety data, data that Merck did not provide, he raised the issue of transparency in his lectures. A Merck official later called Stanford to complain that Dr Singh's lectures were "'irresponsibly anti-Merck and specifically anti-Vioxx,' ... The Merck official 'suggested that if this continued, Dr. Singh would 'flame out' and there would be consequences ... for Stanford." A second professor, this one at the University of Minnesota, also discussed possible side-effects from Vioxx and got a call from the same Merck official. "We had a very direct conversation that I wouldn't call friendly ... It had a tone to me of, 'You better be careful of what you're saying'" (Mathews and Martinez, 2004, p. 1).

Perhaps the best-known cases where companies tried to suppress researchers from either publishing or speaking out about safety concerns involve Betty Dong and Nancy Olivieri. Flint Laboratories, the maker of Synthroid, a product for patients with hypothyroidism, had hired Dr Dong to do work to show that its brand was superior to the less expensive generic versions of the drug. Flint, and later Boots Laboratories which acquired Flint, approved of Dr Dong's study design and her conduct of the study. When the research was completed it actually showed that all the versions of the drug were the same. Dr Dong made preparations to publish her research, but she had also signed an agreement with Flint that the company had to consent to the publication of any data. Boots refused to allow her to publish and, when Dr Dong went ahead anyway, Boots threatened to sue her (Rennie, 1997). Dr Olivieri, who was doing research on L1, a product to be used in the treatment of iron-overload in thalassemia patients, had also signed a confidentiality clause. The clause gave Apotex, the Canadian generic company with the rights to the drug, the right to control communication of trial data for one year after termination of the trial. When Dr Olivieri became concerned about the safety of L1 she contacted Apotex and explained to the company that she needed to inform the patients in the trial of these new safety concerns. Apotex, which disputed her interpretation of the safety data, refused and threatened to take legal action against her if she went public with her concerns (Downie, Baird, and Thompson, 2002).

Beside these cases there are others where there were no confidentiality clauses or even a prior relationship with the pharmaceutical company. The Canadian Coordinating Office for Health Technology Assessment (CCOHTA, now the Canadian Agency for Drugs and Technologies in Health) prepared an assessment regarding the comparability of the statin group of drugs, which are used to lower cholesterol. The report concluded that all of the statins available at that time were equivalent in their benefits. Bristol-Myers-Squibb, makers of Pravachol (pravastatin) took CCOHTA to court to stop the release of the report. Although the case was thrown out when it finally was heard by a judge, it delayed the release of the report by a full year and cost CCOHTA 13 percent of its annual budget on lawyers' fees (Hemminki, Hailey, and Koivusalo, 1999).

Finally, Dr Anne Holbrook of McMaster University was hired by the government of Ontario to produce a report on gastrointestinal medications. Her report concluded that AstraZeneca's drug, Losec (omeprazole), was no better than two less expensive products in the same drug class. As a consequence of her conclusion she received a letter from a law firm representing AstraZeneca, claiming that if her report was released, she would be contravening Canadian federal law and that "In the event that you proceed notwithstanding this warning you should assume that our client will take appropriate steps including the commencement of appropriate legal proceedings in order to protect its interests and to obtain compliance with the law" (Shuchman, 1999, p. A1). AstraZeneca quickly apologized to Dr Holbrook and claimed that the letter had been misdirected to her and should have instead been sent to the Ontario government ("Talking points," 2002).

Conclusion

In an unpublished paper, the British economist Alan Maynard notes that:

> *Economic theory predicts that firms will invest in corruption of the evidence base wherever its benefits exceed its costs. If detection is costly for regulators, corruption of the evidence base can be expected to be extensive. Investment in biasing the evidence base, both clinical and economic, in pharmaceuticals is likely to be detailed and comprehensive, covering all aspects of the appraisal process. Such investment is likely*

> *to be extensive as the scientific and policy discourses are technical and esoteric, making detection difficult and expensive. (Maynard, 2001, n.p.)*

This chapter has shown that Maynard's prediction has a factual basis: pharmaceutical companies have tried to corrupt the content of clinical research and the application of that research at every stage in its production.

Defenders of the pharmaceutical industry have tried to minimize its role in biasing clinical research by pointing out that the pursuit of profits is not the only motivation behind trying to influence the outcome and use of clinical research, and that individuals, government, and medical journals are equally guilty (Hirsch, 2009). Hirsch is correct, bias can come from many sources, but no individual or organization has the resources and ability to influence the entire process in the way that the pharmaceutical industry can. In this respect, the industry is in a class of its own. Moreover, beyond the forms of corruption that this chapter has discussed, there are other avenues that industry can use to ensure that the way in which pharmaceuticals are used works in its favor. Among other things, conflict of interest between academics and industry is rife (Campbell et al., 2007; DeAngelis and Fontanarosa, 2008; Kassirer, 2006), industry executives have pleaded guilty to misleading the government (Hughes, 2009), and companies have bribed doctors to use their products (Murphy, 2002).

We can reasonably ask that pharmaceutical companies not break the law in their pursuit of profits, but anything beyond that is unrealistic. Companies such as Pfizer have promised to reform their behavior only to "sin" again (Evans, 2009). Government efforts to date have amounted to fines that have no deterrent value because companies still find it more profitable to engage in corruption even if they are subsequently caught. What is needed to curb and ultimately stop the corruption that we have seen is a paradigm change in the way in which we view what are legitimate activities of pharmaceutical companies.

References

Abraham, J. and Sheppard, J. (1999) *The Therapeutic Nightmare: The Battle over the World's Most Controversial Sleeping Pill*, London: Earthscan Publications Ltd.

ACCME (2009) *ACCME Annual Report Data 2008*, Chicago, IL: Accreditation Council for Continuing Medical Education. Available at: http://www.accme.org/

dir_docs/doc_upload/1f8dc476-246a-4e8e-91d3-d24ff2f5bfec_uploaddocument. pdf (accessed July 2010).
Bass, A. (2008) *Side Effects: A Prosecutor, a Whistleblower, and a Bestselling Antidepressant on Trial*, Chapel Hill, NC: Algonquin Books.
Berenson, A. (2006) "Drug files show maker promoted unapproved use," *New York Times*, December 18, p. 1.
Bosch, X. (2004) "Spanish editor sued over rofecoxib allegations," *Lancet*, 363, 298.
Braithwaite, J. (1984) *Corporate Crime in the Pharmaceutical Industry*, London: Routledge & Kegan Paul.
Campbell, E. G., Weissman, J. S., Ehringhaus, S., Rao, S. R., Moy, B., Feibelmann, S., et al. (2007) "Institutional academic-industry relationships," *Journal of the American Medical Association*, 298, 1779–1786.
DeAngelis, C. D. and Fontanarosa, P. B. (2008) "Impugning the integrity of medical science: The adverse effects of industry influence, *Journal of the American Medical Association*, 299, 1833–1835.
Dembner, A. (2002) "Report raps drug firms' 'post-approval' studies," *Boston Globe*, June 25.
Downie, J., Baird, P., and Thompson, J. (2002) "Industry and the academy: Conflicts of interest in contemporary health research," *Health Law Journal*, 10, 103–122.
Dunbar, C. E. and Tallman, M. S. (2009) "'Ghostbusting' at Blood," *Blood*, 113, 502–503.
Eichacker, P. Q., Natanson, C., and Danner, R. L. (2006) "Surviving sepsis— practice guidelines, marketing campaigns, and Eli Lilly," *New England Journal of Medicine*, 355, 1640–1642.
Elliott, C. (2004) "Pharma goes to the laundry: Public relations and the business of medical education," *Hastings Center Report*, 34(5), 18–23.
Evans, D. (2009) "Big pharma's crime spree," *Bloomberg Markets Magazine*, December, 72–86.
Fisk, M. C., Lopatto, E., and Feeley, J. (2009) "Lilly sold drug for dementia knowing it didn't help, files show," *Miami Herald*, June 13, p. C3. Available at: http://www.miamiherald.com/business/v-print/story/1095411.html.
Friedman, M. A., Woodcock, J., Lumpkin, M. M., Shuren, J. E., Hass, A. E., and Thompson, L. J. (1999) "The safety of newly approved medicines: Do recent market removals mean there is a problem?" *Journal of the American Medical Association*, 281, 1728–1734.
Fugh-Berman, A. (2005) "The corporate coauthor," *Journal of General Internal Medicine*, 20, 546–548.

Garland, E. J. (2004) "Facing the evidence: Antidepressant treatment in children and adolescents," *Canadian Medical Association Journal*, 170, 489–491.

Gøtzsche, P. C. (1989) "Multiple publication of reports of drug trials," *European Journal of Clinical Pharmacology*, 36, 429–432.

Graham, D. J., Campen, D., Hui, R., Spence, M., Cheetham, C., Levy, G. et al. (2005) "Risk of actue myocardial infraction and sudden cardiac death in patients treated with cyclo-oxygenase 2 selective and non-selective non-steroidal anti-inflammatory drugs: Nested case-control study." *Lancet*, 365, 475–481.

Grant, B. (2009) "Merck published fake journal," April 30, at: http://www.the-scientist.com/blog/print/55671/ (accessed December 2009).

Harris, G. (2004) "Pfizer to pay $420 million in illegal marketing case," *New York Times*, May 14, p. C1, at: http://www.nytimes.com/2009/09/03/business/03health.html (accessed July 2010).

Harris, G. (2009) "Pfizer pays $2.3 billion to settle marketing case, *New York Times*, September 2, at: http://www.nytimes.com/2009/09/03/business/03health.html.

Healy, D. and Cattell, D. (2003) "Interface between authorship, industry and science in the domain of therapeutics," *British Journal of Psychiatry*, 183, 22–27.

Hemminki, E., Hailey, D., and Koivusalo, M. (1999) "The courts—a challenge to health technology assessment," *Science*, 285, 203–204.

Heres, S., Davis, J., Maino, K., Jetzinger, E., Kissling, W., and Leucht, S. (2006) "Why Olanzapine beats Risperidone, Risperidone beats Quetiapine, and Quetiapine beats Olanzapine: An exploratory analysis of head-to-head comparison studies of second-generation antipsychotics," *American Journal of Psychiatry*, 163, 185–194.

Hill, K. P., Ross, J. S., Egilman, D. S., and Krumholz, H. M. (2008) "The ADVANTAGE seeding trial: A review of internal documents," *Annals of Internal Medicine*, 149, 251–258.

Hirsch, L. J. (2009) "Conflicts of interest, authorship, and disclosures in industry-related scientific publications: The tort bar and editorial oversight of medical journals," *Mayo Clinic Proceedings*, 84, 811–821.

Hole, O. P., Winther, F. Ø., and Straume, B. (2001) "Clinical research: The influence of the pharmaceutical industry," *European Journal of Clinical Pharmacology*, 56, 851–853.

Hughes, D. A. (2009) "Corporate news: Former Bristol-Myers aide pleads guilty," *Wall Street Journal*, April 7, p. B6.

Huston, P. and Moher, D. (1996) "Redundancy, disaggregation, and the integrity of medical research," *Lancet*, 347, 1024–1026.

Johansen, H. K. and Gotzsche, P. C. (1999) "Problems in the design and reporting of trials of antifungal agents encountered during meta-analyses," *Journal of the American Medical Association*, 282, 1752–1759.

Kassirer, J. P. (2006) "When physician-industry interactions go awry," *Journal of Pediatrics*, 149, S43–46.

Kauffman, M. and Julien, A. (2000) "Scientists helped industry to push diet drug medical research: Can we trust it?" *Hartford Courant*, April 10, p. A1.

Kondro, W. and Sibbald, B. (2004) "Drug company experts advised staff to withhold data about SSRI use in children," *Canadian Medical Association Journal*, 170, 783.

Kowalczyk, L. (2002) "Use of Pfizer drug Neurontin soars despite controversy," *Boston Globe*, November 25. Available at: http://www.encyclopedia.com/doc/1G1-94907963.html.

Laidlaw, S. (2009) "Merck publishing scandal widens, June 5, at: http://thestar.blogs.com/ethics/2009/06/merck-publishing-scandal-widens.html (accessed December 2009).

Lasser, K. E., Allen, P. D., Woolhandler, S. J., Himmelstein, D. U., Wolfe, S. M., and Bor, D. H. (2002) "Timing of new black box warnings and withdrawals for prescription medications," *Journal of the American Medical Association*, 287, 2215–2220.

Lenzer, J. (2003) "Whistleblower charges drug company with deceptive practices," *British Medical Journal*, 326, 620.

Lexchin, J. (2009) *Drug Safety and Health Canada: Going, Going, Gone?* Ottawa: Canadian Centre for Policy Alternatives.

Lurie, P. and Wolfe, S. (2005) "Misleading data analyses in salmeterol (SMART) study," *Lancet*, 366, 1261–1262.

Mathews, A. W. and Martinez, B. (2004) "Warning signs: E-mails suggest Merck knew Vioxx's dangers at early stage," *Wall Street Journal*, November 1, p. 1. Available at: http://www.marshall-attorneys.com/Press/2004_11_01_WSJ.htm.

Maynard, A. (2001) "Regulating the market for corruption in the pharmaceutical industry," unpublished paper.

Meier, B. (2007) "In guilty plea, OxyContin maker to pay $600 million," *New York Times*, May 10, at: http://www.nytimes.com/2007/05/10/business/11drug-web.html (accessed July 2010).

Melander, H., Ahlqvist-Rastad, J., Meijer, G., and Beermann, B. (2003) "Evidence b(i)ased medicine—selective reporting from studies sponsored by pharmaceutical industry: review of studies in new drug applications," *British Medical Journal*, 326, 1171–1173.

Miners, A. H., Garau, M., Fidan, D., and Fischer, A. J. (2005) "Comparing estimates of cost effectiveness submitted to the National Institute for Clinical Excellence (NICE) by different organisations: Retrospective study," *British Medical Journal*, 330, 65–69.

Moses, H. I., Dorsey, E. R., Matheson, D. H. M., and Thier, S. O. (2005) "Financial anatomy of biomedical research," *Journal of the American Medical Association*, 294, 1333–1342.

Mundy, A. (2001) *Dispensing with the Truth: The Victims, the Drug Companies, and the Dramatic Story behind the Battle over Fen-phen*, New York: St Martin's Press.

Murphy, S. (2002) "US probes drug firm incentive at Lahey," *Boston Globe*, August 3, p. A1.

Ninan, P. T., Poole, R. M., and Stiles, G. L. (2008) "Selective publication of antidepressant trials," *New England Journal of Medicine*, 358, 252–260

Patsopoulos, N. A., Ioannidis, J. P. A., and Analatos, A. A. (2006) "Origin and funding of the most frequently cited papers in medicine: Dababase analysis," *British Medical Journal*, 332, 1061–1064.

Petersen, M. (2003) "Court papers suggest scale of drug's use," *New York Times*, May 30, p. 1.

Psaty, B. M. and Kronmal, R. A. (2008) "Reporting mortality findings in trials of rofecoxib for Alzheimer disease or cognitive impairment: A case study based on documents from rofecoxib litigation," *Journal of the American Medical Association*, 299, 1813–1817.

Rennie, D. (1997) "Thyroid storm," *Journal of the American Medical Association*, 277, 1238–1243.

Rising, K., Bacchetti, P., and Bero, L. (2008) "Reporting bias in drug trials submitted to the Food and Drug Administration: Review of publication and presentation," *PLoS Medicine*, 5, e217.

Rochon, P. A., Gurwitz, J. H., Simms, R. W., Fortin, P. R., Felson, D. T., Minaker, K. L. et al. (1994) "A study of manufacturer-supported trials of nonsteroidal anti-inflammatory drugs in the treatment of arthritis," *Archives of Internal Medicine*, 154, 157–163.

Ross, J. S., Hill, K. P., Egilman, D. S., and Krumholz, H. M. (2008) "Guest authorship and ghostwriting in publications related to rofecoxib: A case study of industry documents from rofecoxib ligitation," *Journal of the American Medical Association*, 299, 1800–1812.

Shuchman, M. (1999) "Drug firm threatens suit over MD's product review," *Globe and Mail*, November 17, p. A1.

Singer, N. (2009) "Medical papers by ghostwriters pushed therapy," *New York Times*, August 5, p. 1.

Sismondo, S. (2008) "Pharmaceutical company funding and its consequences: A qualitative systematic review," *Contemporary Clinical Trials*, 29, 109–113.

Smith, R. (2006) "Lapses at the New England Journal of Medicine," *Journal of the Royal Society of Medicine*, 99, 380–382.

Spielmans, G. I. (2009) "The promotion of olanzapine in primary care: An examination of internal industry documents," *Social Science and Medicine*, 69, 14–20.

"Talking points re: media reports—Dr. Holbrook and AstraZeneca" (2002) at: http://www.canadapharma.org/Media_Centre/Backgrounders/Holbrook 99_e.html (accessed March 2003).

Taylor, R. and Giles, J. (2005) "Cash interests taint drug advice," *Nature*, 437, 1070–1071.

Turner, E. H., Matthews, A. M., Linardatos, E., Tell, R. A., and Rosenthal, R. (2008) "Selective publication of antidepressant trials and its influence on apparent efficacy," *New England Journal of Medicine*, 358, 252–260.

Turner, E. H. and Tell, R. A. (2008) "Selective publication of antidepressant trials," *New England Journal of Medicine*, 358, 2181–2182.

Vedula, S. S., Bero, L., Scherer, R. W., and Dickersin, K. (2009) "Outcome reporting in industry-sponsored trials of gabapentin for off-label use," *New England Journal of Medicine*, 361, 1963–1971.

Whittington, C. J., Kendall, T., Fonagy, P., Cottrell, D., Cotgrove, A., and Boddington, E. (2004) "Selective serotonin reuptake inhibitors in childhood depression: Systematic review of published versus unpublished data," *Lancet*, 363, 1341–1345.

Writing Group for the Women's Health Initiative Investigators (2002) "Risks and benefits of estrogen plus progestin in health postmenopausal women: Principal results from the Women's Health Initiative randomized controlled trial," *Journal of the American Medical Association*, 288, 321–333.

Yank, V., Rennie, D., and Bero, L. A. (2007) "Financial ties and concordance between results and conclusions in meta-analyses: Retrospective cohort study," *British Medical Journal*, 335, 1202–1205.

PART V
Reducing Crime and Corruption in Organizations

10

How to Minimize Corruption in Business Organizations: Developing and Sustaining an Ethical Corporate Culture

Mark S. Schwartz

Introduction

Of all the issues faced by society, one could argue that corruption is one of the most significant in terms of its potential negative impact on society, while remaining one of the most difficult for society to properly address. While many tend to associate corruption with bribery, many other activities have also been defined as acts of corruption, including: receiving and giving gifts and entertainment; kickbacks; extortion; nepotism; favoritism; abuse of power; misappropriation of public funds; illegal political party and electoral campaign funding; money laundering; improper use of insider information; use of intermediaries; conflicts of interest; facilitating payments; or even tipping (see Argandoña, 2005). If one accepts corruption as relating essentially to "dishonesty for personal gain" (Encarta, 2009), other criminal or unethical acts would be included as well (e.g., fraud or aggressive accounting). Unfortunately, one doesn't have to look very far over recent years to see significant examples of crime and corruption within or on behalf of business organizations and the negative impact such scandals have had on investors, employees, customers, and society in general (e.g., Enron, WorldCom, Tyco, Hollinger, Livent Inc., Parmalat, Siemens, Madoff Investments, etc.).

While a vast array of potential solutions has been presented to address corruption from the perspective of business firms (see, e.g., Hess and Dunfee,

2000, 2003), many argue that the presence of an "ethical corporate culture" is a necessary (although insufficient) condition if the extent to which corruption or other illegal or unethical activity is taking place is to be minimized (e.g., Ferrell and Gresham, 1985; Treviño, 1986; Brass, Butterfield, and Skaggs, 1998). Organizational culture has been defined in many different ways, but might be considered as "... the shared assumptions, values, and beliefs and is the social glue that holds the organization together" (Treviño and Nelson, 2007, p. 259). Whether an "ethical" corporate culture will actually make a difference is debatable in the case of all employees and managers, however. There are some, for example, who accept a "20-60-20" rule (see Brooks and Dunn, 2010, p. 256)—in other words, 20 percent of a given workforce will always do the right thing (e.g., act legally or ethically) regardless of the circumstances or their work environment. Another 20 percent will always engage in illegal or unethical behavior when the opportunity exists, the rewards are sufficient, and there is little chance of getting caught. The remaining 60 percent of the workforce, however, may or may not engage in illegal or unethical behavior, depending on the environment in which they work (e.g., managerial pressure, peer pressure, reward systems, etc.). It is this 60 percent that arguably can potentially be most influenced to do the right thing when they work within an ethical corporate culture, and thus this is the target group that is the focus of this chapter.

If a majority of employees are in fact influenced by their work environments with respect to their behavior, it potentially becomes extremely important for organizations and their managers to understand how to best develop and sustain an ethical corporate culture. While recognizing that there may not be a "one size fits all" solution for all business organizations (see Treviño and Nelson, 2007, p. 257), one can certainly postulate in general that certain core elements should be in place at a minimum if one is to have the greatest chance of developing and maintaining an ethical corporate culture. This chapter, rather than providing a comprehensive "to do" list for organizations, will argue that three key elements or fundamental building blocks must exist if crime, corruption, and other illegal or unethical activity within organizations is to be minimized through developing and sustaining an ethical corporate culture. The three elements are:

1. the existence of a set of *core ethical values* infused throughout the organization in its policies, processes, and practices;
2. the establishment of a *formal ethics program* (e.g., code of ethics, training, hotline, ethics officer, etc.); and
3. the continuous presence of *ethical leadership* (i.e., "tone at the top" as reflected by the board of directors, senior executives, and managers).

While each of these three elements is distinct, they also overlap, relate to, and potentially reinforce each other. Each of the three key elements necessary to develop and maintain an ethical corporate culture is discussed below.

Core Ethical Values

The existence of a set of core ethical values appears to be critical in establishing an ethical corporate culture. For example, "Corporate values have long been referred to as the central dimension of an organization's culture ..." (Hunt, Wood and Chonko, 1989, p. 79). An ethical corporate culture has in turn been recognized as important to ethical decision-making. O'Fallon and Butterfield, as part of their extensive literature review on ethical decision-making, state: "The research generally supports the notion that ethical climates and cultures have a positive influence on ethical decision making" (2005, p. 397). Despite the recognized importance of core ethical values, however, research suggests that many employees perceive their firms as lacking ethical values. For example, in a survey of 23,000 US employees, only 15 percent felt that they worked in a high-trust environment, only 13 percent had highly cooperative working relationships with other groups or departments, and only 10 percent felt that their organization holds people accountable for results (Covey, 2004).

Of course, several issues remain: for example, which set of core ethical values should a firm utilize? On what basis should the ethical values be selected? Should they be selected because they currently exist within the firm, or because their existence is desired? What happens when the core ethical values conflict with each other, or with the bottom line? Which should take priority?

Although there are a number of potential ethical values to choose from, it could be argued that one needs to attempt to identify those ethical values which can be considered to be universal in nature. In other words, to the greatest extent possible, the selected moral values should retain their significance despite differences in culture, religion, time, and circumstance. The values should be accepted by a large number of diverse individuals and social groups as being of fundamental importance in guiding or evaluating behavior, actions, or policies. In a sense, universal moral values might be considered as being similar to "hypernorms," described by Donaldson and Dunfee as "deep moral values" (1999, p. 27) representing "... a convergence of religious, political, and philosophical thought" (1999, p. 44). Hypernorms are considered "...so fundamental that, by definition, they serve to evaluate lower-order norms [while] ... reaching to the root of what is ethical for humanity" (1999, p. 44).

In an earlier study by Schwartz (2005), a comparative analysis was conducted of three separate sources in order to generate a set of universal moral values. Those three sources included: (1) companies' codes of ethics; (2) global codes of ethics; and (3) the business ethics literature. The objective was to identify a set of moral values which both emerge from and recur within a number of different sources, and can thus be classified as being potentially universal in nature. The goal was to identify moral values which are not only mutually exclusive, but also sufficiently comprehensive so as to incorporate a wider range of values. The study generated the following list of core ethical values:

1. *trustworthiness* (including honesty, integrity, transparency, and loyalty);
2. *respect* (including notions of respect for human rights);
3. *responsibility* (accountability, accept fault, don't blame others);
4. *fairness* (including notions of process, impartiality, and equity);
5. *caring* (including the notion of avoiding unnecessary harm); and
6. *citizenship* (including notions of obeying laws and protecting the environment).

It can then be argued that all business firms should attempt to infuse these core ethical values throughout their organizations. There are several ways through which this can take place: (a) policies; (b) processes; and (c) practices. Each of these is discussed below.

POLICIES

First, the core ethical values must be made explicit in the firm's policy documents whenever possible. The most important document in which the values should be present is the firm's code of ethics, and they should be stated upfront (other aspects of codes are discussed further below). The values should also be included in the firm's annual report, public accountability statement or social report, and should be indicated as clearly as possible on the homepage of the firm's website. Although being explicit about ethical values might expose a firm to additional critique from NGOs, customers, or even employees, this should be considered a necessary step toward establishing an ethical corporate culture. Of course, even firms such as Enron, despite being quite explicit (e.g., in its office banners and training videos) about their core ethical values (e.g., "integrity," "honesty," and "respect"), failed to live up to them, thus making it clear that the values must be incorporated into other processes and practices as well.

PROCESSES

The values only become alive, leading to a more ethical corporate culture, when they are infused and observed throughout the firm's processes. The first process involves hiring: "When considering an ethical culture, organizations can avoid ethical problems by recruiting the right people and by building a reputation that precedes the organization's representatives wherever they go" (Treviño and Nelson, 2007, p. 272). There are various methods that can be used to build in ethical values such as honesty and integrity into the hiring process, such as testing and interviews. Questions like "Have you ever faced an ethical dilemma before? If so, how did you handle it?" have the potential to reveal an applicant's awareness of ethical issues and perspective on ethical decision-making. The answer "I don't think I've ever faced an ethical dilemma" suggests a lack of awareness and might represent a red flag during the hiring process. In general, ethical values should be considered as the filter or "gate" which a potential employee must get through before performance factors should even be considered. In addition, firms might consider utilizing a group decision-making approach when hiring at the senior levels (as opposed to a one-on-one hiring interviews), as this process might be better at raising ethical "red flags" (see Schwartz, 2009).

The values (in addition to the code of ethics, see below) should also be part of any orientation process, such as ethics training: "The organization's values and guiding principles can be communicated in orientation programs. By providing ethics training, the organization ... communicates that ethical behavior is valued and that ethical dimensions should be considered in decision-making" (Treviño and Nelson, 2007, p. 276). Performance appraisals should also incorporate consideration of employees' behavior with respect to the ethical values: "An effective performance management system is a key component of the ethical culture and plays an essential role in alignment or misalignment of the ethical culture" (Treviño and Nelson, 2007, p. 277). While it is sometimes more difficult in a performance appraisal to measure behavior that conforms to the ethical values, it is easier to identify employees' actions that fail to reflect the values. Decisions regarding promotion must also be based on the ethical values. Employees who are promoted only on the basis of their financial performance, when they have not lived up to the values, only reinforces the perception, for other employees, that the firm does not consider ethical values to be important; this can have a severe potential impact on the firm's ethical corporate culture. Disciplinary or even dismissal decisions should also be based on whether the values are being lived up to. Possibly most important is that the firm aligns its reward system, including compensation, as far as reasonably possible with the firm's ethical values (Treviño and Nelson, 2007).

PRACTICES

In general, if the firm has a set of core ethical values, it needs to be perceived to live up to them—that is, it must "walk the talk" (Messmer, 2003, p. 13; Gibbs, 2003, p. 41). Without this general perception, the ethical values become meaningless. To prevent this from occurring, there are a variety of practices that should explicitly incorporate the firm's values. In general, all decision-making and behavior at all levels and functions should be based on the firm's ethical values, whenever possible. This would include not only executives, managers, and employees, but at the board of directors level as well (see Schwartz, Dunfee, and Kline, 2005). Surveys of employees and customers should also attempt to include performance of the firm and its agents with respect to the ethical values. All meetings, additional training efforts, and speeches (especially by senior managers) should make reference to the core ethical values as well. All these actions reinforce the core ethical values, helping to sustain an ethical corporate culture.

Another method is to build the ethical values into "stories" about the actions or decisions of employees, managers, or senior executives: "Organizational myths and stories explain and give meaning to the organizational culture" (Treviño and Nelson, 2007, p. 287). This includes both positive stories, whereby an employee, manager, or even the CEO acted consistently according to the values despite pressure to do otherwise, as well as negative stories, whereby the firm failed to live up to its values (but discussion then takes place as to why mistakes were made and how to avoid such mistakes in the future).

Formal Ethics Program

Most agree that a formal, comprehensive ethics program is necessary to help establish and ensure an ethical corporate culture, particularly for larger organizations. In fact, changing regulations have virtually made it a legal requirement for large firms or public firms to ensure that they have such programs in place. For example, the US *Federal Sentencing Guidelines for Organizations* (FSGs), enacted by the US Sentencing Commission (1991), are applied when judges sentence organizations for violating US federal law. The FSGs permit firms to have their fines reduced if they have established that they possess an "effective compliance and ethics program." The *Guidelines*, revised in 2004, now suggest that an ethical "organizational culture" is necessary before a firm can be considered to have an "effective compliance and ethics program" which is designed to prevent illegal and unethical behavior. The

FSGs (Section 8B2.1) state: "To have an effective compliance and ethics program an organization shall promote *an organizational culture that encourages ethical conduct* and a commitment to compliance with the law" (emphasis added). They go on to identify the minimum requirements for a firm to be considered as possessing an "effective" program, including a code of ethics, ethics training, an individual responsible for the ethics program (e.g., an ethics officer), and a reporting system (e.g., a whistleblowing hotline) for improper behavior. In a similar fashion, the US Sarbanes-Oxley Act (2002) (SOX), also requires firms to ensure the presence of certain elements of an ethics program. Not only are public firms essentially required to possess a code of conduct (or ethics), but SOX also suggests a minimum content for the code, while requiring that firms have established appropriate whistleblowing channels.

So while US government regulation now provides certain guidance on how to best establish an effective ethics program (i.e., one based on an ethical organizational culture), what is not clearly provided are the details regarding each of the elements of the program. As just a few examples, although a code of ethics is necessary, what specific content should it include? How lengthy should the code be? Should the code merely be positive and aspirational in tone, or more specific and negative in tone? What about the ethics training? Who should conduct it? What format should be used? What should a whistleblowing hotline involve? What protections should be given? Should employees be forced, with threat of discipline, for failure to blow the whistle? Given the lack of agreement over these issues, the following sections will review the key recommendations that have been provided, based on three sources: (i) the US *Federal Sentencing Guidelines for Organizations* (US Sentencing Commission, 1991); (ii) academic researchers and ethics organizations; and (iii) research conducted by the author (Schwartz, 2004). In terms of the latter source (Schwartz, 2004), 57 interviews were conducted of employees, managers, and ethics officers at four large North American business firms for their views on what elements are important in leading to an effective ethics program. Several quotes from the respondents will be provided below as examples related to the various elements of an effective ethics program.

While there are several definitions and types of ethics programs (e.g., compliance- or integrity-based—see Paine, 1994), one might also discuss an effective ethics program based on: (1) the *development* of an ethics program (e.g., code of ethics); (2) the *implementation* of the ethics program (e.g., ethics training); and (3) the *administration* of the ethics program (e.g., ethics hotline/helpline, ethics officer, auditing effectiveness) (see Schwartz, 2001, 2004). The following will summarize some of the major recommendations regarding the development of ethics programs based on these stages of development.

DEVELOPING A CODE OF ETHICS

The starting point for an ethics program is to ensure the existence of a distinct and formal document known as a code of ethics or code of conduct. While the studies on codes are somewhat inconclusive as to whether they actually affect employee behavior (see Kapstein and Schwartz, 2008), one study (Schwartz, 2001) found that while codes may not necessarily influence ethical behavior directly, they often do so in several indirect ways. For example, the code can act as: (a) a "sign-post," leading employees to *consult* other individuals or corporate policies to determine whether certain behavior is appropriate; (b) a "shield," allowing employees to better *challenge* and resist unethical requests (e.g., from suppliers, customers, or even managers); (c) a "smoke detector," leading employees to try to *convince* others and warn them of their inappropriate behavior; and (d) as a "fire alarm," encouraging employees to *contact* the appropriate authority (e.g., the ethics office) and report violations. Overall, codes should be considered a necessary component of any ethics program.

Code content   In terms of code content, as discussed above, the code must explicitly indicate the firm's core set of ethical values. In addition, the Sarbanes-Oxley Act (2002, s.406) now indicates several provisions that essentially should be included in any code of ethics:

1. honest and ethical conduct, including the ethical handling of actual or apparent conflicts of interest between personal and professional relationships;
2. full, fair, accurate, timely and understandable disclosure in reports and documents;
3. compliance with applicable governmental laws, rules and regulations.

Clearly, codes must address additional topics than those indicated in Sarbanes-Oxley Act. Although a number of researchers have both examined the content of codes and made recommendations in terms of appropriate code content, a useful starting point might be Berenbeim's (1999) major study of the codes of large global companies. Berenbeim identified the following content: bribery/improper payments (92 percent); conflict of interest (92 percent); security of proprietary information (92 percent); receiving gifts (90 percent); discrimination/equal opportunity (86 percent); giving gifts (84 percent); environment (78 percent); sexual harassment (78 percent); anti-trust (76 percent); workplace safety (71 percent); political activities (71 percent); community relations (62 percent);

confidentiality of personal information (52 percent); human rights (50 percent); employee privacy (48 percent); whistleblowing (46 percent); substance abuse (42 percent); nepotism (28 percent); and child labor (15 percent).

Be easy to read and understand   All code commentators agree that codes of ethics must be written in easy-to-understand language—that is, written in plain English (Ethics Resource Center, 1990, p. III-1; Raiborn and Payne, 1990, p. 883; Brooks, 1989, p. 124; Pitt and Groskaufmanis, 1990, p. 25) and use an attractive layout (Ethics Resource Center (1990, p. III-2; Moore and Dittenhofer, 1996, p. 29). In relation to this, a further possible concern with respect to code content is when the code is perceived as being too legalistic (i.e., written by a lawyer) and therefore too difficult to understand and apply (Gibbs, 2003, p. 40; Sanderson and Varner, 1984, pp. 28–31). In addition, the provision of examples either in the code document itself or at least during the training on the code has been considered to be a very important means by which to facilitate an employee's understanding of the code's provisions and ultimately code effectiveness (Gibbs, 2003, p. 40; Murphy, 1995, p. 731). Another possible factor affecting whether codes are understood by employees is documents that are too lengthy and thereby require too much time to be properly read (Treviño and Nelson, 1995, p. 246). However, codes should not be too concise, since they need to be used as reference documents. This requirement conforms to that found in the literature, namely codes must consist of enough detail to provide sufficient guidance on expected behavior (Pitt and Groskaufmanis, 1990, p. 1638; Laczniak and Murphy, 1991, p. 269).

Avoid a negative tone   One of the most serious charges against codes by code commentators is that they are often too negative in tone, a series of "thou shalt nots," which does little to inspire employees to do the right thing (Austin, 1961; Harris, 1978, p. 315; Ethics Resource Center, 1990, p. III-2; Raiborn and Payne, 1990, p. 883). In this sense, the code is used as more of a controlling, top-down instrument, and may ultimately be less effective in influencing behavior in a positive fashion. In addition, activities that are not expressly prohibited by the code may be seen by employees as being permissible (Harris, 1978, pp. 314–315; Murphy, 1995, p. 730). It may be, however, that a balance needs to be achieved between the use of a positive tone in the code's language as a whole and more specific negative tone. For example, one respondent in Schwartz's (2004) study suggests that a code written in a negative tone provides clearer expectations than one written in a positive fashion:

> *No, I think it should be negative ... Because it's clearer to understand. And that's what I mean by the black and white issue. If there were gray*

issues ... people would take that and misconstrue it and they could go back and say, well it doesn't really say ... yes or no, do it or don't. I think you'd just be opening up yourself for a lot of misinterpretation ... but if it's clear and concise, negative or not, it doesn't matter, it needs to be very clear ... No, I don't find it offensive at all. (Schwartz, 2004, p. 329, emphasis added)

Be relevant and realistic Another concern is whether companies are providing their employees with codes that address activities that are deemed to be relevant to the employee in question (Pitt and Groskaufmanis, 1990, p. 1639; Brandl and Maguire, 2002). One respondent comments:

... I definitely did not pay a lot of attention to it because I didn't really need it in my everyday life, right now. You know there are some things that you overlook because it is not pertaining to what evolves around you now. (Schwartz, 2004, p. 330)

If companies expect their employees to engage in behavior as set out in the code, and this behavior is perceived by employees to be unrealistic or unattainable, the code may potentially lose its legitimacy (Murphy, 1988, p. 909; Ethics Resource Center, 1990, pp. V–1; Harris, 1978, p. 312).

Include expected behavior and sanctions Everyone appears to agree that codes must include specific descriptions regarding expected conduct, conduct that constitutes violations of the code, and the punishments for non-compliance (Raiborn and Payne, 1990, p. 884). Laczniak and Murphy (1991, p. 269) also suggest that the code must contain sanctions in order to be enforceable. In other words, codes should be blunt and realistic about violations (Murphy, 1988, p. 909) and must include a definite mechanism for enforcement (Molander, 1987). Pitt and Groskaufmanis also state that "[u]pon reading the code, employees should have no doubt that a violation of its terms will subject the employee to discipline and possible discharge" (1990, p. 1649).

Involve the employees It has also been suggested that employees should be directly involved in the code creation process (Messmer, 2003, p. 14). One of the reasons for this suggestion is based on the practical consequence of enhancing the employees' sense of ownership over the code (Ethics Resource Center, 1990, pp. II–3; Montoya and Richard, 1994, p. 714; Arndt, 1990; Sweeney and Siers, 1990, p. 34; Molander, 1987, p. 628). While the majority of respondents felt that their participation in the creation of the code would not necessarily increase their buy-in, their participation would, however, increase the chances that the code's content would be relevant and realistic (Schwartz, 2004).

Get support from senior management and the board of directors One of the factors affecting code effectiveness mentioned in the literature is the necessity of employees knowing that senior management supports their company's code (Montoya and Richard, 1994, p. 714; Ethics Resource Center, 1990, pp. II–1; Brandl and Maguire, 2002; Treviño and Nelson, 1995, p. 252). For example, Jordan believes that "[t]he single most important task in ensuring an effective, successful code of conduct is garnering the full, enthusiastic support of the company's board of directors and senior management" (1995, p. 305). The respondents in Schwartz's study confirmed the importance of perceiving senior management support. Some of the examples employees were able to point to included hearing management speak about the code, seeing managers lead by example, and discovering that managers know and understand the code. For example, all respondents believed that it was a good idea to see a letter from the CEO: "… he is endorsing it. He is saying that yeah, I buy into this concept … I am bound by the same rules you are" (Schwartz, 2004, p. 332).

Application In order for the code to be effective, it should apply and be distributed to everyone within the firm, as well as to key stakeholders (Benson, 1989, p. 318). For example, Hosmer (1991, p. 186) states that ethical codes will work only if the standards apply to everyone—that is, not only the personnel at the operating level. In addition, virtually everyone agrees that all employees must receive a copy of the code (Pitt and Groskaufmanis, 1990, p. 25). Some go further and recommend that shareholders, recruitment agencies, industry organizations, customers, and suppliers should also receive a copy of the code (Webley, 1988, p. 15).

Sign-off process There is general consensus in the literature that in order for codes to be effective, they must be accompanied by a sign-off provision whereby employees acknowledge that they have read, understood, and/or complied with the code (Gibbs, 2003, p. 41; Pitt and Groskaufmanis, 1990, p. 24; Lane, 1991, p. 31). Others, however, raise concerns this process might provoke possible cynicism among employees (Treviño and Nelson, 1995, p. 247). A number of respondents in Schwartz's (2004) study pointed out some of their concerns with respect to the sign-off procedure. The concerns include: (i) general hesitation; (ii) the request of unions not to sign; (iii) lack of utility; (iv) reflects lack of trust; and (v) suggests "pushiness" on the part of their company.

In terms of "pushiness," one respondent indicated:

> ... I feel handing out the booklet is fine. I don't feel that they need to have people sign a copy though. I mean, I think that's being a little pushy. I think just the fact that they hand out the booklet to people ... I think that's good enough. They should not ... need to sign something to say they've read it ... (Schwartz, 2004, p. 333, emphasis added)

Other respondents suggested that requiring employees to sign off on the code is a good idea, primarily because it would increase awareness and provide an incentive to read the document. Several respondents indicated that it was important that their managers appeared to take the annual sign-off process seriously in order for them to take it seriously.

ETHICS TRAINING

According to the commentary on the US *Federal Sentencing Guidelines* (US Sentencing Commission, 2004): "Section 8B2.1(b)(4) makes compliance and ethics training a requirement, and specifically extends the training requirement to the upper levels of an organization, including the governing authority and high-level personnel, in addition to all of the organization's employees and agents, as appropriate." All code commentators concur that, without sufficient training, codes remain ineffective in influencing behavior (Pitt and Groskaufmanis, 1990, p. 24; Gellerman, 1989, p. 77; Lane, 1991, p. 131; Benson, 1989, p. 318; Gibbs, 2003, p. 40; Messmer, 2003, p. 13). For example, firms are using a variety of methods including lectures, role-playing, online training, videos, ethical dilemmas, or cases (Ethics Resource Centre, 1990; Treviño and Nelson, 2007). While some still doubt the value of such training, others suggest that business ethics training can lead to more "... positive perceptions of organizational ethics" (Valentine and Fleischman, 2004, p. 386), or "... can positively influence ethical behavior in the workplace" (Weber, 2007, p. 61).

According to Gellerman (1989, p. 77), the purpose of an ethics workshop is not merely to restate principles, but also, and more importantly, to sensitize people to circumstances in which those principles could lie hidden and indistinct. Ethics training should be based as much as possible on an examination of cases, preferably taken from real life, and even more preferably taken from the experiences of those in the workshop. Lane (1991, p. 31) suggests that two types of case be used during training. One set would present general scenarios reflecting ethical dilemmas faced by managers. A second set would be designed in-house to place managers in daily business situations. While training was perceived positively by most of the respondents in Schwartz's (2004) study, too much training could be perceived by employees to be a waste of time and money, which may reduce the legitimacy of the code.

Several respondents noted the value in training. Essentially, training sessions provide the explanation required in order to raise employees' awareness of the code's usefulness, or at least to indicate the importance the company attached to the code:

> *[The training sessions] are how you make it real to everyone ... by showing them backing up a book. Anyone can create a book, big deal. You back it up with the session where you give examples why we're doing it, why do we have integrity, why is this so important, how can your actions impact a [multi-million dollar] company? (Schwartz, 2004, p. 333, emphasis added)*

Some commentators suggest that the decision on who should conduct the training might have an impact on how employees perceive the code (Treviño and Nelson, 1995, pp. 249–250). The majority of Schwartz's respondents believed that it should be conducted in-house (i.e., by managers or ethics officers) as opposed to being conducted by outside consultants. For example, managers were perceived as understanding better the particular corporate culture, rendering them better equipped to do the training. Greater buy-in from employees is also achieved when the manager conducts the training. There were several reasons proposed, however, as to why an outside consultant, as opposed to a manager, should conduct training. Some managers may not have the ability to engage in code training or lack the legitimacy to conduct the training due to their own lack of ethics. In addition, training sessions would not be as "open" if certain managers were to conduct the training.

REINFORCEMENT

Reinforcement through newsletters, department meetings, notices, e-mails, or executive speeches, has been suggested as playing a role in code effectiveness (Pitt and Groskaufmanis, 1990, p. 24; Treviño and Nelson, 2007, pp. 248–253). This was confirmed by Schwartz's respondents who indicated that, without constant reinforcement, the code would tend to have only a minimal impact on employee behavior. Reinforcement appears to allow employees to perceive the seriousness and importance their company places on compliance with the code. Otherwise, the document becomes less of a concern, and more easily disregarded:

> ... it's just a document. A document doesn't change the culture, it doesn't change values, it doesn't change behavior ... without everything else the document is just a document. You need the constant education, re-education, awareness, examples and build that example base and present it on a regular basis. Just putting in a document, no. (Schwartz, 2004, p. 334, emphasis added)

Appoint an administrator Section 8B2.1 of the US Federal Sentencing Guidelines requires the firm to appoint an individual to be responsible for the firm's ethics program: "Specific individual(s) within the organization shall be delegated day-to-day operational responsibility for the compliance and ethics program." In large US firms, this person is typically referred to as an "ethics officer" or "compliance officer," who may oversee an entire staff within the firm's ethics office. This person must be responsible for the ethics program's operations, and employees must have at least one number to call with day-to-day questions about the code's application. All ethics program commentators support this, and confirm the need for the board of directors to maintain responsibility for the ultimate oversight of the ethics program (Pitt and Groskaufmanis, 1990, p. 1642).

Set up a reporting mechanism All ethics program commentators recommend that a reporting mechanism be set up by companies (Ethics Resource Center, 1990, pp. VII–1; Pitt and Groskaufmanis, 1990, p. 1645; Gellerman, 1989, p. 78). In fact, under section 8B2.1 of the US Federal Sentencing Guidelines, organizations are now required:

> ... to have and publicize a system, which may include mechanisms that allow for anonymity or confidentiality, whereby the organization's employees and agents may report or seek guidance regarding potential or actual criminal conduct without fear of retaliation.

This provision is backed up by many ethics program commentators as being critical. Jordan (1995, p. 312) provides a cautionary note however on setting up a reporting system: "... a telephone hot line—evoking images of 'Big Brother'—may not be consistent with the corporate culture of many companies. Company-wide 'suggestion boxes,' interoffice mail, or electronic mail systems are alternatives." Almost all of Schwartz's respondents believed that having a hotline served an important purpose. For example: "... sometimes you don't feel comfortable talking with the people around here ... who you going to report [the violation to] if you don't want to talk to your manager?" (Schwartz, 2004, p. 336).

Enforcement Many commentators suggest that consistent enforcement of the code (as well as the communication of enforcement) is essential to a code's effectiveness (Pitt and Groskaufmanis, 1990, p. 25; Sweeney and Siers, 1990, p. 39, Gibbs, 2003, p. 40; Messmer, 2003, p. 14). It has even been suggested that the perception of justice (e.g., code enforcement) can directly influence the misconduct of the observer (Treviño, 1992, p. 647). The penalty applied should be fair and proportionate to the violation (Raiborn and Payne, 1990, p. 888; Molander, 1987, p. 630). Schwartz's (2004) respondents made it clear that without consistent and unbiased enforcement, the code may not be taken seriously.

Monitoring/auditing/revision Finally, the effectiveness of the program should be audited, now also a requirement under Section 8B2.1. of the US Federal Sentencing Guidelines (US Sentencing Commission, 2004):

> *The organization shall take reasonable steps (A) to ensure that the organization's compliance and ethics program is followed, including monitoring and auditing to detect criminal conduct; [and] (B) to evaluate periodically the effectiveness of the organization's compliance and ethics program... .*

Jordan (1995, p. 312) discusses the use of regular and random audits to test employees' adherence to, and efficacy of, the code. He also suggests using an employee survey by which to monitor the effectiveness, identify weaknesses, and make improvements to the code of ethics. Several commentators recommend that a code be updated periodically (Murphy, 1988, p. 909; Pitt and Groskaufmanis, 1990, p. 25; Driscoll, Hoffman, and Petry, 1996, p. 156).

All of these measures are part of developing a comprehensive and effective ethics program. Ultimately, the program should be based on the core ethical values discussed above. But a firm that possesses core ethical values infused throughout its policies, processes, and practices, even when supported by the establishment of a comprehensive ethics program, may not be sufficient. The presence of ethical leadership is also necessary, as will now be discussed.

Ethical Leadership

Beyond infusing ethical values throughout the organization and developing a comprehensive ethics program, it has also been argued that in order to achieve an ethical corporate culture, an ethical "tone at the top" must also exist (Schwartz, Dunfee, and Kline, 2005; Sheeder, 2005; Weaver and Treviño, 1999). In fact, many suggest that an ethical corporate culture is contingent upon ethical leadership: "... the moral tone of an organization is set best by top management ... workers generally get their ethical cues by observing what their bosses do" (James, 2000, p. 54). In addition, "[l]eaders are clearly viewed as key to the development and maintenance of a strong ethical climate in their organizations" (Treviño, 1990, p. 203). According to Brown, Treviño, and Harrison, "[l]eaders should be the key source of ethical guidance for employees" (2005, p. 117). Others have even suggested that a relationship exists between ethical leaders and the presence of values within an organization: "Ethics is central to leadership because of the ... impact leaders have on establishing the organization's values" (Northouse, 2001, p. 255).

The relationship between ethical leadership and ethical behavior has also been observed. According to Hitt, "[t]he results of research studies demonstrate that the ethical conduct of individuals in organizations is influenced greatly by their leaders" (1990, p. 3). Perceptions among employees that their managers possess a set of core ethical values and act upon them have been shown to have a significant impact on the ethical corporate culture of the firm. According to a study by Treviño et al., based on a survey of over 10,000 US employees:

> When employees perceived that supervisors and executives regularly pay attention to ethics, take ethics seriously, and care about ethics and values as much as the bottom line, all of the outcomes [i.e., less unethical/ illegal behavior, greater awareness of ethical/legal issues, employees more likely to look for advice within the firm, willing to deliver bad news to management, report ethical violations, and more committed to the organization] were significantly more positive. (Treviño et al., 1999, p. 142)

Despite the recognized importance of ethical leadership within business, there appears to be a perception that such leadership is lacking. For example, a Gallup survey found that only 20 percent of over 1,000 US adults perceived business executives as having "very high" or "high" honesty and ethical standards, even lower than auto mechanics (26 percent) and TV reporters (23 percent) (Gallup, 2004). In a 2009 survey of 1,024 of its readers from around the world, *Harvard Business Review* magazine found that 76 percent of those surveyed had less trust in US senior management than they had the previous year, and 51 percent had less trust in senior management at non-US companies (Podolny, 2009). Canadians' perceptions of ethical business leaders were similar. In an Ipsos-Reid (2003) survey, 1,007 Canadian adults were asked "Whom do you trust?" CEOs were only trusted by 21 percent of respondents, significantly below auto mechanics (33 percent), journalists (31 percent), and lawyers (29 percent), while only being more trusted than car salespeople (10 percent) and national politicians (9 percent). The research suggests that there is significant room for improvement in society's perception of the ethical values of business leaders.

So how exactly do managers and executives exemplify ethical leadership? In most cases, employees will not have direct contact with their senior managers, and thus the firm's leaders must develop a reputation for ethical leadership. Various studies have examined how this reputation is developed. Treviño, Brown, and Pincus-Hartman. (2003) suggest that there are two dimensions to ethical leadership: a "moral person" dimension and a "moral manager" dimension. The moral person dimension (e.g., the manager acts with integrity, honesty, and trustworthiness) is based on being observed to do "… the right thing, showing concern for people and treating them with dignity and respect, being open/listening, and living a personally moral life" (Treviño and Nelson, 2007, p. 265). The moral manager dimension is affected by "… visibly role-modeling ethical conduct, by communicating openly and regularly with employees about ethics and values, and by using the reward system to hold everyone accountable to the standards" (Treviño and Nelson, 2007, p. 266).

Probably the most significant means of demonstrating ethical leadership is to ensure that all decision-making is in accordance with the ethical values (as discussed above). This becomes even more apparent when executives are seen to make such decisions even when there is a financial cost to the firm. In other words, the ethical values must be seen to take priority over other interests, or they quickly become irrelevant. In one famous example, at age 28, Arthur Andersen, as the founder of his accounting firm, refused to "approve" the books of an important railway client. He lost the client as a result, but when the client later went bankrupt, Arthur Andersen developed a reputation as someone who could be trusted to act with integrity (Toffler and Reingold, 2003). This decision set an ethical tone for the firm for many years, leading to Arthur Andersen later acting as a watchdog over the entire accounting industry. Unfortunately, such ethical behavior did not continue long-term at Arthur Andersen, when the billing revenue culture of its consulting practice (especially in relation to its client Enron) began to take precedence over the ethical values underlying its auditing business (Treviño and Nelson, 2007, pp. 292–293).

In another famous example, former Johnson and Johnson CEO James Burke relied on his firm's credo in order to not only withstand the 1982 Tylenol tampering crisis, but also derive a competitive advantage from it years later. The firm (through Burke's leadership) did so by relying on its credo's values, which placed safety ahead of financial considerations; it recalled the product nationwide, despite the cost (Treviño and Nelson, 2007). Similarly, former CEO of Alcoa, Paul O'Neil, developed a reputation for caring about the safety of his employees. He managed this by visiting plants and indicating to employees that there would be no budget for safety matters, and that they should spend money to fix any safety hazard regardless of the cost. He also gave his home phone number for employees to report safety problems, and would personally fly anywhere in the world to visit employees who had been injured (Treviño and Nelson, 2007, pp. 266–267). As another example, following a series of scandals at the Canadian bank CIBC (related to its dealings with Enron and a Can$2.4 billion settlement with investors), the new CEO decided to voluntarily accept a compensation package that delayed the vesting of his share options extensively, and also included a provision that his compensation could be taken away retroactively if a scandal was later discovered during his term as CEO of the bank (CNW, 2005). Such actions could be seen to demonstrate a commitment to ethical values, leading to a perception of the CEO as an ethical leader.

Unfortunately, however, there are too many examples of companies that failed to establish such an ethical "tone at the top," leading to significant scandals and sometimes causing their downfall (Gini, 2004). For example, US firms (and their former CEOs) such as WorldCom (Bernie Ebbers), Tyco International (Dennis Kozlowski), and Adelphia (John Rigas), Canadian firms such as Hollinger (Conrad Black) and Livent (Garth Drabinsky), and Italian firm Parmalat (Calisto Tanzi) appear to have been lacking an appropriate tone at the top. Even Enron, despite possessing a comprehensive compliance or ethics program, collapsed at least partly due to an inappropriate tone at the top led by former CEO Jeffrey Skilling, who emphasized bottom-line results as opposed to ethical values (Watkins, 2003). Kenneth Lay, also former CEO and chairman of Enron, demonstrated a lack of ethical leadership when he requested that Enron's managers use his sister's travel agency for all of their overseas flights (Thottam, 2002). Harry Stonecipher, former CEO of Boeing, was asked to resign following the discovery that he was having an intimate relationship with an executive. Stonecipher had been instrumental in both turning the firm around financially and leading a new emphasis on ethical behavior at Boeing through a revised code of ethics. According to Boeing's non-executive chairman: "It's not the fact that [Harry Stonecipher] was having an affair that caused him to be fired, but as we explored the circumstances surrounding the affair, we just thought there were some issues of poor judgment that ... impaired his ability to lead going forward" (Merle, 2005, p. A01).

In other words, an ethical leader is trustworthy, honest, transparent, responsible, caring, respectful, fair, acts with integrity, and puts the interests of the firm and other stakeholders before his or her own personal interests. All of this must be demonstrated through the leader's actions, not just through words (in fact it may only create greater cynicism among employees if the leader talks about the importance of ethical behavior but does not act accordingly). Without ethical leadership across the organization, there is little chance of establishing and sustaining an ethical corporate culture: "Senior leadership represents an important component of an organization's ethical culture, as integrity (or the lack of it) flows from the top down and employees take their cues from the messages sent by those in formal leadership roles" (Treviño and Nelson, 2007, p. 264).

Conclusion

Figure 10.1 summarizes the interaction of all three elements necessary to develop and sustain an ethical corporate culture within a firm.

Figure 10.1 The three elements of an ethical corporate culture

Once an ethical corporate culture is developed, the assumption is that the extent of crime, corruption, and unethical activity within organizations or on behalf of their agents will be minimized. Unfortunately, it is often difficult to measure the success of an ethical corporate culture, as one cannot always identify the scandal that was avoided as a result of an ethical work environment. In any event, while significant and sustained efforts by firms must be undertaken to ensure high ethical standards, they must take place along with the decisions and actions of other stakeholders, including: governments (e.g., regulation and enforcement); employees (e.g., where to work); customers (e.g., which companies' products to buy or services to use); suppliers (e.g., which companies to work with); creditors (e.g., where to lend); shareholders (e.g., where to invest); and NGOs (e.g., through involving the media). Collectively, all of these stakeholders create pressure on firms to engage in legal and ethical behavior.

With respect to the efforts of the firms themselves, it is argued above that there are three fundamental elements that form the basis of an ethical corporate culture: (1) the existence of a set of *core ethical values*; (2) the establishment of a *formal ethics program*; and (3) the continuous presence of *ethical leadership* (i.e., "tone at the top"). While all three elements are distinct, they also reinforce and support each other. Nevertheless, due to human nature crime, corruption, and other illegal or unethical activity is unlikely ever to be completely eliminated, certainly for a certain percentage of the workforce, regardless of whatever efforts are undertaken. However, business firms do have an ethical obligation to make reasonable attempts to minimize the presence of crime and corruption, for the good of all society.

References

Argandoña, A. (2005) "Corruption and companies: The use of facilitating payments," *Journal of Business Ethics*, 60, 251–264.

Arndt, S. (1990) "Discussion of ethics needed," *National Underwriter (Life, Health/Financial Services)*, 93(43), 3–13.

Austin, R. W. (1961) "Code of conduct for executives," *Harvard Business Review*, September/October, 53.

Benson, G. C. S. (1989) "Codes of ethics," *Journal of Business Ethics*, 8, 305–319.

Berenbeim, R. E. (1999) *Global Corporate Ethics Practices: A Developing Consensus*, New York: The Conference Board.

Brandl, P. and Maguire, M. (2002) "Codes of ethics: A primer on their purpose, development, and use," *The Journal for Quality and Participation*, 25(4), 8–12.

Brass, D. J., Butterfield, K. D., and Skaggs, B. C. (1998) "Relationships and unethical behavior: A social network perspective," *Academy of Management Review*, 23(1), 14–31.

Brooks, L. J. (1989) "Corporate Codes of Ethics," *Journal of Business Ethics*, 8, 117–129.

Brooks, L. J. and Dunn, P. (2010) *Business and Professional Ethics* (5th ed.), Mason, OH: South Western Cengage Learning.

Brown, M. E., Treviño, L. K., and Harrison, D. A. (2005) "Ethical leadership: A social learning perspective for construct development and testing," *Organizational Behavior and Human Decision Processes*, 97(2), 117–134.

CNW (2005,) "CIBC adopts new CEO compensation model," December, at: http://www.newswire.ca/en/releases/archive/December2005/01/c1382.html.

Covey, S. (2004) *The 8th Habit*, New York: Free Press.

Donaldson, T. and Dunfee, T.W. (1999) *Ties That Bind: A Social Contracts Approach to Business Ethics,*, Boston, MA: Harvard Business School Press.

Driscoll, D. M., Hoffman, W. M., and Petry, E. S. (1996) "Nynex regains moral footing," *Personnel Journal*, June, 147–156.

Encarta (2009) Definition of corruption, at: http://ca.encarta.msn.com/dictionary_1861600531/corruption.html.

Ethics Resource Center (1990) Creating a Workable Company Code of Ethics, Washington, DC: ERC.

Ferrell, O. C. and Gresham, L. (1985) "A contingency framework for understanding ethical decision making in marketing," *Journal of Marketing*, 49, 87–96.

Gallup (2004) "Nurses top list in honesty and ethics poll," at: http://poll.gallup.com/content/default.aspx?CI=14236.

Gellerman, S.W. (1989) "Managing ethics from the top down," *Sloan Management Review*, Winter, 73–79.

Gibbs, E. (2003) "Developing an effective code of conduct," *Financial Executive*, 19(4), 40–41.

Gini, A. (2004) "Business, ethics, and leadership in a post Enron era," *Journal of Leadership & Organizational Studies*, 11(1), 9–16.

Harris, C. E. (1978) "Structuring a workable business code of ethics," *University of Florida Law Review*, 30, 310–382.

Hess, D. and Dunfee, T. W. (2000) "Fighting corruption, A principled approach: The C² principles (combating corruption)," *Cornell International Law Journal*, 33(3), 595–628.

Hess, D. and Dunfee, T.W. (2003) "Taking responsibility for bribery: The multinational's role in combating corruption" in R. Sullivan (ed.) *Business and Human Rights: Dilemmas and Solutions*, Sheffield, UK: Greenleaf Publishing, pp. 260–271.

Hitt, W.D. (1990) *Ethics and Leadership: Putting Theory into Practice*, Columbus, OH: Battelle Press.

Hosmer, L. T. (1991) *The Ethics of Management* (2nd ed.), Boston, MA: Irwin Inc.

Hunt, S. D., Wood, V. R., and Chonko, L. B. (1989) "Corporate ethical values and organizational commitment in marketing," *Journal of Marketing*, 53(3), 79–90.

Ipsos-Reid (2003) "So, whom do we trust? Reader's digest trust survey finds that pharmacists, doctors and airline pilots top the list as Canada's most trusted professions," at: http://www.ipsos-na.com/news/pressrelease.cfm?id=1716.

James, H. S. Jr (2000) "Reinforcing ethical decision making through organizational structure," *Journal of Business Ethics*, 28(1), 43–58.

Jordan, K. S. (1995) "Designing and implementing a corporate code of conduct in the context of an 'effective' compliance program" in *Corporate Counsel's Guide To Business Ethics Policies*, Chesterland, OH: Business Laws, pp. 301–314.

Kapstein, M. and Schwartz, M. S. (2008) "The effectiveness of business codes: A critical examination of existing studies and the development of an integrated research model," *Journal of Business Ethics*, 77(2), 111–127.

Laczniak, G. R. and Murphy, P. E. (1991) "Fostering ethical marketing decisions," *Journal of Business Ethics*, 10, 259–271.

Lane, M. R. (1991) "Improving American business ethics in three steps," *CPA Journal*, February, 30–34.

Merle, R. (2005), "Boeing CEO resigns over affair with subordinate," *Washington Post*, March 8, A01, at: http://www.washingtonpost.com/wp-dyn/articles/A13173-2005Mar7.html.

Messmer, M. (2003) "Does your company have a code of ethics?" *Strategic Finance*, 84(10), 13–14.

Molander, E. A. (1987) "A paradigm for design, promulgation and enforcement of ethical codes," *Journal of Business Ethics*, 6, 619–631.

Montoya, I. D. and Richard, A. J. (1994) "A comparative study of codes of ethics in health care facilities and energy companies," *Journal of Business Ethics*, 13, 713–717.

Moore, W. G. and Dittenhofer, M. A. (1992) *How to Develop a Code of Conduct*, Altamonte Springs, FL: The Institute of Internal Auditors Research Foundation.

Murphy, P. E. (1988) "Implementing business ethics," *Journal of Business Ethics*, 7, 907–915.

Murphy, P. E. (1995) "Corporate ethics statements: Current status and future prospects," *The Journal of Business Ethics*, 14, 727–740.

Northouse, P. G. (2001) *Leadership Theory and Practice* (2nd ed.), London: Sage Publications.

O'Fallon, M. J. and Butterfield, K. D. (2005) "A review of the empirical ethical decision-making literature: 1996-2003," *Journal of Business Ethics*, 59(4), 375–413.

Paine, L. S. (1994) "Managing for organizational integrity," *Harvard Business Review*, March/April, 106–117.

Pitt, H. L. and Groskaufmanis, K. A. (1990) "Minimizing corporate civil and criminal liability: A second look at corporate codes of conduct," *The Georgetown Law Journal*, 78, 1559–1654.

Podolny, J. M. (2009) "The buck stops (and starts) at business school," *Harvard Business Review*, 87(6), 62–67.

Raiborn, C. A. and Payne, D. (1990) "Corporate codes of conduct: A collective conscience and continuum," *Journal of Business Ethics*, 9, 879–889.

Sanderson, G. R. and Varner, I. I. (1984) "What's wrong with corporate codes of conduct?" *Management Accounting*, July, 28–31.

Schwartz, M. S. (2001) "The nature of the relationship between corporate codes of ethics and behaviour," *Journal of Business Ethics*, 32(3), 247–262.

Schwartz, M. S. (2004) "Effective corporate codes of ethics: Perceptions of code users," *Journal of Business Ethics*, 55(4), 321–341.

Schwartz, M. S. (2005) "Universal moral values for corporate codes of ethics," *Journal of Business Ethics*, 59(1), 27–44.

Schwartz, M. S. (2009) "Ethical leadership training: An Aristotelian approach," *Conference Proceedings* (electronic), European Business Ethics Network, September.

Schwartz, M. S., Dunfee, T., and Kline, M. (2005) "Tone at the top: An ethics code for directors?" *Journal of Business Ethics*, 58(1), 79–100.

Sheeder, F. (2005) "What exactly is 'tone at the top' and is it really that big a deal?" *Journal of Health Care Compliance*, 7(3), 35–38.

Sweeney, R. B. and Siers, H. L. (1990) "Survey: Ethics in America," *Management Accounting*, June, 34–40.

Thottam, J. (2002) "Time, family business: Lay's sister had a sweet deal too," February 11, at: http://www.time.com/time/magazine/article/0,9171,1001781,00.html.

Toffler, B. L. and Reingold, J. (2003) *Final Accounting: Ambition, Greed, and the Fall of Arthur Andersen*, New York: Broadway Books.

Treviño, L. (1986) "Ethical decision making in organizations: A person-situation interactionist model," *Academy of Management Review*, 11, 601–617.

Treviño, L. (1990) "A cultural perspective on changing and developing organizational ethics," *Research in Organizational Change and Development*, 4, 195–230.

Treviño, L. (1992) "The social effects of punishment in organizations: A justice perspective," *The Academy of Management Review*, 17(4), 647–676.

Treviño, L. and Nelson K. A. (1995) *Managing Business Ethics*, New York: John Wiley & Sons,.

Treviño, L. K. and Nelson, K.A. (2007) *Managing Business Ethics* (4th ed.), New York: John Wiley.

Treviño, L. K. Brown, M., and Pincus-Hartman, L. (2003) "A quantitative investigation of perceived executive ethical leadership: Perceptions from inside and outside the executive suite," *Human Relations*, 56(1), 5–37.

Treviño, L., Weaver, G. R., Gibson, D. G., and Toffler, B. L. (1999) "Managing ethics and legal compliance: What works and what hurts," *California Management Review*, 41(2), 131–151.

US Sarbanes-Oxley Act (2002), at: http://www.sec.gov/about/laws/soa2002.pdf.

US Sentencing Commission (1991) *U.S. Federal Sentencing Guidelines for Organizations*, at: http://www.ussc.gov/2007guid/tabconchapt8.htm.

Valentine, S. and Fleischman, G. (2004) "Ethics training and businesspersons: Perceptions of organizational ethics," *Journal of Business Ethics*, 52, 381–390.

Watkins, S. (2003) "Pristine ethics: Who do you trust?" *Vital Speeches of the Day*, 69(14), 435–440.

Weaver, G. R. and Treviño, L. K. (1999) "Compliance and values oriented ethics programs: Influences on employees' attitudes and behavior," *Business Ethics Quarterly*, 9(2), 315–336.

Weber, J. A. (2007) "Business ethics training: insights from learning theory," *Journal of Business Ethics*, 70(1), 61–85.

Webley, S. (1988) *Company Philosophies and Codes of Business Ethics: A Guide to their Drafting and Use*, London: Institute of Business Ethics.

11

Confronting Corruption Using Integrity Pacts: The Case of Nigeria

Wesley Cragg, Uwafiokun Idemudia, and Bronwyn Best

Introduction

Transparency International (TI), the global coalition against corruption, defines corruption on its website as "the abuse of entrusted power for private gain." John Noonan, in one of the seminal explorations of the subject, defines bribery as "an inducement improperly influencing the performance of a public function meant to be gratuitously exercised" (Noonan, 1984, p. xi). For the purposes of this discussion, bribery will be understood as any attempt, whether successful or not, to persuade someone in a position of responsibility to make a decision or recommendation on grounds other than the intrinsic merits of the case, with a view to the advantage or advancement of him or herself or another person or group to which he or she is linked through personal commitment, obligation or employment, or individual, professional or group loyalty. The virtue of this more comprehensive definition is that it recognizes that bribery and corruption can be motivated by a wide range of considerations, including friendship, family loyalty, and the fulfillment of family obligations and group or institutional values that, taken on their own or considered in the abstract, would normally be regarded as commendable.

As we have defined it, bribery and corruption are no strangers to business or to those engaged in business. For some, acquaintance with bribery will be first-hand. This is not surprising. Transparency International describes bribery as an epidemic in many countries of the world. This view is backed up by the results of three surveys published in the form of indices, a *Corruption Perceptions Index* (CPI), a *Bribe Payers Index*, and an index of the business sectors in which corruption is most likely to occur.[1] These studies all confirm that bribery and corruption have become a serious and entrenched problem worldwide.

Why, it might be asked, is this the case? The answer is complex, in part because bribery has many uses. Enterprises and their suppliers may use bribery to cut costs by avoiding health, safety, or environmental regulations. Corruption of this kind is alleged to have played a significant role in the Chernobyl disaster in Russia, the collapse of buildings in Turkey and Mexico as a result of earthquakes, the devastation caused by Hurricane Mitch in the Honduras, and illegal cutting and deforestation in Latin America and Asia, to cite just a few examples. Bribery can be used to influence purchasing decisions in supply chains, as Wal-Mart has discovered recently in Canada. Corporations may be tempted to influence governmental policy through illegal contributions to politicians and political parties. The Watergate scandal in the US in the 1970s is perhaps the best-known illustration of this form of corruption, though clearly, it is not limited to that country. Charges and allegations of illegal contributions to a political party in Germany and reports of massive corruption on the part of government officials in countries like Russia, Indonesia, and Nigeria offer additional illustrations. The Canadian Bre-X scandal,[2] which involved dishonest claims with respect to an allegedly massive gold deposit in Indonesia and questionable use of family members to gain influence with the Suharto government on the part of a number of companies competing for the right to develop what turned out to be a non-existent gold deposit, illustrates how corruption can affect business practices and investment decisions. And the Barings Bank scandal, allegations of misrepresentation and manipulation of hedge funds, and the recent financial crisis show that not even financial institutions are immune.

Transparency International describes corruption in its mission statement as "one of the greatest challenges of the contemporary world." The seriousness of the challenge lies in the impact of corruption. As TI points out:

> *It undermines good government, fundamentally distorts public policy, leads to the misallocation of resources, harms the private sector and private sector development and particularly hurts the poor. Controlling it is only possible with the cooperation of a wide range of stakeholders in the integrity system, including most importantly the state, civil*

---

1 All available, for various years, from: http://www.transparency.org/.
2 Bre-X, a Canadian gold mining company based in Calgary, Canada, purchased a property in Busang, Indonesia, in 1993. The price of its stock soared over the next several years and then collapsed in 1997 when the samples on which estimates of the gold at the site were discovered to be fraudulent. For a discussion of the scandal see Canadian Encyclopedia (2009).

society and the private sector. There is also a crucial role to be played by international institutions. (TI, 1997)

Nigeria is a graphic illustration of the truth of this claim.

Combating Corruption: The Integrity Pact Model

Many tools have been developed to reduce corruption domestically and internationally. Of these, legal instruments have played the most prominent role. An example is the Foreign Corrupt Practices Act, passed by the US Congress in 1979, in response to the Watergate scandal. For many years, the US was the only country with a law of this kind on its books. In the view of many American corporations, the existence of a law of this nature put them at a significant competitive disadvantage vis-à-vis non- American corporations. Resulting lobbying on the part of American corporations over the following decade did lead to changes in the law. It also led to a determined effort on the part of the US government to "internationalize" the US legislation with a view to "leveling the playing field" for American corporations in international markets.

Whether the US law indeed had the effect of disadvantaging American corporations in international markets is a matter for debate (Cragg and Woof, 2002). Be that is it may, the OECD was eventually persuaded to take action, producing, in 1997, the OECD Convention on Combating Bribery of Foreign Public Officials (OECD Anti-Bribery Convention). Since that time there have been a series of international conventions adopted by various international institutions, including the Organization of American States, and the United Nations.

More recently, Publish What You Pay (PWYP), an international NGO, has lobbied national governments to require that resource extraction companies publish what they pay in taxes and royalties to governments of countries in which they are active. The Extractive Industries Transparency Initiative (EITI) is a response. It is a government-led initiative whose purpose is to persuade governments, particularly in the developing world, to put in place a framework for the disclosure and auditing of payments and revenues. The Nigerian government is a participant.

Transparency International has also been active in this field. It led the way in the internationalization of the American Foreign Corrupt Practices Act, resulting in the OECD Anti-bribery Convention. It has published scientifically grounded assessments of the state of corruption in countries around the world, including the *Corruption Perceptions Index* and the *Bribe Payers Index*, which help identify where corruption is most endemic. However, persuaded that there was a need for practical tools to help eliminate corruption from government transactions, TI has also developed the concept of an Integrity Pact.

The Integrity Pact tool (IP) was developed by TI in the mid-1990s, to help governments, business and civil society work together in combating corruption in the field of public contracting. Law enforcement is largely a reactive process. IPs, on the other hand, are a proactive instrument. They are designed to prevent corruption, not just punish it when it occurs. Although greeted with skepticism by international institutions like the World Bank when it was first developed, Integrity Pacts are now being employed by TI throughout the world in a variety of sectors from telecommunications to transportation, utilities, finance, and information systems. The Integrity Pact concept has been put to work by TI chapters in Colombia, Italy, South Korea, and Pakistan, to name just a few.

The IP is a process that generates an agreement between a government (at the federal, national or local level) or government department and all bidders for a public-sector contract. It requires an agreement on the part of all parties that there will be no offers, demands, payments or acceptance of bribes in bidding for the contract to which the IP applies. Further, it requires a public commitment not to engage in collusion with competitors in bidding for the contract or contracts covered by an IP or, on winning the contract, in carrying the contract out. Bidders are required to disclose all commissions and similar expenses paid by them to anybody in connection with the contract. Sanctions specified in the IP and agreed to by all participants apply, should violations of the IP occur.

What gives Integrity Pacts their credibility is the requirement that the implementation be monitored by an arm's-length third party—for example, an NGO such as a national chapter of TI. The agreement binds those participating to allow the inspection of accounts and the constant monitoring of bidding and contract implementation. It requires public reporting on the part of the monitor as the pact is implemented and when the contract has been completed. The monitor's final report confirms publicly and on the basis of extensive investigation that the process from beginning to end has been corruption-free and the terms of the contract have been fulfilled.

IPs are an option for contracting where there are:

- a central, local or municipal government, a government's subdivision, or even a state-owned enterprise (the "principal") with a project to be contracted out; and
- private-sector companies (the "bidders") interested in obtaining such a contract, or in charge of implementing it.

An IP covers the planning, design, construction, installation or operation of assets by the principal, the privatization of assets, the issuing by the principal of licenses and concessions, and corresponding services, such as consulting services and technical, financial, and administrative support. Since the aim is for maximum transparency, wherever possible, an IP covers all activities related to the contract from the pre-selection of bidders and bidding terms, the actual bidding phase and contracting, through implementation to completion and operation—all steps which offer an opportunity for corrupt behavior.

The two primary objectives of an IP are:

1. to enable *companies* to abstain from bribing by providing assurances that:
    a) their competitors are also committed to refrain from bribing; and
    b) government procurement, privatization or licensing agencies are committed to preventing corruption, including extortion, by their officials and to following transparent procedures; and
2. to enable *governments* [including aid organizations] to reduce the high cost and distortions by corruption of public procurement, privatization or licensing. (TI, 2002, p. 4).

While the IP has taken on some permutations in certain contexts, the main criteria are:

- a pact (contract) among a government office (inviting contractors or suppliers to submit tenders for a public sector project—the "principal") and those companies submitting a tender for this specific project (the "bidders");
- an undertaking by the principal that its officials will not demand or accept any bribes, gifts, etc., with appropriate disciplinary or criminal sanctions in case of violation;
- a statement by each bidder that it has not paid, and will not pay, any bribes [or collude with competitors] "in order to obtain or retain this contract" (thus excluding facilitation payments);
- an undertaking by each bidder and its chief executive officer to disclose all payments made in connection with the contract in question to anybody (including agents and other middle men as well as family members, etc., of officials);

- the explicit acceptance by each bidder that the no-bribery commitment and the disclosure obligation as well as the attendant sanctions remain in force for the winning bidder until the contract has been fully executed;
- a pre-announced set of sanctions for any violation, by a bidder, of its statements or undertakings, including some or all of:
  - denial or loss of contract
  - forfeiture of the bid security
  - liability for damages to the principal and the competing bidders
  - debarment of the violator by the principal for an appropriate period of time (this sanction is usually the most effective) (TI, 2002, pp. 4–5).

Some key findings, which have come to the fore in implementing successful IPs, include the following:

- Because an IP establishes contractual rights and obligations of all parties, it eliminates uncertainties as to the quality, applicability and enforcement of criminal and contractual legal provisions in a given country—that is, the IP concept can be done anywhere without the normal lengthy process of changing the local laws.
- There is a need to establish political will at the highest possible level; IPs tend to exist more at the municipal than at the regional or national levels.
- Civil society plays a critical role in overseeing and monitoring the correct and full implementation of the IP through an external independent monitor; this helps create confidence and trust in the public decision-making process in general, thus leading to a more hospitable investment climate and local public support.

In some countries, the government will not allow civil society to play such a monitoring role. Where this is the case, the government must:

1. employ an "Independent Private Sector Inspector General"—that is, a private-sector company or individual with appropriate expertise; or
2. commit itself to provide full public disclosure of all relevant data, regarding the evaluation of the competing bids, the evaluation criteria and confirming evidence affirming that they were fully

applied, a list of the bidders and their prices, a list of the bids rejected and why, reasons for allocating the contract to the winning firm, and the government's cost estimate for the project (TI, 2002).

The Internet has played a significant role in the posting of all the specifications. Public hearings have also proven to be effective.

TI has developed and adjusted the IP model on the basis of extensive discussions with governments and international agencies, such as the World Bank, the Inter-American Development Bank, the Asian Development Bank, the UNDP, the International Finance Corporation, and the Court of Arbitration of the International Chamber of Commerce.

The key to implementing IPs is their *flexibility* in application and their adaptability to different legal settings. In some jurisdictions they are used in their complete form; in other jurisdictions only essential elements are used. Sometimes they are voluntary, at other times, they are imposed. Each situation is different, and only country-specific strategies developed in full partnership with civil society have proven to be successful.

With IPs, everyone is a winner. For governments, they help increase their credibility and legitimacy; when public officials are honestly concerned about corruption and transparency issues, costs are reduced, including legal costs associated with enforcing contracts and the law more generally. For corporations, the bidding process is made easier and transaction costs are reduced. Corruption, after all, is not free of charge or cheap—winning and losing fairly is for, the most part, less costly. For civil society, it is an effective and efficient way of generating changes in public policy and its administration. The impact can be felt financially, economically and environmentally, on health, human safety and innovation.

As of 2008, more than 300 IPs have been, or are being, successfully instituted around the world, with independent monitoring included in the implementation.[3]

Oil and Nigeria: Background Context and Issues

The 1914 forced amalgamation of the southern and northern protectorates that was driven by British colonialist political and economic interests, as opposed to the concerns or aspirations of the indigenous people, marked the birth of

---

3 Further information concerning IPs is available at http://www.transparency.org/integrity_pact/index.html; also available from TI are the CD-ROM, *The Corruption Fighters' Tool Kit*, and the *Handbook for Curbing Corruption in Public Procurement*.

the modern Nigerian state-nation. The nature of this amalgamation, and its political and economic consequences, has had significant ramifications for post-colonial state-society relations. For instance, due to the state-nation status of the Nigerian state as a result of the forced amalgamation, questions of ethnicity, nationalism, and citizenship are often a subject of contestation, which has had significant negative ramifications for the country's national development.

At independence, the post-colonial Nigerian economy was largely dependent on agriculture as the three major regions that made up the country specialized in the production of certain agricultural products. For example, groundnuts were produced in the North, cocoa in the West, and rubber in the East. However, the discovery of oil in 1956 and its subsequent extraction in 1958 have transformed the Nigerian economy over the past 30 years from an agriculturally-based economy to one that is essentially dependent on oil. For example, between 1960 and 1973, oil output exploded from just over 5 million barrels per day to over 600 million barrels per day, and government revenue also rose from N66 million (naira) in 1970 to over N10 billion in 1980 (Watts, 2007). Today, the *rentier* status of the Nigeria state is emblematic of the fact that oil accounts for 40 percent of its GDP, 95 per cent of exports and 83 per cent of government revenue. This centrality of oil in national politics against the backdrop of pre-oil politics facilitated the full manifestation of the "resource curse." In economic terms, between 1965 and 2004, per capita income fell from US$250 to US$212. Between 1970 and 2000 the number of people subsisting on less than US$1 a day grew from 36 percent to more than 70 percent—from 19 million to about 90 million (Watts, 2007). Income distribution deteriorated, such that 90 percent of oil revenue accrued to 1 percent of the population, while, in addition, between 1960 and 1999 the country lost as much as US$380 billion to corruption and waste (HRW, 2007). Indeed, Watts (2007) noted that, in 2003, 70 percent of the country's oil wealth was either stolen or wasted. At the time of writing (2009), Nigeria is ranked 158th out of 182 countries in the UNDP's human development index (UNDP, 2009). Politically, oil wealth has also transformed the Nigerian state into an effective tool for primitive accumulation.[4] Consequently, military coups and counter-coups with military dictatorships were the dominant form of government in Nigeria for over 30 years from 1960 on. For example, the administration of Babangida who ruled between 1985 and 1993 saw the disappearance of US$12.2 billion, and General Abacha's regime is believed to have embezzled US$1–3 billion dollars.

The advent of democracy in 1999 saw the "instrumentalization of disorder" as a means of winning elections and holding on to power, largely

---

4 By primitive accumulation we mean the use of rent-seeking and patronage strategies, as well as corruption, for self-aggrandizement.

in order to gain access and control over oil money. To make matters worse, the region where crude oil is mainly extracted in the Niger Delta (see Figure 11.1), one of the world's largest wetlands characterized by lagoons, creeks, marshlands, and rivers and a home to over 40 different minority ethnic groups in an estimated 3,000 communities, is endemic with poverty, environmental degradation, and unemployment levels that are higher than the national average (NDDC, 2004).

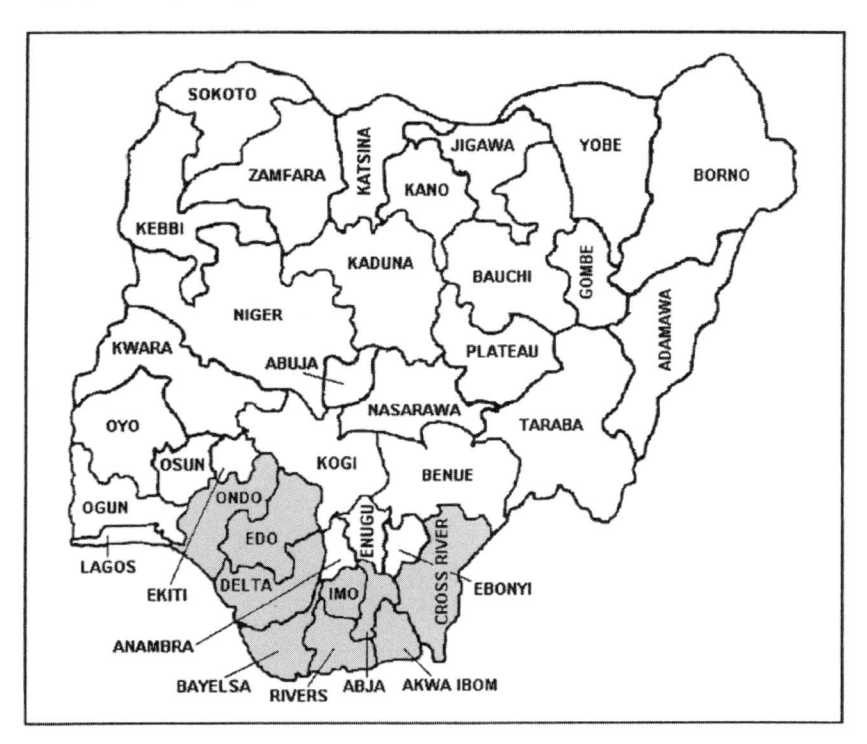

Figure 11.1   Constituent states of the Niger Delta, Nigeria

In addition, 70 percent of the Niger Delta people live in rural areas with no access to basic social amenities such as tap water, good roads, electricity, and healthcare facilities. This paradox of poverty amidst plenty (i.e., oil wealth) has meant that conflict is also endemic in the Niger Delta. Incidence of oil bunkering, kidnapping and ransom demands, electoral violence, and inter/ intra-community violence occur almost on a daily basis. As one analyst put it in 2000, the question in the Niger Delta was no longer whether there would be violence; rather, it had become a question of when and where (Ibeanu, 2000; alos Idemudia, 2009a).

Despite this, oil has also become the organic glue holding the country together. The centralization of oil revenue and the subsequent overdependence of all other tiers of government on the centre (i.e., federal government) essentially allow the federal government to purchase compliance from the various state governments. Hence, the federal government has been able to enforce some degree of political cohesion within the fragile Nigerian federation largely because of oil wealth since the bloody civil war of 1967–1970.

Efforts to address the dysfunctionalities brought on by the resource curse in Nigeria have generally focused on the creation of two types of new institution. The first type is those institutions designed to address the specific grievances of the Niger Delta people by directing more oil revenue to the region. Examples of such institutions include the Oil Mineral Producing Area Development Commission (OMPADEC) that was created in 1992, the Niger Delta Development Commission (NDDC) created in 2000, and the Ministry of the Niger Delta created in 2008. While Frynas (2000) has described OMPADEC as a tool for public relations and a device for siphoning off oil revenue, Omotola (2007) asserts that the NDDC has been a failure.

The second set of institutions is made up of those set up to fight corruption. Notable examples include the Independent Corrupt Practices and Other Related Offences Commission (ICPC) in 2000, the Economic and Financial Crime Commission (EFCC) in 2002 and the Nigeria Extractive Industries Transparency Initiative (NEITI). The EFCC claims that it has successfully prosecuted more than 82 people on charges of corruption and fraud and recovered more than US$5 billion in stolen money (HRW, 2007).

Despite these efforts to fight corruption that have yielded some dividends, the HRW (2007) noted that success has so far been limited and that corruption continues to remain rampant at all levels of government. Today, Nigeria still ranks 130th out of 180 countries in Transparency International's *Corruption Perceptions Index* (TI, 2009). This can be partly attributed to the fact that the Nigerian government has failed to push through key pieces of legislation that would have complemented its participation in EITI by making government expenditure at all levels more transparent. For example, at the time of writing, the government has yet to pass into law the fiscal responsibility bill that would introduce new measures of integrity, transparency and uniformity of budget-making and government expenditure at all levels. This inaction by government is both due to, and complicated by, structural and systemic deficiencies inherent in the Nigerian state-nation (Idemudia, 2009b). Consequently, addressing the issue of corruption is not just critical to good governance in Nigeria, but also a necessity if sustainable development is to be an achievable goal in the volatile Niger Delta region.

Integrity Pacts and the Niger Delta Development Commission

Every year TI convenes an annual meeting of its board, staff, and representatives of national chapters to review progress over the past year, develop new policies, and prepare action plans for the year to come. In November 1999 the annual meeting was hosted by South Africa and held in Durban. TI-Canada representatives went to that meeting with the intention of discussing the use of the Integrity Pact concept in the Niger Delta.

There were many reasons for TI-Canada to undertake this initiative. Canadian companies were actively involved in the extraction of oil in the Delta. One of those companies, Nexen, a leading Canadian anti-corruption champion, was represented on the TI-Canada board of directors. Canada had acquired both prominence and respect for its leadership in exposing and refusing to cooperate with the military dictatorship of General Abacha and for having led the initiative to have Nigeria suspended from the Commonwealth until democracy was restored. Canada was an oil-producing country with experience in efficient and largely corruption-free operations. And the head of Transparency International Nigeria, Ishola Williams, a former general in the Nigerian armed forces and vocal critic of corruption in Nigeria, had visited Canada and, in discussions with TI-Canada, had expressed an interest in developing a partnership with the Canadian NGO.

Initial discussions in Durban were very promising. An informal agreement to pursue a Canadian-Nigerian TI partnership to address corruption issues in the Niger Delta was formed, and planning was begun. What follows is a description of the evolution of that partnership.

From the beginning, it was agreed that the project would have a number of distinct features. Unlike many anti-corruption initiatives, this project would start small. The target was to be the Niger Delta Development Commission, an institution set up by the Nigerian government to funnel development funds generated by oil revenues back to communities in the Niger Delta to stimulate economic development. It was not the goal of the planned initiative to reform the Commission's contracting system: the culture of corruption was much too deeply embedded for that to be a feasible option. Equally important, the capacity to institute corruption-free contracting on a wide scale was almost certainly absent.

The alternative was to begin with just a very few contracts of manageable size and demonstrate two things on a case-by-case basis to local communities in the Delta. First and most important was to demonstrate to local communities, the Commission, and its contactors that corruption-free contracting was a genuine possibility. A second objective was to begin to develop the capacity to monitor

Integrity Pacts. Training the people who would monitor the IP projects, one contract at a time, was the way to accomplish both goals. It was also agreed from the outset that the initiative would not succeed unless funding for its implementation came from neutral sources. This ruled out the major oil companies active in the Delta (e.g., Shell Oil), all levels of government and government departments, and the Niger Delta Development Commission itself. It would be impossible to persuade anyone in Nigeria that the project was corruption-free, if funds came from any of those sources. Canadian government funding, however, was not viewed in Nigeria with the same skepticism. This opened the door to two funding sources: the Canadian International Development Agency (CIDA) and the Canadian High Commission in Nigeria. In subsequent years, both funding sources were successfully tapped. A third funding source was the Canadian company Nexen, which was in the process of building a strong reputation for corruption-free operations in Nigeria. The same was true for Statoil, the Norwegian state oil company that was also building a strong, anti-corruption persona in Nigeria. Both companies were persuaded to support the project financially.

As it turned out, getting to apply the concept to actual NDDC contracts would prove to be a long journey—one that is not yet complete 11 years later.

The first task was to explain the initiative to key players in Nigeria and to win their support. This required an action plan that could be used both to raise funds and garner the support of key Nigerian stakeholders. The plan that emerged proposed that the project should develop in four phases. The first phase would be a national conference in Abuja for the purpose of introducing the Integrity Pact concept to government, NGO, and private-sector stakeholders and win their endorsement for testing the concept using NDDC contracts in the Niger Delta. Clearly, for this idea to be successful, it would have to win the endorsement of not only the NDDC itself, but also the government at all levels and Nigerian civil society which had become increasingly skeptical about any possibility for reform involving the NDDC.

The second phase would be to work with the NDDC itself and local (Delta) stakeholders to explain the concept, win stakeholder endorsement, and begin to identify a small number of contracts that could serve to launch the project. A third phase would create and train an initial team of monitors. The final phase would be to put the concept to work around a limited number of manageable contracts. As it turned out, the plan would undergo considerable refinement and strategic adjustment during the following years.

With a general plan in place, TI-Canada approached both Nexen and CIDA for funding to launch the project. Both responded positively with a Can$15,000 grant from Nexen and Can$50,000 from CIDA. With these funds in hand, the project was launched.

The first task was to introduce the concept to key stakeholders in Nigeria. Armed with some initial thoughts about an agenda for the opening conference, a trip to Nigeria was undertaken by Wesley Cragg, who was at the time the chair and president of TI-Canada. In December 2001, accompanied by a Transparency International Nigeria (TIN) colleague, Shade Lawal, Dr Cragg met with key stakeholders in Lagos, Abuja and finally Port Harcourt, where they were joined by Ishola Williams for a meeting with the NDDC. The plan received a cautious but positive reception from Shell Nigeria, the Nigerian Anti-Corruption Commission, a number of professional societies, labor representatives, and the Movement for the Survival of Ogoni People (MOSOP). The Niger Delta Development Commission also endorsed the idea, though it was clear that senior management was not convinced that they needed help in removing corruption from their own operations.

With this endorsement by key stakeholders, planning for a first conference began. Two additional partners were recruited: one, Statoil, to provide additional financial support with a contribution of US$10,000, and the second, TI-Norway, with a view to broadening the project's partnership base. As it turned out, however, and despite what appeared to be strong foundations on which to move ahead, convening the first conference would take an additional three years.

Three years after the initial trip, the stars finally aligned themselves, and an initial conference, designed to introduce the concept and win the endorsement of both government and the private and voluntary sectors, took place in Abuja on May 27 and 28, 2004. The conference was attended by some 75 people representing 52 organizations.[5]

The opening session was chaired by Dr (Mrs) Oby Ezekweseli, Senior Special Assistant to the President, Head, Budget Monitoring and Planning Unit, and Coordinator, National Stakeholders' Working Group on EITI. The conference was addressed by Chief Olusegun Obasanjo-GCFR, President of the

---

[5] Ijan Youth Council; Bayelsha State Youths Federation; Publish What You Pay (Nigeria), Centre for Voluntary and Community Services, Statoil, TIN, PENGASSAN, Exam Ethics Project, FRCN, IATN, Centre for Responsive Politics, Niger Delta Initiative for Development, Women's Right to Education Program, National Assembly, IAFN, MOSOP, Shell, Centre for the Development of Civil Society, British High Commission, NUPEN, UNDP, Oxfam, Institute of Human Rights and Humanitarian Law, African Network for Environment and Economic Justice, Ministry of Petroleum Resources, Independent Corrupt Practices and Other Related Offences Commission, House of Representatives, CIDA, Global Rights Partners for Justice, Norwegian Embassy, Women's Environmental Program, Canadian High Commission, Poverty Alleviation Institute of Nigeria, Public and Private Rights Watch, Business Day, State House, NNPC-NAPIMS, Media Right Agenda, NLNG, Citizen Communications, Ijan National Congress, Africa Leadership Forum, CWSL, CAPP, NGO Coalition for Environment, Ministry of Finance, Ministry of Commerce, Niger Delta for Professional Development, TI-Canada, TI-Norway, TI Secretariat.

Federal Republic of Nigeria. A number of other dignitaries were also invited to speak. Unfortunately, the chair of the opening session neglected to invite the chair of the NDDC board to say a few words—a mistake that would lead to the departure of the NDDC participants and set the project back in a serious way.

Themes discussed throughout the conference included the Nigerian government's decision to join the Extractive Industries Transparency Initiative and to require the publication, by the oil companies actively extracting oil in Nigeria, of the taxes and royalties paid to the government, and to have those reports independently verified. Participants discussed the challenge posed by corruption in the oil and gas sector as faced by government, industry, labor, and NGOs. The concept of an Integrity Pact, as developed by Transparency International, was introduced, and the potential for its application was discussed. The ground rules for the discussion and for moving ahead were set out. Most importantly, a "no-go" principle was put in place; the initiative would not proceed to Phase 2 without the consensus of conference. It was also agreed that this principle would operate throughout all phases of the project.

The discussion that followed was emotional, sometimes very angry and accusatory, and frequently skeptical about the possibility of building the kind of industry-voluntary sector-government alliance that would be required to introduce the IP concept in the Niger Delta. Remarkably, however, as the potential of the idea for the Niger Delta emerged more clearly, participation and attendance increased. On the second day, all those who had been invited, with the exception of NDDC senior management, attended and participated actively in the discussion.

On the final afternoon, participants addressed the following topics in break-out sessions:

- key challenges,
- pact partnerships, and
- monitoring and implementation.

The break-out groups reported back a series of resolutions that were then discussed in a final plenary session. Six resolutions were adopted by vote following discussion and debate:

> *1. That we have accepted the Integrity Pact (IP) as a key tool to attaining transparency and the elimination of corruption in public procurement contracts, and it should be encouraged and implemented;*

2. That the President has endorsed the IP in principle and that governments must show commitment to IPs in order for them to be effective;

3. That a network be built between Transparency International Nigeria (TIN) and other domestic and international bodies to promote the implementation of IPs in Nigeria, beginning with the oil and gas sector;

4. That TIN and Transparency International (including other National Chapters and the Secretariat) target capacity building for Nigerian civil society, relevant government agencies and, in particular, the oil-bearing communities;

5. That freedom of information is a required foundation for effective IPs; for this reason, TIN should work with the existing supporting agencies to push for a speedy enactment of the Freedom of Information Act;

6. A follow-up workshop on the application of the Integrity Pact to a particular agency, namely the NDDC should be held as soon as possible.

Fourteen participants were then designated to meet to initiate planning for the next steps in implementing the IP concept for NDDC contracting in the Niger Delta. The planning meeting was held the next day and included:

- five members of Transparency International Nigeria (TIN)—the President, Vice-President, two board members and the conference organizer;
- two members of Transparency International Canada (TI-Canada)—the Chair/President and the National Coordinator;
- one member of Transparency International Norway (TI-Norway)—the National Director;
- one member of the Transparency International Secretariat (TI-S)—the Integrity Pacts and Public Contracting Programme Manager;
- one representative from Statoil;
- four representatives of Niger Delta NGOs—MOSOP, Ijan Youth Council, Niger Delta for Professional Development; and
- one other person who is not identified in the records of the meeting.

The agenda for this meeting was the following:

1. Identify and clarify next steps.
2. Identify the purpose and location of the next meeting.
3. Address Niger Delta Development Commission (NDDC) issues.
4. Explore and agree on funding for the remainder of the project.

In the meeting that followed, agreement emerged around all agenda items.

1. The next steps were identified as follows:
   - The endorsement of the Nigerian President should be requested, and planning to introduce the idea of ultimately implementing an Integrity Pact (IP) in specific projects with the NDDC should now be undertaken.
   - The second workshop was to describe the IP in detail, plan how it could be applied in development contracts of the NDDC, and invite buy-in for the IP concept by the participants.
   - Following the second workshop (to take place in Port Harcourt), steps should be undertaken to develop and ensure a monitoring scheme for the implementation of the IP. This would require capacity building.
   - The final step would be to structure an actual contract, using an IP.
2. In preparing for the next phase of the initiative, it was agreed that:
   - Issues affecting all aspects of the proposed project should be discussed.
   - The potential for tapping into monitoring structures already in existence in the Niger Delta should be studied and perhaps employed.
   - Core people should be brought together—for example, the Niger Delta States' representatives and commissioners—with a view to creating an in-depth understanding of the IP before the second workshop was held.
   - Capacity building must be a key objective.
   - The possibility of extending the use of IPs, state-by-state should be considered.
   - It would be important to build on things that are already on the ground.
   - Because workshops are a common occurrence in the Niger Delta, this second workshop would need to generate concrete results.
   - The NDDC would need to be re-engaged.

With this in mind, a number of goals were set for the second workshop:
- Communicate the concept of the IP and create "buy-in" for the idea.
- Initiate training for monitoring.
- Bring in representatives of communities, NGOs and NDDC officials involved in awarding contracts.
- Focus on the implementation of an IP with the NDDC as a pilot project/experiment/test run.

It was also agreed that the workshop would last two days and take place end of September (29–30) or mid-October (13–14, 2004), and be held in Port Harcourt. In addition, it was agreed that, to accomplish these objectives, it would be necessary to bring others, particularly the NDDC, to the same level of understanding and acceptance of the IP concept as that of the participants of the May 27–28 conference.[6]

3. Addressing NDDC issues posed a particular challenge. The NDDC had shown interest in the concept in a face-to-face meeting in Port Harcourt in December 2001. It had been approached for participation in the conference. As a result of a perceived snub, however, the NDDC Chair had left the conference at the first opportunity, and NDDC participation in the conference had effectively ended. A strategy for bringing the NDDC back to the table was therefore the most pressing challenge, if the initiative was to proceed.

4. Funding for the second workshop and beyond was discussed. The Canadian High Commissioner and Nigeria-based CIDA staff remained interested in continuing to support the project. It was agreed that it would be appropriate to ask the NDDC to cover some costs. Nexen and Statoil were endorsed as credible funders and further support was to be solicited. TI's Partnership for Transparency Fund was also identified as a future source. It was agreed that it would be important to diversify sources of funding but that no contribution should be allowed to compromise the image or the mission of the project and its participants. Finally, it was agreed that the international partnership of TIN, TI-Canada and TI-Norway provided a strong foundation on which to move ahead with the initiative.

With all agenda items addressed, the meeting adjourned, with a clear understanding that, above all else, rebuilding the relationship with the NDDC

---

6 The NDDC has 26 board members, nine of whom represent the governors of each of the Niger Delta states.

remained as the most pressing concern. It was agreed therefore that TIN would make every effort to schedule a meeting with the senior management of the NDDC to report on the conference, discuss next steps, and raise the possibility of an interactive workshop with the NDDC management itself. Dr Oby Ezekwesili would be asked to contact the Chair of NDDC to apologize for the oversight in the opening ceremonies. The Canadian High Commissioner would be asked to request a meeting with the Chair of NDDC to discuss the Nigeria Project, when he was scheduled to be in Port Harcourt to open an Honorary Consulate, the week following the conference.

Unfortunately, despite the fact that the Chair of the NDDC was an appointee of the President of Nigeria and stated that the NDDC "remains willing to participate"—a statement that was reiterated in a subsequent meeting between Howard Strauss, the Canadian High Commissioner, and the Chair of the NDDC board—progress toward Phase 2 of the initiative was to be set back for several months.

It was not until the following December that TIN was able to arrange a meeting with the NDDC Director of Rural and Community Development. The meeting was positive, and TIN was told that the NDDC accepted the idea of experimenting with the Integrity Pact idea, in principle. However, leadership changes were under way, TIN was told, and it would be advisable to postpone further discussions until a new NDDC board had been appointed.

In a congratulatory letter following the appointment of a new board, TIN reminded the NDDC board about the commitment in principle to pursue the IP initiative and asked if an interactive session could be arranged to inform NDDC about the nature and the goal of the IP and to request its participation in the Phase 2 workshop. On June 28, 2005, the chairman of the NDDC, Sam Edem, replied and invited TIN to an interactive session with the board of directors on July, 14, 2005, in Port Harcourt, Rivers State.

Word of the proposed meeting reached Wesley Cragg in London, while in transit to a workshop in Hungary, He was able to obtain a visa on very short notice to travel to Nigeria and join his TIN colleagues for the interactive session.

On July 14, a TIN delegation, accompanied by a representative of the organization put in place to implement the Nigerian Extractive Industries Transparency Initiative, and Dr Cragg, met with the full board of the NDDC. In their presentation to the board, Dr Cragg and Dr H Assisi Asobie, Chair of TIN, described what was being proposed in the following way:

> *Integrity Pacts have many of the characteristics of the Extractive Industries Transparency Initiative, though on a smaller scale, in*

which Nigeria is playing a leading role. Every Integrity Pact draws voluntary non governmental organizations (NGOs), business and the government into a partnership in which the parties cooperate and work together to achieve a common goal. Each Integrity Pact is transparent. Each Integrity Pact requires public reports at specific stages of a project on how effectively the Integrity Pact is working and what has been accomplished and how it has been accomplished to date. And each Integrity Pact includes a comprehensive report by the voluntary sector partners on the successful completion of an Integrity Pact project.

Integrity Pacts are not designed to expose corruption or embarrass public or private officials. Their purpose is build public trust and confidence by showing in a fully transparent and accountable way that public funds are being used to achieve important public objectives efficiently and effectively and free of corruption.

They went on to say:

Integrity Pacts are particularly useful for projects involving economic development. Economic development is most effective when it has the support and confidence of the communities it is designed to benefit. In the case of the Niger Delta Development Commission, this involves government, local communities, contractors, the oil companies and voluntary sector NGOs. We have discussed the idea of applying the Integrity Pact idea in the Niger Delta with many key voluntary sector, business and government stakeholders. Last year we organized a conference in Abuja at which the Integrity Pact idea was introduced. At the end of the conference there was a strong consensus that we should move to the second phase of the project with a workshop to be held in Port Harcourt.

The purpose of this second workshop is to introduce the Integrity Pact idea in detail to the people in the Niger Delta. As was the case for the first conference, the goal of the workshop will be to explain how Integrity Pacts work. Actual examples of how Integrity Pacts work will be examined and discussed. The merits of putting the idea to work on economic development projects in the Niger Delta will be discussed. If there is consensus including, of course, the NDDC that the idea should be developed, we will move directly to the third phase of the project.

The purpose of our meeting today with the Board of the NDDC is to win your support for holding a workshop on the Integrity Pact idea and how it might apply to NDDC-sponsored economic development projects in the Niger Delta. We need to move quickly to the next phase in which the applicability of the idea to economic development projects in the Niger Delta can be evaluated. The workshop will be an excellent opportunity for an open discussion with all stakeholders on how best to adapt the Integrity Pact model to economic development in the Niger Delta. If there is consensus to proceed, planning for the next phase of the project will begin immediately following the workshop.

In his response on behalf of the NDDC Board, Mr Timi Alaibe, the Commission's Acting Managing Director, thanked the representatives of TIN and TI-Canada for their initiative, gave his full support and commented on the persistence of TIN in pursuit of NDDC involvement. The Managing Director's message was then reiterated by the chair of the board, Mr Edem, who, as it turned out, knew Canada well by virtue of the fact that he had served as Nigeria's High Commissioner in Ottawa.

What then followed was a hiatus of several years. Elections saw President Olusegun Obasanjo replaced by Umaru Yar' Adua. This was followed by changes in leadership in the NDDC and TIN.

In November and December 2007, e-mails suggesting that the project be reactivated began to circulate. The political situation in Nigeria was becoming more stable, a new team was in place in the NDDC, and EITI Nigeria was under way. An agenda for a Port Harcourt workshop, now being described as Phase 2b of the project, was developed, and contact with the NDDC was re-established.

In September and October 2008 things began to move very quickly. Over a very short space of time, the NDDC and TIN were proposing to hold a workshop between November 24 and 28 in Port Harcourt. However, things were now moving too fast for TI-Canada, and a last-minute postponement was required when Dr Cragg was unable to obtain the required entry visa in time to participate in the workshop.

The workshop was rescheduled, with NDDC concurrence, to January 18-20, 2009. This time, travel arrangements were successfully arranged, and the workshop took place as planned. It had a threefold purpose:

1. To sensitize the public in general and stakeholders in particular to the existence and usefulness of Integrity Pacts for combating corruption.
2. To educate senior officials of the Niger Delta Development Commission (NDDC), on how to implement the Integrity Pact in

its procurement process, starting with one or two projects before giving it a wider application.
3. To set up modalities and a time line for implementing the Integrity Pact in the NDDC procurement process.

Topics covered included

- a general overview of the Integrity Pact
- Integrity Pact (IP) best practices—where and how it has been used
- how IP works—successful implementation of the IP
- application of the IP to NDDC contracts
- components of the IP
- sanctions for violation
- monitoring and evaluation issues and challenges.

The workshop was well attended with the participation of about 60 people drawn from the Niger Delta region. The largest numbers of participants were from civil society organizations. There were also a significant number of local government officials in attendance and a large contingent from the NDDC itself.

The workshop accomplished all of its goals, the most important of which was to reach an agreement with the NDDC to experiment with the use of Integrity Pacts in contracting for NDDC economic development projects. The Managing Director of the NDDC, Mr Timi Alaibe, participated in the opening of the workshop and spoke very positively about the need to focus on integrity issues in the NDDC. An informal meeting with Mr Alaibe followed during the first break to request a meeting with him after the workshop in order to discuss the introduction of Integrity Pacts into NDDC contracting. Mr Alaibe agreed to meet with a TIN/TI-Canada delegation at his office and to share important planning documents with us at that time.

The workshop provided an opportunity to discuss the merits of using the Integrity Pact concept in NDDC contracting with those present. Everyone left with a good fundamental understanding of the concept, including members of the NDDC management, who participated throughout.

Immediately following the close of the workshop, a small TIN/TI-Canada delegation then met with Mr Alaibe, at his office. He was very forthcoming about NDDC plans and his intention to work with TIN to introduce Integrity Pacts into NDDC contracting. He shared with the delegation a planning document entitled "Measuring Corporate Performance at NDDC: Objectives and Key Performance Metrics." The document set out six strategic objectives for the NDDC, the first item of which was to "Entrench integrity, transparency and accountability" as an internal objective. The key action to be taken in implementing that objective was the "(f)ormation of a partnership with Transparency International on institutionalizing the Integrity Pact." The planning document indicated that the formation of that partnership was already in progress.

In his follow-up account of the meeting, Mr Alex M. Sharta, South Zonal Coordinator of TIN, concluded his report of the workshop and follow-up meeting with the NDDC with the following words:

> *The workshop ended on a happy note full of optimism that the embers of the IP will soon be kindled in NDDC to leaven its procurement system. This will make the NDDC an island of integrity which can hopefully be replicated in other Government Agencies all over Nigeria.*

In subsequent correspondence with TIN and Mr Timi Alaibe, it was emphasized that the most important element in TI's Integrity Pact concept was independent monitoring of the contracting process at every stage from preparing specifications, to competitive bidding, to selecting a contractor, to implementing the contract, to preparing a final audit. It was indicated that, in the first instance, at the very least, this would require that funding for the monitoring of the initial contracts be provided by a completely independent non-government source. Finding independent funding would therefore be the next task for TI-Canada as a partner in the NDDC/Integrity Pact initiative. The offer to help find funding for this next phase of the initiative was communicated by Dr Cragg in an e-mail dated January 25, 2009, in which he pointed out that:

> *As you will recall, there was a good deal of discussion at the Port Harcourt workshop about ensuring that the monitoring of the Integrity Pacts to be formed for two or three initial NDDC contracts is independent and is perceived to be independent. One important element in ensuring independence is to ensure an independent source of funding for the monitoring process. It will be important to ensure that the monitor or monitors are adequately compensated financially for their work and have the funds required to cover expenses associated with carrying out their duties effectively. Determining how best to do this over the long run will be something that will have to be decided as the program develops. However, in the first instance, I believe that everyone agrees that the best option is to have funds provided from sources that have no connection at all to the NDDC or to contractors or communities or governments in the Niger Delta.*

I indicated to you that I would help to achieve that goal and that I would ask TI-Canada to support an effort to find independent funding for this very important initiative. However, before I can begin to approach potential funding sources, I will need the following things.

1. *I will need to know what two or three contracts have been identified by TIN in consultation with the NDDC for application of the Integrity Pact. I will need a description of the work to be accomplished by those contracts, where that work is to take place, why the work is being undertaken, and the period of time that will be required to fulfill each of the contracts.*

2. *I will need a job description for the monitors. This will have to be a detailed description of the tasks the monitors will be expected to carry out.*

3. *I will need a fairly detailed preliminary budget for the monitoring of each of the contracts.*

4. *I will need minutes of Board meetings that confirm that the Board supports the initiatives to be undertaken, agrees with the contracts to which the Integrity Pact process is to apply, and has studied and approved a detailed preliminary budget.*

This case study was written in October 2009. To this point, there have been no further developments with regard to introducing the Integrity Pact concept into NDDC contracting.

Conclusions

It is the view of the authors of this case study that the use of IPs offers an important opportunity for the fight against corruption and the realization of sustainable development objective in Nigeria. The flexibility of IPs allows them to be adopted at the local-, state-, and federal-level government, which means that they perfectly complement other efforts (e.g., NEITI) to fight corruption that often mainly focus on the federal level of Nigerian society. In addition, IPs' emphasis on preventing corruption as opposed to just exposing corruption provide an important opportunity for the gradual development and reinforcement of the culture of transparency and accountability that is

Table 11.1   The IP implementation plan and progress achieved

Phase	Activities	Outcomes
Phase 1	National Conference in Abuja to introduce the Integrity Pact Concept	Consensus on moving ahead with a regional workshop in Port Harcourt
Phase 2 (a)	Meetings with the NDDC to secure support for the initiative	Agreement to participate in a regional stakeholder workshop in Port Harcourt
Phase 2(b)	Regional stakeholder workshop in Port Harcourt	Consensus formed to proceed with Phase 3
Phase 2 (c)	Meetings with NDDC senior management	General agreement to proceed and establish a working plan for implementation
Phase 3	Selection contracts for initiating IP implementation and train monitors	Not yet undertaken
Phase 4	IP implementation on experimental basis with two or three NDDC contracts	Not yet undertaken

lacking in a country like Nigeria with its history of corruption in business-government interactions. Similarly, because IPs emphasize partnership among government, business, and civil society, they allow for intersectoral learning and the development of trust that is needed to ensure durability of anti-corruption measures. However, as the case study above shows, if there is to be significant progress in reducing the incidence of corruption in Nigeria, there will have to be significant changes in patterns of behavior on the part of government leaders, the multinational oil companies active in the Niger Delta, the voluntary sector, and the NDDC itself. In addition, the failure or success of IPS will ultimately depend on changes at a grassroots level where the benefits of removing corruption from procurement practices can be experienced by the people most harmed by those practices. The NDDC-Integrity Pact initiative is being undertaken to both illustrate and test that perspective. What is clear from this story, however, is that engendering change at a local level can be a painstakingly slow process.

References

Canadian Encyclopedia (1997) "Bre-Ex bubble bursts," April 7, at: http://www.canadianencyclopedia.ca/index.cfm?PgNm=TCE&Params=M1ARTM0011316 (accessed August 2010).

Cragg, W. and Woof, W. (2002) "The U. S. Foreign Corrupt Practices Act: A study of its effectiveness," *Business and Society Review*, Spring, 98–145.

Frynas, George (2000) *Oil in Nigeria: Conflict and Litigation between Oil Companies and Village Communities*, Munster, Germany: LIT.

Human Rights Watch (HRW) (2007) *Chop Fine: The Human Rights Impact of Local Government Corruption and Mismanagement in River State, Nigeria*, New York: Human Rights Watch,

Ibeanu, Okechukwu (2000) *Oiling the Friction: Environmental Conflict Management in the Niger Delta, Nigeria, Environmental Change and Security Project Report 6*, Washington, DC: Woodrow Wilson International Centre, 19–32. Available at: http://www.wilsoncenter.org/topics/pubs/Report6-2.pdf (accessed February 2003)

Idemudia, U. (2009a) "The changing phases of the Niger Delta conflict: Implications for Conflict escalation and the return of peace," *Conflict, Security and Development*, 9(3), 307–331.

Idemudia, U. (2009b) "The quest for the effective use of natural resource revenue in Africa: Beyond transparency and the need for compatible cultural democracy in Nigeria," *Africa Today*, Winter, 3–24.

Niger Delta Development Commission (NDDC) (2004) *Niger Delta Regional Development Master Plan: Draft 3*, Directorate of Planning, Port Harcourt, Nigeria: NDDC.

Noonan, John T. Jr (1984) *Bribes*, New York: Macmillan.

Omotola, J. Shola (2007) "From the OMPADEC to NDDC: An assessment of state responses to environmental insecurities in the Niger Delta, Nigeria," *Africa Today*, 54, 573–89.

Transparency International (TI) (1997) *The Fight Against Corruption: Is the Tide Now Turning?* Berlin: Transparency International (TI).

Transparency International (TI) (2002) *The Integrity Pact: The Concept, the Model and the Present Applications: A Status Report as of December 31st, 2002*. Available at: http://www.transparency.org/global_priorities/public_contracting/integrity_pacts'

Transparency International (TI) (2009) *Corruption Perceptions Index 2009*, at: http://www.transparency.org/policy_research/surveys_indices/cpi/2009/cpi_2009_table.

UNDP (2009) *Human Development Report 2009. Overcoming Barriers: Human Mobility and Development*. Available at: http://hdr.undp.org/en/reports/global/hdr2009/.

Watts, Michael (2007) "Petro-insurgency or criminal syndicate? Conflict and violence in the Niger Delta," *Review of African Political Economy*, 114, 637–660.

12

Easy Prey Canadians

L.S. (Al) Rosen

Context

Canada is one of the world's top tourist attractions if you happen to be a non-Canadian securities swindler. Researchers ought to include Canadian data and scenarios in their multi-country comparative studies, because Canada is likely to provide an excellent testing ground for the comprehensiveness and effectiveness of any proposed securities protection hypotheses. Any "principles-based" corruption monitoring concepts, for example, would have to be supplemented with selective tough rules, or the principles would be inadequate, inefficient or pointless in a Canadian setting. Briefly stated, the Canadian courts typically look for violations of clear rules, and tend to ignore departures from vague principles. The peculiarities of the few Canadian corporate crime investigations that are publicly available for study merit careful research thought when formulating regulatory research hypotheses.[1] In general, investor protection processes that have been followed in Canada have repeatedly been unsuccessful for several reasons. Many clues and ideas can be developed from Canada's serious regulatory mistakes, including minimal oversight, or deregulation. Much of the consequences of Canada's securities market corruption have been self-inflicted by various participants.

Many international researchers who work with Canadian corporate data make the same huge errors. That is, they use the public, audited data as is, even though it has often been grossly manipulated by many of the corporations. Unless the dollar figures are adjusted for commonplace trickery, the real facts are simply being ignored by the researchers. Accordingly, any research conclusions can be precisely what the securities tricksters want the investing public to believe: protection exists (when, in fact, the opposite is the reality).

---

1 For a listing of Canadian financial collapses see Rosen and Rosen (2010).

What Protection?

Before listing the financial reporting trickery that is popular in Canada for deceiving investors and creditors, the essential background must be tabulated. As difficult as it may be to try to comprehend what Canada has done to itself since the 1929 stock market crash, realities have to be incorporated into any contemplated research design. Far too much rosy material has been published about Canadian companies (such as banks), all of which has directly caused investor losses when reality is eventually uncovered, years later.

Noteworthy realities of Canada include the following:

1. A national or nationwide securities regulatory and prosecution system does not exist. As a consequence, comprehensive investigation and conviction data is not readily available. A thoroughly false impression is left by the available, incomplete, and misleading statistics. The few prosecutions in Canada falsely indicate that the country is relatively free of white-collar crime. But the international securities tricksters know otherwise, and that's why they come to Canada for a few years, to work their pyramid schemes and Ponzi frauds. Many such embezzlements are never reported because investment fund managers do not want to publicize their weaknesses. Egos win; investors lose.
2. Some international con artists make the mistake of not limiting their financial fleecings to Canadians. They con Americans as well, in a North American scheme, and thereby enter into the clutches of the US SEC. Most of the nastier prosecutions of Canadian securities scams commence with the US authorities detecting the problems and then investigating and prosecuting. Canadian provincial securities regulatory bodies may or may not follow up with criminal proceedings, even though the US has already successfully prosecuted the swindlers.
3. Most of the publicized Canadian securities frauds constitute civil court actions designed to recover some of the stolen money. Class action securities cases are still in their infancy in Canada, but a few have been successful. In essence, deep-pocket plaintiffs are usually needed to finance the civil litigation, which tends to drag out over several years. Absent civil litigation, nothing happens and the investors lose everything that was turned over to the securities tricksters.
4. Similar to the SEC success with some Canadian cases, a successful civil case does not assure that criminal proceedings will be

commenced in Canada. In an important sense, securities con artists are given considerable freedom in Canada to work their scams. Their contempt for the ineptitude of Canadian securities regulators leads to copycat repetitions of similar scams.

5. Unlike in most larger industrialized countries, in Canada the accounting, financial reporting and auditing rules and concepts have been written by the financial statement auditors' umbrella body. Not surprisingly, many of the rules are weak, thereby lowering auditors' obligations. Examples involve the search for corporate fraud and reporting of self-dealings or related party transactions. Considerable additional management compensation, for instance, can be obtained when executives of publicly-owned companies are permitted to own their own companies that in turn transact with the public company at unknown prices.

6. The monitoring and investigative branches of Canada's provincial securities commissions are still heavily staffed with former auditors, mainly from the large public accounting firms. Independence can be lacking in prosecutions because of long-standing allegiances with former colleagues, and acceptance of low standards based on previous personal experience.

7. Federal versus provincial/state bickering over jurisdictional matters, such as securities regulations and standards, leads to extensive fragmentation. Names and operating procedures of known and suspected financial tricksters have not been coordinated for prosecution purposes. Consequences are widespread. A major deficiency is that the politicians have nowhere to turn to obtain an independent opinion on the merits of auditors' proposals, such as to deregulate. Thus, weakness can take on a life of its own.

8. In 1997 the Supreme Court of Canada delivered an astonishing decision concerning auditors' obligations to investors for audits of annual financial statements. In essence, auditors generally cannot be successfully sued by investors for having approved of, in their audit reports, materially misleading annual financial statements of publicly-traded companies. The case, *Hercules Managements* (1997), despite its far-reaching implications, is not well known in Canada and elsewhere. Yet, the *Hercules* case has prevented the pursuit of many dozens of other allegations against auditors for alleged acceptance of financial misrepresentations. Thus, Canadian statistics dealing with misleading annual financial statements or securities fraud allegations can be misleading from 1997 onward.

A false appearance of safety in securities trading has been created by this one single court case. Consequently, potential plaintiffs have been discouraged from proceeding with a variety of cases, despite the facts, including where there are consequent financial failures of the companies.

9. An interesting contrast to the Supreme Court's decision involving annual financial statements is the situation where audited financial statements form part of a prospectus that is offering new shares or debt to investors in the public company. The Appeal Court in British Columbia set a higher standard because inclusion of the financial statements in a prospectus clearly meant that they should be being used for investment decisions. In the leading case (*Kripps*, 1997) the auditors were held liable because they did not meet societal standards requiring "full and fair disclosure," among other matters. The Supreme Court of Canada declined to hear the appeal of the Big Four public accounting firm (Deloitte), which meant that *Kripps* became a "leading case."

The benefits of the *Kripps* decision are far outweighed by the negative effects of the *Hercules* decision. Approximately 95 percent of securities trading in Canada occurs in the "secondary market,"[2] which excludes prospectus contracts. Most analysts utilize annual audited financial statements for their valuation modeling. Thus, misstated annual financial statements can easily lead to, and have caused, disastrous investment outcomes.

Yet, investors in Canada cannot legally claim financial recoveries against the auditors who accepted, or perhaps participated in drafting, the faked numbers. Those who are aware of the court cases know that audited annual financial statements are close to useless in providing assurance concerning the dollar figures and note descriptions. Those who are unaware of the *Hercules* court decision operate at a distinct disadvantage and can be serious victims of corruption and corporate fraud. Canadian investors have been exposed to a steady stream of surprise financial failures during the twenty-first century.

10. White-collar securities scams have been tolerated in Canada for at least 80 years. The resourced-based nature of Canada (especially oil and gas and mining) requires that corporate development

---

[2] The "secondary market" is one that does not involve investment cash flowing into or out of the company that issued the securities. "Secondary market" trades are typically between or among pension funds, mutual funds and individuals, for previously-issued securities.

costs be financed. The most likely participants are above-average risk-takers. The Vancouver Stock Exchange, in particular, gained a worldwide reputation into the 1990s as a haven for fraudsters. An endless chain of suspect companies exist in the country, but the politicians largely choose to ignore suspicious antics. Somehow, an assumption has been made that those who choose to enter the stock market casinos deserve their fate.

Various feeble attempts have been made in Canada to introduce coordinated enforcement but, in the absence of serious political leadership and appropriate operational finances, the investigators and prosecutors lose enthusiasm. Thus, major financial collapses such as Nortel Networks and non-bank Asset-Backed Commercial Paper (ABCP) are virtually daily life for investors in Canada.

To summarize, in many respects, given the absence of acceptable investor protections, it is somewhat surprising that investors continue to place their money in Canadian companies, other than in the role of being majority shareholders. Successful companies largely tend to be in resource fields such as mining, oil, and gas, although, large financial institutions and real estate corporations have also generally been successful and have attracted investors over the years. However, exceptions occurred in the mid-1980s and early 1990s when several financial institutions failed.

Corruption?

Medium-sized public companies in Canada have to be watched particularly carefully. The group comprises an unfortunate combination of the honest and trustworthy and many that require particularly close investigation. Factors such as Canada's granting of immunity to auditors associated with bogus annual audited financial statements, the few legal obligations on directors, the minimal number of governmental investigative bureaus, lengthy and often unsuccessful court proceedings, and few jail terms for false reporting and pyramid trickery all provoke suspicion about what is being disclosed to potential investors. Fairness of reporting is a myth. The concept of the "shareholder's auditor" was abandoned long ago.

Canada has also had a long history of weak business analysis. What is reported in newspapers or shown on television is often influenced by corporations' advertising budgets. Many important court cases receive little media attention, thereby fostering inappropriate beliefs that Canada is relatively crime-free. All too often, if the US SEC had not chosen to prosecute a Canadian-based fraud, Canadian investors would not even be aware of serious financial problems and trickery.

In the late 1980s Canadian politicians ceased holding public judicial inquiries into the causes of large financial failures. In the mid-1980s two Canadian banks failed, leading to the discovery of many questionable or misleading financial reporting practices. In addition, dozens of corporations collapsed as a result of the recession in 1980-1983, revealing further deficiencies in Canada's accounting and financial reporting standards. Left uncertain is whether the financial embarrassments of the 1980s caused politicians to pretend that investors did not need to learn more about financial shenanigans. The net result was that seniors and savers became "set-up" to be fleeced every few years, because they had not been taught to protect themselves.

The extent to which investors had become neglected became clear as the twenty-first century began. A series of collapses, publicized around the world but only partially in Canada, occurred in quick succession: the Bre-X Minerals fraud (non-existent gold); the collapse of Nortel Networks; several business income trust pyramid schemes and frauds; and non-bank Asset-Backed Commercial Paper (ABCP) scams. Each highlighted major flaws in Canada's securities regulation practices. However, the politicians did not commence judicial inquiries, or try to improve the system. Whatever of importance that was learned came from civil court proceedings in Canada or investigations by the US SEC.

Overall, Canada has benefited from living next-door to the US. Several huge successful investigations have been handled by the SEC. But too many investors have not looked carefully at the causes of the steady stream of financial failures and their close relationship to unacceptable behavior on the part of the politicians, courts, regulators, auditors, brokers, underwriters, and related persons or groups. A financial climate that encourages investment in Canada for a person's retirement years is just another fairy tale.

It would be particularly worthwhile to undertake a study or research project to determine why the interests of others is being held to be of such greater importance than those of investors. The politicians' reliance on the advice of seriously conflicted auditors is both astonishing and irrational. It's the investors who provide the capital to create jobs. Yet, Canadian laws and investigative practices all too often treat the few available investors' rights with contempt.

Ponzi Frauds

Between 2005 and 2010 Canadian investors had to suffer an epidemic of securities-based pyramid schemes and Ponzi frauds, after having endured lesser volumes in 2000–2004. Bernie Madoff should have operated his frauds out of Canada. Then, instead of being sentenced to 150 years' imprisonment, he would be out on the street awaiting trial in Canada, and perhaps would never get sentenced. If fraudsters are accused and convicted at all in Canada, they receive terms of two to seven years, and, typically, five-sixths of the sentence is not served in jail. Often, cases do not reach the courts for a variety of reasons, including lack of enthusiasm by prosecutors, given the indifference or agenda of the politicians.

One batch of the 2000–2006 pyramid schemes arose because politicians, securities administrators, and auditors essentially remained silent over several years as fake investment yields were publicized. The basic trickery centered on "rejecting," through false advertising, a company's net income results and replacing it with a figure 50–200 percent higher, called "distributable cash". Thus, a net income of Can$1million could be manipulated into distributable cash of Can$3 million. A yield of 4 percent (Can$1 million on an investment of Can$25 million) could become, using fakery, 12 percent (Can$3 million on the investment of Can$25 million).

In an era of low interest rates, an apparent 12 percent yield on an investment seemed very attractive. Many savers and seniors took the bait and got hooked. The difficulty was that, to get from the Can$1 million to the Can$3 million figure, a wide variety of financial shenanigans had to take place. Many expenses were ignored, including taxes, depreciation, amortization, and similar.

The Can$3 million equivalent figure was not sustainable into the future, because cash was needed to operate the business. Yet, to maintain the aura of a 12 percent yield, the Can$3 million had to be distributed to investors each year (through a mechanism called an "income trust").

To keep the company/trust out of bankruptcy, more money had to be brought in each year, by borrowing or selling more shares/units. Hence, the Ponzi scheme had to get into high gear by borrowing from, or selling shares/units to, new suckers to pay off the previously-conned investor-suckers.

In the business (as opposed to real estate, or oil and gas) segment of these income trusts, well over 100 entities became suspect. Several collapsed after two or three years, resulting in investors losing more than Can$25 billion. Despite extensive published warnings from a few writers (mainly forensic accountants), no serious action was taken by those who are supposed to be on the look-out for scams—namely, securities regulators, auditors and politicians. These became especially dark days for the country.

Terrible companies were sold for up to ten times their realistic value during the income trust era, as stock underwriters promoted a seriously flawed product using many nasty tricks. Entire sections of newspapers and hour-long television programs hyped what could only be called "lies." No serious discipline ensued.

Sadly, that's Canada. Timely interference with an ongoing scam is rare. A fascinating series of questions therefore center on "Why does this continue to happen?" Several parties, including naïve investors, add to losses. But, comprehending the depth of cozy alliances and friendships is a significant problem for independent investors.

Most fundamentally, investors do not have a powerful friend in Canada. Heavy advertising from stock promoters intimidate publishers and news directors, it seems. The politicians, in turn, astonishingly ask, of all people, the auditors and provincial securities administrators whether everything is OK. In short, in the absence of a powerful equivalent of the US SEC, the politicians are asking the people who are causing the problems whether the current system is adequate. Exactly what caliber of response are the politicians expecting?

The five- to six-year business income trust era in Canada could only be described as shameful and disgraceful. The victims were mainly seniors, many of whom lost their life savings. Unfortunately, the number of income trust prosecutions, including civil cases, can be counted on one hand.

During this same period, dozens of other Ponzi schemes were being operated, primarily in the provinces of Alberta and Quebec. Money managers were faking results, while simultaneously sending stolen cash to offshore hiding places. The economic downturns of 2008 and 2009 made the task of finding new suckers particularly difficult. Accordingly, many Ponzi schemes collapsed when the cash dried up in the economy.

What is still missing is the investor learning. Canada is ripe for the next batch of Ponzi and pyramid schemes because the politicians have not taken corrective action.

Mixed Mandates

Both the provincial securities regulators and the so-called shareholders' auditors face competing, yet conflicting, obligations or mandates. The securities regulators believe, as judged by their actions, that their real job is to make life easier for entities that want to raise more money. Investors therefore rank far down the priority list. One startling, but typical, example involved Nortel Networks. Fines levied in Canada were a small fraction of what the US SEC assessed and received for alleged deceptive financial reporting. Seemingly, investors were viewed as close to irrelevant in Canada, and certainly did not receive compensation for losses.

The auditors' perceived role, as set forth in corporations and securities acts (i.e., being the supposed shareholders' auditor) is not how auditors officially see their priorities. In the *Hercules Managements* case, argued at the Supreme Court of Canada in December 1996, the auditors' barristers amazingly stated that annual audited financial statements were not assembled to assist shareholders in their investment decisions. Shockingly, the Supreme Court's justices accepted such a thesis, despite what the corporations and securities acts state.

Thus, by default, auditors have to be the servants of corporate management with the consequence that nobody is overseeing management and their opportunities for financial misbehavior (to cover up their mistakes or enhance their bonuses, and similar objectives). Such a role becomes exceedingly frightening when Canada's auditors push inferior, full-of-holes International Financial Reporting Standards (IFRS) into the financial legislation in 2011, as planned. Corporate management then becomes eligible to utilize every weakness of the IFRS (which number in the hundreds) to report virtually whatever numbers they want, until the inevitable financial crises arise and become public.

Determining exactly how a blatantly obvious negative outcome for investors was not stopped quickly in its infancy would prove to be immensely beneficial research. Out-of-control collaborations have major ripple effects in that investors elect to avoid equities and countries associated with these, leading to fewer jobs and a lowered quality of life. Canada fits this description.

The expression "there's a sucker born every minute" seems to have been embraced by Canadian "investment" promoters. With essentially nobody other than the investors themselves being available to prevent swindles, and with many naive investors still in existence, Canada is more than inviting to international financial tricksters.

Investor Protests

From time to time investors form various groupings to object to the one-sided approach of minimal investor protection in Canada. However, most groups disband within a few years, out of frustration because they are unable to make progress with politicians.

For example, in 2009–2010, the Canadian government proposed amendments to the Criminal Code. The draft legislation called for a minimum sentence of two years for certain types of fraud over Can$1 million. What made the proposed legislation laughable was the usual Canadian practice of releasing people from jail after they had served one-sixth of their sentence for a white-collar crime. In brief, the politicians too often behave as though they would like to see more securities criminals reside in the country.

Corrupt Reporting

There is a strong probability that investors in many countries will be drawn into significant losses within the next decade. Several countries have adopted variations of IFRS, which are based on hidden but incredibly naive financial reporting assumptions. One major IFRS assumption is that the managers of a company know its operations better than others, and therefore should be given freedom to report what they see.

In a country like Canada, too many managements see golden opportunities to pay themselves huge bonuses and engage in extensive self-dealings that assure them of lifelong comfort. Yet, IFRS build in few prohibitions and restrictions to prevent excessive reporting trickery.

Hence, a more than likely outcome is that many managements will use the accounting laxity embedded in the IFRS to conceal their mistakes and increase their personal pay. However, consequences are waiting round the corner, in various forms. A few are:

- The company runs out of cash after four to six years, and the lenders become suspicious.
- The cover-ups become too large to hide: for example, in the second year of a scam, the trickster accountants not only have to make the second year's results look great, but also have to continue to cover up the first year's fictions. As a result, if last year's fake numbers have to be exceeded by 10–15 percent, while previous years' fictions still have to concealed, each year adds that much more of a burden.
- A financial analyst begins to suspect that "the numbers look too good to be true." Often, certain relationships among the numbers that are reported fall beyond logical boundaries. Further investigation shows that several fake transactions occurred, and additional evaluation reveals that the fraud has been occurring for five years or so.

Only rarely do the so-called shareholders' auditors discover serious problems and blow the whistle, which should tell investors something about the worth of most audits.

When a company commences its unraveling process, a batch of inevitable lawsuits can divert attention from the main objective of running an honest business. Typically, a company could have been employing perhaps a dozen principal dirty tricks to keep up an appearance of success. As in the case of

Nortel Networks which issued four financial statement restatements of its previously audited numbers, corporate survival was not possible, and the company went bankrupt. Creditors and investors just do not know what to believe when financial statements have to be revised, and the Nortel bankruptcy outcome should not be ignored.

Diagnosis

Given that financial statement cover-ups and other financial trickery have an important role to play in companies that engage in various forms of suspect behavior, several paragraphs have to be devoted to basic diagnostic procedures.

The purpose of these explanations is not to train more potential securities criminals, but to alert researchers to bread-and-butter techniques that may indicate paths leading to other suspect activities. As forensic accountants, we often do not know the nature and origins of a particular scam. Initially, all we know is that financial reporting has been chosen to cover up some nastiness, and that big money is involved. Having discovered the cover-up, we next have to pin down which specific financial mess is being unfairly "repaired."

The most commonly-seen cover-ups are:

1. Converting various operating expenses into assets to be shown on a balance sheet or position statement, rather than on some profit or income computation financial statement, wherein the effect would otherwise have been to lower profit;
2. Reducing liabilities (such as potential liabilities for warranty repairs) by recording them as expense reductions or sales revenue increases—again, the purpose is to give the appearance of increased profits or income;
3. Hiding liabilities and expenses by neglecting to record future obligations that have arisen from operating activities that have already occurred. An example would be a mining company that has sold its ore, but has not recorded the liability for the cost of restoring the land to whatever the environmental laws require;
4. Overstating assets (and, as a consequence, falsely increasing the shareholders' recorded "worth") by using a variety of loose techniques. The IFRS will be especially nasty to investors because of the wide choice of valuation techniques that are available for hiding cover-ups. Often, overvalued assets remain at high levels for years

because vague IFRS principles do not require that the amounts be written down to cash trading values.

In addition to the above, there are plenty of other issues that can point to the possibility of financial fraud:

1. Off-balance-sheet liabilities were a major cause of Enron's collapse. Many reporting loopholes have since been closed for what are called variable-interest entities (VIEs). But, other trickery still exists for some pension obligations, asset securitizations, and hybrid liabilities. False impressions of the adequacy of a company's equity occur when debt is much higher than what is being reported to investors.
2. Self-dealing and non-arm's-length transactions are a monstrous problem in Canada. Executive-owned companies can transact business (e.g., provide sales, or services) with the publicly-owned company that the executives manage, theoretically on behalf of shareholders. However, the purchase and sale prices that are used for self-dealing trading purposes can be a little too friendly, for the benefit of the executives. Nevertheless, most self-dealing accounting and auditing rules are extremely weak and do not force disclosure of departures from utilizing fair market value trading prices. What is more disturbing is that the IFRS have even weaker accounting and reporting rules than previously existed in Canada. Accompanying audit procedures for the IFRS do not require searches for unfair trading prices. Abuses can only grow, against investors, as the IFRS begin to be used in countries that permit widespread "cooking the books."
3. Other executive compensation issues, in addition to self-dealing, can tell much about managements' ethics and modes of behavior. Additional compensation can flow to executives through bonuses, stock options, excessive expense accounts, loans at low or no interest rates with no specified repayment terms, paid extra vacations, being listed on multiple payrolls of related entities such as joint ventures, high insurance coverage payable to the executive's estate and much more. Aside from inviting some income tax implications, boards of directors generally are far too tolerant of such activities. Many executives lobby with their friends on boards of directors, to obtain fat compensation packages.
4. Laws that require only the disclosure of executives' salary, bonuses, and stock options are "years behind the times." The existence

of companies owned solely by executives could yield double compensation and yet be unknown to shareholders.
5. Revenue inflation, in addition to that arising from lowering liabilities as mentioned above, is out of control around much of the world. IFRS will cause these problems to become much worse because of the vagueness on matters such as collection of amounts owing. Further commentary follows shortly.
6. Note disclosure can all too often be misleading or incomplete. Unless words in notes are studied carefully, to observe the exceptions and disclaimers, misinterpretations of financial statements can easily occur. As a generalization, many companies provide lengthy notes on unimportant matters and ignore far more crucial descriptions of pending problems. All too often, note disclosure attempts to provide comfort to investors instead of telling a full story, especially about important downsides.

Not only do several variations exist for each of the above financial reporting "creations," but many dozens of additional scams could be illustrated. Certain scenarios are virtually always suspect, but some are cleaner than others. An example meriting suspicion would be when a business purchases another one, and issues shares of the purchaser company plus some additional cash to the sellers. The prices that are placed on each acquired asset and liability of the purchased company for financial reporting purposes can be just too accommodating and hypothetical. For example, if the acquiring company wants to increase its profits/income in the year after the company's purchase (in order to look attractive and sell more shares to the public, or to increase management bonuses) several elementary tricks are available.

At the date of the corporate acquisition, low values can be placed on acquired assets such as inventory and receivables. A few months later, on receipt of cash for the sold inventory/collected receivables, extra profits automatically pop up, because a low price was assigned at the date of the company's purchase. The new managers appear to be geniuses for generating high profits in the new company grouping, when the real applause should be directed to a creative accountant (who probably should be in jail).

The corporate purchase scenario has led to nonsense conclusions in many research studies over the years. Various "before-and-after a merger" profit tabulations seemingly conclude that a particular business acquisition or consolidation was a brilliant corporate decision, leading to a variety of "savings" and "profit enhancements." But such conclusions can be false unless the accounting gimmickry is removed from researchers' numbers. For example, various intangible assets that were acquired by the purchasing company could be hugely overstated in value, and kept that way for years, simply by utilizing the most optimistic of valuation assumptions. In reality, a merger could have been complete foolishness, because too much was paid to acquire a company. Yet, tricky accounting could easily show otherwise.

Another corporate scenario that is too often a balloon awaiting its explosion involves "consolidators" who buy private companies to "consolidate" an industry, thereby reducing the number of so-called less productive "mom and pop" (or family-owned or small) businesses. Sometimes, consolidation makes sense when cost savings can actually be received. But, the "consolidator" scenario is open to significant abuse when the real agenda involves buying private companies at low prices and peddling their profits/income record to public shareholders at unrealistic earnings multiples.

Here's how this gimmickry works. A group of private companies (e.g., pharmacies, or funeral homes) could conventionally be viewed as being individually worth about four times their annual cash profits. However, publicly-owned companies in the same line of business could be selling for eight times annual cash profits, partly because they are "public" companies listed on stock exchanges. Thus, if the private companies can individually be acquired for a multiple of four times, and dumped into the public company to be valued at eight times cash profit, a supposed doubling of "value" takes place automatically.

The secret for tricksters is to delude the public investors into thinking about the wonders of prospective savings from having consolidated drug stores/pharmacies, or from similar industries. The next crooked step is to ensure that the "eight times" multiple is steadily used by the investors in the marketplace. Various lunches with financial analysts and speeches and TV appearances are needed to maintain the myth of "eight times" for the particular group of acquired companies.

In reality, a multiple of perhaps "five" or "four" times cash profit would be more logical in the public company because not much profitability has changed. The public company is really just a collection of yesterday's private companies. In essence, the private stores have not changed their operations, but lower costs may exist for some purchases (e.g., cosmetics costs sold by the drug store/pharmacy could be reduced through arranging for bulk purchases, but, wages, rent and other costs would remain about the same).

Overall cash profits may increase slightly from the reduced expenses, leading to a higher stock market price for the consolidator company. But, why should the price/earnings multiple itself increase from four to eight when the business risks are essentially the same? Private has become public, but not much more has occurred.

When the purchases of the private businesses are transacted over a period of several years, the tricksters have a better chance of conning investors into believing that "eight times" is reasonable. In mathematical terms an "eight times" multiple equates to believing that the consolidator company earns over 12 percent on its shareholders' equity. Tricky accounting can be employed to maintain the myths.

In summary, investors and researchers have to watch out for companies that engage primarily in buying private companies. Only some situations are legitimate. Too often, the real agenda is not the attaining of cost savings, but conning investors into paying "eight" times, instead of "four" times (i.e., double) for their shares in the consolidator company. When the savers are buying shares, guess who is selling them?

It is these types of long-standing, favorite swindles that make a mockery of the "principles-based" and deregulation political movements. Deregulation is a gift to criminals because it means that no regulator is watching out for elementary trickery. When the securities con artists have never bothered to acquire ethical "principles," they have only one reason to learn the latest financial reporting principles, such as IFRS. They want to locate the loopholes, areas of silence, weak wording, evasive topics and similar. Then, they can get back into their main business of swindling the naive.

Canada provides plentiful evidence for researchers. What may be successful in one country could very well be destructive in other countries for basic reasons: culture, ethics, traditional business practices, enforcement or lack thereof, and similar. Canada's politicians pretend that securities fraudsters are rarities. Thus, the country is attractive to swindlers.

Revenue Enhancements

Faking the revenue/turnover/sales line in an income/profit/operations financial statement is exceedingly popular. During the dot com hype years at the beginning of the twenty-first century, company valuations based on income were not possible, simply because most of them were not generating profits. Valuers therefore had to place a valuation multiple on something else. Large numbers of analysts decided that a multiple of sales revenue was convenient, as some sort of proxy for "future profits."

The tricksters caught on quickly and invented higher sales revenue numbers, which were able to be audited given the weak accounting and auditing rules that then existed in many countries. Ideally, a sale of goods or services should be recorded in the company's financial statements: when a form of contract and selling price have been agreed, the buyer receives the goods or services, and cash collection of the selling price is essentially guaranteed. But, different types of contract or agreement can be arranged, which require some modifications of the ideal principles. For example, a warranty may have to be provided for five years covering parts and labor repair costs. If so, the question arises as to whether more than one sales date should be set, to recognize the delay in having to conduct warranty repairs. Obviously, a variety of other circumstances could be contemplated for different industries, such as those engaged in long-term construction.

The looser the accounting principles, rules and guidance, the greater are the chances that management will fiddle with the numbers to keep the company's stock price high, along with the value of any options held by the management executives. For example, some companies will engage in bartering. A magazine publisher and a trade show organizer may barter. An advertisement may appear in the magazine advertising a trade show, wherein a booth would be provided at the trade show so that magazine subscriptions can be sold. No money is exchanged. Is this type of transaction a sale or revenue enhancement?

Companies that are valued by analysts based on a multiple of sales revenue will probably record the estimated sales revenue in a barter arrangement. The higher the revenue, the higher the stock price. But, such transactions do not produce any profits. Costs equal revenues. That is, revenue is chosen by some analysts as a proxy for profitability. With a barter transaction, no profit appears; yet, costs may be incurred in designing and publishing an advertisement. Thus, it is possible that profits are negative, until the advertising generates customers. Tight rules concerning what must occur so as to record sales revenue would help analysts when they compare companies. No rules; more fiddling with the numbers.

The barter transaction is hardly the most serious of the questionable or dirty tricks that are played with sales revenue/turnover. Some of the more commonly-chosen scams are:

- inventing a customer
- inflating the sales price and reducing it months later
- prematurely recording revenue
- selling to a customer with a dreadful credit rating and worrying about the consequences later
- selling to a partially-owned company and recording some of the sales and profit even though the goods have not been resold to an end-user customer.

Combinations and variations of the above are frequently seen, including in audited financial statements.

What is amazing to many forensic accountants is that an obvious target for committing securities frauds—sales/revenue/turnover—is not accompanied by especially tough financial reporting rules that limit scam opportunities. That is, if the heart of a corporation's success flows from selling goods or services, surely the financial controls over revenue tampering should be at their height. The fact that considerable looseness is available, especially under IFRS, says paragraphs about the sources of power and corruption in countries. If securities administrators and auditors are merely "going through the motions" in some faked shareholder protection exercise, investor deception has to be their top priority. If so, for research purposes, many groups from politicians down the legislation chain to investors have to be interviewed and perhaps investigated to rank the weaknesses and causation chain of events.

The invent-a-customer scam, for example, has to commence within a corporation, but at its higher levels. For the scheme to be successful, a combination of agreeable politicians, accounting rule-setters who believe in laxity, uninterested auditors, weak boards of directors, and out-of-touch securities regulators have to exist. If so, the invent-a-customer variations can continue for years in a particular company.

Here's how some of the invent-a-customer trickery functions. The objective is to keep the stock price and executive bonuses high. Sales revenue has to appear to be on an upward trend, to give the impression, albeit false, that all is well. When sales slow down, sales have to be made up by discounting prices, more advertising, higher sales commissions, and similar. But the most successful sales generator of all, in the short term, is to sell much volume to customers who are fictions or cannot afford to pay.

Sometimes, goods are shipped to a rented warehouse under a name very similar to that of a large corporation, which typically buys from the fraudster-seller. High prices are commonly charged on the fictitious sales invoice. After a few months, a credit note may be issued to reduce some of the receivable amount that is owing. Next, possibly months later, the unpaid account receivable can be converted into an investment in shares of the fake or near-bankrupt company. Such a worthless investment may then sit on the seller company's balance sheet for years. The result is that sales have been increased, but no cash has been generated, whereas expenses have had to have been paid.

All too frequently, what was actually shipped to the rented warehouse was otherwise unsaleable merchandise. Alert auditors should be able to catch such trickery. But, under the current Canadian system of minimal legal liability for auditors, risks and consequences from conducting pointless audits are few.

Investors unfortunately have to be their own auditors, watching for unusual matters, such as unexplained investments in smaller companies.

The gimmick of inflating sales prices and then later reducing them arises when some extra sales revenue money is needed in the current year to enhance bonuses, comply with creditors' restrictions, or to meet some other short-term objective. In essence, revenue gets added to one quarter and subtracted from another quarter or year. Therefore, the tricks are a variation of the next-discussed item: premature revenue recognition.

The scam of recording sales revenue in the current period instead of the next one has existed for many years. Investors have to be on guard for various types of circumstances, such as when a company needs money for expansion or to cover up for losses and mistakes. The financial statements have to be made to look as attractive as possible. The conventional trick involves recording as much revenue as can be squeezed out of the available contracts, even though various required services have not yet been performed (e.g., the purchased machinery still is not functioning at 100 percent and several technical adjustments have to be made). A result is that future periods show little revenue, but include the costs of having to perform services or construct whatever had previously been invoiced.

As with most of these types of financial trick, several factors have to be in place to allow the swindle to continue: weak auditing concepts and procedures; lazy or indifferent auditors; uncaring securities regulators; soft accounting rules; indifferent attitudes of politicians and boards of directors; inattentive media; and similar. The longer the timespan between occurrence and trying to correct the problem situations, the tougher the solutions become.

While politicians, for example, procrastinate for years, the securities swindlers have more time to refine their trickery. With few chances of being caught and much less of being prosecuted, and even less of occupying a jail cell, why not earn a living by conning investors? In Canada, securities crimes involving multi-millions of dollars committed over 20 years ago have still not resulted in convictions. Cold cases? Not really—they are still crawling their way through the legal system. Researchers thus have to be aware that Canadian statistics do not convey what is really happening today.

Financial Industry

Several interesting examples have occurred in the financial services industry in which a combination of weak governance, inept securities regulation, and misdirected or worthless auditing have led to massive financial collapses.

Recurring themes are that none of the supposed corporate and societal checks and balances or oversights was able to compensate for negligence or corruption elsewhere in the alleged investor protective network. Investors were left with huge financial losses, because theoretical safeguards crumbled when buck-passing excuses were permissible and quickly became accepted norms.

Revenue-recording trickery played the most significant role in allowing the non-recognition of the depths of inappropriate lending being made by the financial institutions. A combination of the scams noted above was chosen so as to grossly overstate the institutions' loans receivable assets and interest revenues. In effect, even though cash was (and is) the very essence of financial institutions' businesses, each entity was scraping by daily on pennies. Small amounts of cash were being recycled and re-used rapidly each day to give the impression that large cash sums actually existed within each institution.

A favorite shenanigan involved "pretending" that cash had been received and was then quickly loaned out to other borrowers. But, because no new cash had actually been received from a previous borrower in partial repayment of a loan, no cash existed to loan to other customers. Not to worry; bring loose accounting to the rescue.

The deception would be successful as long as regulators and auditors cut corners instead of checking the receipts and disbursements of cash. "Successful" is precisely the word that describes what has repeatedly happened in Canada in several instances over many years. Corruption has worked well.

Here's how the scam functions. A cash loan is made (perhaps to a "friend") so that property may be acquired by the borrower (e.g., a building, hotel, shopping centre or similar). Enough "money" is loaned so that interest due on the loan can be paid back to the financial institution for two or three years. Often, this extra loaned "money" never leaves the offices of the loan company or bank, but is held to supposedly pay interest. Usually, no cash exists for the extra sum, which gets called a "deferred revenue" for financial reporting purposes. As a consequence, for two or three years, the loan is kept up-to-date on its interest obligations by lowering "deferred revenue" and increasing "revenue." The interest is recorded as revenue on the profit or income statement, and the financial institution appears to be very successful. All that has really happened, however, is that non-existent money has been recycled by shuffling the deferred revenue liability into revenue.

The secret of loaning the extra amount of faked cash for future interest obligations involves being able to receive a generous property appraisal from a pliable or friendly appraiser, who sees roses everywhere. Next, securities regulators who avoid getting their hands dirty by actually reading the documents are required. Discrepancies and absurd assumptions cannot be pursued if the bubble is to be kept intact. Finally, inexperienced auditors are essential, to readily accept the appraisers' figures and fail to notice the absence of cash.

Several variations of the basic scam are widely available once a fraudster has the cast of characters in place: pliable appraiser, sleepy or indifferent securities or banking regulator, auditor lacking curiosity, and weak oversight at company board level. For example, loans may be made to phantom companies that then pass the cash within minutes to a previous borrower who pays overdue interest.

Most of the schemes result in the loans receivable assets increasing appreciably, and interest revenue being recorded on the income or profit or operating financial statement each year. The flaw is that the loans grossly exceed the value of underlying property. When the cash eventually runs out, bankruptcy occurs. Blame can be attached across a wide group of people. The safety nets did not work. Investors lose everything.

No End in Sight

The Canadian picture is especially troublesome because various plans to improve the safety net system will not work. The current holders of power, who have installed a corrupt network, can be expected to lobby fiercely to retain the power and daily control. Artificial oversight using the same caliber of people cannot possibly lead to improvements for investors.

Principles-based regulatory concepts are too vague to be accepted in criminal courts, where the level of proof is "beyond a reasonable doubt." Ill-conceived financial reporting approaches, such as IFRS, which place full control in the hands of management, encourage financial cover-ups of endless numbers of scams.

Pension plans that consist heavily of shares of public companies can easily be fictions as managements place glowing values on mediocre assets. The very fact that IFRS-type deregulation can become accepted in a country like Canada shows the absence of thought about tomorrow's inevitable financial collapses.

As stated at the outset, research on corporate corruption has to include Canada as one of its "lab rats." Selfish and foolish behavior by Canada's leaders and citizens has been duly observed by the world's financial swindlers. They know a haven from prosecution when they see one, and make regular visits.

Researchers must visit Canada as well, to observe another viewpoint: a system that works very well for the unprosecuted financial mobsters.

Knowing "why" should be exceedingly beneficial for researchers and policy formulators.

References

Hercules Managements Ltd et al. v. Ernst & Young et al., Supreme Court of Canada (1997).

Kripps et al. v. Touche, Ross/Deloitte, Supreme Court of British Columbia, Appeal Court Division, (1997).

Rosen, L. S. and Rosen, M. (2010) *Swindlers*, Toronto, OH: Madison Press, forthcoming.

Index

Note: page numbers in *italic type* indicate tables; those in **bold type** indicate figures.

20-60-20 rule 274

Abacha, General 304, 307
Abbas, Mahmoud 15
ABCP (Asset-Backed Commercial Paper) 327, 328
ability 123, 125, 135, 136
absence (withdrawal behavior) 187, 189–90, 193
  study 195, 196–7, 199, **200**, 202–3
academic integrity 102–4
academic journals, fake 11, 258
academic misconduct 48, 98–9, 100, 102, 106, 215–16, 218–22, 238–40
  causes of 223–31
  consequences of 222–3
  and CWB 103
  field and organizational interventions 237–8
  overcoming 231–8
academic work 217–18
  taxonomy of ethical dimensions *221*
accounting 29, 30, 180
accounting rules
  Canada 325
  IFRS (International Financial Reporting Standards) 331, 333, 334, 335, 339, 342

acquisitions 335–6
active bribes 17
addictions 47
Adelphia 5, 290
adjustment 100, 106, 108, *109*, **110**
ADVANTAGE study, Merck 251
adverse drug events (ADE) 253
affective autonomy 150, **152**
affective commitment 194, 195
  study 198, 199, 200, **200**, **201**, 202, 203, 204
affinity fraud 26
Afghanistan 14, 17, 18, 39
agency theory 34
agreeableness 101–2, 103, 106, 230
AIG 77, 78
Ajzen, I. 98
Albrecht, Chad 17, 36, 47, 163–84
Albrecht, Conan C. 17, 36, 47, 163–84
Albrecht, W.S. 36, *165*, 176, **176**
Alcoa 290
Aleynikov, Sergei 4
Aliabe, Timi 316, 317, 318
Allen, N. J. 194, 198
Alonso, Fernando 22
Amylin Pharmaceuticals Inc. 11
Anand, Vikas 6, 36, 44, 46–7, 129, 143–58
Andersen, Arthur (founder of company) 289
Anderson, Geraint 9
animals, treatment of in research *221*

Antes, Alison L. 48, 215–40
antidepressants 254, 255
Antigua, Financial Services
 Regulatory Commission 7
Ao Man-long 69
Apotex 262–3
appeal to higher loyalties
 (justification) *146*, 147, 152–3
arms trade, corruption in 16
arrogance 28
Arthur Andersen (company) 289
Ashforth, B.E. 3, 6, 36, 129, 143, 144,
 145, *146*, 148, 153, 154, 155, 156
Asian Development Bank 303
Asobie, H. Assisi 314–16
Asset-Backed Commercial Paper
 (ABCP) 327, 328
Association of Certified Fraud
 Examiners 4, 37, 178
Astor, Brooke 69
AstraZeneca 263
athletics, corruption in 20–2
auditors
 Canada 325, 331
 conflict of interest of 19–20
Australia 18, 98
autonomy 150, **152**, 153, 154, 156

background (pre-employment)
 checks 124, 129, 133, 174, 277
bad apples (individual
 characteristics) 23, 97, 98
bad barrels (organizational
 environment characteristics)
 24, 97, 98
bad cases (moral issue characteristics)
 24, 97, 98
BAE Systems Plc 8
bail-outs 73, 121
Ballard, Harold 42
Bangkok Bank of Commerce 7

Bank of America 8, 27
Bank of Montreal (BMO) 7–8
bank robbery 69
bankers
 bonuses 78
 public dislike of 8, 30, 32
banking sector 27–8
Barings Bank 76, 298
barter transactions 338
Bartol, K.M. 86–7
baseball players, steroid use 70
Bayer AG 11
Bear Stearns 72–3, 79
behavior, unusual 180
behavioral norms 98
benevolence 123, 125, 126, 129, 130,
 131, 133, 133–4, 135, 136
Benmosche, Robert 77
Berenbeim, R.E. 280
Besito and Company 261
Best, Bronwyn 49, 297–320
Bextra (valdecoxib) 11, 40, 249, 260
Bhutto, Benazir 14
bias, in research 218, 251, 254, 264
Big Five personality factors 101–2,
 104–5, 106, 111
billionaires 79
Black, Conrad 37, 290
Blankfein, Lloyd 32
BMO (Bank of Montreal) 7–8
Boeing 290
Bongo, Omar 16–17
bonuses 27, 28, 73, 78, 88
Boots Laboratories 262
Brazil, police killings 31
Bre-X Minerals 298, 328
Bribe Payers Index 298, 300
bribery 4, 49, 297–9
 by companies 15–16
 cross-cultural views on 17
 definition of 297

kickbacks 3, 4, 17, 41, 43, 69, 70, 179
  see also corruption; Integrity Pacts
Bristol-Myers-Squibb 263
Brown, Gordon 74
Burke, James 289–90
Burke, Ronald J. 3–50, 69–88
Burma (Myanmar) 18
business leaders, public opinion of 75
business practices 220, *221*, 226
business scandals 131
business students, cheating 22–3, 34–5, 46, 78, 102, 104

Calderón, Rafael 15
Callan, Erin 77
Canada
  abuse of Afghans by forces 39
  cheating in colleges and universities 98
  executive pay 76
  fraud level 18
  government regulation 42
  laws on whistleblowing 40
  Ponzi schemes 72
  securities frauds 50, 323, 342–3
    corrupt reporting 332–3
    corruption 327–8
    diagnostic procedures 333–7
    financial services industry 340–2
    investor protests 331
    lack of protection 324–7
    mixed mandates 330–1
    Ponzi schemes 328–30
    revenue enhancements 337–40
  tax fraud 8
  white-collar crime 18, 42
Canada Revenue Agency 8
Canadian Coordinating Office for Health and Technology Assessment (CCOHTA) 263

Canadian International Development Agency (CIDA) 308, 313
Canadian Rights and Democracy 74
cancer studies 18, 70
capital reserves, of banks 27
capitalism 44, 87
CardioNet Inc. 19
Caribbean 76
caring 276
caring ethical climate 191, 192
  study 195, 197, 200, **201**, 202, 203, 204, 205
CCOHTA (Canadian Coordinating Office for Health and Technology Assessment) 263
celebrity lifestyles 81
Cephalon 11
CFA (Chartered Financial Analysts) 35
CFA (Confirmatory Factor Analysis) 107–8
Chacon, Jesse 15
Chad, fraud level 18
Chartered Financial Analysts (CFA) 35
Chavez, Hugo 15
cheating
  financial benefits of 78
  in schools and universities 22–3, 34, 46, 98–9, 100, 103–4, 105, 106, 108, *109*, **110**, 112–13
  by business students 22–3, 34–5, 46, 78, 102, 104
  cheating behavior 105, 106, 108, *109*, **110**, 112–13
  reporting of 100, 104, 105, 106–7, 108, *109*, 110, **110**, 113
Chernobyl nuclear accident 15, 298
children, and materialism 81, 87
China
  billionaires 79
  contaminated baby formula 42

fraud level 18
  government corruption 15
  manufacture of counterfeit goods 81
Chirac, Jacques 15
CIBC 290
CIDA (Canadian International Development Agency) 308, 313
citizenship 276
civil litigation, in securities frauds 324
class actions, in securities frauds 324
clinical guidelines 260–1
clinical research 249–51
CMD (Current Medical Directions) 257
CME courses 260–1
codes of ethics *see* ethics, codes of
coercive power 173
Colvin, Richard 39
companies, and Integrity Pacts 300–3
compensatory forms 204
compliance officers 36, 286
condemning the condemner (social excuse) 148, 155
confidential data, theft of 127–8, 130
confidentiality, in academic research 221
Confirmatory Factor Analysis (CFA) 107–8
conflicts of interest 18–20, 37, 70, *221*
conscientiousness 101–2, 103, 106, 112, 230
"consolidators" 336
conspicuous consumption 80
consumer fraud *165*
contextual excuses *146*, 147, 148–9, 155–7
  see also excuses; social excuses
continuous commitment 194–5
control systems 134–5, 170, 175, 180

corruption 273, 297–9
  control of 35–43
  costs of 16, 30–3, 47–8
  cultural views on 17–18, 46–7
  definition of 3, 297
  extent of 4–6, 20–3
  government 14–17
  high corruption countries 166–7
  international 43
  monitoring 43
  normalization of 143–4
  progress against 43–4
  reasons for 22, 23–9
  recovery from 32–3
  reduction of 33–5, 48–9
  spread of within an organization 6–7
  see also bribery; Integrity Pacts
Corruption Perceptions Index (CPI) 298, 300, 306
Costa Rica, government corruption 15
counterfeit goods 81
counterproductive work behavior *see* CWB
Court of Arbitration 303
Cragg, Wesley 49, 297–320
Cressey, D. 128–9
cricket 71–2
crime
  extent of 4–6
  General Theory of Crime 103
  reasons for 22, 23–9
  reduction of 48–9
criminal proceedings, in securities frauds 324–5
cross-cultural views 17–18
Cullen, J.B. 191, 197
cultures
  and corruption 17–18, 46–7, 144–5, 149, 151–7

cultural dimensions 149–51
Current Medical Directions (CMD) 257
customer fraud *165*
customers, "invent-a-customer" scam 339–40
customs officers, betrayal of trust 31
CWB (counterproductive work behavior) 46, 99, 100, 104–5, 111, 113–14, 192
    and academic integrity 102–4
    CWB-C checklist 107
    personality as an antecedent of 101–2
    relationship to OCB 100–1
cycling 20–1
cynicism 230, 239

Dalal, R.S. 101
Darling, Alastair 28
data management 220, *221*, 226
data theft 127–8, 130
data-driven fraud detection 181–3
Davis, James 6
Davis, J.H. 122–3, 129, 130, 133, 136
Dawson, S. 82
Defining Issues Test (DIT) 235
degrees, "fake" 13, 70–1
demographic factors 23
Deng Xiaoping 79
denial of illegality (contextual excuse) *146*, 148, 149, 156–7
denial of injury (justification) *146*, 147, 152, 153
denial of responsibility (contextual excuse) *146*, 148–9, 156
denial of victim (social excuse) *146*, 148, 154, 155
Denmark, fraud level 18
derivatives fraud 164–5, **166**

Diener, E. 83, 85
diet pills *see* Redux
DiPascali, Frank 6
disciplinary actions against employees 277, 282
distributable cash 329
distributive justice 192
    study 195, 198, 199, **200**, 202, 203, 204
DIT (Defining Issues Test) 235
Donaghy, Tim 21
Dong, Betty 262
Douglas, Jennifer 16
Drabinsky, Garth 28, 42, 76–7, 290
Dresdner Kleinwort 9
drugs testing, in athletics 20–1

Eagleson, Alan 42
East Germany, corruption in athletics 20
Ebbers, Bernie 290
Economic and Financial Crime Commission (EFCC), Nigeria 306
Ecuador, fraud level 18
Edem, Sam 314, 316
EDM (Ethics Development Model) 176–7, **176**
EFCC (Economic and Financial Crime Commission), Nigeria 306
Effexor (venlafaxine) 254–5
egalitarianism 150, 151, **152**, 153, 154, 155, 157
eHealth 75
EITI Nigeria *see* Nigeria Extractive Industries Transparency Initiative (NEITI)
Eli Lilly 11, 12, 258–9, 260, 261
Ellison, Larry 25
Elsevier 11, 258

embeddedness 150, 151, **152**, 153, 154, 155, 156
embezzlement 4, 128–9, *165*
emotional stability 101–2, 106
employee theft 4, 38, 44, 46, 108, *109*, 110, **110**, 113–14, *165*
  as job enrichment 14
  perspectives on 123–5
  practical applications 132–6
  and trust 46, 121–2, 125–31
employees
  and business ethics information 40–1
  expense account abuse 37
  involvement in codes of ethics 282–3
  training 174–5
  trust in employer 130–1
employers, trust in employees 125–30
employment of staff from fraudulent firms 9–10, 77
enforcement, of codes of ethics 277, 282, 287
engineering 216
Enron 29, 131, 163, 276, 290, 334
  Enron Broadband Section (EBS) 19
Ernst & Young 15–16
ethical behavior 223
ethical climate 191
  study 195, 197
  see also ethical organizational culture
ethical decision-making 289
  influences on 227–31
  sense-making model 223, 224–6, **224**, *225*, 235–6, 239
ethical leadership 41, 274, 287–91, **291**, 292
ethical organizational culture 29, 33, 49, 174, 274–5, 291–2, **291**

core ethical values 274, 275–8, **291**, 292
ethical leadership 41, 274, 287–91, **291**, 292
formal ethics programs 274, 278–87, **291**, 292
  see also ethical climate; organizational ethics
ethics
  codes of 29, 40, 232, 276, 279, 280–4
  cultural views on 17–18
  education and training 34–5, 77, 133–4, 232–7, 239, 240, 277, 284–5
  information for employees 40–1
Ethics Development Model (EDM) 176–7, **176**
ethics officers 36, 286
evidence, destruction of 12
excessive risk 27
excuses 47, 145, *146*, 147–9
  see also contextual excuses; social excuses
executive pay 75–6, 334
  excessive 27, 73–4, 78
executive protection services 74
Exerpta Medica 256
expense account abuse 37
  MPs' expenses scandal, UK 74–5
experiences, and happiness 85–6
experiential learning 229–30
expert power 173
Extractive Industries Transparency Initiative (EITI) 299
  see also NEITI
extraversion 230
Ezekweselu, Oby 309–10, 314
Ezzedine, Salah 71

fabrication (academic misconduct) 48, 219, 221
  see also FFP
fairness 276
  see also organizational justice
fake goods 81
falsification (academic misconduct) 48, 219, 221
  see also FFP
families, role in reducing greed 87
family satisfaction 83
Faour, Youseff 71
Fatah 15
FDA (Food and Drug Administration), and pharmaceutical industry 252, 253, 254, 255, 259, 261
Federal Sentencing Guidelines for Organizations (FSGs), US Sentencing Commission 278–9, 284, 286, 287
FFP 219, 220, 221, 222
  see also fabrication; falsification; plagiarism
fiddles 131
field interventions, and academic integrity 237–8
field socialization 227–8
figure skating 21
financial crisis 45
financial fraud 7–10, 37–8
financial goals 29
financial reporting
  Canada 325, 332–3
  fraud 29, *165*
  IFRS (International Financial Reporting Standards) 331, 333, 334, 335, 339, 342
financial services industry 27–8
  Canada 340–2

loss of trust in 32
Financial Services Regulatory Commission, Antigua 7
Finland, fraud level 18
Fistful of Dollars, A: Lobbying and the Financial Crisis (IMF) 28
Flint Laboratories 262
Follett, Barbara 75
football 22
Foreign Corrupt Practices Act (1979) 299
formal ethical climate 191, 192
  study 195, 197, 199, **200**, 202, 203, 204, 205
Fosamax (aledronate) 262
France, government corruption 15
fraud
  auditing 175
  by misrepresentation 10–13
  and culture 17–18, 143–58
  detection 178–83, **178**
  effects on organizations 164–7
  extent of 4
  fraud triangle 47, 168–72, **168**
  government 14–17
  innocent victims of 9–10
  as job enrichment 14
  levels in different countries 18
  perpetrators 167
  prevention 173–7
  recruitment 172–3
  reduction of 47, 48–9
  symptoms 179–80, 182–4
  types of 163–4, *165*
Frustaglio, Steve 19
Fujimori, Alberto 14
Fuld, Richard 77
full mediation model 105, 108, 110, *110*, 111

Gabon, government corruption 16–17
Galleon Group 7
gambling 21
General Motors 166
General Theory of Crime 103
ghostwriting, of academic papers 11, 12, 49, 256–8
gibberish 9
Gilovich, T. 85
giving 86
GlaxoSmithKline 249, 253, 255
Global Economic CrimeSurvey (PwC) 4
Goldman Sachs 4, 32, 73
Gottfredson, M.R. 103
Gottlieb, Myron 76–7
governance 174
governments
 fraud and corruption 14–17
 and Integrity Pacts 300–3, 301, 302–3
 regulations 42–3
graduate students
 academic misconduct 99
 and work environment 228–9
greed 27, 45, 47, 69–86
 and children 81
 reduction 87–8
Gregory, Joseph 77
Guerber, Amy 46–7, 143–58

Haiti, fraud level 18
Halcion (triazolam) 252
happiness, and money 80–7
harmony 151, *152*
Harrison, D.A. 23–4, 97–8, 102, 103, 112
health sciences, sense-making in 227
heart disease 252, 256
Helton-Faulth, W. 220, *221*, 225
Henry, Thierry 22

Hercules Managements case, Canada 325–7, 331
Hertz Global Holdings, Inc. 19
Hester, Stephen 76
hierarchy 150–1, 151, *152*, 154, 155, 156, 157
Hil, N.C. 176, **176**
Hill, G. 85
Hirko, Joseph 19
Hirschi, T. 103
Hogan Personality Inventory *see* HPI
Holbrook, Anne 263
Holland, Daniel V. 47, 163–84
Hollinger 37, 290
Home Depot 29
honesty tests 124, 129
Hong Kong, fraud level 18
honor codes 34
hotlines, for reporting ethical breaches 34, 49, 134, 274, 279, 286
Howell, R. 85
HPI (Hogan Personality Inventory) 106
 Reliability Scale 102, 105
HRT (hormone replacement therapy) 215, 256
hubris 28
Human Rights Watch (HRW) 31, 306
Hwang Woo-suk 12, 215
hypernorms 275

Iceland, fraud level 18
ICPC (Independent Corrupt Practices and Other Related Offences Commission), Nigeria 306
Idemudia, Uwafiokun 49, 297–320
identity theft 6
IFRS (International Financial Reporting Standards) 331, 333, 334, 335, 339, 342

Ijan Youth Council 311
Ikea, withdrawal from Russia 16, 70
illegal behaviors 4, 46
illegality, denial of (contextual excuse) *146*, 148, 149, 156–7
IMF (International Monetary Fund) 28
Imperial Tobacco Canada 12
income level, and happiness 83–5
income tax fraud 172
Independent Corrupt Practices and Other Related Offences Commission (ICPC), Nigeria 306
India 79, 164
individual characteristics (bad apples) 23, 97, 98
individual differences orientation 124, 125, 129, 133
Indonesia 298
Infectious Diseases Society of America 261
informed consent *221*
informers 175, 178
injury, denial of (justification) *146*, 147, 152, 153
institutional review boards *221*, 232
institutionalization 143
integrity 123, 125, 126, 129, 130, 131, 133, 133–4, 135, 136
Integrity Pacts (IPs) 49, 288–303
  Nigeria 307–20, *320*
  see also TI (Transparency International)
integrity tests 102, 105, 124, 129, 132, 133, 134
Intel Corp. 3
intellectual autonomy 150, **152**, 155, 156
intellectual property *221*

intent to leave (withrawal behavior) 187, 190, 193, 194
  study 195, 197, 200, **201**, 202, 203
Inter-American Development Bank 303
International Chamber of Commerce 303
international corruption 43
International Finance Corporation 303
International Financial Reporting Standards (IFRS) 331, 333, 334, 335, 339, 342
International Journal of Cross Cultural Management 17
International Monetary Fund (IMF) 28
International Olympic Committee 21
"invent-a-customer" scam 339–40
investigation 175–6
investment fraud *165*
Iran, fraud level 18
Iraq, fraud level 18
Ireland 75
Israel 16
  schoolteachers' withdrawal behavior study 47–8, 195–205
Izzo, J. 84

Jagri, Reshma 70
Janulis, Ted 77
Japan, fraud level 18
Jawahar, I.M. 46, 97–114
Jeffries & Co. 19
job enrichment, and employee theft 14
job loss, and data theft 127
job satisfaction 84
Johnson and Johnson 289–90
Jones, Earl 26, 70
Jones, Susan 169

Joshi, M. 6, 36, 129, 144, *146*, 148, 153, 154, 155, 156
Journal of the American Medical Association 11
journals, fake 11, 258
JP Morgan Chase & Co. 3, 72
justification 47, 145, *146*, 147, 157
 and culture 152–3

Karzai, Hamid 14, 22
Kasser, T. 84
"keeping up with the Joneses" 81
Kennedy, Brian 19
Kenney, Martin 76
Kenya, fraud level 18
Kerik, Bernard 5
Kerviel, Jérôme 35–6
kickbacks 3, 4, 17, 41, 43, 69, 70, 179
King, Melissa 72
Kisamore, Jennifer L. 46, 97–114
Kish-Gephart, J.J. 23–4, 97–8, 102, 103, 112
Kopchinsky, John 40
Kordan, Ali 13
Kozlowski, Dennis 37, 290
Kripps case, Canada 326
Kumar, Anil 7

L1 262–3
labeling, of unethical behavior 174
LaPorte, Joan-Ramon 262
lateness (withrawal behavior) 187, 189, 193
 study 195, 196, 199, **200**, 202, 203
lawn-bowling 21
lawyers, betrayal of trust 31
Lay, Kenneth 290
leadership, ethical 41, **76**, **176**, 177, 274, 287–91, **291**, 292
Leamer, L. 71, 80

Lebanon 71
ledger, metaphor of the (contextual excuse) *146*, 148, 149, 157
Leeson, Nick 76
legal system 149, 156
"legitimacy lies" 12–13
legitimate power 173
Lehman Brothers 72, 77
Lewis, Ken 8
Lexchin, Joel 48–9, 249–64
Liechtenstein, tax evasion 8
lifestyles, extravagant 180
Livent 76, 290
Locke, E.A. 86–7
Losec (omeprazole) 263
loss prevention industry 134

Macao 69
McCabe, D.L. 23, 34, 98–9, 100, 103–4, 106, 107
McCain Foods 32
McCallion, Hazel 19
McDade, Bart 77
McGee, Hugh 8
McGwire, Mark 21
McKinney, Rich 77
McMaster University 263
Madoff, Bernard 6, 9, 10, 25, 43, 71, 168, 329
Madoff, Peter 9–10
Malik, Hafiz 72
management fraud *165*
marketing, of pharmaceuticals 10–11, 252
Marshall, Anthony 69
mastery 151, *152*
match-fixing 21
material affluence 84
materialism 80–2
Mayer, R.C. 122–3, 129, 130, 133, 136

INDEX

MBA students 34–5, 70
Medicaid 70
medical communication companies 257
medical research 11–12, 18–19, 217
medicines, marketing of 10–11, 252
Medvedev, Dimitri 16, 70
Melander, H. 254
Melnetizer, Julius 42
menopausal women, HRT (hormone replacement therapy) 215, 256
Merck 10–11, 12, 70, 251, 253, 254, 257–8, 261–2
mergers 335–6
Merrill Lynch 8, 27–8
metaphor of the ledger (contextual excuse) *146*, 148, 149, 157
Mexico, fraud level 18
Meyer, J.P. 194, 198
Ministry of the Niger Delta 303
Mintzberg, H. 88
Misick, Michael 70
misrepresentation 10–13
modeling, of ethical behavior 174
money
    and greed 69–88
    and happiness 80–7
    motivation 25–8, 45, 86–7
    see also greed
money-laundering 12–17, 16
monitoring 175
moral development 24–5, 223, 233
moral disengagement 25
moral identity theory 223
moral intensity dimensions 98
moral issue characteristics (bad cases) 24, 97, 98
moral manager (ethical leadership) 289
moral person (ethical leadership) 289

mortgage lenders 28
motor racing 22
Movement for the Survival of Ogoni People (MOSOP) 309, 311
MPs' expenses scandal, UK 74–5
Mumford, Michael D. 48, 215–40

narcissism 230, 231
Nardelli, Robert 29
National Audit Office 15
National Basketball Association 21
National Retail Foundation (US) 5
negative tone, in codes of ethics 281–2
NEITI (Nigeria Extractive Industries Transparency Initiative) 306, 310, 314, 316
    see also Extractive Industries Transparency Initiative (EITI)
Netherlands, fraud level 18
Neurontin (gabapentin) 249, 259–60, 260
neuroticism 230
New Century Financial Corp. 3–4
New Jersey, government corruption 26–7
New York, government corruption 26–7
New Zealand, fraud level 18
Nexen 307, 308, 313
Niger Delta for Professional Development 311
Nigeria
    government corruption 16
    oil industry 49–50, 303–6, **305**
    Niger Delta Development Commission (NDDC) 306
    and Integrity Pacts 307–20, *320*

Nigeria Extractive Industries
   Transparency Initiative (NEITI)
   306, 310, 314, 316
Nigerian Anti-Corruption
   Commission 309
non-profit organizations, and
   employee theft 127
Noonan, John 297
normalization of corruption 143–4
normative commitment 194, 195
   study 198, 200, **200**, **201**, 202
Nortel Networks 30, 73, 327, 328,
   330, 332–3
Norwegian Medicines Control
   Authority 262

oaths, to behave ethically 34
Obama, Barack 27, 28, 78, 88
OCB (organizational citizenship
   behavior) 46, 99, 100, 104–5,
   111, 112, 133
   and academic integrity 102–4
   personality as an antecedent of
     101–2
   relationship to CWB 100–1
O'Donoghue, John 75
OECD Anti-Bribery Convention 299
off-label prescription of drugs 258,
   260
Office of Research Integrity (ORI) 232
offshore accounts 8
Oil Mineral Producing Area
   Development Commission
   (OMPADEC), Nigeria 306
Okun, Edward 7, 42, 72
Olivieri, Nancy 262–3
Olympic Games
   Beijing (2008) 20
   Montreal (1976) 20
   Salt Lake City (2002) 21

Vancouver (2010) 21
O'Neil, Paul 290
online fraud 163
Ontario Lottery and Gaming Corp.
   75
Ontario Securities Commission 9
openness 230
OPMADEC (Oil Mineral Producing
   Area Development
   Commission), Nigeria 306
Optionable, Inc. 7–8
Organization of American States 299
organizational citizenship behavior
   see OCB
organizational commitment, as
   mediator between withdrawal
   behaviors and
  organizational ethics 194–5, 202, 204
organizational culture 228–9
   see also ethical climate; ethical
     organizational culture
organizational environment
   characteristics (bad barrels) 24,
     97, 98
organizational ethics 187, 191–2
   and withdrawal behaviors 188,
     193–5, 195–205
   see also ethical organizational
     culture
organizational interventions, and
   academic integrity 237–8
organizational justice 192
   study 195, 197–8
     see also distributive justice;
       procedural justice
organizational reduction of greed 87–8
organizations, effects of fraud on
   164–7
ORI (Office of Research Integrity)
   232

Pakistan, government corruption 14
Palestine, corruption 15
Palm Beach, Florida 71, 80
Parke-Davis 259
Parmalat 290
partial mediation model 105, 108, 111
passive bribes 17
pasta-makers, Italy 4
Paxil (paroxetine) 249, 255
peer review system 218
Peled, D. 191, 197
pensions 73, 342
perceived opportunities **168**, 169–71, 172
perceived pressures **168**, 169, 172
performance appraisals 277
personality variables, as predictors of dishonest behavior 100, 104–11
Peru, government corruption 14
Pfizer 11, 12, 40, 249, 257, 259–60, 260
pharmaceutical industry 10–12, 48–9, 249–50, 263–4
  attempts to silence critics 261–3
  betrayal of trust 31
  biasing the content of CME and clinical guidelines 260–1
  communication of safety issues to regulators 251–3
  conflicts of interest 18–19, 70
  funding of research 250–1
  ghostwriters 11, 12, 49, 256–8
  marketing 10–11, 252
  promotion of drugs for unapproved indications 258–60
  selective and misleading publication 253–5
philanthropy 86

Picower, Jeffry 25–6
Piquet, Nelson Jr. 22
plagiarism 12, 48, 98, 100, 219, 221
  see also FFP
Poehlman, Eric 215
police officers, betrayal of trust 31
politics, corruption in 22
Ponemon Institute 127–8, 130
Ponzi schemes 6–7, 8–9, 25, 26, 71, 72, 164
  Canada 50, 328–30
post-marketing studies, in clinical research 251
Pound, Richard 21
power, of one person over another 173
PPH (primary pulmonary hypertension) 253
Pravachol (pravastatin) 263
pre-employment checks 124, 129, 133, 174, 277
Premarin, Prempro (HRT drugs) 256
pretence of richness 81
primitive accumulation 304
problem-solving models 233
procedural justice 192
  study 195, 198, 200, **201**, 202, 203, 204
production deviance 108, *109*, *110*, 113
professional practices 220, *221*, 226
progressive model 187, 191
  study 195–205
propensity to trust 122–3
prosecution policy 175–6
Prozac (fluoxetine) 255
prudence 100, 106, 108, *109*, *110*
psychological contract 194, 203
psychological factors 23
public contracts, and Integrity Pacts 300–3

Public Health Service 232
publication of academic research 221, 253–5
Publish What You Pay (PWYP) 299
Purdue Pharma 249
PwC (Pricewaterhouse Coopers) 4, 18
pyramid investment fraud see Ponzi schemes

Radler, David 42
Rajagolpan, Aparna 46–7, 143–58
Rajaratnam, Raj 7
Raju, B. Ramalinga 164
randomized controlled trials see clinical research
rationalization 47, 129, 143, 145, *146*, 147–9, **168**, 171–2
  and culture 151–7
RBC Dominion 8
RCMP (Royal Canadian Mounted Police) 31
recession 121
recruitment, pre-employment checks 124, 129, 133, 174, 277
red flags 179–80, 182–4
Redux (dexfenfluramine) 252–3, 256, 260
referect power 173
reinforcement of codes of ethics 285–7
religious organizations, and employee theft 127
Renault Formula One team 22
reporting mechanisms, for codes of ethics 34, 49, 134, 175, 274, 279, 286
research participants, treatment of 219, *221*
"resource curse" 304, 306
respect 276

responsibility 276
  denial of (contextual excuse) *146*, 148–9, 156
resumés, lying on 13
retail shrinkage 5
reward power 173
Richins, M.L. 82
Rigas, John 5, 290
Rio de Janeiro, police killings 31
risk 134–5, 175
'risk-taking in the relationship' 123, 126, 127, 129–30, 131, 136
Rogers Communications Inc. 13
Romania, fraud level 18
Rosen, L.S. (Al) 43, 50, 323–43
Rosenblatt, Zehava 47–8, 187–205
Rothstein, Scott 26
Roy, Jean-Louis 74
Royal Bank of Scotland 76
Royal Canadian Mounted Police (RCMP) 31
Russia 16, 18, 70, 79

sabotage 108, *109*, 110, *110*, 113
sales representatives 4
Sanders, Matthew L. 47, 163–84
São Paulo, police killings 31
Sarbanes-Oxley Act (2002) 279, 280
Satyam 164
Saxena, Rakesh 7
Schoorman, F.D. 122–3, 129, 130, 133, 136
Schwartz, Mark S. 49, 273–92
Schwartz, S.H., cultural framework 47, 149–51
Schwarzman, Stephen 25
Scrushy, Richard 6
SEC (Securities and Exchange Commission, US) 3–4, 8–9, 43, 324, 328, 330

securities frauds, Canada 50, 323–43
security measures 171
security orientation 124, 125, 129, 133
security professionals 130–1
"security through obscurity" 170–1
"seeding" trials 251
selective serotonin reuptake
 inhibitors (SSRIs) 254, 255, 257
"selective social comparison" 154–5
self-control 103
selfishness 79–80
Semenya, Caster 21
sense-making model 223, 224–6, **224**, *225*, 239
 and ethics education 235–6
Sentencing Commission (US), *Federal Sentencing Guidelines for Organizations*
 (FSGs) 278–9, 284, 286, 287
sepsis 261
Serevent (salmeterol) 253
Shabaneh, Fahmi 15
Shapira-Lishchinsky, Orly 47–8, 187–205
Sharta, Alex M. 318
Sheldon, K.M. 84
Shell Nigeria 309
shoplifting 5
Siemens AG 29
sign-off process, for codes of ethics 283–4
simple lifestyles 82, 87
Singapore, fraud level 18
Singh, Gurkipal 262
situational risk 129, 130, 131, 134–5, 136
Skilling, Jeffrey 290
"slippery slope effect" 7
Smith, Adam 79–80
smoking 12

sociability 100, 106, 108, *109*, *110*
social concensus 98
social exchange theory 124, 194, 195
social excuses *146*, 147–8, 153–5, 157
 see also contextual excuses; excuses
social norms 124
social orientation 124, 125, 129, 133
social weighting (social excuse) *146*, 148, 154–5
social-loafing behavior 193
socialization 143
Société Générale 35–6
Solomon, Elaine 9–10
Somalia, fraud level 18
Sorenson, Gary 72
South Africa, fraud level 18
spending patterns, and happiness 86
spillover model 204
Spitzer, Eliot 33
sport, corruption in 20–2, 70
Squillari, Eleanor 9
Srivastava, A. 86–7
SSRIs (selective serotonin reuptake
 inhibitors) 254, 255, 257
Stanford Financial Group Co. 6–7
Stanford, Sir Allen 6, 71–2
Stanford University 262
statins 263
Statoil 308, 309, 311, 313
stem-cell experiments 12, 216
Stone, Thomas H. 46, 97–114
Stonecipher, Harry 290
stress at work 189, 218
structural equation models 105, 108, 110, **110**
students
 absenteeism 190
 impact of teachers' withdrawal behavior 193
study conduct 220, *221*, 226

Sudan, fraud level 18
suicide 31–2
Sun, Peng 13
Supreme Court of Canada 325–7, 331
Surviving Sepsis Campaign 261
Sutton, Willie 69
Sweden 18, 254
Switzerland 8, 18, 22
Synthroid 262

Tang, Weizhen 9
Tanzi, Calisto 290
tasers 31
task performance 99, 112
tax fraud 5, 8, 172
teachers, withdrawal behavior 193–4, 195–205
tendency to misbehave 192
    study 195, 198, 200, **201**, 202, 203, 204
Tenth Global Fraud Survey (Ernst & Young) 15–16
testing of drugs 10–12
Thain, John 27–8
Theory of Planned Behaviour (TPB) 98
TI (Transparency International) 18, 43, 49, 297–9, 299–300
    see also Integrity Pacts
TI-Canada 307, 309, 310, 313, 316, 317, 318
TI-Norway 309, 310, 313
TIN (Transparency International Nigeria) 307, 311, 313–14, 317–18
tips 175, 178
tobacco industry 12
Tomlinson, Edward C. 44, 46, 121–36
"tone at the top" 174, 274, 287, 290, 292

see also ethical leadership
Toronto Dominion Bank 42
TPB (Theory of Planned Behaviour) 98
training, of employees 34–5, 77, 133–4, 174–5, 232–7, 239, 240, 277, 284–5
transparency 170–1
Transparency International *see* TI
Treviño, L.K. 23–4, 34, 97–8, 98–9, 100, 102, 103–4, 106, 112
trust
    betrayal of 31–2
    definition 122
    and employee theft 46, 121–2, 125–31, 132–6
    organizational trust 122–3, 125
trustworthiness 123, 276
    of employers 130, 135–6
    evaluation of 133
Turkey, fraud level 18
Turkmenistan, fraud level 18
Turks and Caicos 70
Turner, E.H. 254–5
Tyco International 37, 290
Tylenol 289–90

UK
    cheating in colleges and universities 98
    fraud level 18
Ukraine 15, 18
UNDP 303, 304
unethical behaviors 4, 46
unethical work practices 229
unfair treatment 124
United Nations 299
universities
    cheating in 22–3
    "fake" degrees 13, 70–1

relationship with industry 12
University of Michigan 70
University of Minnesota 262
University of Toronto, 'fake' degrees 13
UNODC (UN Office on Drugs and Crime) 17
unusual behavior 180
Upjohn 252
US
   billionaires 79
   cheating in colleges and universities 98
USB Bank 8
Uzbekistan, fraud level 18

values, ethical 274, 275–8, **291**, 292
Van Boven, L. 85
Vancouver Stock Exchange 327
"vanguard companies" 50
variable-interest entities (VIEs) 334
vendor fraud *165*
Venezuela, government corruption 15
victim, denial of (social excuse) *146*, 148, 154, 155
Victor, B. 191, 197
Vioxx (rofecobix) 10–11, 251, 252, 253, 254, 257, 262
Visting Important Professor Program (VIPP) 260
voluntary simplicity 82, 87

wages of sin 76–7
Wal-Mart 298

Watergate scandal 298, 299
Watson Wyatt 131
Wealth of Nations, The (Smith) 79–80
whistleblowing 34, 38–40, 104, 111, 175, 223
white-collar crime, Canada 18, 42
Williams, Ishola 307, 309
wire fraud 21
withdrawal behaviors 47–8, 108, *109*, 110, **110**, 114, 187
   and organizational ethics 188, 193–5, 195–205
   withdrawal syndrome 188–91
Women's Health Initiative (WHI) 256
work environments *see* organizational culture
work and spend treadmill 81
work stress 189, 218
working hours 81
workplace deviance *see* CWB
World Bank 303
World Bank Institute 15
World Class Developments 19
WorldCom 163, 290
Wyeth 252–3, 254–5, 256–7, 260

Xigris (drotecoginalfa) 261

York University, "fake" degrees 13

Zafirovski, Mike 73
Zagreb University 23
Zardari, Asif Ali 14
Zoloft (setraline) 257